5.00

Introduction to Sociology

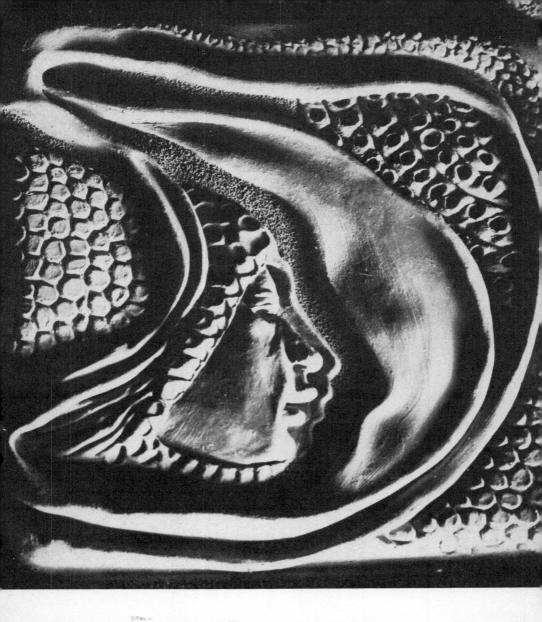

Introduction to Sociology

SECOND EDITION

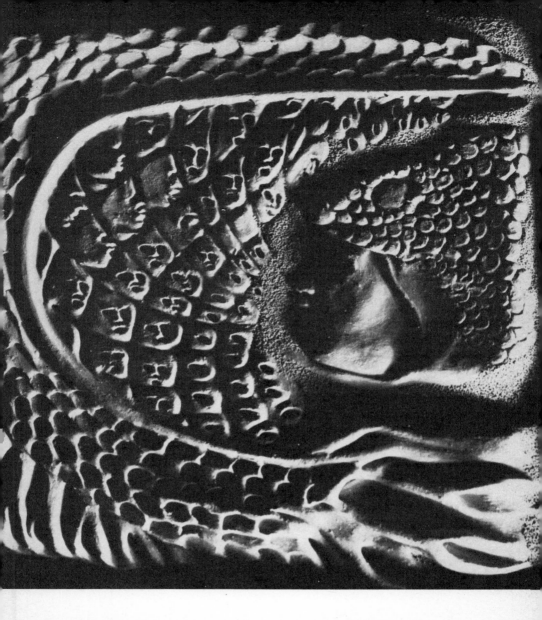

McGRAW-HILL BOOK COMPANY
New York   St. Louis
San Francisco   Düsseldorf
Johannesburg   Kuala Lumpur
London   Mexico   Montreal
New Delhi   Panama
Paris   São Paulo
Singapore   Sydney
Tokyo   Toronto

ELBERT W. STEWART
Chairman, Department of Sociology
and Anthropology
Bakersfield College

JAMES A. GLYNN
Assistant Professor of Sociology
Bakersfield College

Introduction to Sociology

Library of Congress Cataloging in Publication Data

Stewart, Elbert W
 Introduction to sociology.

 Includes bibliographical references.
 1. Sociology. I. Glynn, James A., joint author.
II. Title. [DNLM: 1. Sociology. HM51 S849i 1975]
HM51.S898 1975 301 74-7357
ISBN 0-07-061321-4

1 2 3 4 5 6 7 8 9 0 KPKP 7 9 8 7 6 5 4

This book was set in Optima by Holmes Composition Service. The editors were Lyle Linder and Ronald Kissack; the designer was Janet Bollow; the drawings were done by Richard Leech and Judi McCarty; the sculpture was done by Sue Sellars, photographed by Nedda Rovelli; the production supervisor was Judi Frey.
Kingsport Press, Inc., was printer and binder.

TITLE PAGE ART: Siva seeks to redesign the social fabric that Brahma and Vishnu have woven. On the left side of the composition Siva is moving into the social fabric (symbolized by Vishnu's fish scale structure), seeking to redesign it. By Siva's movement the pattern begins to be modified. The dark area in the center is Brahma, penetrating everything. On the right side of the composition he is sending out pattern seeds in an organic, open channel that curves in front of Vishnu's field of vision. Vishnu recognizes Brahma's pattern and manifests his design of the social order in his scale structure.

Brahma is the force everywhere that in all ways gives form to everything. Vishnu traditionally is shown with scaly skin and finlike hair because the Hindus believe his first incarnation was as a fish. Siva is depicted with the cobra entwined in and about his hair, according to Hindu tradition.

Ron Kissack, in memoriam

Contents

Preface

There is no single way to capture the totality of the madness and mirth of human society, of its heroism and its foibles, of the daily rhythm of its routine activities, and the shocks of its recurrent tragedies. Folk tale, proverb, and prophecy have made shrewd comments upon the human scene; philosophy has searched it for meaning, and poetry and drama have heightened its emotional impact and sensitized it with an empathic touch.

Sociology examines the same human scene in another manner—the systematic, objective manner of modern science. The drama of human life is in no way deadened by the sociological approach; in fact, it is often enlivened by new discovery, but there is always an insistence on regularity and order in method and explanation. Although all sociologists search for an understanding of the development and cohesion of human societies, their detailed studies are wide ranging, and their total field of interest is enormous. How, then, can the sociological view of the vast social milieu be brought within manageable proportions for a brief, introductory book?

To a great extent our introduction to sociology will center on three facets of human society, or possibly, three faces of reality. In the mythological genius of Hinduism, three great principles are presented as a triad of gods: Brahma the Creator, Vishnu the Preserver, and Siva the Destroyer. Sociology must also look into these three faces because they are as real to the modern world of science as to the world of Hindu religion. The forces that mold human groups into societies and cause them to develop their distinctive cultures represent the creative force, the Brahma, of sociological science. The socialization processes and the institutions that tend to become rigid and encrusted with age represent the sociological Vishnu, the Preserver. Perhaps the most important god of modern society is Siva, the force of change and the subverter of old orders, who constantly seeks to redesign the societies' fabric, a fabric that the other gods have woven and sought to preserve. Although only our final chapter speaks of social change in its title, "Siva" will be found constantly at work in this analysis of society, changing socialization patterns, altering religions, undermining economic systems, broadening and changing political orders, ripping up the old and time honored, and lending voice to a hundred movements of protest.

Social institutions also are discussed at length in this text, although they are presented always in a framework of change. They are given considerable space because they are the culmination of the creative processes of society and servants of its values. Institutions, in an age of challenge, can also be the vortices around which swirl the forces of social change. In an age of polarization and economic conflict, it seems highly appropriate to give ample space to the institutions of government and economics. When society fears a decline of its religious values, such values cannot be ignored as irrelevant. Religion changes as it struggles with the secular, scientifically oriented society, but the personal and societal needs that gave rise to religion remain. The prevailing belief in and concern about generation gap and family instability must be examined and explained, and so must the charge of irrelevance in the educational institution. All institutions must be examined in terms of their contribution to the social order, and their required changes must be seen in the same terms.

To be faithful to sociological perspectives, social systems must be shown as on-going concerns, with self-preservation mechanisms that operate even in times of disturbance. This view is necessary also to prevent making sociology nothing more than a dreary recitation of societal failure. Nevertheless, we who inhabit today's world see it as a planet of strife, uncertain of its future, convulsed by war and internal conflict. We are antagonized by any evasion of problems and challenges. For this reason the present text invades the field of social problems to a limited degree, because it has seemed the logical and natural way to illustrate sociological concepts and endow them with life and meaning.

We have spoken of the gods of creation, preservation, and change but perhaps have said too little of the god of science—a hard master to serve. Sociology prides itself on scientific method and theory and strives for objectivity. Attention has been given to several great theorists of sociology: Durkheim, Weber, Simmel, Merton, and Parsons. Many have been omitted, of course, partly because this book is too brief to include them all and partly because writers, try as they will to be objective, are more engrossed in one man's ideas than another's. This book does not attempt to be a compendium of sociological knowledge but only a brief introduction and, hopefully, a goad to further study. Where opinions have inevitably crept in—those of the authors or of the authorities cited—they should add heat to the discussion, and the discussion itself can generate the light.

A major purpose in keeping an introductory book concise is to give it flexibility. The basic concepts introduced here can be supplemented by studies of the surrounding community or by revealing and relevant articles in journals or books of readings. There are many specialty books available—books about minority struggles, deviants and contracultures, student movements, conservative suburbia, the urban crisis, and the hundreds of issues that are the reason for a constantly growing interest in sociology. We hope this introduction will add to that interest and help to bring the patterns and details of the social order into sharper focus.

ELBERT W. STEWART
JAMES A. GLYNN

PART ONE ART: Brahma has just turned from the right side of the illustration to the left.
The impression of his face is shown on the right; his face itself is on the left. Siva is emerging
from the far right, elevating a subculture so swiftly that it sends waves of motion across the panel. The
motion goes through Brahma, causing him to turn his head so quickly that his impression is left
on the right side. The waves of destruction set in motion by the raising of the subculture topple the
old, coroded structure of empty tradition. Vishnu rises on the left from his reclining position and
tries to stabilize the old order.

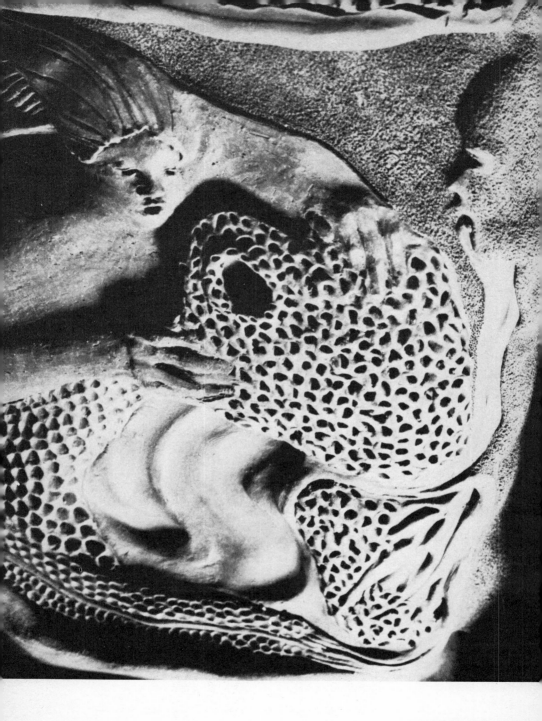

Part One

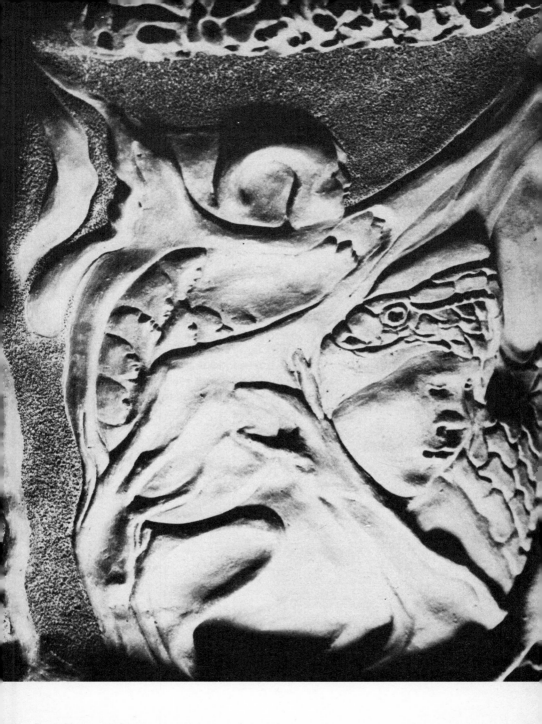

The Group Basis of Society

To encompass all classes and conditions of people, a science specializing in human relationships should search for principles unbounded by time, place, or phase of development. Such a science is obviously very difficult of achievement and can only be approached, not fully realized. If only two of the great gods mentioned in the preface—Brahma the Creator and Vishnu the Preserver—were responsible for human affairs, the task would be greatly simplified. There are, as these gods would will it, many creative and preservative forces in human societies. We need each other economically, physically, and emotionally; therefore we create social groups and all the customs and habits, rules and regulations, mythologies and traditions that go with them. In our attempts at social preservation we teach our living patterns and beliefs to our children, hoping to preserve what has been ours and somehow to make ourselves and our little systems immortal.

If order and its preservation were the total substance of social life, there would be no need for a social science. We would need nothing more than rule books—The Five Classics, the Laws of Manu, the Bible, Torah, or Koran. However, new forces intrude into old social systems. In the first chapter we shall note that the pace of social change has dethroned tradition. Sociology was born in the early days of an age of science, and it has matured in the midst of social conflict. Most typically, sociology and the other social sciences must grapple with societies in transition, adjustments to technological change, upward-striving minority groups, new nations demanding their place in the sun, and eternal conflicts for control of power structures and the economic wealth of the earth.

To define clearly the meaning of sociology, the first chapter considers the questions sociologists ask, their methods of seeking answers, and the variety of their interests and viewpoints. Chapters 2 through 4 will appear at first to be a recitation solely of the creative and preservative forces of society, dealing as they do with the compulsive need for group life, with cultural patterns, and with the process of indoctrinating the young. Even here, however, the third god, the Destroyer of Old Ways, will be seen in the background, undermining the old order with subcultural divisions and individual differences and causing new group norms to develop among entire cohorts of the young. Old traditions crumble, and suddenly Siva, God of Change, emerges as the compelling reality of the modern world. Later sections will emphasize the changes resulting from internal divisions along class and ethnic lines, population growth and concentration, and other sources of stress and strain. At present we shall describe the first phenomena of social existence: the need for human groups and a science explaining them, the growth of cultures, and the attempt, however futile, to preserve them as they are.

Chapter 1

Developing a Science of Society

Know that the problems of social science . . . must include both troubles and issues, both biography and history, and the range of their intricate relations. Within that range the life of the individual and the making of societies occurs; and within that range the sociological imagination has its chance to make a difference in the quality of human life in our time.[1]

C. Wright Mills
The Sociological Imagination

In many ways the twentieth century seems to be the ultimate age of enlightenment. New knowledge is produced in hundreds of laboratories and research centers throughout the world, with all the brightest scientific minds drawn into the investigative effort. Science is undaunted by the vastness of the heavens, the depths of the oceans, or the invisibility of atomic structure. Everything is researched, from the amino acids that

---

[1]C. Wright Mills, *The Sociological Imagination*, Oxford University Press, Fair Lawn, N.J., 1959.

6

build the proteins of life to the processes of decomposition of life and of matter itself; from the communications systems of dolphins to the visual acuity of the lowly slug; from the pecking order of chickens to the memories of flatworms. The mind of man is similarly researched: emotions, senses, neurons, origins, capacities, and genetic structure. Everywhere the thirst for knowledge grows faster as the amount of knowledge expands. As the old French proverb says, "The appetite comes with the eating."

Yet much of the knowledge poured out so lavishly in recent years is of a technical nature, improving our potential to live and multiply in the world but often disturbing the social patterns by which we have lived. The material inventions of the last few centuries have had the cumulative effect of increasing human numbers, concentrating people in cities, and disturbing old ways of life. Technological changes have thrown together people of different social and cultural backgrounds, often increasing awareness and resentments of long-existing inequalities. Industrial workers have been concentrated together in great masses, and more recently the same has been true of white-collar workers and students. Current technological changes have led to feelings of unease about gigantic filing systems and banks of computer information that invade the lives of individual and group alike. Above all, the traditional bases of intimate human interaction are shaken—family, neighborhood, community, church. At the same time, other types of social organization grow portentously—governmental, industrial, and military bureaucracies, financial structures, and both national and international corporations. Such changes have made society less comprehensible to the individual than it once seemed to be and have led to an increasing interest in and need for the systematic study of social systems.

WHAT IS SOCIOLOGY

What is clearly needed is an approach to knowledge that attempts an understanding of society, that seeks the constant and relevant in social systems, and that tries to increase man's understanding of his fellow man. From its very beginning sociology has aspired to accomplish this task. Sociology has also been interested in the dilemma of rapid material progress that seems to outrun society's capacity to adjust, as well as the search for basic principles of social organization. Sociology is a systematic and scientific discipline seeking knowledge of people as social animals: their societies and subsocieties and their adjustment to them, their customs and institutions and the patterns of stability and change that they develop.

Characteristics of Sociology As Peter Berger[2] noted, not all that sociology says will be startlingly new, but it will cast a new light on things barely noticed before. Students of geology or physical geography suddenly discover new interest in a landscape that they have often passed without notice because now they are trained to see the features of erosion, uplift, and volcanic activity. Students of paleontology find that the old sediments they have observed before are full of treasures revealed to them only after they have been trained to see them. Similarly, students of sociology will discover a new world, a world that was always there but previously was little observed: the ethnic groups of their city, the social-class divisions, the blighted areas, the varied religious denominations, sects, and cults, the distinctive and little-observed worlds of poverty. They will find the world of deviant behavior closer to their own world than they care to know. They will see many variations in life-chances for the young. They will discover that education—the open sesame for the majority of people—is a closed door for some, regarded either as unimportant or impossible. They will find that a nation pledged to equality has a type of stratification which many informed observers have called "racial caste." They will find that the emotions roused in mobs and riots are not as foreign to their nature as they would like to believe. They will perhaps agree with Emerson that there is no type of behavior too low for them to have followed had the circumstances been different.

Relation of Sociology to the Other Social Sciences All the social sciences seek greater understanding of people and society, although their approaches are somewhat different. Sociology and anthropology are both extremely broad in their perspectives; they try to study societies in their entirety, not just as political systems, economic systems, or systems of belief and value. Anthropology has focused a majority of its studies on preliterate societies, and sociology has focused on contemporary societies, but both look for universal patterns of human relations behind the varying details. The other social sciences are somewhat more specialized, but their areas of investigation are also important to the total understanding of human societies. Psychology studies the mental and emotional side of human nature; economics studies the systems of production and distribution of goods; and political science studies the systems by which social power and authority are institutionalized, exercised, and regulated. History, in its careful recording of the past, gives all the social sciences a body of evidence from which to draw. The

[2]Peter L. Berger, *Invitation to Sociology*, Doubleday & Company, Inc., Garden City, N.Y., 1963, pp. 20–24.

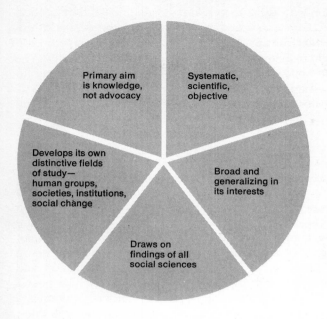

social-science disciplines are interrelated, of course, and profit from each other's studies; sociology cannot ignore any of them.

"If there is one rule of conduct which is incontestable," said Émile Durkheim, one of the greatest contributors to sociology, "it is that which orders us to realize in ourselves the essential traits of the collective type."[3] Human beings are social animals, living together, creating societies of various kinds. The distinctive field of sociology is the study of these societies, how they form, change, and differentiate. The word "society" has a number of meanings, but unless otherwise specified it is used in sociology to refer to people welded together by common patterns of interaction, institutions, and means of social control. In the modern world the term is almost synonymous with "nation." Obviously, societies have grown through human history from small hunting and gathering bands into modern states, studied in different ways by the social sciences.

Unlike anthropology, sociology does its studies mainly in modern industrial societies rather than in preliterate societies. Unlike history,

[3]Émile Durkheim, *The Division of Labor in Society,* The Free Press, Glencoe, Ill., 1947, p. 396.

sociology looks mainly for explanations and developmental trends when it studies the past rather than searching carefully for the details of the story. Sociology differs from psychology in its greater emphasis on the group rather than the individual. All the social sciences are of value. We believe that for the college student sociology offers particularly useful insights for the understanding of self and society. As we turn to an analysis of the types of questions pursued by sociologists, this point will become increasingly clear.

WHAT QUESTIONS DO SOCIOLOGISTS ASK

Sociology encompasses so many areas of research that in some respects it seems impossible for a brief text to introduce the entire discipline. In a more important respect, however, a concise introduction to the field remains possible because all phases of society and its problems are interrelated. A study of any major part of society sheds light on the whole; a study of the problems of any ethnic group reveals much about the entire human race. The problems of the family and of the education and socialization of the young are the problems of the total society. The ghetto casts its shadow over the affluent world beyond its borders; poverty and malnutrition are the problems of all people, contributing to crime rates, welfare costs, and hostility and despair. Intergroup conflict, whether it grows out of struggles between classes, political factions, or races, sends its shock waves throughout society. Industrialization, an almost imperceptible force in the eighteenth century, now sweeps the entire world, crushing older production systems under its weight of goods and uniting much of the world in the common paradox of miraculous productivity and rapid despoliation of the natural environment. The questions sociologists ask, then, range all the way from those about the nature of human beings in all their social class and ethnic variety to those dealing with society's major institutions and how societies are perpetuated and how they change in values, organization, and complexity.

The Group Basis of Society   The first questions must be asked about people as social beings. How does social life help and protect individuals? How does it limit and encircle them? What new problems of human interrelationship arise in complex societies dominated by formal organizations?

We must also ask some questions about contrasts in societies. Why are societies so different in their beliefs, values, and views of reality? The antiquated idea of race used to be considered an answer to this question; now we have at last laid the racial explanation to rest and seek answers in the sociological concepts of cultural habits, values, and opportunities.

Also in connection with society and culture, the idea of socialization must be examined. How do children learn the ways of their society and take on its ideas about right and wrong? It is hard to ask such a question without asking why people deviate from the standards set by society. Is deviation to be explained as plain wickedness on the part of the individual, or does it result largely from defects in the society itself? To what extent is deviation merely a matter of how society defines the term?

Differentiation Within Societies   Societies become differentiated in many ways, but two areas of difference that have been studied most diligently by sociologists are those of stratification into social classes and differential treatment accorded people on the basis of race, ethnic group, and sex. What are the differences in life-opportunities among people of different social class and ethnic backgrounds? What are the myths and stereotypes about racial and ethnic minorities and the female of the species, and what are the consequences of the myths?

Trends in Demography and Collective Behavior   The population of the world has grown at unprecedented rates in recent decades and continues to do so, in spite of a slowing of the growth rate in many industrial societies. What are the possible consequences for the future? Not only has population grown, but it has changed into a mainly urban and suburban population. What are the results of greater crowding of population? Together with a study of urbanization are questions about collective behavior—crowd actions, riots, demonstrations, fads, social movements, and the formation and manipulation of public opinion. Are there connections between urban societies and such types of mass behavior?

Institutions and Social Change   Because institutions such as family, religion, and government are standardized and generally accepted patterns for achieving the essential needs of society, their study is basic to sociology. All institutions are undergoing change, and with them the entire fabric of society changes. How is the traditional family changing? Will it continue to meet the needs of individuals and society, or will alternate life styles become increasingly prevalent?

With the increasing secularization of society, what is the place of religion? Why is religion deeply meaningful to some and irrelevant to others?

Why are educational systems under increasing strain? What are their basic functions, and are they meeting them? Why is a large segment of college youth so critical of society?

Family	Continuous or divided generations
Education	Opportunity or frustration
Religion	Meaning or irrelevance
Economic system	Equity or exploitation
Political system	Democracy or military-industrial complex

What is happening to the economic system as economic advisors try to cope with the problems of inflation, unemployment, and international exchange? Certainly our economy has changed from a small-business to a huge organizational system. Will it provide equity and opportunity for all, or is it becoming a concentrated means of exploitation by a wealthy elite? Almost the same question can be asked of governmental institutions. Can they be made responsive to the will of the people, or is government growing into a secret, unapproachable bureaucracy, dominated by some kind of military-industrial complex?

Finally, what kinds of forces account for the massive change observable in modern societies? Is the societal system capable of keeping pace with scientific and technological change, or are dangerous disparities developing?

These questions are not the only ones that concern sociologists, but we see them as some of the most important. They are questions that relate to the ensuing chapters and give some idea of what an introductory sociology course is about. Few of the questions can be answered definitively at this stage of sociological knowledge, but an examination of findings and informed opinions of sociologists will widen greatly the student's perspectives on modern society, its organization, trends, and problems.

HOW SOCIOLOGISTS SEEK ANSWERS

As the level of complexity of society increases, the wisdom of the past becomes less adequate and less relevant to sociological understanding. The common-sense answers people once regarded as infallible are becoming increasingly open to doubt. Much of the common sense of the past turns out to have been common ignorance. Modern society recoils at the thought of burning "witches," trials by ordeal, torturing the insane, or bleeding the sick, but all these practices have at one time or another seemed like good common sense. More recently, such policies as denying voting rights to women, denying equal educational rights to black Americans, forcing Indians onto reservations and later off the same reservations, and flogging mariners, criminals, and children have all been defended as common-sense policies.

Not all commonly held views of the past are as offensive as the ones just cited, and not all are to be repudiated, but all ideas and policies must be open to the light of scientific examination. Are present policies based upon false premises? Were they ever useful and functional to the society? If so, are they still functional to the societies of today?

Observational Studies   The most obvious route to knowledge is through direct observation, but this does not imply that all observations are careful and accurate. The conflicting accounts of witnesses at trials, different accounts of the same event in newspapers and magazines, and even arguments over entries in autobiographies are good indications of the difficulties encountered in casual observation. Individual biases enter the picture, helping the observer to see mainly what he wishes to see; selective memory later helps to weed out other unacceptable details of observation.

In spite of its problems, however, observation must be depended upon, and many highly creditable observational studies are done. Observational studies depend upon training and reflection, knowing what to look for, and careful recording of all observed behavior so as not to select in terms of preconceptions. Some classical cases of observational studies in sociology are the studies of William I. Thomas and Florian Znaniecki involving Polish peasants adjusting to life in the United States, and William Whyte's *Street Corner Society*. In both cases the researchers spent long periods of time with their subjects and came to know them thoroughly. Lewis Yablonsky's *The Hippie Trip* and Leon Festinger's *When Prophecy Fails* (a study of a flying-saucer cult) are interesting examples of more recent observational studies. Erving Goffman spent a year as observer in a mental institution and wrote *Asylums*, a disturbing analysis of what he calls "total institutions," i.e., institutions that have total control over the individual.

Theories and Concepts   Observation of events naturally leads to interpretation and the search for explanation. Some sociologists are more preoccupied with analysis and interpretation than simply with the gathering of data, but, as in any science, both the collection and interpretation of facts are important. New explanations make sense of the knowledge gained and can become the basis for policy. For example, the germ theory of disease made the old practice of bleeding the patient seem absurd, and also it swept away explanations of disease as the result of witchcraft or sin. Environmental theories of delinquency suggest possibilities for correction, whereas older explanations of "bad blood in the veins" did not.

Sociology, then, as any science, looks for theoretical explanations. A *theory* is a logical and scientifically acceptable principle to explain the relationships between known facts. The theory of evolution, for example, is a well-known principle explaining the relationships between all living species. Some attempts have been made at broad general principles in sociology, but many theories are more limited in scope, explaining types of delinquency, variations in divorce rates, the appeal of new religious sects, social movements, urban riots, and many other social phenomena.

Not all sociological tools of analysis can be called theories. Sociology also develops a number of *concepts,* which are abstract ideas generalized from particular cases and usually having wide applicability. Many sociological concepts will be introduced later in this text, but some are already familiar enough in common speech to make recognizable examples: *norms* (behavioral expectations), *folkways* and *mores, status* and *role, culture, social class, elites,* and *subcultures,* to name a few.

Models of Society Similar to concepts in analytical value are models for the viewing of society. Sometimes the models are of an analogy type, as when society is compared with a living organism. A model that will be referred to in several of the later chapters is that of *functionalism*—a model which views society as a system of interrelated parts and stresses how each part contributes to the whole. It is easy to apply a functional analysis of education, seeing how it contributes to the maintenance of the entire social system by such functions as passing along tradition, promoting citizenship, training personnel, and researching areas in which new knowledge is needed. If these are the expected results of education for society, then it can be seen that new courses and methods must be developed as society changes, or the educational system can become ineffective or even detrimental—a condition sociologists call *dysfunctional.* Similar analyses can be made of all social customs and institutions.

For some purposes a developmental or cultural-evolutionary model can be used, showing the tendency for many societies to go through similar stages of change, especially after industrialization occurs. Yet another model of society is one that sees society as a struggle between

opposing forces—social classes, conservative and liberal ideas, or minority groups versus entrenched majorities. The conflict model is often
preferred by radical sociologists, but it is also fairly traditional to political
scientists as a means of viewing political processes.

   Statistical Validation   When observation and logical analysis suggest a relationship between phenomena, some attempt must be made to
validate the conclusion by examining all available evidence. Occasionally the offhand evidence may seem to point in opposite directions. For
example, a welfare worker observing families in the poorer sections of
town will note very large numbers of families broken by divorce. Another
person, reading the society page, will be impressed by the number of
divorces that occur in the upper circles of society. Is there an actual
relationship between social class and divorce? Do wealthy people get
more divorces than the poor, or does it just seem that way because more
attention is paid to their social lives? The answer is readily at hand in
national statistics and can be stated very briefly: The higher the income
and educational level, the lower the divorce rate. William J. Goode has
collected statistics from the United States and many other countries that
generally validate this statement. He finds that in most cases the poorest
levels have the highest divorce rates and the wealthy the lowest. The only
exceptions occur where divorces are very expensive or desertion without
divorce is extremely easy.[4]
   A short introductory text cannot go into detail on statistical method.
It should be mentioned, however, that usually the matter is much more
complex than in the example just given. If the information is not available
in Census Bureau reports, the researcher may have to develop his own
statistics through extensive questionnaires and interviews. If he is trying to
find a relationship between two phenomena (such as social class and
premarital sex relations), he will have to know enough about statistics to
know whether his results are statistically valid, based upon enough
examples and showing a strong enough correlation to eliminate the
possibility that findings are mere coincidence.

   Experimental Method   Experimental studies, as well as statistical
and questionnaire studies, are possible in sociology. They depend upon
formulating hypotheses, isolating a variable, and employing experimental
and control groups. A *hypothesis* is a supposition or conjecture of a
tentative nature to try to explain known facts. A *variable* is one of many
factors of a changeable nature that might account for a particular

---

[4]William J. Goode, "A Cross-Cultural Analysis of Class Differentials in Divorce Rates," *International
Social Science Journal*, vol. 14, no. 3, 1962, pp. 507–526.

phenomenon. An *experimental group* is a group in which one variable is deliberately changed. A *control group* is a group in which all variable factors are left the same so that the comparison with the experimental group can be made. A simple illustration will make these concepts clear.

Let us pose a hypothesis to account, in part, for the failure of low-ability students to improve their work in school. Our hypothesis will state that unfavorable self-image is an important cause of failure to improve. This hypothesis can be tested by dividing the students seeming to show low ability into two groups: one experimental and the other control. The experimental group will be given much encouragement, and many statements will be made to lead them to think that they actually have good potential. The control group will be taught in the same manner, except that this type of encouragement will not be given. We must watch to be sure that other variables do not enter the picture. Both groups should be equal in all significant ways, especially in measured ability and attitudes, and both should be given equally good teachers and equally favorable classrooms and periods of the day for study. If both groups are not equal, there will be no certainty whether we are measuring the variable of favorable self-concept or simply the difference between two teachers or classroom situations. If the hypothesis is proved, as sociologists would expect, we should find a measurable and statistically significant difference between the two groups in the amount of progress made by the end of the semester.

Scientific Attitudes   Whatever the method of research used, scientific method depends upon several basic attitudes and practices. The first is *objectivity*—the willingness to accept the facts as ascertained and to avoid biases. It is a disappointment to do extensive research work and then find that one's treasured hypothesis is not proved, but objectivity calls for admitting such failures. Even disproving a hypothesis can make a contribution to knowledge, but distorting the facts cannot.

Precision, reexamination, careful attention to critics, and an open-mindedness, even about favorite theories, are all attitudes necessary for good scientific research. The task in sociology is more difficult than in many areas of physical science, partly because emotional involvement and prejudices are harder to overcome. It seems also to a student of the social sciences that the complexity of the field and the number of variables involved are much greater than in the physical sciences. It might be some consolation to the social scientist to know that the physical scientist can feel just as enmeshed in complexities. Such fields as physics and astronomy become infinitely more baffling as greater knowledge is gained. Sociology is not alone in such problems; as do all sciences,

Methods	Attitudes
Observation	Objective
Theories	Systematic
Concepts	Open-minded
Analytical models	
Experiments	

sociology must refine its techniques of study to cope with growing complexities.

HOW DID SOCIOLOGY DEVELOP

As a scientific discipline sociology has had a brief but interesting and stormy career. There was, of course, much interest in human societies long before the origin of the concept of a science of society. No doubt our most remote ancestors were concerned with ways of holding together their bands and tribes. Folk wisdom of all societies is full of proverbs about social norms and responsibilities. Ancient Hebrew prophets raged against the oppressors of widows and orphans and other violators of the moral law. In China the confucian philosophers concentrated on human relationships between ruler and ruled and between older and younger generations. Confucius (557–479 B.C.) taught that the status quo of a society must not be disturbed, because only through changelessness could social relations be orderly and moral. This thought so dominated the values of the people that two centuries later Hsun Tse wrote, "The essence of good conduct . . . is the unfailing repetition of tradition."[5] Obviously such ideas could not lead to a science of critical investigation that might challenge the authority of tradition, and tradition was almost as strong in the Western world as in China.

Breaking the Bonds   A few social philosophers of the old Greek-Roman world almost freed themselves from the ties of tradition, but tradition returned in full force to medieval societies. It was only after the

---

[5]Howard Becker and Harry Elmer Barnes, *Social Thought from Lore to Science*, Dover Publications, Inc., New York, 1952, p. 69.

end of the medieval period that the bonds of tradition were broken. In England, John Locke (1632–1704) wrote persuasively that government should depend upon the consent of the governed—a theme found later in the American Declaration of Independence. Voltaire (1694–1778) devoted much of his long life to the struggle for religious liberty and general freeing of the human mind. Jean Jacques Rousseau (1712–1778) wrote vehemently against the evils of the old order, as did many of the intellectuals of France and the American colonies. Great revolutions occurred in France and America, proclaiming the end of kings and aristocracies and rule instead by voice of the public. The time had come to search for a science of society which could give enlightenment to that public.

The Premature Science: Auguste Comte   In the United States the revolution succeeded in establishing a stable order. In France the revolution led to rule by the guillotine, with hundreds of heads rolling in a violent bloodbath. Next came Napoleon, and then, after twenty years of victory, a French defeat and the return of the kings. What had gone wrong?

Two French writers of the period, Claude Henri, Comte de Saint-Simon and Auguste Comte, concluded that societal failures had resulted from a lack of scientific knowledge, which could be supplied only by a science of society. Comte (1798–1857), the better known of the two, is the man usually given the title Father of Sociology. Greatly impressed by the progress being made in such sciences as physics and chemistry, he reasoned that scientific method should also be applicable to the study of society. He coined the name "sociology" for the new science and expected it to be the crowning achievement of the scientific age. He dreamed of a "high priest of humanity" who would reform society through the use of the new knowledge. The weakness of Comte, though, was that he did not turn to the careful investigative and experimental methods needed for gaining the new knowledge. Much of his thinking constituted "a premature jump from the level of observation and inference to the level of theory."[6] The development of a science took more than mere advocacy and easy optimism about a beautiful future for humanity.

The Premature Science: Herbert Spencer   Much later in the nineteenth century a number of social philosophers became infatuated with another aspect of modern science: darwinism. Guided by the

[6]Nicholas S. Timasheff, *Sociological Theory: Its Nature and Growth*, Random House, Inc., New York, 1957, pp. 28–29.

biological principles of Charles Darwin, and adding their own view about the need for a highly competitive economic system, they developed the idea that social struggle for survival is the key to the future. The British philosopher Herbert Spencer was the most influential proponent of such ideas. He plunged into the great task of trying to fit all geological, biological, and social theory into a grand scheme of evolution. Societies with intellectual and economic freedom and a dedication to science would eventually free humanity from oppression and the superstitions of the past. As in biological evolution, however, the weak and "unfit" would have to be eliminated on the way as a part of nature's law of survival of the fittest.[7]

In the United States, William Graham Sumner became associated with very similar ideas, feeling that the reformists of his time were only meddling with the laws of nature. This brief mention of Spencer and Sumner fails to do them justice because they were both very good critics of much of the accumulated folklore and nonsense of tradition. Spencer became the vogue among the informed readers of his time. Sumner's ideas of folkways and mores and ethnocentrism have become part of the vocabulary of sociology and will be encountered in later chapters.

In the present context, though, the main point to make is that Comte in his way, and Spencer and Sumner in theirs, had all found too simple a key to human society. Although not aristocrats, they saw the world from the viewpoint of the educated and well-bred. Their sociologies left little room for the views of an alienated lower class, which Marx had begun to champion before the end of the life of Comte and before either Spencer or Sumner had achieved prominence.

The View from Below: Karl Marx (1818–1883) Karl Marx is a little difficult to deal with in sociology. Because he was primarily an advocate and a revolutionist, he does not fit the prevailing opinion that sociology should be scientific, objective, and value-free. Furthermore, he was not accepted as a sociologist by his leading contemporaries in the field or by any of the universities. Marx is also difficult to deal with without bias, because he has been enshrined as a saint in communist ideology and looked upon as the archfiend by many capitalists. Nevertheless, Marx cannot be ignored. He turned the attention of the world to phenomena that had been almost entirely ignored by the academic world before his time. He saw that while upper-world intellectuals were describing the beautiful onward sweep of civilization, there was a class of laborers sweating sixteen hours per day in the heat of smelly, unsanitary factories,

[7]Randall Collins and Michael Makowsky, *The Discovery of Society*, Random House, Inc., New York, 1972, pp. 67–70.

crawling through coal mines, living lives of bitterness and despair, and dying young. This, to Marx, was the reality of social life. Marx saw economics as the moving force of history, and a developing class struggle as the compelling economic fact of his time.[8]

More will be said about Marx when we consider social class. We shall point out that many of his predictions have not materialized and that he would probably despair over some of the governments which claim to follow him. However, Marx showed that society is not necessarily a smooth, harmonious system, nor can it be seen and understood the same way from lower-, middle-, and upper-class positions. To anti-Marxists, his slogan to workers, "You have nothing to lose but your chains," sounds exaggerated and unreal, but how equally exaggerated and unreal are the optimistic and complacent views of upper classes to the oppressed and impoverished.

Summarizing the previous pages, we could say that Comte looked for progress through science, Spencer through evolution, and Marx through revolution. The next two men to be considered were fully aware of both the conservative and revolutionary theories of their time and of the onrush of science, but neither was tempted to accept a simple key to the future. Both dealt with the complexities of science and of social change in such a manner that sociology could no longer be called a premature science. With the theoretical breakthroughs of Émile Durkheim in France and Max Weber in Germany, sociology was coming of age.

The First Breakthrough: Émile Durkheim (1858–1917)   Marx concentrated his attention on the class conflict within society. Durkheim, born ten years after Marx had issued his *Communist Manifesto*, was aware of internal conflicts, but he also saw that societies generally hold together in spite of conflicts of interest. To him, social solidarity was the overriding theme. Consequently, he asked some of the fundamental questions of sociology: What binds societies together? What happens to the binding forces of society when faced by industrial change? How do the various parts of society interrelate? How is the individual affected by the presence or absence of social cohesion?

Durkheim was so intellectually productive that his ideas will be encountered more fully in later chapters, but several comments are needed here to show his historical importance. First of all, Durkheim found the roots of social cohesion in approximately what is now called the culture concept (see Chapter 3). We are held together by common

[8]*Ibid.,* pp. 36–38.

ways of speaking, perceiving, thinking and believing, and these common points are reinforced by such collective representations as flags, parades, installations, ceremonies, monuments, commemorations, and national celebrations. We have a language, a national identity, and a religion "ready and waiting for us at birth," and to a great extent we simply absorb these characteristics of the social pattern. Furthermore, we tend to see our social order as "right" because we are accustomed to it, but even more so because there has to be at least a modicum of common agreement on rules, regulations, and contracts or society could not work. In this sense, society, said Durkheim, is a type of moral order.

Durkheim saw also that society was changing. Much of the source of this change was a result of an ever more complex division of labor in society. People have increasingly specialized jobs, are less alike than in the past, and need new rules to maintain a sense of social solidarity. Consequently, science and technology do not necessarily lead to a utopia. Perhaps in the long run a new order will be better than the old, but Durkheim foresaw much alienation and social wreckage on the way.

Much of the subject matter of sociology was explored by Durkheim, and the right questions were asked. Whether cohesive or divisive forces are stronger is still a question. World War I at first seemed to prove Durkheim right. The Marxists of Germany rallied to the Fatherland rather than seizing an opportunity to rebel. However, before the end of the war Russian soldiers mutinied, joined forces with the workers and peasants, and helped raise the red flag of revolution. Durkheim had died by that time. His son was killed in the war, and Émile sank into a depression that took his life within a few weeks. In Germany, another great sociologist, Max Weber, correctly foresaw the Russian Revolution and even speculated that the event might someday repeat itself in China.[9] Weber's attention to the master trends of history gave him a foresight rare among scholars in any discipline.

The Master Trends: Max Weber (1864–1920)   Born and educated in Germany in the days of the Empire, Weber was recognized for his brilliance at a very early age. His first writings were in the field of economics. He was highly productive of new ideas in economics, politics, and the history of civilizations. Like Marx, Weber was strongly aware of economic and social-class issues, but he found flaws in the complete economic determinism of Marx. Weber sought to prove that sometimes religious and political philosophies can be as much moving forces in history as economic interest, an idea developed in his *Protestant*

[9]Hans Gerth and Saul Landau, "The Relevance of History to the Sociological Ethos," *Studies on the Left,* vol. 1, Fall 1959, pp. 6–14.

Ethic and the Spirit of Capitalism, which will be discussed later in Chapter 12 under the topic of religion.

Above all, Weber took an interest in what he saw as the master trend of history—the disenchantment of the world (die entzauberung der welt).[10] As seen by Weber, the movement of the world was toward massive bureaucratic organization, toward rationalization of production, and away from the religious, the mythical, and the poetic. The trend was also away from personal loyalty (fealty) as a means of social cohesion and toward impersonal, formal, bureaucratic organization. In his opinion the Marxists had failed to see the bureaucratic nature of the modern economy. When the Russian Revolution triumphed, Weber remarked that "The dictatorship of the official and not the proletariat is on the march."

Early American Sociology   So far we have mentioned no American sociologists except William Graham Sumner, who was hardly typical of early American sociology. Many more American sociologists of the time were strongly reform-oriented. This was particularly true of Lester Frank Ward (1841–1913), who became the first president of the American Sociological Association. Ward was influenced by Spencer's ideas of evolutionary progress, but he did not follow the theory through to its bitter struggle-for-survival conclusion. Instead, he was an active reformer, working for free public education, equality for women, and child labor laws. He was typical of the leaders of the field in his day, optimistically believing in inevitable progress and also in conscious human effort to hasten it along.

American sociologists also became interested in the field of social psychology, which was strongly influenced by Charles Horton Cooley (1846–1929) and George Herbert Mead (1861–1931), who will be discussed at some length in Chapter 4 (socialization).

Later Developments in American Sociology   Early American sociology tended to be based too exclusively upon deductive logic rather than upon research, and it was also too blandly optimistic. The experience of two world wars and an age of social convulsions eventually led to a new sociology, one that was no longer convinced of the inevitability of progress but was aware of the fact that the road to a science of society lay through long, painstaking research. For many years the University of Chicago became the center of American sociology and contributed a number of leaders, most notably William I. Thomas (1863–1947) and

[10]Collins and Makowsky, *op. cit.,* pp. 111–117.

Robert Park (1864–1944). Both men and their students went directly to the people to conduct investigations rather than drawing upon library research and purely deductive logic. Also at the University of Chicago, the first sociological studies in urbanization were carried on, outlining patterns of growth, development, and decline of urban areas.

American sociology grew to be a major discipline in the majority of colleges and universities. Some characteristics of the discipline, especially in the 1940s and 1950s, were very strong concentration on research work and a decline in theorizing. American sociology became far more precise and statistical than European sociology, but theorizing almost fell into disrepute.[11] More recently there has been greater balance between research and theory. The gathering of facts without attempts at explanation can eventually become rather pointless, just as too much theorizing without careful checking of facts can lead to very doubtful conclusions. Talcott Parsons and Robert K. Merton, both of Harvard, are two of the leading American theorists in sociology.

Modern American sociologists agree quite well on the need for both research and theory and for constant reexamination of data. Nevertheless, there are disagreements within the field. Some would like for sociology to be a pure science, concerned with investigation but avoiding involvement in issues or work at the request of government agencies or industries. Others feel that their research should be applied and that sociologists should make good advisors in the applications of their findings.[12]

The other conflict in sociology is largely a matter of values. The conservative school remains devoted to explaining the functioning of society and tends to believe that such modern societies as ours are making fairly rational adjustments to the needs of industry, urbanization, and technological change. The more radical school is highly critical of the vast bureaucratic institutions of contemporary society and more concerned with how systems malfunction than with how they function, especially with regard to poverty, inequality, and the problems of minority groups. However, controversies within academic disciplines are almost inevitable and are by no means detrimental. Often they have the effect of intensifying interest and stimulating ideas and research. The worst possible fate for any science of human affairs would be to degenerate into a polite society in which no one would dare disagree with prevailing opinion. At present there seems to be no danger of such a fate for sociology.

---

[11]Alan P. Bates, *The Sociological Enterprise*, Houghton Mifflin Company, Boston, 1967, pp. 32–33.
[12]*Ibid.*, pp. 33–34.

WHAT OCCUPATIONS DO SOCIOLOGISTS PURSUE

Part of what sociologists do has just been discussed in connection with the history of sociology: Sociologists analyze, explain, and criticize modern society and institutions and provide information that can be used in the redirection of policies. Occasionally sociologists are even appointed to commissions to advise the President or Congress, as was the case with recent Commissions on Crime and Justice, Violence, Population, and Obscenity and Pornography. The final decisions, though, are made by politicians, and scientific findings are often thrown out as politically inexpedient. In spite of such setbacks to investigatory commissions, the facts are ascertained and publicized and may eventually move the public and its elected representatives to more enlightened policies.

Turning to the more usual and immediate answer to the question concerning sociological pursuits, there are a number of choices, depending upon the level of sociological study one wishes to reach. Raymond Mack reported in 1969 that "Seventy-nine percent of the sociologists whose primary employment is known are affiliated with colleges and universities."[13] Most of these people hold advanced degrees in sociology. Reading such figures might lead one to the erroneous conclusion that sociologists do nothing but teach others to teach sociology. This is far from true because most teachers in the field also do research work, and large numbers of people who neither teach nor regard themselves as professional sociologists nevertheless engage in sociological work.

Sociology at the Bachelor of Arts Level   Students who take a strong interest in sociology naturally wonder what their opportunities are if they set their sights on the completion of a four-year course in this field. People who are not well-acquainted with the breadth of the field assume that social work is the most likely possibility. This is a numerically minor occupational goal for the sociology major, although it is one possibility. Often social work is approached through psychology; as Peter Berger says, "American social work has been more influenced by psychology than by sociology in the development of its theory."[14] Also, many colleges and universities have established separate schools of social welfare, designed to produce graduates with specializations geared to meeting the needs of state and local welfare agencies. Such schools, of course, require considerable work in psychology and sociology.

A student with a bachelor's degree in sociology might also consider a career as a *probation or parole officer*. The man or woman making this decision should begin early in the junior year to enroll in course work

[13]Raymond Mack, "A Career in Sociology," The American Sociological Association, Washington, D.C., 1969, p. 7.
[14]Berger, *op. cit.,* pp. 3–4.

Premature theories	Auguste Comte	Herbert Spencer and William Sumner
	Father of Sociology	Social evolution through struggle for survival
	Suggests a science of society	

A view from below	Karl Marx	
	Class struggle, conflict, and alienation	
	Contrasting views of society	

The breakthroughs	Émile Durkheim	Max Weber
	The sources of social solidarity	The master trends: bureaucracy, rationalism, disenchantment
	Division of labor in society	

American beginnings	Lester Frank Ward	C. H. Cooley G. H. Mead
	Commitment to social reform	Social psychology

Modern American sociology	Improved methodology; balance of research and theory	
	Remaining ideological conflict: pure or involved science	

relevant to this occupation. Many young graduates in sociology are particularly attracted to the field of youth probation because they feel that through their sociological understanding and personal guidance the young offender may be steered toward an adulthood of productivity.

Personnel work is an appropriate field of employment for a graduate in sociology. As a personnel assistant, one screens applicants for jobs in industry, helps in the preparation of job descriptions, and coordinates or mediates interdepartmental matters. Sociology students might qualify also for such related fields as public relations and advertising.

There are many other areas in which sociology will provide a valuable start. ''An undergraduate major or minor in sociology will provide an especially valuable background for the student who plans eventually to become a *clergyman, attorney, economist, psychologist, political scientist,* or *historian. . . .* ''[15] So to answer the student's question as to what fields are open to the holder of a bachelor's degree in sociology, we would respond, ''You can do almost anything that, at a preprofessional level, is concerned with the direction, motivation, and effective organization of people.''

There are also by-products of sociological learning, as there are in all intellectual tasks. The sociologist should be well-trained in the kind of critical thinking that can be applied effectively in all occupations, especially those dealing with customs, institutions, and social groups. The trained social critic should also be able to provide community leadership in proposals for political and social change and citizens' movements of various kinds.

The Master's Degree At the master's degree level one's opportunities in sociology widen. There are occasional opportunities in administration or research in government or industry, and the M.A. is also the usual requirement for community college positions. Some sociologists with a master's degree are employed in state colleges or universities, although most state colleges and universities require completion or near completion of a doctorate before hiring a sociologist.[16]

Often the master's degree is accepted in lieu of experience in many of the fields we have discussed. In this case new employees enter the occupation with better status and better pay than if they have only a bachelor's degree. Not only is the beginning position better, but chances for advancement are greatly improved.

The Doctor's Degree Men and women who are willing to invest another two or three years of time in classes and seminars may earn the degree of Doctor of Philosophy. At this point they are sociologists. Now they are qualified to direct research projects for private enterprises,

[15]Department of Sociology, University of Kentucky, ''Should You Be a Sociologist?'', in Edgar A. Schuler et al. (eds.), *Readings in Sociology*, Thomas Y. Crowell Company, New York, 1969, pp. 839–844.
[16]Mack, *op. cit.,* pp. 8–9.

Doctor's degree
Sociologist

Research for
  Government
  Industry
  Universities
  Foundations

Master's degree
Research

Junior college
  instructor

State college
  instructor

Professor of Sociology in
  Urban problems
  Demography
  Race relations
  Criminology
  (And many more)

Bachelor's degree
  Personnel work
  Probation, parole officer
  Juvenile advisor
  Social work

Administrator in
  Social work
  Probation
  Juvenile work

Higher degree increases pay and opportunity for promotion in all areas.

Sociological knowledge serves youth, minority groups, and the impoverished.

educational institutions, or state and federal agencies; or they may be specialists in urban problems, demographic trends, rural sociology, social gerontology, race relations, or any of a number of other categories of interest to sociology. As mentioned, most holders of Ph.D.'s in sociology are affiliated with educational institutions and are involved in both research and teaching.

Social Service   Strongly idealistic students might be less concerned about the particular job they will hold, or even the pay scale, than they are about what they can offer society and what they can do to improve the conditions around them. Although it should be made clear that sociology is not a synonym for social reform and that, as an academic discipline, it is concerned with investigation and understanding rather than advocacy, it nevertheless will have much to offer young idealists. Sociologists often are called upon for help in the formulation of plans for reform in many institutions of society. Recently the specialist in urban sociology has been called upon to offer suggestions for relieving the pressures created by increasingly rapid urban growth; the criminologist is sought for advice on prison reforms; the individual with a background in medical sociology is called upon to help facilitate the rehabilitation of wounded veterans, mental patients, and people with physical handicaps caused by illness, injury or congenital ailments.

Students with an undergraduate major in sociology are excellent candidates for the Peace Corps or VISTA. Also, their understanding of

27

human interaction is invaluable in working with Target Area programs in the nation's minority communities. The specialist in race relations is asked for methods to alleviate the conditions that have given the black community the stigma of ghetto. The student with some understanding of sociology also is needed to work in programs directed toward the alleviation of poverty among migrant Mexican-American farm workers, poor whites in Appalachia, and Puerto Ricans in New York. For some students of sociology such programs become short-term learning experiences, but for an increasing number of individuals these projects become lifelong occupations.

SUMMARY

All the social sciences become increasingly necessary in an age of rapid social change and expansion of knowledge. The special characteristics of sociology are its great breadth of interest in all aspects of the group life of mankind, in the trends and developments of social systems, and in the causes of social change and social problems. The questions asked by sociologists cover a wide range, including the reasons for the development of social cohesion and group-centered attitudes, the analysis of cultures, the socialization process, racial and ethnic groups, population and urbanization, and the major institutions of society.

The methods of sociology are similar to those of any other science or social science, stressing careful observation, the development of theories, concepts, other tools of analysis, and sometimes experimental designs. Whatever method if used, sociologists attempt to be systematic, logical, and open minded.

A brief glance at the history of sociology reveals much about its basic orientation and how it has changed emphasis to remain abreast of the times. Auguste Comte had several good suggestions for the development of a science of society, although he was not a leader in the actual application of scientific methods. Sociology to Comte, and later to Herbert Spencer, was considered scientific, but not enough actual research work was done to achieve anything like a scientific level of knowledge. Also, conflicting interests and viewpoints within society had to be recognized, as was done by Karl Marx, along with greater awareness of basic social cohesion (supplied by Émile Durkheim), and the trends of modern society, as emphasized by Max Weber. Although modern sociologists hope their findings will help humanity, they see their task as primarily the intellectual quest for knowledge and explanation. Several American sociologists of earlier times (especially Lester Frank Ward) were interested in sociology as a reforming field of knowledge. On the other hand, William Graham Sumner contended that any attempt of man to improve social justice would end only in a decline of the human species. Later sociological research became much more research-oriented, but the old conflict between a detached viewpoint and a strongly involved and critical viewpoint has reemerged.

Sociology provides a good background for a number of fields of employment, including some that are only indirectly sociological, such as probation and parole work, welfare, many kinds of juvenile work, and advisory positions in aid to the poor. For the person moving directly on to a higher degree, sociology offers opportunities for supervisory jobs in the above fields of work, but more typically in college teaching, college research, and governmental and industrial research. Finally, it must be added that much of what sociology has to teach about society and social class will be helpful to any idealistic person going into community service, work with youth groups, or such organizations as the Peace Corps or VISTA.

The field of sociology has expanded rapidly in the last few decades, and until recently there has been a shortage of sociologists. Indications are that sociology will continue to be a growing field in the future in college, government, and industry. A complex, dynamic society requires study by experts, careful in their methods and objective in their conclusions.

Chapter 2

The Human Group

Socially the hunting ape had to increase his urge to communicate and to co-operate with his fellows . . . . With the new weapons to hand, he had to develop powerful signals that would inhibit attacks within the social group. On the other hand he had to develop stronger aggressive responses to members of rival groups.[1]

Desmond Morris
The Naked Ape

Judging by all contemporary societies and by what little is known of the remote past, the human being is and always has been a social animal. Reasons for our social traits are rooted deeply in our biological nature, a nature in which sex interest is a continuous rather than a seasonal phenomenon; an extremely undeveloped and helpless infancy calls for

[1]Desmond Morris, *The Naked Ape,* Dell Publishing Co., Inc., New York, 1967. p. 23

constant warmth and attention; and a lack of instinctive ways of facing the problems of life calls for a long process of learning from others. Although nearly all primates and a majority of other mammals as well are social in their habits, human beings have carried social traits further than any other species, subordinating and controlling biological urges for the good of the group.[2] Societies create their own rules regarding mating and marriage and the duties and obligations of kith and kin and define their own groups, bands, tribes, and communities in contrast with those of the outsider. In their evolutionary past men and women had to learn cooperation in their constant search for food lest they be the hunted rather than the hunters. One man alone was helpless. To be ostracized by the group was to be virtually sentenced to death. Now, after hundreds of thousands of years of human development, the physical possibilities of surviving alone are greatly increased, but it is a rare individual who chooses to live alone. As John Donne wrote, "No man is an island, entire of itself . . . ."

THE IMPORTANCE OF GROUP IDENTITY

In a society that has a tradition of individualism, it may seem strange to emphasize the study of groups of people rather than individuals. We like to see individuals with minds of their own, and we decry anything that looks like slavish conformity. Yet all of us are influenced in basic attitudes and values by our families, conform to some of the norms of our peer groups in childhood, and are sensitive to the judgments of our neighbors, associates, and fellow workers. We look to friends and kinsmen for moral support and psychological security; the achievement goals we seek are generally meaningful and worth our strife only if they are highly regarded by the groups to which we belong. Group pressures help us to obey the laws in most cases, but membership in deviant gangs can encourage disobedience. Group pressures can make cowardly conformists of us in some cases, and under other circumstances they can make us into self-sacrificing heroes. The group can impose its tyranny upon us, but it can also be our protector. It is not an exaggeration to say that the presence or absence of meaningful ties can be the determining factor as to whether we wish to live or die.

To Live or Die: Durkheim's Study of Group Influence A major contribution of Durkheim was that of defining a distinctive field for sociology. Sociological facts, he believed, should be explainable in terms

---

[2]Marshall D. Shalins, "The Origin of Society," *Scientific American*, vol. 203, no. 3, September 1960, pp. 76–85.

of sociological causes. One of his major works, *Suicide*, published in 1898, clearly demonstrates social causes for the desperate decision to take one's own life.[3]

First, Durkheim demonstrated with careful use of statistics that neither race nor climate had any bearing upon suicide rates, although they were both rather popular explanations of suicide rates in those days. He also argued that to describe suicide as the result of a psychological malady, *suicidal mania*, simply was to supply a name for a puzzling phenomenon but not an explanation. Durkheim reasoned that instead of examining the psyche of the person who killed himself (something nearly impossible to do), we should examine his group relations.

When a man commits suicide he is not only destroying his own life but severing his relationships with others. If these relationships mean enough to him, his emotional ties should surely act as a bulwark against suicide. Suicide, then, must be more characteristic of the isolated individual than of the man with a strong sense of belonging. In this negative sense suicide can be thought of as a social phenomenon.

Durkheim carefully checked all the available statistics relative to various indexes of social integration. What about married people as opposed to single? What about people with children as opposed to childless couples? In both cases the importance of belonging was demonstrated. Married men and women are much less prone to suicide than single people, and married people with children are even less prone. Not only is family a protection against possible suicide, but Durkheim's statistics indicate that the same is true of belonging to closely knit communities, such as the old-fashioned European village. Even national group identity has a demonstrable effect. In wartime the suicide rate consistently goes down; Durkheim explained that war, despite its ills, solidifies the nation, giving everyone a sense of belonging, identity, and purpose. Religious identification also has a measurable effect upon suicide rates. The suicide rate in France of Durkheim's time was highest for nonchurch members, second highest for Protestants, low for Catholics, and even lower for Jews, although all three religions teach suicide is wrong. Durkheim reasoned that the differences between the three religious groups was a matter of the closeness of emotional union. The Jews are linked together by closer community feeling than either the Protestants or the Catholics. Catholicism, however, holds people into closer bonds than does Protestantism. Catholicism stresses organizational membership, spiritual leadership, and, in a philosophical sense, does not leave man alone before God as does Protestantism. Those not belonging

[3]Émile Durkheim, *Suicide*, John Spaulding and George Simpson (trans.), The Free Press, New York, 1966.

to churches lack the group identity of the religious groups, and this, to Durkheim, was the major explanation of their higher rates of suicide.

Suicide rates also increase with age. Again Durkheim found the explanation in group solidarity: Old age tends to become a period of increasing isolation as old friends die, and deafness and senility often alienate the individual from others.

What about social expectations? Do feelings of right and wrong have their influence? After all, the family man or woman is bound by duties as well as by love, and churchgoers would consider self-destruction a major sin. Durkheim's conclusion was that suicide rates are also higher among people who are not held in line by society's rules, either because they have never internalized the rules or because they are plunged into a situation in which the rules they have learned no longer seem to apply. The problem of changing or inappropriate norms was part of the explanation Durkheim gave for the higher rate of suicide in the city than in the village. Suicide rates were highest among the recent immigrants to the city; it was they who were lost, rootless, and normless, not knowing the ways of urbanism. Other cases of suicide related to normative problems are those of people who were once well off and then lost status or sank into poverty (recently demonstrated in a New Orleans study).[4]

Durkheim concluded that suicide rates were increasing in Europe at the beginning of the twentieth century and that greater isolation of individuals from old home ties and greater detachment from the norms of an older society were part of the reason. Both types of detachment were typical of the growing industrial societies. He called the suicide resulting from isolation *egoistic*. *Ego* means self; the word "egoistic," as used by Durkheim, can best be thought of as referring to the isolated self. Durkheim applied the word "anomic" to the suicide resulting from detachment from the norms. *Anomie,* a word very much in the vocabulary of sociology ever since Durkheim's time, refers to normlessness or confusion over the norms. Durkheim also applied the word to the socially uprooted.

The concepts of egoistic and anomic suicide do not tell the whole story of self-destruction. Durkheim realized that there were societies in which people were closely bound by rules and regulations and by relationships to kinsmen, but suicide rates were, nevertheless, high. Japan was an important example. In Durkheim's days the practice of hara-kiri was more prominent than now, although it still exists. *Hara-kiri* is the practice of cermonially taking one's own life by disemboweling himself with a knife. The reason for hara-kiri was not isolation or anomie but

---

[4]Warren Breed, "Occupational Mobility and Suicide," *American Sociological Review*, vol. 22, no. 2, April 1963, pp. 179–188.

essentially a matter of sacrificing for others. If the identification with the group is too strong, and, as Durkheim said, "The importance of life is beyond the individual life itself," then it is easy to die. This is the essence of sacrifice in war, but it is also the essence of hara-kiri. The Japanese committed suicide if they had brought disgrace to the family, the community, or the nation. One could protect the honor of others only through self-sacrifice. Puccini expressed the idea correctly in *Madame Butterfly:* "If one can no longer live with honor, then one must die with honor." This form of suicide was termed *altruistic.*

Durkheim's three types of suicide are diagrammatically presented here. The circle indicates an optimum condition in which the individual is held closely in group bonds but not so subordinated as to make life impossible without them. The circle indicates a nearly zero suicide rate (no country actually has this), and the arrows leading in three directions indicate an increasing suicide rate for each of the reasons given. Anomic and egoistic suicide are shown close together because they are similar types. An individual might be both isolated and anomic, but the altruistic case is completely opposite.

In summary, group membership functions to give the individual a sense of identity and worth, obligation, and mutual benefit. So great are the psychological functions of the group for the individual that group membership can help usually to protect him against self-destructive urges, but under some circumstances it may even prompt him to lay down his life for the common good.

To Fight or Surrender   Durkheim's use of the term *altruistic suicide* comes very close to our term *heroic self-sacrifice* in some cases, especially when one willingly lays down his life for his country. Durkheim's study suggests that this type of heroism is most likely to occur when one's group is more important than his life. Research work from World War II bears out Durkheim's conclusions. In an investigation of why men were willing to face the enemy, several variables were tested.[5] Was indoctrination in love of country the primary source of bravery? Or was bravery most strongly developed as a result of hatred of the enemy? Neither explanation was primary. The strongest factor in this type of bravery was found to be group opinion. One cannot show cowardice in the eyes of his comrades-in-arms. Similarly, public opinion has pressured millions of men into joining the armed services in time of war; better to face the enemy than to face the contempt of one's peers. If the Vietnam war was unsuccessful in attracting many volunteers, it may be because

[5]Samuel A. Stouffer, "A Study of Attitudes," *Scientific American,* vol. 180, no. 5, May 1949, pp. 11–15.

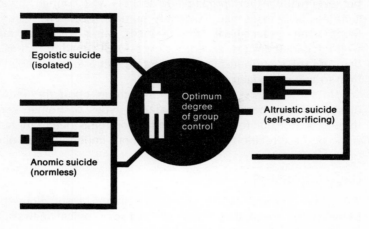

group pressure was far from unanimous, with opponents of the war ready to give moral support to those who resisted the draft.

A study of the German Wehrmacht shows how strong the influence of close group organization and sentiment can be.[6] The German army was organized with group integration in mind. Squads were trained together for long periods, went on furloughs together, and, if transferred, were reassigned together. Everything was done to maintain the social solidarity of the fighting team. Seldom has fighting morale remained so high for such long periods, even after ultimate defeat began to seem inevitable. After Stalingrad fell there were no reassuring German victories, only a long series of reverses. Yet desertions were rare, and it took an unbelievably long time before demoralization set in. The surrenders were most likely to occur among units hastily formed toward the end of the war and among those whose intensive primary-group identity had not emerged. Others with a high surrender rate were those men who had never fit in with the group or the unwillingly recruited soldiers: Austrians, Moravians, Czechs, and other outsiders.

Soldiers were constantly reassured that all was well at home and that they would be cruelly treated by the enemy if they surrendered. There were even cases where deliberately cruel treatment of civilian populations was encouraged to convince the men that they could expect no quarter. A common rumor was that they would be castrated if captured,

[6]Edward A. Schills and Morris Janowitz, "Cohesion and Disintegration in the Wehrmacht in World War II," *The Public Opinion Quarterly*, vol. 12, 1948, pp. 280–294.

but eventually Allied propaganda leaflets and counterrumors led the Germans to believe that reasonably humane treatment would be given them. Even under these circumstances surrenders were rare among well-integrated groups, except for occasional squad decisions to surrender. The study attributes the high-morale factor to group solidarity more than to any other factor.

In the analysis of effects of the group upon the individual, no distinction has been made yet among types of human groups. The importance of our relationships with people has been emphasized, but some of these relationships are much more important than others.

GROUP CLASSIFICATIONS

The term "group" has a special meaning in sociology because it represents a concept that is central to any sociological analysis. A *group* is a collectivity of people sharing some common interest or having some basis for interaction. The possibility of reciprocal communication is also an essential element. Therefore families, friendship circles, and close neighborhoods are usually classified as groups. Their interaction and communication extend over rather long periods and are generally inclusive.

Associations are organizations of people bound together for relatively limited and specified purposes. People enter associations to promote or satisfy their individual interests. Clubs, protective and benevolent organizations, and certain business organizations are associations. The proliferation of associations in the United States accounts for the fact that many foreigners view us as a "nation of joiners."

Chapters 11 through 15 will examine the five major institutions found in every society. An *institution* is an established pattern of behavior that is organized to perpetuate the welfare of society and to preserve its form. The family, religion, education, economy, and government are the major social institutions, although many minor institutions develop in some societies.

A *society* is the largest meaningful group to which the individual belongs and is almost identical to nation or nation-state. There are some exceptions to the identity of nation and society, however, as when strong feelings of brotherhood cross national boundaries. Such feelings of societal identity bound Zionist Jews together long before they had succeeded in creating the present state of Israel. Their Arabic opponents are also bound together in the cause of Islam and Arabic unity more than by mere identity as citizens of Jordan, Saudi Arabia, or Kuwait.

There are also collectivities of people that do not constitute groups, such as a statistical category of "all people over sixty-five years of age" or "all middle-income families." There are also differences in degree of group identity. People generally feel more loyal to their family and close friends than to the companies for which they work. The small, intimate groups are so important in some respects that they are called *primary*.

Primary Groups   Charles Horton Cooley in 1909 was the first to use the term "primary groups" to describe such groups as family, neighborhood, and children's play groups. Such groups were, in Cooley's phrase, "the nursery of human nature," where the essential sentiments of group loyalty and concern for others could be learned. Cooley was not creating an entirely new concept, but he contributed the word "primary," along with a sensitive description of the meaning of primary-group relationships.[7]

The characteristics of the primary groups Cooley described are those of face-to-face interaction, sentiments of loyalty, identification, emotional involvement, close cooperation, and concern for friendly relations as an end in themselves, not as a means to an end. The primary group is usually rather small, but size is much less important than sentiment. The primary group gives the individual his "first acquaintance with humanity." To Cooley (and the idea is typical of sociological perspectives), the group is of overwhelming importance. "Human nature is not something existing separately in the individual, but a group-nature or primary phase of society."[8] Human nature "comes into existence through fellowship and decays in isolation." Primary groups are, obviously, a great source of emotional psychological security. They are also, for a child, a school for learning the ways of human interaction and the give-and-take of working and playing together. Quarrels within primary groups can and do occur, and feelings can be hurt because the members are emotionally close to one another, but indifference is impossible. How often have we, as children, said to a brother or sister, "I'll never speak to you again!," only to have our resolution collapse within an hour?

Cooley concluded that the positive and affectionate characteristics of the human being grow in families, neighborhoods, and children's play groups in all societies and that hatred, bigotry, and intolerance are, to a great extent, a failure of these sentiments to spread beyond the small group. In later pages of his book *Social Organization* he speculates about

[7]Charles Horton Cooley, *Social Organization,* The Free Press of Glencoe, Inc., New York, 1958, pp. 23–31.
[8]*Ibid.,* p. 30.

the possible spread of primary-group sentiments to wider areas of mankind as improved communication makes people more aware of others and as social organization grows and improves to prevent the division of humanity into hostile groups. Although Cooley's hopes have not been realized, few would deny the desirability of his suggestion for a more thorough mutual understanding of the peoples of the world.

Cooley's analysis of primary groups and their functions may be even more relevant to society today than it was in 1909. The analysis of the spread of something resembling primary-group sentiments to wider and wider areas of the world has not been continued in Cooley's terms, but some of the implications of primary groups have been stressed even more by modern writers. A dichotomy between primary and secondary groups, perceived but not elaborated upon by Cooley, has become an analytical tool for describing certain types of societal change.

Secondary Groups   *Secondary groups* are the more formal and less intimate types of groups to which people belong. To start with clearly definitive examples, the United States Army, General Motors, and a large state university are secondary groups. As organizations, secondary groups do not give people the feeling of close identity that primary groups give. Considerable effort must be devoted to making people proud of the corporation for which they work, and this type of pride, if it is achieved at all, is not a primary-group sentiment. One can still be lost in the great organization; there is not the same sense of psychological security. There is a greater possibility of one feeling uprooted and alienated.

If large secondary organizations are completely replacing primary groups, then there is much to worry about in modern mass society. Loss of identity and alienation in the mass society are common themes in literature. There are arguments for feeling that the drift of modern society is toward the secondary group. The military service can seize the individual and take him from his family, friends, and neighbors. The demands of education also can take people away from their primary groups and lodge them in a giant university, and often the demands of business can cause them to move far from home. Primary groups are either helpless to resist or do not wish to interfere with the modern demands of career opportunities.

Two observations that must be made about primary groups lessen the dreariness of the picture just presented. First, primary and secondary groups are *ideal types,* that is, types represented as opposite poles for the sake of analysis. In concrete life situations most relations are not purely primary or secondary but have characteristics of each, and the two groups become intertwined. A man who has just moved from Arizona to Detroit to take a new job with a giant corporation will take his family with him. He might also transfer his membership in the Elks Club from the chapter in his home town in Arizona to a club in Detroit. In this case he will still belong to a family (Cooley's prototype of primary group) and to an association that has certain primary traits.

The second reservation about primary-secondary group class-ifications is that primary groups form within secondary groups. The man from Arizona might make a number of close friends on his new job, even though the corporation remains a distant and aloof entity. In as gigantic a secondary organization as the army, friendship ties are sometimes unusually close, especially in combat crews. Clubs and little friendship circles form in great universities, even though such large institutions of learning seem cold and impersonal compared with the small-town schoolhouse. There are, however, sometimes "loners" within such large organizations.

A recent study by Litwak and Szelenyi[9] indicates that in the industrial society primary groups are broken up more easily than they were in agricultural societies, but they are also formed more easily by most people. The better educated people required by industrial societies are more accustomed to making new friends and even to forming neighbor-hood associations when needed. In a small, agricultural community newcomers might be regarded as strangers for years; in the modern community, where the turnover is rapid, the newcomers are "old residents" almost as soon as they have finished unpacking. Litwak's research indicates that neighbors are still the first people to be called upon in short-term emergencies (especially in a disaster such as flood or earthquake), relatives still help with long-term problems, and newly found friends fill the need for sociability and a sense of belonging in the new community. Litwak's study says more about well-educated people, however, than it does about the less educated. The latter are less likely to join associations and less likely to adjust quickly to new circumstances. Many people miss the ties of the small community, in spite of its having been a place of gossip and intrusiveness. Nostalgia for a simpler way of life is quite common.

Reference Groups   A reference group is a group to which one refers for normative behavior patterns or other important aspects of life. A reference group can be one of a person's primary groups, but not

[9]Eugene Litwak and Ivan Szelenyi, "Primary Group Structures and Their Functions: Kin, Neighbors, and Friends," *American Sociological Review*, vol. 34, no. 4, August 1969, 465–481.

necessarily. People are often influenced strongly by groups to which they do not belong but to which they aspire: occupational groups, theatrical circles, upper classes, and the best clubs. There can also be negative reference groups, which are groups whose ways one would avoid. White society can constitute a negative reference group for black militants. In older societies positive reference groups were often strictly rural, and country people thought of city life in terms of negative reference groups. Modern societies give wide possibilities for reference groups, just as they offer many alternative ways of life.

Societal Analyses Communities and societies have been analyzed in a manner paralleling the primary-secondary types of group relationships just discussed, and sometimes the analysts show a nostalgia for an older order. The German sociologist Ferdinand Tönnies used the word *gemeinschaft* to describe communities characterized by many primary-group relationships. Picture an old-fashioned European village with its homespun games and entertainments, its traditional festivals, communal baking ovens, a village common for sheep or cattle, and achievement in arts and crafts measured by village standards, not national standards. In such a place families have known each other for generations; it would seem unlikely that one would worry about alienation. One might, however, be hounded by village gossip and ridicule. The opposite type of society in Tönnies' analysis is called *gesellschaft*—a businesslike, contractual society, emphasizing efficiency rather than primary personal ties. Durkheim and Weber were both aware of such contrasting types of societies. Weber spoke of the trend toward bureaucracy and rationalization of means of production, and Durkheim described a shift toward organic solidarity. By *organic solidarity* he meant the kind of solidarity that arises in a society whose members are as interdependent as cells in a living organism, each doing a different type of work. The idea of organic solidarity is not entirely pessimistic. Durkheim said that in time the new interdependent society would be better than the old, but much chaos could be expected for the immediate future—a period of adjustment to a new style of life. In Durkheim's terms, the older societies had *mechanical solidarity,* with members as alike as products of a machine.

In the discussion of primary and secondary groups and societies attention has been focused on groups to which we belong. Primary-group loyalties are strong and affectionate. Secondary-group belonging can be based on purely utilitarian values rather than affection; but in both cases the individual is a cooperating member of the group. What about the outside group—the people across the tracks, or across the ocean? What feelings develop relative to the outsider?

Cooley's primary group concept

Primary group

Examples
 Family
 Children's play groups
 Close-knit neighborhood

Traits
 Emotional involvement
 Close cooperation
 Face-to-face interaction
 Identity
 Psychological security
 Belonging an end in itself

Secondary group

Examples
 Giant corporation
 State university
 United States Army

Traits
 Unemotional
 Competitive
 Less intimate
 Identity less relevant
 Economic efficiency
 Belonging a means
 to an end

Additional comments

Not all groups are strictly primary or secondary but come somewhere between: school, church, lodge.

Primary groups exist within secondary groups.

Societal types similar to primary-secondary relationships

Tönnies
 Gemeinschaft
 (person-centered)

Gesellschaft
(business-centered)

Durkheim
 Mechanical solidarity
 (members all alike,
 as though turned
 out of a machine)

Organic solidarity
(members all different,
held together
by interdependence)

INTERGROUP ATTITUDES

Conflicts have been so frequent and terrible in the human race that we sometimes wish all people could be blended into the same social system and all differences disappear. Yet a little more reflection makes us realize that such a world would be dull, undifferentiated, and devoid of the constant and largely unconscious experimentation with social systems that has been the major preoccupation of the human species. Some of these social systems insist upon maintaining their own separate identities even within larger societies. Those societies holding pluarlistic values would say they should have this right.

Conflict Groups   Georg Simmel, an early German sociologist, wrote that "The unity of groups frequently disappears if they have no enemies."[10] In this phrase he was describing what are often called *conflict groups,* groups living within a society but in a state of normative conflict with it. Throughout many centuries of Western history, religious dissenters have been good examples of conflict groups. Such groups, especially if they feel threatened, close ranks, displaying great unity and cohesion. Throughout most of their history the Jewish people have lived as a conflict group in one society or another. By surrendering their ideals, perhaps they could have lived unmolested, but at the price of surrender of their religion and their cultural identity. Simmel tells us that many Protestant nonconformist groups resisted attempts at compromise with the established churches because "otherwise the solidarity of their opposition would disappear, and without this they could not further struggle." The very fact of opposition to others preserves group solidarity.

In-groups and Out-groups   Sumner used the terminology of "in-group" and "out-group" to describe similar types of group feelings, but Sumner's terms have wider applicability. The groups to which we belong are *in-groups,* and groups to which we do not belong are *out-groups,* especially if we look upon them with a certain amount of antagonism. The in-group versus out-group concept is applicable to friendly rivalries between schools, clubs, and associations, but it is also applicable to much more hostile groups. On a small scale it is descriptive of violent neighborhood gangs; on a larger scale it is descriptive of wars between nations.

The in-group versus out-group concept is intimately linked to *ethnocentrism,* which means, literally, centered in the culture, and it can be characterized as the idea that one's own group is best and others are to be judged on its terms. Ethnocentric attitudes are mentioned most frequently relative to national rivalries, but ethnocentrism has many applications. One can be ethnocentric about his community, state, social class, or even his race. Strong and exaggerated ethnocentrism regarding nation and race is fraught with danger and possible conflict. Sumner was

[10]Georg Simmel, "The Sociology of Conflict," *American Journal of Sociology,* vol. 9, 1904, pp. 517–518.

a pessimistic thinker on the subject of human hostilities, concluding that people would always be ethnocentric and divided into antagonistic groups and would always have wars.

The essential reason for ethnocentrism is that a society must teach the "rightness" of its ways to its young to give them a sense of values; and if the society's ways are right, other ways must be wrong. Furthermore, group morale demands loyalty and pride. Even the individual ego is bolstered by the belief that one's society is best. The stories of heroes are told and retold to emphasize the societal virtues, and rising generations are not allowed to forget the evil ways of the enemy and all his past transgressions.

Isolated in the hills of Western New Guinea live the Dugum Dani, a Stone Age people not contacted by Western civilization until the 1960s.[11] Each tribe of the Dugum Dani is indistinguishable from the others, but they are mortal enemies, each tribe seeing its people as good and the outsiders as bad. Year after year intermittent war goes on between pairs of tribes. A member of one tribe is killed and is buried amid impressive ceremonies and agonies of tears. After the burial, as soon as a good day for fighting arrives, the war is resumed until a Dugum Dani from the other side is killed to avenge the act of "those evil people." No one knows when the war started because it is older than the memory of any living man, and its origin was unknown to his father or even to his father's father's father. Nor is there any expectation that the war will ever end because all wicked deeds must be avenged so that departed spirits can rest in peace and the righteousness of the tribe can be reaffirmed.

The recent history of Western civilization also contributes many examples of ethnocentric behavior. During World War II both Axis and Allied troops prayed to the same God to make them victorious over the enemy. Each combatant nation was sure that it had "God on its side."

In fact, ethnocentric attitudes have often served as justification for violent acts. The Ku Klux Klan has used the pretext of "protecting white womanhood" to rationalize its lynching of blacks. Our ancestors drove the Indians from their land because it was a matter of "manifest destiny" that God intended it for us.

Reducing Out-group Hostility Is the account of the Dugum Dani actually a kind of parable about the human race? Sumner would have said "Yes"; Cooley would have said "No." Sumner saw a destructive degree of ethnocentrism as inevitable, growing out of our respect for our own customs and values. Cooley saw the possibility of the spread of

[11]Robert Gerdner and Karl Heider, *Gardens of War: Life and Death in the New Guinea Stone Age,* Random House, Inc., New York, 1968, pp. 135–144.

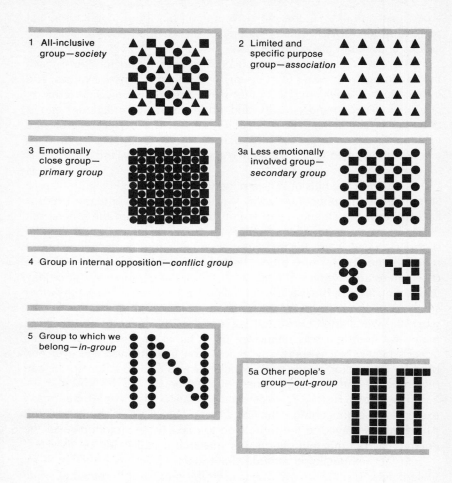

1 All-inclusive group—*society*

2 Limited and specific purpose group—*association*

3 Emotionally close group—*primary group*

3a Less emotionally involved group—*secondary group*

4 Group in internal opposition—*conflict group*

5 Group to which we belong—*in-group*

5a Other people's group—*out-group*

feelings of sympathy for our fellow man during an age of worldwide communication, and he saw also the possibility for larger organizations that would sweep old enemies together into common societies, as happened long ago in England and Scotland.

Another possible hope for the human race is in greater education and awareness of others. The most narrowly and dangerously ethnocentric individual is apt to be poorly educated and to have little experience with other types of people. Such a person is often referred to as an *authoritarian personality,* a term developed in the 1940s by Adorno,

Flowerman, and others and widely used since. Authoritarian types tend to think that only one way is right, that there is not much room for argument, and that there should be strict obedience to leaders. Such people are usually highly intolerant of foreigners and draw complete and easy distinctions between "good guys" and "bad guys."

Education, especially education in the social and behavioral sciences, probably causes a slight decline in narrowly ethnocentric attitudes. Greater experience of the world and of various groups of people, not necessarily gained just in the classroom, is also helpful in broadening the mind. The type of perspective that social scientists would like to substitute for ethnocentrism is that of cultural relativism.

Cultural Relativism   *Cultural relativism* is the attitude that all people should be judged in terms of their own cultures and that various customs and practices we would avoid might be appropriate in the context of the cultures which follow them. Nearly all present-day Americans are capable of seeing that such Indian leaders as Tecumseh, Joseph Brant, and Crazy Horse, although they fought against our ancestors, were great men as measured by their own standards. We are also open-minded enough to realize that in some cultures a man can have four or five wives because it is the custom.

Cultural relativism is a viewpoint that enables students to step outside their own circle of values and see unfamiliar social customs as their practitioners see them. This does not mean, of course, that the cultural relativists are without values of their own, but they at least withhold judgment of other cultures as they study them.

There are, however, some strains in the cultural-relativist concept. Most cultural relativists would find it difficult to remain purely objective about a society whose ideals call for conquering all its neighbors or for practicing cannibalism, slavery, or headshrinking; nor would they be objective about the atrocities of nazism on the theory that they were part of a cultural system. Even the cultural-relativist view of human societies has its limitations, not in ethnocentric attitudes but in terms of the common welfare and survival of mankind. The United Nations Declaration of Human Rights is a first faltering attempt to define rights and wrongs in terms of the welfare of mankind as a whole. The declaration avoids being a mere ethnocentric statement of the values of the Western world, and it also avoids the above-mentioned pitfalls of cultural relativism. Whether mankind can ever agree to certain human rights and make them more than an unenforceable statement remains to be seen. Many different cultural values would have to be considered because cultures vary widely, as we shall see in the next chapter.

SMALL-GROUP RESEARCH

Considerable study has been done in the field of group research to test degrees of conformity and other patterns of group interaction. Are the judgments of people badly distorted by group pressures? Do patterns of leadership emerge naturally? Does interaction generally promote friendliness? Are there cases in which group and leadership pressures constitute dangers?

Conformity Studies   One of the best-known studies in group conformity (conducted among college men) was undertaken by Solomon Asch.[12] The subject of the experiment compared the length of lines on white cards. He and several others sat in separate booths, and he was led to believe that the other people were also subjects of the experiment. The system was rigged in such a way that he could hear the judgments made by the other men being tested. What he did not know was that all the others had been instructed to give the same wrong answer. The question was whether the subject would have enough independence of mind to rely upon his own judgment or whether he would go along with the opinions of the others. The answer was obvious enough so that errors could be expected in only about 1 percent of the cases. Yet under the influence of group pressure, 36.8 percent of the subjects gave the wrong answer.

Some variations on the experiment were also tried. If some of the people who were wise to the test were instructed to give a different wrong answer from that of the majority, then the subject's resistance to group pressure was increased. Standing alone against a unanimous group is more difficult than facing a disunited opposition.

A similar type of experiment was conducted by Muzafer Sherif, also with college men.[13] In Sherif's experiment men were asked to watch a single pinpoint of light in a totally darkened room and to describe its movements. Sometimes four or five men watched it together, and sometimes individuals watched alone. The light actually did not move, but the circumstances made it very easy to imagine movement. The men got together to decide what the movements were. Those who had to watch alone readily agreed with the group about the direction of the light movement. It was as though under conditions of confusion and bewilderment there was a great reassurance in finding group norms. Sherif

[12]Solomon Asch, "Opinions and Social Pressure," *Scientific American,* vol. 193, no. 5, 1955, pp. 31–35.

[13]Muzafer Sherif, "Group Influences upon the Formation of Norms and Attitudes," in Eleanor E. Maccoby, Theodore M. Newcome, and Eugene L. Hartley (eds.), *Readings in Social Psychology,* Henry Holt and Company, Inc., New York, 1958, pp. 219–232.

concludes that people may sometimes feel too constrained by group norms, but the absence of such norms is much more intolerable.

Building and Resolving Conflict   Sherif also did a lengthy study of group interaction among boys of junior high school age at a summer camp.[14] The boys chosen to attend camp were carefully selected so that such variables as bad reputation, ethnic-group antagonisms, and widely different abilities and backgrounds did not have to be considered. All the boys were intelligent, of good reputation, and from middle-class backgrounds. They were selected from different schools so that they did not know each other before summer camp began.

In the relatively unstructured first days of the experiment, friendships formed quickly, and leadership emerged. Leadership seemed to be natural and spontaneous. One experiment proved that the popular, leadership types were overrated in their performance in competitive games.

After friendship cliques were formed and leadership emerged, the boys were divided into two groups—the Eagles and the Rattlers—cutting across friendship lines. The Eagles and Rattlers were always made antagonists in sports and contests. Old friendships dissolved rapidly, with especially hard feelings toward former friends, who were now seen almost as traitors.

After antagonisms had grown strong, two attempts were made to resolve the conflict situation before it destroyed the summer camp. The boys were allowed to enjoy good times together: motion pictures and special treats at the cafeteria. This plan did not work. The two groups pushed and shoved in line and vented their hostility toward one another. The next part of the experiment was to see whether they could be brought back together by tasks in which they had to cooperate for their mutual good. It was arranged for the water supply to break down so that the boys had to work on the system. A truck was stuck in the mud, and everyone had to cooperate to get it out. Almost immediately, the antagonisms began to dissolve. The experiment had an acceptable outcome, and by the end of six weeks in summer camp old friendships were restored.

To what extent can the experiences of a group of boys in summer camp be generalized? Certainly there are many other situations in life where repeated contests rouse hostility. Sportsmanship is hard to maintain if tensions run too high between rival schools, for example. But what about the other side of the case? Can a need for cooperation unite people

[14]Muzafer Sherif, "Experiments in Group Conflict," *Scientific American*, vol. 195, no. 5, 1956, pp. 54–58.

who have long been antagonistic? The experience of integration of the
Armed Forces would indicate that the answer is a qualified "Yes."

Experiments in Integration   Samuel Stouffer reports about the experiments in integrating the Armed Forces toward the end of World War II.[15]
Previously, black and white troops had been assigned to separate units
and separate tasks. It is appalling to think that we were fighting a war
against the racism of the Nazis but were fighting it with a racially
segregated army.

Questionnaires were given to a control group and an experimental
group. The control group consisted of white soldiers who had had no
experience with integration, and the experimental group was one in
which integration had been tried.

The question asked of the control group was "How would you like
integration with black troops?" The replies were overwhelmingly negative, with approximately two-thirds saying they would dislike the idea
very much, 11 percent saying it would be all right, and the remainder
mildy opposed. In the experimental group, after integration had been
tried for several months, similar questions were asked. The replies were
almost the exact reverse of the control group. Sixty percent expressed
approval, seven percent disliked it intensely, and the remainder expressed only mild disapproval.

Not all types of integration have worked out as well as that of the
Armed Forces. It must be admitted that men in uniform are under orders
that cannot be openly defied. There are, however, some of the same
implications as those found in the study of boys in summer camp. The
armed services bring men into a situation in which they have the same
complaints, in which they are ordered around in the same manner, and in
which they are deprived of the privileges of civilian life. They must
cooperate for their mutual good in training and sometimes in a subtle
defiance of the system through "goldbricking" (looking busy without
doing anything). Under combat conditions their lives depend upon each
other, and color becomes completely irrelevant.

Neither the Korean nor Vietnam war has resulted in strong resistance
to integration; attitudes change as customs change. It is not to be assumed
that all is harmony at all times. Clashes still arise, often the result of hard
feelings over inequalities in assignments and promotions. Under combat
conditions color does not matter. Unfortunately, off the post, in bars and
recreation halls, where the pressures of common interest disappear, a
pattern of self-segregation is still noticeable.

[15]Samuel A. Stouffer, *The American Soldier: Adjustment During Army Life,* Princeton University
Press, Princeton, N.J., 1949, p. 594.

Interaction and Friendliness George Homans has done an extensive study of continuous personal and group interaction and its influence on friendship.[16] In methodical, point-by-point analyses based upon research studies by various writers, he shows the modification of opinions, the growth of sentiments of loyalty and friendliness, and the growth of leader-follower relationships through prolonged interaction. All these sentiments decline if constant face-to-face interaction declines—probably one of the reasons why old-time reunions are enjoyable only for a relatively short time. Eventually the conversation begins to lag; there is not enough in common to talk about because interaction has not gone on in recent years. Homans' work also helps to explain why people are seldom fired from jobs in which a personal relationship has developed. Even rather difficult characters are hard to turn against completely. If they are fired at all it is likely to be before they have become part of the crowd.

The Dangers of the Group Durkheim's suicide study suggests that the control of the group can be too great. In other ways, the studies cited by Asch and Sherif are disturbing because they make us wonder to what extent we surrender our minds to group opinion. The development of group conflicts and ethnocentric attitudes is also disturbing. Certainly the group can both mother and smother us, and it can define our friends and enemies for us.

A disquieting thought about the compulsive power of the group was suggested by Raser in an article titled "The Failure of Fail-Safe."[17] The term "fail-safe" refers to attempts to guarantee against human error in strategic situations fraught with extreme danger, especially in the handling of nuclear weapons. Many United States submarines are equipped with nuclear missiles that could be fired in retaliation against an enemy which resorted to nuclear warfare against us. To make sure, however, that no American commander fires a nuclear weapon on sudden impulse or in a state that the courts might call "momentary insanity," fail-safe systems are employed. A senior officer can fire a missile only with the consent of the other officers aboard and, ordinarily, only after receiving a set of radio signals. However, in case of an extreme emergency it would be possible for the officers to make the fateful decision themselves. An important precaution in fail-safe is that a number of officers must decide jointly. The critical question the author raises is: Knowing what we do of group cohesion, of group thinking, and of the close primary-group loyalty and

---

[16]George Homans, *The Human Group,* Harcourt, Brace and Company, Inc., New York, 1950, and George Homans, *Social Behavior: Its Elementary Forms,* Harcourt, Brace and Company, Inc., New York, 1961.

[17]John R. Raser, "The Failure of Fail-Safe," *Transaction,* vol. 6, no. 3, January 1969, pp. 11–19.

"almost mystical sense of trust" that develops under combat conditions, can we really expect the junior officers to overrule their commander? Raser further shows that human judgment grows more erratic and undependable under conditions of extreme emergency. Adrenaline enters the blood stream to prepare the warrior for fight or flight but not for meditation. It is also under emergency conditions that people look most strongly to leadership and seem least capable of rendering independent judgment. "Even if the subordinates have doubts, there is research showing that they will probably obey the captain's orders."[18] A combination of explosive ingredients develops: fear and hatred leading to restricted vision and imagination and group training and loyalty leading to group thinking. Add to this combination greater power in a single Polaris submarine than has been exploded in all the wars of history, and we shudder in spite of all the reassurances of fail-safe.

SUMMARY

Human beings are social animals who exist in groups, collectivities of people sharing interests, interaction, and communication. The individual identifies with the group, influences it in some cases, and is influenced by it in others. The group itself exerts strong pressure to conform to the standards and behavioral patterns of the overall membership.

A study of suicide has shown that the individual's attachment or lack of attachment to a group may influence him to commit suicide. Anomic suicide occurs when there is loose attachment to the group or when there are simply no norms to follow. If one commits altruistic suicide, his motivation arises from the idea that in taking his own life he will serve the good of the group. If one is isolated from the group, he may commit egoistic suicide.

Groups, associations, and institutions make up the structural fabric of society, the largest meaningful group to which one belongs. However, the *most* meaningful relationship is that which exists between the individual and the primary group, a small, close, and emotionally involved collection of people. Secondary groups are more formal, less emotional, and less intimate.

Conflicts between groups occur when members of a group think of themselves in ethnocentric terms. Ethnocentrism teaches the "rightness" of one's customs and patterns and may justify violent actions against anyone whose attitudes are too divergent from those of the group.

[18]*Ibid.*, p. 17.

However, the attitude of cultural relativism can help to reduce out-group hostilities by pointing out that other customs are the results of different value patterns.

Experiments in creating and reducing conflict between groups, as well as experiments in integration, have shown that it is possible to change hostile attitudes toward a group to friendly, or at least tolerant, attitudes. In each case it is the nature of the group that is the decisive factor in influencing the attitude of the individual.

Chapter 3

Human Societies, Culture, and Subcultures

God gave to every people a cup, a cup of clay, and from this cup they drank their life. They all dipped in the water, but their cups were different. Our cup is broken now. It has passed away.[1]

A "Digger" Indian, Quoted by Ruth Benedict
Patterns of Culture

Culture consists of the thought and behavior patterns that members of a society learn through language and other forms of symbolic interaction—their customs, habits, beliefs, and values, the common viewpoints which bind them together as a social entity. It is what the old Indian in the above quotation meant by the cup from which they drank their life. Cultures change gradually, picking up new ideas and dropping old ones; but many of the cultures of the past have been so persistent and

---

[1]Ruth Benedict, *Patterns of Culture*, Mentor Books, New American Library, Inc., New York, 1946, p. 19.

self-contained that the impact of sudden change has torn them apart, uprooting their people psychologically. When the old Indian said "Our cup is broken now; it has passed away," he was not speaking of physical death "but of something that had equal value to that of life itself, the whole fabric of the people's standards and beliefs,"[2] the entire culture. Cultures of the modern world sometimes change with such rapidity that members of an older generation can easily feel that "Our cup is broken now."

Culture is spoken of here as though it is an actual, tangible thing, but it is, of course, an abstract concept. Cultures are developed by and transmitted through societies, which can be defined as self-perpetuating human groups, usually possessing a territory and government or other means of social control, and often including subgroups within. Society refers to people and their organization; *culture* refers to thought and behavior patterns and means of intercommunication.

The concept of culture is one of the major interests of sociology and anthropology. Much that was once attributed to race and heredity is now seen clearly as the result of cultural training. The Iroquois were not savage fighters because it was in their blood but because it was in their culture. The Hopi are not outwardly calm and imperturbable people because it is in their blood (or more correctly, chromosomes) but because it is in their culture. Cultures train people along particular lines, tending to place a personality stamp upon them reading "Made in the U.S.A.," "Made in France," or "Made in Germany." This is not to say that all people are alike in any particular culture, for people have their own idiosyncrasies and are a blend of heredity, cultural experience, subcultural experience, family experience, and unique, personal experience. Nevertheless, the total experience of growing up in one culture leaves its mark upon the individual, so that a Korean child reared in America can seem typically American, and an Anglo-American child reared in Korea can seem, in cultural respects, Korean. People create culture, but it is equally correct to say that cultures create people.

CULTURAL TRANSMISSION, ACCUMULATION, AND DIFFUSION

Because culture consists of patterns of socially transmitted rather than instinctive behavior, it stands to reason that culture must be acquired through a learning process. All phases of cultural learning involve imitation and observation, and, more importantly, the acquisition of language and other means of symbolic communication.

[2]*Ibid.*, pp. 19–20.

Transmission Through Symbols   All societies have their systems of symbols. A *symbol* is any sign, signal, or word that stands for something else. The most obvious symbolism by which culture is transmitted is language. All words are symbols, having only the meaning assigned them by the speakers of the language. Language among human beings conveys a great variety of meanings that the simple cries of animals cannot transmit. Language not only describes what is here, but it can recall the past and warn of the future. Language includes not only simple names for things but also abstractions such as "justice," "love," and "idealism." Language focuses on the things most important to a culture, changes with a culture, and not only expresses thought but helps to shape the thought processes. Some languages, such as Navajo, depict human beings as pawns in the hands of nature, compelled to live in harmony with her laws or perish; on the other hand, the English language tends to express an active attitude of man toward nature.[3] Some languages, such as Chinese, emphasize the precise, practical, and concrete; others, especially Hindi, are rich in words dealing with abstractions. At least one linguist believes such linguistic differences explain why Buddhism was always interpreted very differently by Chinese and Indian civilizations.[4] Such linguistic differences probably both shape the thinking of a culture and reflect the cultural philosophy.

Cultural symbolism, though, is more than mere language. It includes many other ways of conveying meaning: laughter, smiles, and tears; handshakes, embraces, and kisses; national anthems, love songs, and dances; banners and emblems; military uniforms, epaulets, and stars; Christian crosses, Moslem crescents, and the Star of David; traffic lights, sirens, police badges; bells, bridal gowns, and wedding rings; caps and gowns, processions, diplomas; and a thousand more. We speak commonly too of symbols of status—yachts, elegant dress, exclusive neighborhoods, and social registers. The person foreign to a culture must learn symbols of the above types just as much as he must learn the language. Hand gestures that are signs of friendliness in one culture are obscene in another. A raised, extended hand in America probably means hail or farewell; in Greece it could mean "A curse upon you!" All cultures occasionally require communication by silence, some more than others. Many American Indians are much more circumspect than whites in this respect, never intruding into one's solitude with a gush of words. Some

---

[3]Benjamin Lee Whorff, *Language, Thought and Reality,* The M.I.T. Press, Cambridge, Mass., 1956. The idea of the influence of language on thought patterns has been pursued by other anthropologists, most notably Edward Sapir.

[4]Hajime Nakamura, *Ways of Thinking of Eastern People: India, China, Tibet, Japan,* Philip P. Weiner (trans.), East-West Center Press, Honolulu, 1968.

peoples express emotions strongly; others, such as the Japanese, politely subdue strong emotions, especially of sorrow. Again, one does not know the culture without knowing its symbol system, including the silent as well as the spoken symbols.

Cultural Accumulation Cultures accumulate more techniques, ideas, products, and skills as time goes on, and the more traits a culture has, the more rapidly it grows. The pace of change in modern Western societies is often bewildering. At the same time that new cultural traits are added, certain old ones have to be dropped because they have outlived their usefulness. Buggies and most of the paraphernalia of the age of horses has dropped out of American culture. However, cultures sometimes accumulate customs that are outdated but very hard to drop, such as our cumbersome methods of spelling words, our dividing lengths into inches, rods, furlongs, and miles, and dividing weights into ounces, pounds, and tons. The adoption of a metric system would save hours of mathematical computation, and the adoption of an easier spelling system would make reading possible for many who have had reading problems all their lives. Unfortunately, though, many of the traits accumulated by a culture become set and unchangeable.

Diffusion Cultural ideas and inventions not only accumulate, they diffuse, that is, spread from one area to another. During the Middle and New Stone Ages the knowledge of the bow and arrow spread to all parts of the world except Australia. An alphabet, developed by the Phoenicians, copied by the Greeks and Romans, and modified by them and various other peoples, has spread to encompass all Western civilization and much of the rest of the world. History books are full of illustrations of the spread of the use of gunpowder from the East to the West and its devastating effects on medieval castles and feudalism. The diffusion of the automobile to all parts of the world in recent years is having a similarly drastic effect. Examples of cultural diffusion are so numerous that it is difficult to think of an important cultural trait which has not been involved in the cultural borrowing process.

Although distance is ordinarily a barrier to diffusion, sometimes elements can diffuse over tremendous distances and long periods of time. Versions of such Biblical stories as the Great Flood, the Tower of Babel, and the forbidden fruit of the Garden of Eden have traveled to and from Near Eastern countries and to various parts of Africa, with some changes in details but with the plot recognizable. For example, in an Ashanti version of the Garden of Eden story, a pregnant woman is overcome with an irresistible urge for the fruit of the tahu tree, which the great god

Onyonkopon has warned people not to eat. The moon sees her take the fruit, reports the incident to God, and death is sent down among men.[5] The brothers Grimm found that many of the Germanic fairy tales they recorded were found in nearly all parts of the world.

A study of the gradual diffusion of Chinese ideas and products into the Western world reveals the ubiquitous nature of diffusion. Even back in ancient Roman times silk made its way from distant China to the courts of Rome, where it was dyed purple and used for royal robes.[6] During that same period of history the peach and apricot trees spread to the West. In 751 the Moslems captured some Chinese paper makers, and the making of paper spread through the Arabic world and across North Africa, reaching Spain in 1150. The magnetic compass also spread to the West via the Arabs, as did porcelain and the orange and lemon trees. After the time of Marco Polo, the knowledge of gunpowder and coal spread to Europe, along with less portentous inventions such as dominoes, playing cards, chess (via Persia), and paper money. Later tea, wallpaper, the sedan chair, lacquer ware, kites, and folding umbrellas spread to Europe; and yet later, Chinese gardens, goldfish, azaleas, chrysanthemums, camellias, tree roses, papier mâché, soybeans, firecrackers, and a few of the thousand or more vegetables used by the Chinese became popular in Europe.

Interestingly though, it was only during the eighteenth century, when Europe was very critical of its own civilization, that the ideas and philosophy of China began to spread to the West. For a while Confucius and Mencius were very much the vogue in France, hailed as the greatest sources of wisdom the human race had ever developed.

The fact that ideas spread only under the right circumstances is closely connected with the total understanding of cultures and their ethnocentric attitudes. Often, even when a new cultural idea is accepted it is modified and reinterpreted. The West has never understood Hinduism or Buddhism, even though some of their ideas have diffused. In the East, Christianity is likewise misinterpreted in many cases. The leader of the Taiping Rebellion in late nineteenth century China called himself the reincarnation of Christ, confusing Christian and Buddhist concepts. Westerners try in vain to equate a Buddhist state of nirvana with their concept of heaven, but there is little similarity in the concepts. Ideas that are extremely foreign to a culture are borrowed only under special circumstances, and even then they are bent in the philosophical direction of the receiving culture.

[5]Susan Feldman (ed.), *African Myths and Tales*, Dell Publishing Co., Inc., New York, 1963, pp. 118–119.
[6]Paul Frederick Cressey, "Chinese Traits in European Civilization: A Study in Diffusion," *American Sociological Review*, vol. 10, no. 5, October 1945, pp. 595–604.

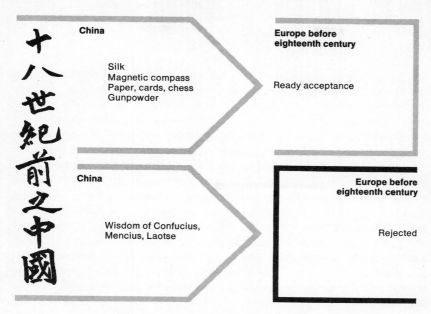

Foreign ideas are seen as more threatening than foreign products.

The wisdom of the East held no interest before the eighteenth century.

There are other limitations on cultural diffusion, such as fear and suspicion of outsiders and their ideas. Even more important are the effects of physical isolation. People who have lived in the greatest isolation have had no chance to borrow from others. Extreme examples would be the Greenland Eskimo, who had lost all contact with other human life until their rediscovery in the early eighteenth century. The Australian aborigines were another people living in total isolation from the outside world, in their case for many thousands of years. Generally speaking, the greater the isolation, the more primitive the society; and the greater the cultural borrowing, the more advanced the society. Naturally, a harsh, unproductive environment, or enervating heat, impenetrable jungles, Arctic permafrost, or precipitous mountain terrain can have a negative effect on cultural advancement. Cultural and environmental factors of this kind, and not race or heredity, explain the different levels of advancement of the cultures of the world. Even in advanced modern societies the most isolated groups tend to advance most slowly: for example, the mountaineers of Appalachia, remote rural communities, and the surprisingly isolated city ghetto areas.

THE FUNCTIONS OF CULTURE

An examination of the functions of culture make it clear why the expression "Cultures create people" is not an exaggeration. Culture defines what the proper *family* structure should be, how many wives a man should have, and whether premarital sexual relations are a proper preparation for marriage or are grossly immoral. There are set rules for the socialization and care of children: when they should be weaned, how they should be cared for, and to what extent they should be trained for independence. An educational system (not always the formal one we know) is found in all cultures for teaching growing children what they must know and how they must behave. Values are culturally defined so that growing children are taught rights and wrongs and what their aims and goals in life should be. Culture provides *heroes* who exemplify what a good man or woman should be and after whom one can pattern his life.

To a great extent culture molds and channels what we think of as the *human condition*, partly deciding even such biological details as how often we get hungry in the course of a day, at what time we have reached marital age, and whether we express our feelings loudly or with restraint. Even the personality differences that we think of as separating feminine from masculine temperament are interfered with to some extent. Hall tells us that in Iran it is perfectly fitting for a man to burst into tears when overwrought.[7] Because man is the stronger of the two sexes, he should show his feelings. Woman, being the weaker sex, should be able to hide her feelings. This is nearly the opposite of what Americans think of as proper behavior patterns.

Culture also *provides for economic needs*, telling how to earn a living, which jobs should be done by men and which should be done by women. Some occupations are assigned high prestige in one culture and only the most debased status in others, for example, prostitution. Tilling the soil might be considered the only sacred way of life in one culture, but in another culture it might be thought of as so demeaning as to be done only by slaves.

Culture provides a means of *social control*. Not all cultures have complicated legal machinery, but all impose sanctions against those who defy their most sacred customs. Sometimes these sanctions are merely ridicule and ostracism, but these can be powerful forces for control in small, self-contained groups. Imagine the misery of the man rejected by

[7]Edward T. Hall, *The Silent Language*, Fawcett Publications, Inc., Greenwich, Conn., 1961, p. 50.

the only people in the world he will ever know! Often primitive cultures can depend upon taboo and fear of the supernatural as a means of control. Modern, secular cultures find the problem of social control more difficult and must depend increasingly upon police power and court procedures rather than upon family and neighborhood opinion. This is but one illustration of the tendency for cultures to grow more complex and institute more formal and specialized officialdoms as they become more advanced and urbanized.

Culture even *defines reality* and a person's relationship to the supernatural. There can be wide variations within such a culture as that of the United States, but even here culture imposes limits, so much so that it would hardly occur to a modern American to worship Quetzalcoatl or to believe in blood sacrifice. In a simpler culture there is little or no variation in sacred belief. In modern cultures, of course, much of existence is defined by science, which greatly enlightens, but takes away much of the mythological wonderment of the past. Even science, however, does not supply answers to the eternal existential questions of people, and they usually look to the religions and philosophies of their culture for a torch to guide them.

Folkways and Mores   Much of the study of culture is the study of the growth of custom. Sumner used the words "folkways" and "mores" to describe the customs of a people.[8] As originally used by Sumner, *folkways* referred to the old customs whose origins are lost in antiquity but that continue to be followed. The types of food we eat, how many times per day we eat, our customs of dress, how we celebrate traditional holidays, and our burial customs are all examples of folkways. It can be seen that some of these customs change, so that often the term "modern folkways" is used.

Mores are also cultural customs, but they are those that are held with strong feeling and whose observation is insisted upon. Eating with a knife instead of a fork would be a violation of folkways and might cause raised eyebrows, but to bake and serve a puppy for dinner would bring screams of outrage—mores would have been violated. In Sumner's analysis the breach of mores constitutes a threat to the group; cannibalism, murder, and treason are extremely good examples. These deviations are easy to understand in Sumner's terms, but it is a little harder to understand why the violation of certain types of food taboos would meet almost as strong opprobrium. The reasoning behind the strong emotions is clear in some cases and less so in others, but always the mores can be thought of as rules whose violation is viewed with great hostility. Obviously there are

[8]William Graham Sumner, *Folkways*, Ginn and Company, Boston, 1940.

some customs that are intermediate between these examples of folkways and mores. How does one classify sacrilegious jokes, vile language, or a failure to salute the flag?

Folkways and mores are rules of behavior or *norms*. Some norms are vigorously enforced and written into law; others are frequently avoided. Sometimes mores and laws seem to be one and the same thing, as in the commandment "Thou shalt not kill." The difference is that laws are formalized, legitimately instituted, and carry the threat of punishment by society. Often laws grow out of the mores, but it is important to note that laws sometimes create new mores. For example, when regulations were changed to bring about the racial integration of the Armed Forces of the United States, the decision seemed to be in conflict with the norms of much of the country. Now the idea of integrated Armed Forces is one of the societal norms, with no noticeable movement to turn back the clock to the old days of a segregated army. Laws do not always succeed in changing norms, however, especially if there is great normative conflict over whether the law should be passed; the experience of the United States with Prohibition is an often cited case.

The norms of society can be thought of as the rules of conduct that flow out of certain *values* or underlying sentiments of right and wrong. A society with strong military values will find it easy to recruit manpower and will probably give high-status awards to the warrior. A society with negative attitudes toward the military service will find recruiting difficult, except in a national emergency, and possibly even then. In our history, Lincoln and Wilson were particularly harassed by this problem, and the Vietnam war is a modern example of the same difficulty. On the other hand, our society has been particularly successful in stressing the values of hard work and success-striving. Leisure has been little admired; hard work has had the greater value.

Status and Role   Reflection upon the values of society gives a good clue to what roles will be most admired and how they will be defined. In sociology we speak of *status* as a position held and *role* as the behavior expected of the person occupying that position. We all hold many statuses and perform many roles. There are kinship statuses, such as father and mother, son and daughter, brother and sister; positions of prestige, such as high priest, king, or president; ordinary occupational roles, such as farmer, carpenter, or grocer; certain inherited (ascribed) statuses, such as male or female, natural-born citizen, family background, race, and many others. The norms define the roles of parents, the roles of men and women, our occupational roles, and the roles of leaders. Consistent with the American value of success-striving, the captains of industry of the nineteenth century were among the most admired people, and the norms allowed great freedom in the pursuit of wealth. However, norms change, and with them the prestige of certain statuses and roles. There is no longer a consistent definition of women's roles, nor is there anything like the adulation of the successful businessman that was encountered in the nineteenth century. The roles of distant kinsmen grow less important; the laborer is no longer as subservient as in the past. Nevertheless, the normative aspect of role remains. People in high position are expected to exemplify the norms of leadership, and the country can feel betrayed when they utterly fail to do so.

An entire society can be analyzed in terms of status and role, with one person replacing another in a particular status or social position without the society's suffering the loss of a status occupant. For this reason the learning of the cultural system by successive generations is largely a matter of learning role behavior—an idea that will be further commented upon in the next chapter.

CULTURAL ALTERNATIVES AND FREEDOM

The norms of a society are in many cases applied to all its members equally. No American can be legally forced into slavery or peonage, and, ideally, all should have equal protection of the laws. Laws against theft and murder are also based on universal norms, the types that apply to all members of the society equally. There is no such universal law against drinking liquor, and yet any practicing Mormon or Seventh Day Adventist will avoid drink. The minister of another church may be allowed to take an occasional social drink, but his or her congregation will be horrified if he or she goes on a bender, whereas the common laborer might meet much less outrage for the same offense. Physical bravery has always been a norm for Marines or policemen, but only recently has it become so for the college president! In other words, a limited amount of choice is permitted in some norms but not in areas where one's position calls for exemplary conduct.

These examples of differences in the rigidness of the norms are only minor examples of the broader area of cultural alternatives. Durkheim once said of more primitive societies that "One's first duty is to resemble everybody else, not to have anything personal about one's beliefs or actions. In more advanced societies, required likenesses are less numerous; the absence of some likenesses, however, is still a sign of moral failure."[9] An examination of examples will point out the truth of Durkheim's statement.

[9] Émile Durkheim, *The Division of Labor in Society*, The Free Press, Glencoe, Ill., 1947, pp. 396–397.

Culture is a way of life that...	Culture is a functioning system that provides...
Is transmitted from generation to generation	A "proper" family type
Is cumulative	Socialization of the young
Diffuses from place to place	Education
Is selective in what it borrows and retains	Values: rights and wrongs
	Heroes to emulate
Provides specialties and a limited number of alternatives	Ways to channelize human nature
Tends to be integrated around central values	An economic system
Defines status and role	Social control
	Definitions of reality and the supernatural
Can be complicated by subcultures and cultural conflict	Norms for guidance: folkways and mores, group pressures and laws

Specialties and Alternatives   In the United States today one has many possibilities insofar as occupation is concerned; these possibilities are referred to in sociological literature as *specialties*. Jobs are assigned partly on the basis of sex, but not nearly as much so in modern industrial societies as in traditional ones. Women are not confined to the home but may pursue any job from nurse or school teacher to steeplejack or jockey. The latter jobs can be taken only in the face of social disapproval, however, because there is still some of the old desire to make people "resemble everybody else." The role of nurse for a man has similar problems, admirable as it is, so other names such as "medical assistant" have been used to avoid the stigma.

Cultural alternatives are the types of choices that allow for differences in ideas, customs, and life styles. Modern, democratic societies offer far more cultural alternatives than have many societies of the past. Religious alternatives constitute one of the areas in which Western civilization has grown greatly in freedom for individual choice. In the United States people may belong to any church or to none at all. Even here, though, traditional practices have sometimes worked to limit those alternatives. Polygyny is illegal even among people whose religion supports the practice. Native American Indian beliefs have not been recognized sufficiently to give their practitioners time off for religious holidays, as is the case with Christianity and Judaism. Atheists are often shunned as though nonbelief constitutes a threat to the entire society.

In older societies in which church and state were combined, a failure of religious conformity was logically regarded as a threat to the state. Now that the state is a political rather than a religious entity, the threat of nonconformity is most likely to be felt in the political sphere. Communists in the United States and anti-Communists in Russia are extremely unpopular, both in the public mind and from the official viewpoint. Nonconformism is much more dangerous to the individual in Russia than here, but even here political dissidents can find themselves under surveillance.

It would be heartening to be able to say that cultural alternatives are completely permitted as long as they do not constitute a threat to the society, but even this is not true in all cases. Many sexual practices are illegal, even between consenting adults, and local communities are apparently free to prohibit theaters, plays, and even literature considered offensive to majority opinion, regardless of redeeming social value. The use of alcohol is permitted in practically all states, but not the alternative of marijuana. Even such trivial matters as styles of hair and dress have been interfered with by employers and local school boards, although at first glance they would seem to be unquestionably in the area of cultural alternatives. In conclusion, we can say that the area of cultural alternatives tends to grow in modern freedom-loving societies but often only as the result of a struggle.

CULTURAL INTEGRATION

The opening comments of this chapter imply that culture is patterned in the sense that it has enough consistency to make life meaningful for its members. If a society is cooperative and peaceful and worships gods who are also cooperative and peaceful, the culture will have a religious consistency about it; it will be *integrated* around a set of beliefs. All parts seem to fit together. Anthropologists describe many primitive societies as having been well-integrated before the impact of modern civilization disrupted them. Thus the life of the Great Plains Indians centered around vision quests that brought bravery and magical protection, and this belief was in keeping with a way of life that stressed warfare, hunting, horsemanship, and the adventurous spirit.

Guy F. Swanson has done a fascinating study on the subject of cultural integration as applied to religions, especially of primitive peoples. By careful statistical analysis of fifty societies he demonstrates that advanced groups with various levels of authority over them usually populate the spirit world with various levels of gods. If they have a supreme chief or king, they are very likely to worship a high God above all others. Those groups with strong interests in lineages are likely to worship ancestors. Tribes with strong differences in wealth and position are more likely than others to attribute their moral rules to the gods, thus strengthening the hand of the upper classes over the lower. The author documents even more examples of this correspondence between culture and religious concepts.[10] Years ago Durkheim developed this same idea but without the documentation that is possible today.

The words "cultural integration" also take on another shade of meaning in the sense that new elements are integrated (fitted) into the culture. The horses of the Great Plains were descended from horses lost by the Spanish explorers, but they quickly became part of the culture of the Indians, making perfect sense in a mobile hunting society.

Many of the white man's cultural traits did not fit in—could not be integrated—into Plains Indian society. Schools, clerical jobs, the idea of saving money, and getting ahead all seemed unmanly and wrong. Erikson's *Childhood and Society* gives an excellent portrayal of how the customs and values of the Sioux created a character type that could hardly be expected to fit into modern American society.[11] Oliver LaFarge's *The Enemy Gods* tells the tragic story of a young Navaho who takes up Christianity and relates his eventual feelings of guilt, isolation, and remorse for having "followed the Jesus trail," a way incompatible with his kinsmen and their culture.[12]

There are many other illustrations of new and incompatible elements in a culture. Actually, modern societies are always full of new elements, only half-digested by the culture, so that the concept of cultural integration is hard to illustrate in such cases. For example, in the United States there are certain basic cultural orientations usually commented upon. Man is seen as the master of nature, the active life is stressed more than the contemplative, and hard work and success-striving continue to be highly regarded. However, even some of these sentiments may not be held as firmly as in the past. As man's attempt to master nature frequently ends in polluting streams, turning lakes into cesspools, and spreading contaminants throughout the world, faith in mastery begins to falter. Americans continue to place great emphasis upon the individual, but as

[10]Guy F. Swanson, *The Birth of the Gods: The Origin of Primitive Beliefs*, The University of Michigan Press, Ann Arbor, 1960.
[11]Erik H. Erikson, *Childhood and Society*, W. W. Norton & Company, Inc., New York, 1950, chap. 2.
[12]Oliver LaFarge, *The Enemy Gods*, Houghton Mifflin Company, Boston, 1937.

the welfare state becomes a more constant force the individual's interests often succumb to those of the state. It is still true that all the sentiments mentioned above, plus a strong belief in the democratic process, run strong in America, but it is questionable whether they are consistent enough to give the sense of cultural integration of which the anthropologists speak. Many elements of Christianity stand in opposition to wordly and materialistic success-striving. Although better than 90 percent of Americans claim to be Christians of some type or degree, who would claim that a thorough understanding of Christianity would give a perfect understanding of modern American society?

COMPLEXITIES OF MODERN CULTURES

Modern societies are complicated by heterogeneous populations made up of people with different interests, different philosophies, different occupations, and different social-class positions. In numerous modern societies, especially in the United States, many racial and ethnic groups add variety to the culture but also make it difficult to describe the culture in simple terms. The dominant values of the majority are not always the values of various subcultural groups. In fact, the society can best be conceived as a system embracing many subcultures, each with its own subcultural traits.

Subculture means a smaller culture within the greater one and a small culture that, despite its distinctive values, is still subsumed under the larger cultural system. The concept is a little tricky. How divergent can a subculture be and still fit the case? Are the extremely isolated old-order Amish a subculture, or are they a distinctive culture? Because they are subject to the laws of the United States and are American citizens and pay taxes, we would probably say that they are a subculture, but the divergence is obviously greater than the meaning implied in such terms as "Midwestern subculture" or "rural subculture."

Much latitude is given in the use of the subcultural concept, and various papers have been written about ethnic subcultures, regional subcultures, youth and age subcultures, deviant subcultures, occupational subcultures, religious subcultures, and many others.

Subcultures can be conveniently divided into three major types. Some are in the process of being assimilated into the general culture and can be called *convergent subcultures*. Many of the ethnic subcultures are of this type, for example, Irish, Italian, Czech, Jewish. Certain religious groups that once seemed very distinctive are no longer as much so, such as Catholics, Mormons, and Greek Orthodox. They are now moving in the direction of the majority culture and are more completely accepted by

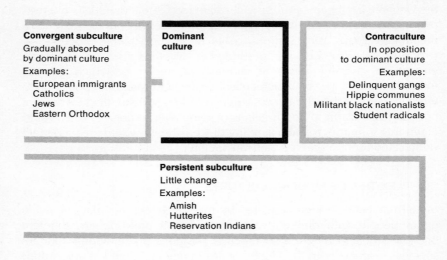

Convergent subculture	Dominant culture	Contraculture
Gradually absorbed by dominant culture		In opposition to dominant culture
Examples:		Examples:
European immigrants Catholics Jews Eastern Orthodox		Delinquent gangs Hippie communes Militant black nationalists Student radicals

Persistent subculture
Little change
Examples:
   Amish
   Hutterites
   Reservation Indians

it than in the past. Other subcultures converge with the main culture more slowly, if at all. The isolated Amish and Hutterites could be called *persistent subcultures* in contrast to convergent subcultures because they insist upon keeping ways of life very different from those who they regard as the ungodly majority. Even they, however, are disturbed by forces, such as the requirements of education, that move them gradually toward modernity and slightly closer to the majority culture. Some of the American Indians on reservations have remained so separate from the culture of the United States as to make an excellent example of persistent subculture. The only problem is that the term "distinctive culture" might fit them better than any subcultural concept could do.

Occasionally a subculture seems to exist mainly as a reaction against the dominant culture. Yinger has coined the word "contraculture" or "counterculture" for such groups. Other subcultures may very well have values that conflict with the major culture, but they have not arisen mainly as a reaction against it. The contraculture is primarily a reaction and "can be understood only by reference to the relationships of the group to the surrounding dominant culture."[13] One of Yinger's examples

[13]J. Milton Yinger, "Contraculture and Subculture," *American Sociological Review*, vol. 25, 1960, pp. 625–635.

is the delinquent contraculture—the type of culture formed by city boys' gangs, especially if they are dominated more by expressions of hostility than by an interest in theft or other remunerative crimes. The beatniks of the 1950s and the hippies of the 1960s are excellent examples of contracultures, explainable only in terms of reaction against the dominant culture. It should be noted, though, that these groups are not entirely rejecting American norms, but they seem to overstress certain values (equalitarianism and ready tolerance, for example) to the utter exclusion of others, such as middle-class striving and respectability. Such groups, dedicated to opposing the norms of the larger society, can never entirely tear themselves loose. Sometimes they display the very hostilities they oppose; often there is a kind of struggle for status, a status that depends upon just the right degree of rejection of the "square" world, but a struggle for status nevertheless.

The distinction between subculture and contraculture can be well illustrated from the experience of the black American cultures. Among some black Americans, a mother-dominated family, although different from the traditional American model, can be seen as merely part of a subcultural pattern; on the other hand, the Black Panthers' rejection of the whole world of the white man is contracultural. However, many groups cannot be neatly categorized into one concept or the other. A poor person might express contracultural points of view toward the wealthy or "the dirty politicians who run the country" but still be a loyal conformist.

Culture conflict—a conflict over cultural values and norms—exists for all kinds of individuals and subcultural groups, whether they are contracultural or not. Southern blacks moving to northern cities have been enculturated into a different culture from the one they will face in the city. Even some of the rights and wrongs are different. Sons of rural Mexican families grow up in the United States with different cultural values. In the last decade much has been written about the "culture of poverty," a culture characterized by feelings of hopelessness and futility, mitigated by hedonistic pleasures on the few occasions when there is money on hand. The Puerto Ricans of New York City form another subculture with different cultural values. The same can be said for certain southern, mountainous areas, where local mores make it virtually impossible for revenuers to collect taxes on liquor. Immigrants from lands where fathers are dominant in the family find it hard to get used to our equalitarian family, and often conflict between generations arises. People from countries where marijuana has been used legally find it hard to understand our inconsistent laws on the matter, just as an earlier generation of immigrants could not understand our Prohibition amendment.

These then are some of the complexities of the culture concept in the intricately varied American society, but the concept is just as important here as anywhere. All people are molded by their cultures, or often even more by their subcultures; but simple or complex, the cultural determinants are powerful. It is these cultural determinants, and not race or heredity, that account for the fascinating variety found in the human species. Whoever seeks an understanding of humanity must first study cultures.

SUMMARY

Culture is the total way of life of the people of a society, including their customs, institutions, beliefs, and values. Culture functions as a binding force, holding people together by common attitudes, beliefs, and traditions.

Culture is learned behavior, transmitted through communication, largely in the form of language. Language is so intimately connected with culture that it links its users in common modes of thought and perception. It raises the level of human possibilities far above those of the animal world because it can relate present to past and future and the close-at-hand to the faraway. Language (especially when written) makes possible the retention of the learnings of the past and their transmittal to younger generations.

Culture accumulates new traits over a period of time, and it drops many traits that are no longer useful. Sometimes, however, ingrained cultural habits make change difficult. Although culture is a vehicle for human survival, it is also a trap of habit and custom from which no one can fully escape.

Cultural traits diffuse from one society to another. Distance is a barrier to cultural diffusion, but sometimes attitudes are even more of a barrier. Cultural traits diffuse if they fit into the needs and values of the receiving culture. Foreign ideas are less likely to be accepted than are products and techniques. Fear of outsiders and extreme physical isolation are very important factors in the prevention of diffusion. Where cultural diffusion is impossible, cultures fail to develop the technologies that the Western world characterizes as advanced. It is difficult to avoid use of the words "primitive" and "advanced," but they should not be taken as descriptive of levels of happiness or psychological well-being.

Some of the functions of culture are those of defining the "right" family type and patterns of rearing the young and "proper" social roles for men and women. Cultures develop values, traditions, and heroes.

Cultures help to regulate human nature, even interfering to some extent with such biological matters as age of maturity, how often the individual should eat, and what he should eat. Cultures define reality, influencing one's perception of the world and explaining the supernatural.

Cultures have their values and norms, standards of behavior. Some societal norms are enforced equally upon all individuals; others place stronger expectations upon people in respected positions than upon the common person. Cultures allow certain alternatives, sometimes in such minor matters as style of dress and sometimes in such major matters as religious and political opinions. There are always limits to such alternatives, however. Where laws do not impose limits, the threat of social ostracism does.

Anthropologists describe cultural integration as the condition that exists when all phases of a culture seem to blend together and be intelligible in terms of certain major values and beliefs. Because of the complexities of modern societies and frequent internal contradictions, the idea of cultural integration is harder to illustrate in the modern world than in the "primitive world."

Integration can refer to a process—the integration of new elements into a culture. Frequently the new elements are but poorly understood and are reinterpreted in terms of the more traditional views of the receiving culture.

Modern societies have so many complexities that variations on the word "culture" must be used for adequate description. Within the culture there are various ethnic, occupational, regional, and religious groups with ways distinctive from the majority. The ways of life of such people are referred to as subcultures, variations on the general culture, but are contained within the same larger society. Some of the subcultures, especially those of ethnic minorities of European descent, can be called convergent in the sense that they gradually lose their distinctiveness as subcultures. Other subcultures are more persistent, trying to cling to distinctive ways, sometimes for reasons of religious conviction.

A special subcultural type arising out of opposition to the prevailing culture is called the contraculture, well exemplified by delinquent gangs, beatniks and hippies, and the Black Panthers. Such subcultures are understandable only as reactions against many of the prevailing societal norms.

Culture conflict is conflict over cultural values and norms. The very discussion of subcultures implies cultural conflict, which is a part of most societies. There are strong differences of opinion as to what the values, norms, and laws should be.

Chapter 4

The Preservation of Societies: Socialization

Old woman: It's easy once you begin, like life and death . . . it's enough to have your mind made up. It's in speaking that ideas come to us, words, and then we, in our own words, we find perhaps everything, the city too, the garden, and then we are orphans no longer.[1]

Eugene Ionesco
"The Chairs"

Socialization is the process by which people acquire the beliefs, attitudes, values, and customs of their culture. It also involves the development of a distinctive personality for each individual because the traits of the group are never absorbed in precisely the same way by all the people. Cultural and subcultural experience, family experience, and unique personal experience interact in complex ways upon individuals whose hereditary endowments differ. The process, then, creates a bewildering variety of personalities, but always within cultural and subcultural frameworks.

[1]Eugene Ionesco, "The Chairs," in *Four Plays*, Donald Allen (trans.), Grove Press, Inc., New York, 1958, pp. 111–160.

THE ESSENTIAL ELEMENTS OF SOCIALIZATION

Human personality does not develop automatically through an inevitable unfolding of potentialities. It is true that a certain level of maturity must be attained before various possibilities can develop, but whether or not human beings develop their full capabilities depends upon *human interaction,* the mastery of *language,* and at least some measure of *affectionate acceptance.* These three essentials of socialization usually interact during the process of social and physical growth.

Through interaction with others people learn appropriate behavior patterns; they learn their rights, duties, and obligations, and they learn which actions are approved and which are forbidden. This learning is accompanied and accelerated by the learning of language. Because people are emotional as well as intellectual beings, they must learn to experience love and to give love in return. For the sake of analysis we shall examine human interaction, affection, and language as though they were separate determinants, although in real-life situations these three essentials of socialization are inseparable.

Human contact and interaction are so important they would seem to need little elaboration, and yet people sometimes assume that real ability can develop without them. The old saying "Genius will out" implies that true genius needs no background or training. A little reflection and an examination of the known evidence, however, indicate that even the greatest talent can be wasted if there is no encouragement for its development.

The Need for Interaction: Experimental Evidence   We can never be certain that experimental evidence from animal studies is entirely applicable to human affairs, but such evidence deserves consideration. Conclusions from animal studies generally agree quite well with what we know of human development, and, of course, certain types of experiments can be performed on animals but not on human beings. Rat experiments indicate that those rats deprived of companionship and an interesting environment are mentally dull compared with rats "educated" in a stimulating environment. In the case of rats it is possible to perform autopsies and weigh the brains. The "educated" rats actually have greater brain weight than those from the deprived environment. Apparently both the physical growth of the brain and its functions are influenced by the environment.[2]

Experiments with human beings must of necessity be more limited, but what experimental evidence exists indicates a similar damaging effect

[2] J. T. Tapp and H. Markowitz, "Infant Handling: Effects on Avoidance Learning, Brain Weight, and Cholinesterase Activity," *Science,* vol. 140, May 3, 1963, pp. 486–487.

from stimulus deprivation. In an experiment performed at McGill University, subjects (volunteer college students) were confined to a small room, isolated, and deprived of anything to stimulate interest; the lights were dimmed and the rooms soundproofed. Feelings of disorientation began within a few hours. Subjects reported that it became increasingly difficult to think clearly. Most of the subjects were having hallucinations within twenty-four hours. Various figures began to appear on the wall in front of them, dancing about erratically. One man was so sure of the reality of his hallucinations that it was hard to convince him they were not real. Measurable differences in brain-wave patterns were also found after a period of isolation, and emotional responses were described as increasingly childish.[3]

The McGill experiment demonstrated, under controlled conditions, what has often been observed before: the mental and emotional regression that takes place with people long isolated from meaningful contact. In the early nineteenth century attempts were made at prison reform by isolating prisoners from each other. The idea was that as long as the prisoners were isolated they could not learn criminalistic behavior from each other. Such experiments were eventually abandoned because of the mental deterioration of prisoners long held in isolation. An unusual case of mental isolation occurred among American prisoners of war in Korea, where clever manipulation by the Chinese sowed the seeds of suspicion of man against man until the Americans did not know who they could trust. The result was little communication with anyone for long periods of time and consequent mental depression, apathy, and decline in the will to live.

Cases of very great deprivation of contact among institutionalized people are by no means uncommon. Such cases occur in prisons (both military and civilian), mental institutions, homes for the aged, and, in the past, commonly in orphanages.

Isolated Children   There have been reports in the past of children (called *feral children*) growing up without human contact. The assumption has been that such children would prove what human nature, unaided by cultural learning, is really like; but the assumption is dubious, and reports of feral children are too unreliable for forming any such conclusions. Although abandoned infants and small children have been found from time to time, there is no way of knowing how long they were abandoned or whether they were normal at the time of abandonment. The closest approach to finding out what happens to the individual who is

[3]Woodburn Heron, "The Pathology of Boredom," *Scientific American*, vol. 196, January 1957, pp. 52–56.

deprived of contact comes from cases of badly mistreated children, occasionally reported in the news, who have been locked up and given almost no attention. The classic cases of such children are two reported by Kingsley Davis: Anna and Isabelle.[4]

Anna and Isabelle were two girls found at about the same time, both showing the effects of extreme isolation. Although the two cases are similar, there are also significant differences. Both were illegitimate children, and in both cases grandparents had attempted to hide them away so their existence would not be known. They were locked in attics, hidden away from society, deprived of adequate sunlight and nourishment, and deprived of human instruction and the chance to engage in play or other childhood activities. Neither child knew any words; both emitted only animal-like sounds, and both seemed to be severely mentally retarded.

The first significant difference was that Anna had been totally isolated while Isabelle had been secluded with her deaf-mute mother. After the girls were found they were given special training, but Anna made only slight progress. She mastered almost no words and continued to be extremely retarded in mental growth. She died four years after her discovery.

By contrast, Isabelle gained command of language. Once she attained her first breakthrough in the grasp of words her progress became rapid. Eventually she was enrolled in school, where she achieved a grade level only slightly below her age and made satisfactory mental and social-emotional adjustment to her classmates. Why did the two girls respond differently to the process of socialization? Of course hereditary differences cannot be ruled out entirely, and Isabelle's training had been better than Anna's, but it seems likely that the greater amount of human contact between Isabelle and her mother was of major importance. There had been at least minimal interaction, more than in the completely empty world in which Anna spent her first six years of life.

Mistreatment of children is frequent enough so that the above case has more than just theoretical importance. We shall return to the problem of mistreatment later, but for the next examples we shall consider cases involving larger numbers of children, culturally deprived by institutionalization or by subcultural experience.

Deprived Subcultural Groups　　In the early years of mental testing it was hoped that means had been discovered for accurately measuring all children and knowing just what their life potential would be. The reason

[4]Kingsley Davis, "Final Note on a Case of Extreme Isolation," *American Journal of Sociology*, vol. 52, March 1947, pp. 432–437.

such a hope proved unattainable is that intelligence tests actually measure the cultural learnings of children, and children coming from a culture for which the test was not intended, or having had little contact with any culture at all, will naturally test low. The test scores sometimes are so low as to make it seem that the children could not possibly function in life outside of an institution. Actually, what seems to be measured is called *academic intelligence,* as opposed to *practical intelligence.* The former declines much more drastically in cases of cultural deprivation than the latter.[5]

One of the first people to realize the degree to which mental tests reflected the cultural environment was Otto Klineberg,[6] who demonstrated that the difference between the test scores of black and white children were to be accounted for by different environmental and educational backgrounds, not by racial difference. He proved his point by showing that both black and white children from backward rural areas scored low on intelligence tests, but if their families moved to areas of better educational opportunity, the intelligence scores of the children went up significantly.

While Klineberg was working on the comparison of rural and urban backgrounds in America, studies were also being conducted in England. English children who lived on canal boats and who had little contact with the cultural environment of the land and virtually no schooling showed a gradual decline in IQ scores from an average of 90 at age five to less than 70 at age eleven. A study of Gypsy children (also in England and without schooling) showed an almost identical drop in intelligence-test scores.

In the United States the English studies were duplicated by a study of Kentucky mountain children, who showed a similar intelligence-score loss. A more encouraging type of study was done on isolated mountain children from Tennessee.[8] By using a longitudinal study covering ten years, the researcher was able to demonstrate a gradual increase in the intelligence-test performance of the children. The reason for the difference was that transportation was improving, there were more schools, and more children were going to school longer.

The importance of such studies for an understanding of socialization into the American culture is obvious. Those who live in a state of isolation from the main currents of life, and especially from good schools, are

[5]"Retarded Children Mislabeled," *Science News,* vol. 93, June 1968, p. 533

[6]Otto Klineberg, "What Psychological Tests Show," in Barnhard J. Stern and Allain Locke (eds.), *When Peoples Meet,* Progressive Education Association, New York, 1942.

[7]Walter S. Neff, "Socioeconomic Status and Intelligence: A Critical Study," *The Psychological Bulletin,* vol. 35, December 1938, pp. 727–741.

[8]Lester Rosin Wheeler, "A Comparative Study of the Intelligence of East Tennessee Mountain Children," in Anne Anastasi (ed.), *Individual Differences,* John Wiley & Sons, Inc., New York, 1965, pp. 203–209.

greatly handicapped. What applies to isolated rural areas applies to a degree to urban ghettos, Indian reservations, isolated ethnic groups in our large cities, and many Mexican-American rural communities of the Southwest.

The Need for Affection   At a 1968 conference of the National Institute for Child Health and Human Development, Dr. Stephen A. Richardson reported an interesting case demonstrating the results of affection in child care.[9] Thirteen orphaned children, less than three years old, had been taken from a state orphanage and transferred to a home for retarded women. Within two years it was noted that the children showed greater mental ability than the children left behind at the orphanage. A follow-up of the orphans after they reached maturity found them all to be normal and functioning well in society. This was not true of all the children who had remained in the orphanage: Several were mentally retarded and needed institutional care as adults. The conclusion of the study was that the love and attention given the children by the women in the mental institution had made a great difference in their favor. The case is particularly surprising because the women were retarded and could not have given very much mental simulation.

The problem for the children who remained in the orphanage was not unusual. Orphanages generally have had a record of poor physical and mental health for the children under their care. In a well-known study of a Belgian orphanage, René Spitz gave an account of the extent of the psychological damage and its causes.[10] The orphanage he described was well-run in terms of cleanliness and diet, but the babies were isolated from each other, lacked maternal care and affection, and had nothing to stimulate interest or play activities. A follow-up study after two years found them all to be below average in development, some severely retarded. Not only was mentality affected, but so was health: One-third of the infants died by the age of four. A group of infants in another institution, used as a control group, had no infant deaths whatever. Although the other institution was not as scrupulously clean as the orphanage, the infants' mothers were with them for the first year of life, and the children were given affection and play activities.

Such studies as Spitz's are given support in experimental studies. Harry Harlow, in a long series of experiments with rhesus monkeys, found that those raised without mothers showed a high degree of anxiety and did not learn to play with each other as normal monkeys do.

---

[9]"Retarded Children," *Transaction*, vol. 6, September 1969, pp. 6, 8.

[10]René A. Spitz, "Hospitalism," in *The Psychoanalytic Study of the Child*, International Universities Press, Inc., New York, 1945, vol. I, pp. 53–72, and "Hospitalism: A Follow-up Report," vol. II, pp. 113–117.

Although they matured physically, they did not display normal interest in the opposite sex.[11]

We do not have exactly the same kind of experiment with human subjects to draw from, but the above-cited study of the orphanage and studies of cruelly treated children give evidence of inadequate development for humans as well as monkeys. Many cases of battered children are discovered by doctors and juvenile authorities. Often the authorities are told that the child fell and hurt himself, but sometimes careful investigation proves that the child has been severely and repeatedly beaten. It often develops that the parents of such children were battered children themselves. Nearly always they were starved for affection in childhood. One mother of the affection-starved type admitted to the doctor that she had never been loved. She thought that if she had a baby he would love her. "He didn't love me, so I beat him," she said.   Just as the emotionally deprived monkey in Harlow's experiment seemed never to achieve emotional normality, so with the emotionally starved human being.

Language and Socialization   Chapter 3 emphasized that culture is transmitted through symbolic communication, including language and many other signs and signals. It is obvious that a person who is unable to learn language or some type of symbolic communication could never absorb the cultural pattern. Isabelle made a breakthrough into the world of people as soon as she began to grasp the meaning of words. Most people know the famous story of Helen Keller, whose mind was locked away from the world by blindness and deafness until her teacher was able to communicate with her. On a dramatic occasion in her life, Helen grasped the idea that her teacher was writing on her hand a symbol which stood for water. The idea that all things had names (symbols), that she could learn somehow, began to waken her mind. Her progress toward education and an outstanding career began at that point.

Ordinarily language is acquired unconsciously by the growing child, with only a few suffering the problems of Isabelle or Helen Keller. For many more children, though, there are definite language problems. It is doubtful that the above-mentioned canal boat, Gypsy, or mountain children had acquired anything like the vocabularies of children with more schooling and contact with the general culture. Leonard Schatzman and Anselm Strauss[13] made an interesting study of social-class differences in the use of language by asking people to describe their experiences in a

---

[11]Harry F. Harlow, "Social Deprivation in Monkeys," *Scientific American,* vol. 207, March 1962, pp. 136–148.

[12]"The Battering Parent," *Time,* vol. 94, Nov. 7, 1969, p. 77.

[13]Leonard Schatzman and Anselm Strauss, "Social Class and Modes of Communication," *American Journal of Sociology,* vol. 60, January 1955, pp. 329–338.

disastrous tornado. The lower-class respondents did not use English as objectively as the middle class, even though the study was made entirely among English-speaking people. Vocabularies were more limited; there was less ability to organize accounts of what had happened, less ability to classify, fewer generalizations and abstract words, and less imagination of how well the account was being comprehended by the listener. All these differences no doubt simply reflected rearing by parents who were poorly educated, but it can be seen that they would make English classes at school much more difficult for lower-class than middle-class children.

If there are linguistic problems across class lines, there are greater ones across ethnic lines. Many Mexican-American and Indian children enter school still thinking in their home languages and translating into English only with difficulty. Often their own languages are treated as though they do not count; the only "proper" language is English. Many times IQ tests are given in English to Spanish-speaking children, and their native capacities are thus rated in an unfair manner. Special help is needed to acquaint them with the total English symbol system; instead, the scores are sometimes taken too seriously, and it is assumed the children have very little ability. Federal law now requires that special instruction be made available to children who are unable to speak English. A unanimous Supreme Court decision of 1974, ruling in favor of Chinese-speaking children from San Francisco, contends that to deny special instruction to such children is to render education useless to them and hence to deprive them of their civil rights. The same principle, obviously, applies to children who understand only Spanish, Navajo, or Eskimo, but it takes time for all districts to conform to such decisions.

Children speaking local dialects or ghetto slang have less trouble with English than children from foreign-language homes, but they too experience failures of communication and the problems of being told their language is not proper. Of course there are advantages to speaking a fairly standard English, but children should be given the reassurance that their home accents are perfectly good in their own location. "Good" in the case of languages simply means capable of communicating. To modern linguists, all languages and dialects are good in this respect.

If the socialization process is to accomplish its aim, the culture must be conveyed to each succeeding generation. Obviously the differences in life experiences are such that the culture is conveyed in varying manners and degrees. Because of differences in the types of people with whom one interacts, differences in one's experience of acceptance and affection, and of considerable differences in symbolic communication, great variety in personality types is produced within the same society. There are other differences in the socialization process connected with the degree of persistence and change in socialization patterns.

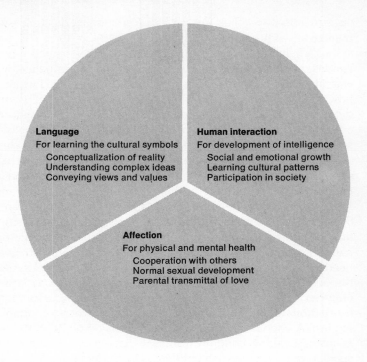

Language
For learning the cultural symbols
Conceptualization of reality
Understanding complex ideas
Conveying views and values

Human interaction
For development of intelligence
Social and emotional growth
Learning cultural patterns
Participation in society

Affection
For physical and mental health
Cooperation with others
Normal sexual development
Parental transmittal of love

PERSISTENCE AND CHANGE IN SOCIALIZATION

Because socialization is the process by which people internalize the values of their cultures, it follows that every culture and subculture will make an attempt to socialize children in its own pattern. Many immigrant groups arriving in America made determined efforts to ensure that their children kept some of the values and customs of the old world from which they had come. Many Chinese children still go to Saturday school to learn the Chinese language, and in the large Chinese community of San Francisco the old tong organizations have only recently begun to lose their influence. For two or three generations Greek children in the United States learned at least some of the Greek language to help retain Greek culture and to make the Greek Orthodox Church Services intelligible.

Persistent Patterns of Socialization   Other examples of the persistence of subcultural socialization are easy to find. Such religious groups as the Amish and the Hutterites have kept their people out of contact with the rest of society as much as possible so that the old traditional patterns might continue. All people of strong religious conviction try to make sure that their children follow the religion of their fathers and learn traditional masculine and feminine roles.

The persistence of socialization patterns also applies to a considerable degree to social classes. People reared in a middle-class pattern are taught to forego the pleasures of today for the sake of tomorrow, especially in the pursuit of success through education. Upper classes try to train their sons and daughters in the proper pattern, the social graces, styles of living, and all that maintains proper status. Similarly, lower-class ways of life tend to be self-perpetuating, not because anyone enjoys poverty but because often there is insufficient knowledge of how to break out of the pattern, and both financial problems and attitudinal values prevent the long-continued education necessary for advance.

There are also different socialization patterns for rural and urban people. In bygone days rural farm life was largely an inherited way of life, and farmers had strongly ethnocentric feelings as to the great worth of the farmer relative to the city dweller. Every attempt was made to instill rural values in the minds of the young. What has been true of the attempt to perpetuate the rural way of life has been equally true of the attempt to perpetuate the Southern way of life, although both are succumbing to the needs of urban-industrial society.

Finally, it should be emphasized that the dominant culture tries to perpetuate a general way of life often referred to simply as the "American way." Some conservative Americans like to see our traditions change as little as possible; some liberals are out to promote gradual and limited change, and radicals would like to see fundamental changes in the pattern. The old-fashioned American way of life has stressed rugged individualism, self-reliance, and a strongly competitive ethic.

Many of the subcultural patterns have undergone change with the passing of time and the changing requirements of society. Old ethnic groups begin to lose their distinctiveness to quite a degree. Slight inroads are made in the separatism of some of the fundamentalist churches. The rural pattern of life has undergone such a definite transformation that in many states the distinction between rural and urban has almost disappeared. Even where a definitely rural subculture still socializes people into a distinctive pattern, the impact on the society is less because the rural farm population has declined to only about 6 percent of the total.

Along with the changing socialization patterns for many subcultural groups, has there also been a change underway for the entire society? Nearly everyone would agree that changes have taken place, but there is much difference of opinion as to the direction of the change, and even wider difference of opinion as to the evaluation of the change. Are we losing our old-fashioned values? Are we becoming slavish conformists? Is the old competitive ethic weakening?

Changes in Socialization   One of the most influential books to try to analyze the problems of changing personality types and socialization patterns is *The Lonely Crowd* by David Riesman.[14] Riesman maintains that the process of internalization of norms through the influence of others can take place in different ways in different cultures. There are societies in which children follow the roles of their parents so automatically that mere imitation of tradition is the mechanism by which the norms are internalized. If we imagine a medieval village or a present-day village in India, we can picture a small community in which there is little conflict in point of view or occupation. Everything is learned through tradition. Riesman would call the people of such a society *tradition-directed*.

In the United States, although we have traditions as do all people, there is enough variety so that tradition alone does not direct us. In Riesman's opinion, in earlier America we were of an *inner-directed* type. Inner-directed men and women actually learn norms from others, but the norms become so strongly internalized that they think of them as their own. Inner-directed people develop a strong conscience and sense of righteousness that has been drilled into them by stern parental teaching. A strong case of this type would be the early Puritan model—a Jonathan Edwards or Cotton Mather.

As seen by Riesman, the inner-directed socialization pattern was just right for the development of the dynamic, compulsively driven type of person to develop the nation's resources and conquer a wilderness. Such a man might not have been pleasant to get along with, but he had an inner sense of direction, a "built-in gyroscope," to use Riesman's description.

With the passing of time, the increase of population, urbanization, and massive school systems, the process of learning the norms and the resultant personality types have changed. The new type of person can be thought of as having antennae that pick up signals from all the people around him, and these signals take the place of the built-in gyroscope. A new character type is developing, says Riesman, that is better for salesmanship and the demands of a consumer-dominated economy. The new type is reinforced by the teaching methods of modern schools, stressing the ethic of social adjustment and assuring the young that the most important point in worldly success is learning to get along with others. This emerging type of personality Riesman characterizes as *other-directed*.

Riesman's work has been widely read and highly praised. As with any work that tries to categorize people into essential types, it may

[14]David Riesman, *The Lonely Crowd,* Doubleday & Company, Inc., Garden City, N.Y., 1953.

	Inner-directed personality	Other-directed personality
Traits	Inner "gyroscope" maintaining self-direction	"Antennae" to pick up signals from others
	Clear sense of right and wrong	Ambiguity about right and wrong
	Relatively rigid	Adaptable
	Drive toward self-determined goals	Drive channelized by expectations of others
Developed by	Strong parental direction	Peer group, school, mass media
	Competitive ethic	Cooperative ethic
Functions for	Independent enterprise	Salesmanship and executive positions
	Taming a wilderness	Crowded urban life
	Basic industry	Consumer goods industries

overstate the case for the sake of clarity. Riesman would not contend that every twentieth-century person is purely other-directed or that every earlier American was purely inner-directed, but he does contend that the emphasis is changing drastically. If he is right, we would expect people to follow new fads and fashions more easily than in the past and for children growing up in school to be more responsive to the subcultures of their own generation than those of their elders.

The old competitive ethic has not vanished entirely, according to Riesman; rather, it shows up in different forms. One once worked hard to succeed by being an independent businessman; one now works hard to learn the ways of the corporation executive, and the future depends upon identification with the firm. Once again the new socialization pattern seems to fit the needs of the society, and yet many are unhappy with the picture of the new character type. We would like to think of ourselves as more independent than the other-directed person. Possibly we are. A further examination of socialization and theorists in the field will show that we can respond to the expectations of others but still retain an independent quality and that something about the human being resists being neatly fitted into a mold.

THEORIES OF SOCIALIZATION

All theories of socialization acceptable to social scientists are based upon the premise that the child is not to be regarded as a miniature adult but as the raw material from which a mature personality can be formed. All these theories also proceed to explain how the child begins to take on adult attitudes and values, how he sees himself as a person, and how he develops a personality distinct from any other. Finally, these theories stress the importance of human interaction, emotions, and symbolic communication.

Mead's Theory of Socialization Among the most prominent theorists in the development of social psychology are Mead and Cooley. Mead has been mentioned in relation to symbolic communication. He was also interested in an analysis of how aspects of personality gradually emerge from childhood play and games.[15] In early childhood play the child observes and attempts to act out adult roles, and in so doing he is gradually learning some of the attitudes that go with the roles.

The process of learning traditional roles by playing at them seems obvious in the play activities of little girls. They take care of dolls and play such realistic roles as mother, nurse, and teacher. For little boys the childhood play is more apt to exist in a never-never land of cowboys and Indians or cops and robbers. Even in this case it could be argued that there is an internalization of the idea of what constitutes "good guys" and "bad guys," and there is definitely a learning of which roles are appropriate for boys and which ones are appropriate for girls.

[15]George Herbert Mead, *Mind, Self, and Society,* The University of Chicago Press, Chicago, 1934, pp. 68–78.

At the next phase of child play, Mead sees a more important aspect of internalization of society's norms: the development of the concept of the *generalized other*. Children no longer play only at pretend roles; they begin to play games that have definite rules. At first a group of small boys will quarrel angrily over a game of baseball, with cries of "Cheater!" and "Liar!" hurled at each other. The game will break up, until little by little the boys learn that the only way to play is by the rules, the rules that "they" have made up. The indefinite "they" in the statement is close to the meaning of Mead's generalized other. The generalized other represents the rules and judgments of others. There is even the beginning of an understanding of others, a development of empathy, because all players in the game have to learn the roles of the others. Thus Mead explains the beginning of taking the role of others and being socialized by others.

Mead, however, does not make the individual appear as a complete pawn in the hands of others. He uses the simple words "I" and "me" to designate two aspects of personality.[16] The "I" is the subjective side, imaginative, creative, innovative. The "me," an aspect of all personalities, is the objective side of the personality, the part that is largely formed through reaction to others. Obviously the relative size of the "I" and of the "me" differs for different individuals.

Cooley and the Looking-glass Process Cooley, the other great founding father of social psychology, also had some stimulating ideas about the socialization process. He too was interested in how the individual takes on the proper attitudes, ideas, sentiments, and habits to make him a cooperative member of his society. Cooley was an extremely perceptive man and a man gifted with empathy, that unusual capacity to feel one's way into the mind and emotions of others. From the study of his own children Cooley arrived at an idea about socialization that he called the "looking-glass process."[17] As people familiar with infants and small children will have observed, the child at first seems to react to the parent's face more than to the spoken word. When his mother says "No!" the child attempts to read her face to see whether she really means it. He looks into her face, Cooley says, for other reasons as well—mainly to see whether he is loved and accepted and whether he is looked upon as good or bad. The essence of Cooley's looking-glass process is that we always look into the faces of others in an attempt to read their attitudes toward us, and that we form our own self-concepts in terms of our imagination of

[16]*Ibid.*, pp. 152–164.
[17]Charles Horton Cooley, *Human Nature and the Social Order*, Charles Scribner's Sons, New York, 1902.

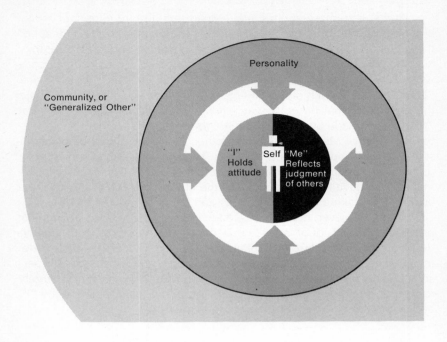

what they think. We literally learn to know ourselves through the eyes of others. There is much wisdom in the old lines from Robert Burns:

> O wad some Power the giftie gie us
> To see oursels as ithers see us!

Cooley does not contend that we always see ourselves as others see us, but what he does say is that we try to do so and that we see ourselves as we imagine others to see us. Cooley also hypothesized that the looking-glass process begins with the very first days of life.

Since Cooley's time there has been considerable argument as to whether the newborn infant perceives much of anything. It has been speculated that sight is so poorly developed that everything is an undifferentiated blur. Evidence from an interesting experiment in infant perception (although not intended as a comment on the looking-glass theory) tends to confirm Cooley's idea. Newly born infants in their first few weeks of life were tested by having a number of objects presented to them, noting which objects they focused their attention upon. The objects

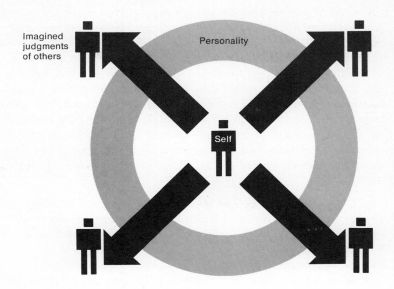

included brightly colored balls and balls with various markings on them. One was marked with the outlines of a human face. Without exception, the face was the object preferred by the babies. The other objects with markings on them received very little attention, and the brightly colored balls were completely ignored.[18]

Cooley's looking glass in infancy would reflect the clearest self-image from the glances of the mother and father. In later years the child becomes more sensitive to his playmates. In the romantic years of early adulthood the sensitivity is greatest to the object of one's love. Always, however, we are interested in what others think about us, and we adjust our reactions to our perceptions of their attitudes. Often we carry this reaction so far as to pretend interest we do not really feel in order to make the right impression.

The rejected child could be understood in Cooley's analysis as one with a destructive self-concept based upon rejection by others. Even the young tough guy can be explained as developing a personality that will win him acclaim from the most important members of his peer group. The important people, the ones we look to for our self-image, are the *significant others*. Although the first examples to come to mind are based

[18]Robert L. Fantz, "The Origin of Form Perception," *Scientific American,* vol. 204, May 1961, pp. 66–72.

85

upon childhood experience, there are significant others throughout life. Kin and close friends are always significant; so also are our professional colleagues. The self-image follows us through life, and we will do fantastic jobs of rationalization to preserve a favorable self-image. Think of such expressions as "I was just not myself when I did that," or "That just wasn't like me," or "If they had been decent to me I would have turned out all right." No one likes to abandon a favorable impression of himself. Reckless and Dinitz[19] did a study supporting the hypothesis that in a neighborhood of high delinquency rates the nondelinquent boys were the ones who had the most favorable self-image. His conclusion was that a self-image of the good boy was a major protection against delinquency.

Criticisms of Cooley and Mead   In spite of these words of praise for Cooley and Mead, it must be admitted that there are criticisms of their concepts and also of the socialization picture developed by sociologists since their time. One who is familiar with the works of Sigmund Freud can see that he perceived much of socialization as a struggle between the individual and society. In this respect the view of psychoanalysis has been in opposition to that of Cooley. Whereas Cooley is inclined to picture a harmonious adjustment to society, Freud saw the individual as constantly desiring to throw off the fetters of society's rules and regulations. Rationally, anyone can see that he has much to gain by conforming to the rules because the very law that prevents him from committing murder or mayhem also protects him from other people of violent intent. Nevertheless, there are always feelings of resentment against rules, routines, customs, time schedules, and the patterns that social life imposes upon us. Even the poetess Amy Lowell ends her famous poem *Patterns* with the line, "Christ! What are patterns for?"

Dennis Wrong[20] wrote an excellent article titled "Oversocialized Conception of Man," in which he contended that sociologists have looked a little too much to the harmonious adjustment between individual and society. A great amount of small-group research has been done on how the individual responds to the group; not enough has been done on why the individual often does not respond and why the human being remains a recalcitrant character. Although there is no definitive answer to the questions raised by Wrong, an examination of the widely conflicting agencies of socialization and pressures upon the growing individual will help to make clear why the socialization process is difficult and fraught with danger.

[19]Walter C. Reckless and Simon Dinitz, "Self-Concept as an Insulator against Delinquency," *American Sociological Review,* vol. 21, December 1956, pp. 744–746.

[20]Dennis H. Wrong, "The Oversocialized Conception of Man," *American Sociological Review,* vol. 28, 1961, pp. 183–193.

CONFLICTING AGENCIES OF SOCIALIZATION

Socialization is a complex process. It does not consist simply of fitting people into social and cultural patterns; in modern societies it calls for the development of a type of person who can adjust to changing patterns and who can help to change patterns to fit changing needs. The required personality type is developed against a background of conflicting agencies of socialization. No longer do family, church, and school work harmoniously together without fear of conflicting influences, if, indeed, they ever did. The generally recognized major agencies of socialization face a vast array of contradictory influences, and they are often in disagreement among themselves.

Conflicts Within Recognized Agencies The major agencies of socialization—family, church, and school—are all discussed in later chapters. For now we shall limit our discussion to pointing out that there are many cases in which one or more of these agencies hardly function at all. Some children are in such constant conflict with the school that enforced schooling becomes purposeless misery; some homes are hopelessly disorganized. The church is often ignored; it seems to be declining as an influence on youth, especially college youth (see Chapter 12). Also, the major agencies of socialization often seem to be working at cross-purposes. A strict, puritanical home may resent a sex-education course given at school, as well as assigned stories, plays, and novels. Parents who are strict disciplinarians may regard the teachers as too weak and permissive; other parents may think the school is tyrannical. There are also indifferent types of parents who do not cooperate with the school, even to the extent of encouraging their children to attend. Children reared in a fundamentalist church may be taught that the evolutionary theories mentioned in biology are wicked nonsense. Often conservative parents resent liberal teachers, and liberal parents resent conservative teachers.

Conflicts in Role Definition As we observed in a previous discussion of status and role, there is a lack of agreement on how social roles should be defined. In the presentation of Mead's theory of role learning, the examples of female roles were of a very traditional type that women no longer accept as the only possibility. The housewife-mother role has its attractions and fulfillments, but so has a career. Role conflict develops for the woman who is torn between the two expectations or attempts to follow both—a situation similar to what Durkheim characterized as *anomie*. The same role conflict develops for the children of immigrants whose parents wish them to follow many of the norms of the old country but whose newly-found peer groups initiate them into new norms.

Sometimes role conflict develops between the expectations of public service on the one hand and financial success on the other. In the political world there is frequent role conflict between the requirements that call for an official to be a friend of his political backers and those which call for impartial service to all his constituents. In many business concerns one must choose between being an upright citizen, repudiating all shady practices, and being "part of the team" and going along with them. It becomes difficult for the young initiate into society to feel certain about its rules and roles.

The Unofficial Agencies of Socialization   Meanwhile, frrom outside the school, church, and family, the individual is being influenced by less recognized but very powerful agencies of socialization: magazines, television, advertisements, movies featuring sex and violence, new types of companions, and the general awareness of a world of bright lights and frivolous pleasures. All kinds of new contradictions come into the teaching of the individual through these agencies. We shall elaborate upon one such conflict in values and mention others only briefly.

The Violence—Nonviolence Dilemma   Among the various conflicts that accompany the socialization process is an ambivalence on the part of society toward violence. Although our official doctrine denounces violence, we are aware of violence all around us. The mass media are often held responsible for playing up violence both in news accounts and drama. In the movies the "good guys" always win, but often they win only by being the fastest with a gun. What does this mean to the growing child? Is the child being conditioned to violence, or building up an immunity to its shock? In *Seduction of the Innocent,* Frederick Wertham maintains that the answer to each question is "Yes."[21] Accordingly, he has long compaigned against violence in comic books and on television. Others have contended that this kind of violence is perceived by the child as existing only in a harmless fantasy world. Some even contend that violent drama might vicariously satisfy the hostile feelings of an individual—feelings that might otherwise be directed against people in the world of reality.

Otto Larsen has edited a well-balanced treatment of the argument concerning violence in the mass media, presenting impressive evidence on both sides. After examining the empirical evidence in the field, he arrives at two important conclusions: (1) Under certain conditions, the

[21]Frederick Wertham, *Seduction of the Innocent,* Holt, Rinehart and Winston, Inc., New York, 1954.

observation of mass-media violence can "reduce inhibitions against violent behavior and provide cues that aggression is socially acceptable. . . . " (2) The laboratory evidence, supported by data from the field and clinic, tends to suggest "that exposure to media violence does *not* drain off aggressive tendencies."[22] Larsen reminds us that violence is not just a matter of the mass media:

> . . . *The indicators of an abiding fascination with violence are all around us, as witness the popularity of certain athletic events, such as professional football (sometimes referred to as "Mayhem on a Sunday afternoon"), the booming Christmas sales of toy weapons, ranging from gun-shaped teething rings to simulated atom bombs, and the continued attraction of both real and fictional accounts of war and crime.*[23]

Whatever the result of psychological studies and investigations of violence may eventually be, there is no doubt that the young boy, told by his mother that he should not fight, is being bombarded by contradictory stimuli.

A similar analysis of many other types of contradictory stimuli could be made in such areas as the Vietnam war, violence of both demonstrators and police, drug abuse, inconsistencies in court action, hypocrisy in sexual norms, and "respectable" alcoholism. The socialization process presents an infinity of confusions and conflicts. As we go down the road of life we find it plastered with billboards carrying conflicting messages. We will be advised to follow the straight and narrow way but also to be sports, take a chance. Members of our own generation may tempt us to try marijuana; when our parents hear of it they will be badly shaken and will need another drink to steady their nerves! We will be confronted with the patriots and superpatriots and with the radicals and protestors. We will have choices to make about early employment or a college career, whether to follow the Puritan norms in sex or to have our affairs before marriage, whether to adopt a moralistic or a hedonistic philosophy, whether to follow a competitive business orientation or a social-service ethic. And all these conflicts will be within the range of acceptable behavior as seen by significant segments of society. There are, of course, other possibilities—those that lie along the roads of delinquency and crime—to be discussed in the next chapter.

[22]Otto N. Larsen (ed.), *Violence and the Mass Media,* Harper & Row, Publishers, Incorporated, New York, 1968, p. 117.
[23]*Ibid.,* p. 19.

SUMMARY

Socialization is the process by which one internalizes the attitudes, beliefs, and values of his culture. Socialization requires (1) interaction with others, (2) the experience of emotional acceptance, and (3) symbolic communication, mainly through language. There is much evidence, observational and experimental, to prove the necessity of interaction with other people and contact with the culture for mental growth. That affection is needed for normal development is demonstrated by studies of isolated children, orphanages, and battering parents who were themselves deprived of affection.

Language is not only a means of communication, but to a great degree it is a means of perception and thought. Ethnic groups whose knowledge of the use of the English language is deficient have serious difficulties at school. This applies not just to foreign-language groups but to all groups whose use of English is unusual enough to impair communication.

Cultural and subcultural groups try to preserve their identity by socializing children into their own pattern, but socialization patterns change. David Riesman suggests that societies can socialize children into three possible patterns: tradition-, inner-, or other-directed. America was never very strongly tradition-directed in its socialization pattern, but in the past it was inner-directed; that is, strong feelings of right and wrong were internalized by growing children as the result of the teachings of stern parents and teachers. The modern pattern is toward an other-directed personality, guided mainly by the expectations of others of one's own generation. The new character type is one's adaptable for salesmanship and working with others but lacks the independence of decision characteristic of the earlier American society, according to Riesman.

The founding fathers of American socialization theory were George Herbert Mead and Charles Horton Cooley. Mead analyzed the process of internalization of the norms through successive stages of childhood play—first at imitating specific roles and later learning generalized rules through the rules of the game. Cooley thought of the socialization process as one of responding to the wishes of others through the looking-glass process. In Cooley's view, we study the faces of others for looks of approval and support, attempting to form a favorable self-image.

Dennis Wrong calls Cooley and Mead's views "oversocialized conceptions of man," implying that they overemphasized people's tendency to conform to expectations. He feels that sociology has not devoted enough attention to why people misbehave and to negative sanctions.

It is obvious that one of the reasons for a failure of the individual to conform to societal expectations is that there is no solid agreement about what those expectations are. Not only do such primary agencies of socialization as family, church, and school sometimes fail to agree, but they find themselves in conflict with unofficial agencies of socialization: the mass media, advertising, exposure to violence, delinquent crowds, conflicting political preachings, propaganda, and demonstrations.

PART TWO ART: Siva whispers across the darkness into the ears of the minorities, telling them to recognize the power in their hands. Brahma is in the center, emanating from all directions. His profile faces Siva on the right. The minorities occupy the lower portion of both panels. The startled middle class is above, looking toward Siva. A few members of the lower class, who have heard the message, are beginning to stand erect, while Siva, with his snaky body, pushes the rest of the group across the unknown (dark area).

Part Two

Differences Within Societies

The God of Preservation works through norms, laws, and holy books to make sure traditions are unchanged, but in his zeal he sometimes makes rules that are impossible to follow. Furthermore, Siva, our God of Change, sees to it that conflicting rule books enter the land so that norms are not quite the same in successive generations or in different classes and ethnic groups. Worse yet for the cause of preservation, people are not all alike, not even to the extent of being capable of full socialization into society's norms, nor do many of them burn with desire to follow all the rules faithfully and meticulously.

What actually happens in the people-making process is that no perfect models appear. Some people violate the rules ever so slightly; others, in the pursuit of self-interest, break the rules flagrantly. The system fights back, usually punishing the law violators from the lower rungs of the social ladder but showing great leniency to those on the upper levels. There are others whose violations of laws are based not upon self-interest but upon a will to defy unjust and outmoded laws. Such violators are the would-be forerunners of important social changes, the conscious agents of Siva himself.

Just as individuals vary in their experience of social life and their reactions to it, so do social classes. The upper classes tend to agree with Vishnu that all should be preserved in this best of all possible worlds.

From below, and sometimes even from the middle, the perspective is different. Upper circles can explain why social class is necessary to maintain an orderly, smoothly running world. The poor and dispossessed see the class system as the outcome of avarice and greed or the spin of the wheel of fortune. Strong forces are at work to keep all the same people at the top of the class structure, but occasionally one slips, or another rises from the middle or, much more rarely, from the bottom. Revolutions have been known to alter the whole structure, but a social-class system always rises again in some new form.

The Creator made people of different colors and appearance, with males and females of each type so they could multiply their kind. Vishnu gave out different rule books for the different groups and also separate rules for men and women. Societies decided that some colors are good and should belong mainly to middle and upper classes and that others are not so good and should be left mainly in lower classes; regardless of class or color, they decided women should follow behind men. Eventually, though, Siva whispered into the ears of the darker people, "You are good! You are beautiful! There is power in your hands!" The message went from the black people to the brown and the red and finally to the women of all colors. Since the dissemination of that message, minorities have become restive and societies are no longer the same.

Chapter 5

Social Deviance

Children's games constitute the most admirable social institutions. The game of marbles, for instance, as played by boys, contains an extremely complex system of rules, that is to say, a code of laws, a jurisprudence of its own.[1]

Jean Piaget
The Moral Judgment of the Child

In Part One we examined some of the processes that produce conformity to the norms of a society or culture. Basically these processes involve internalizing of social norms, identifying with group expectations, and abiding by the advice of authority and tradition. However, this process of socialization does not always produce people acceptable to society; sometimes the failure of socialization results in delinquency, crime,

[1] Jean Piaget, *The Moral Judgment of the Child,* Collier Books, The Macmillan Company, New York, 1962, p. 13.

alcoholism, various addictions, and other pathologies. Other times, a peculiarity within the process may result in the development of innovators, people ahead of their times, who have insights that others lack. Such people may become heroes or prophets, given certain social conditions and a particular set of social values, or they may become psychopaths whose ingenuity can destroy lives or society itself.

Because the process of socialization or its failure may produce diverse and often threatening behavior patterns, the subject of social deviance is of major concern to society and produces constant debate as to its extent, cause, and cure. Even the problem of defining deviance is difficult. In the discussion of culture in Chapter 3, norms were explained and classified into folkways and mores. The violator of folkways is often considered merely odd; the violator of mores is considered wicked, although even in this category there are different degrees of wickedness. If the mores have been formalized into criminal law, the violator is by definition a criminal, but not all crimes are looked upon as equally reprehensible. A study of deviance, then, is a logical place for starting a study of degrees of differentiation within society.

Differences in degrees of public feeling about norm violation have to be taken into consideration in a study of deviance, as well as the fact that folkways, mores, and laws are culturally determined. To quite a degree, rights and wrongs differ from time to time and place to place. It is true that all societies have rules against some kind of incest and murder, but there is far less agreement in laws regarding sex behavior, abortion, marriage and divorce, drinking, marijuana use, and gambling, to name but a few. Thus deviance is culturally relative, and it could be expected to vary in kind and degree in different societies and at different times. Since the earliest days of sociology much theorizing has been done about definition and cause of deviance.

THE CLASSICAL THEORIES OF DEVIANCE

To better understand deviance it is helpful first to trace the line of sociological thought about the topic. Theorists have always reasoned that the amount and type of crime would be closely connected with other characteristics of society, with new forms of deviance arising and older forms of deviance being reevaluated. For example, we no longer worry much about such once-shocking crimes as witchcraft, heresy, or breaking the Sabbath, but in recent years our concern over crimes against property, violence, and drug addiction has increased. Such changes would not surprise a classical theorist like Durkheim.

Durkheim: Anomie and Deviance   Durkheim's concept of *anomie* was to form a basis for sociological interpretations of deviance for decades after his death. Recall from Chapter 2 that one of the three types of suicide discussed by Durkheim was called *anomic,* from the word "anomie." To Durkheim, anomie had several similar meanings: It meant a failure to internalize the norms of society, an inability to adjust to changing norms, or even the tension resulting from conflict within the norms themselves. In Durkheim's view the new social trends in urban-industrial societies result in changing norms, confusion, and lessened social control over the individual.[2] Individualism becomes greater, new life styles emerge, perhaps giving greater freedom but also increasing the possibilities for deviant behavior. The close ties of the individual to family, village, and tradition in the old days were confining upon the individual, but they helped to hold him in line. In modern societies the constraints on the individual weaken.

Eventually, perhaps, Durkheim reasoned, societies would get accustomed to new ways of life and form new types of moral bases to society, but for a long intervening period there would be more anomie, more rootlessness, and consequently more deviance and crime. Modern statistics seem to bear out Durkheim's thesis in many respects: Areas of rapid movement, economic instability, and urban congestion are generally areas of high rates of both anomie and deviance. Such areas are characterized by a clash of values, resentment of societal leadership and norms, and delinquent or rebellious subcultures, or even retreat into alcoholism and addiction. Much deviance, then, could be explained as a natural consequence of societal characteristics.

William Graham Sumner: The Deviant as Unfit   We mentioned that there were clashes of opinion among the early sociologists. Durkheim's suggestion about anomie and deviance was that something should be done to create closer bonds of union among people, possibly through workers' groups. Sumner, whose views on the "struggle for survival" were previously noted, felt that drunkards, delinquents, and other deviates are simply the dropouts of the struggle for survival. "If we do not like the survival of the fittest," he wrote, "we have only one possible alternative, and that is the survival of the unfittest."[3] Competition must inevitably weed out the unfit. Sumner's views in this respect have had far less effect on sociology than those of Durkheim, but they are opinions still

[2] Émile Durkheim, *Suicide,* John A. Spaulding and George Simpson (trans.), The Free Press, New York, 1966.

[3] Cited in Maurice R. Davie, *William Graham Sumner,* Thomas Y. Crowell Company, New York, 1963, p. 16.

encountered among many people who view both the indigent and deviant as worthless and beyond redemption.

In spite of his strong belief in individualism, Sumner did not believe in anarchy. He felt that societies, by a process of trial and error, had worked out an organized way of life based upon the folkways and mores previously discussed. People should compete, but only within such rules. Even for individualists there had to be some measure of conformity. Note, though, that Durkheim stressed the importance of conformity to social norms much more than Sumner, the rugged individualist. A later American, William I. Thomas, turned his attention to a problem of deviance previously implied. In American society we are often condemned for being slavish conformists, and yet a fairly good simile for "nonconformist" is "deviate." When does one cease to be a respectable nonconformist and become instead a deviate?

William I. Thomas: The Problem of Conformity   Between 1918 and 1920, Thomas conceived of a synthesis of the conformist and nonconformist in his revered work *The Polish Peasant in Europe and America.* His examination of personality types lead him to develop three basic ideals that are never actually found in their pure form. The first is the Philistine, who is in total agreement with the values of society. This "stable" individual is not likely to engage in deviance as conceptualized by society as a whole, but neither is he likely to develop useful new ideas. The opposite personality is that of the Bohemian, whose character is not fully developed and who may easily be tempted toward antisocial behavior. However, a third possibility exists, the Creative Man, who is a perfect compromise between the previous character types.[4] If Creative Man is the perfect combination of elements, then we are left with the conclusion that under some circumstances the behavior of the conformist, as well as that of the nonconformist, is maladaptive.

Ordinarily the Philistine has, according to Thomas, a "definition of the situation" which corresponds to that of society as a whole. Sometimes, however, social definitions are erroneous or outmoded, as, for example, proper definitions of the "proper place" for women or minority groups. The creative type can assess new situations and form better "definitions of the situation."

Although stated very differently, Thomas' views have something in common with those of Durkheim in that the individual is considered less bound by group definitions of the situation in modern society than in more traditional societies. Partly as a result of his study of the adjustment

[4]William I. Thomas and Florian Znaniecki, *The Polish Peasant in Europe and America,* Richard G. Badger, Boston, 1918–1920.

of Polish immigrants to American society, Thomas concluded that the transition to urbanism and industrialism has upsetting consequences for society and personality. Deviance increases. There is less regard for folkways because, in his view, folkways are developed in the small community. In the modern world the sense of community declines, and with it the informal controls of neighborhood opinion:

> ... In the immediacy of relationships and the participation of everybody in everything, it (community) represents an element which we have lost and which we shall probably have to restore in some form of cooperation in order to secure a balanced and normal society—some arrangement corresponding with human nature.[5]

NEOCLASSICAL THEORIES

Several contemporary writers in sociology can be called neoclassical, from "neo," meaning new, and "classical," meaning their ideas are a continuation of those of some of the earlier classical writers. Probably the most prominent of these theorists are Talcott Parsons, Robert K. Merton, and Robin Williams. Parsons is extremely difficult for an introductory text, so we shall limit the discussion to Merton and Williams. It will be seen that both of them, like Durkheim, stressed ways in which characteristics of the society result in certain types of crime. Such types of crime could be called *functions* (a word used in sociology to mean "consequences") of societal requirements, customs, and institutions—a view referred to in Chapter 1 as functionalism.

Robert K. Merton: Goals and Means   Merton elaborates upon the idea that a type of anomie results from a conflict within the norms themselves.[6] If the rules of society tell us to do contradictory things or set goals that are impossible of achievement, then we are in a state of anomie. This, says Merton, is precisely what happens in modern American society. American society is unusually firm about judging people's worth on the basis of whether they succeed, and success generally means making money. All societies have prescribed *goals* of striving and also prescribed *means* of achieving the goals. In our case monetary success is the goal, and the means should be honest.

In Merton's scheme of analysis (see page 101) the person who adheres to both the goals and the honest means receives a plus score,

[5]William I. Thomas, *The Child in America*, Alfred A. Knopf, Inc., New York, 1928, p. 572.
[6]Robert K. Merton, *Social Theory and Social Structure*, The Free Press of Glencoe, Inc., New York, 1957, chap. 5.

Means	Goals		
+	+	=	Conformist (rich and honest)
−	+	=	Innovator (rich but devious)
+	−	=	Ritualist (poor but honest)
−	−	=	Retreatist (rejects goals and means)
±	±	=	Rebel (demands new rules)

Ways of coping with strong social expectations for success, according to Robert K. Merton, given in order of social acceptability. The norms demand success but do not give equal access to success goals by honest means.*

*Adapted from Robert K. Merton, *Social Theory and Social Structure.* The Free Press of Glencoe, Inc., New York, 1957, p. 140.

denoting high honors in both cases, and is called a *conformist,* the preferred type. If we placed overwhelming emphasis on honesty at any price, we would give second honors to the ritualist, the person who makes a ritual of honesty even though unable to succeed. However, says Merton, we actually give second honors to the person who succeeds by clever but devious means (as long as he does not get caught), so the temptation to succeed by dishonest means is very great. The problem is made worse by the fact that many people cannot succeed by honest means, either because they are the victims of racial discrimination or because they come from environments that do not teach them the means to success.

As Merton sees the matter, there are two ways to adjust to the difficult problem of success-striving. One adjustment is simply to give up, not caring about either success goals or honest means. His original illustration of such an adjustment was that of the vagrant or hobo, but a more contemporary example would be the addict, a *retreatist* from both goals and means. Finally, it is possible to believe in some of the means and some of the goals, but not all, and therefore to wish to revolutionize society. Both Fascists and Communists are examples of the latter and possibly other types of angry militants and ''rebels without a cause.''

Merton's analysis is quite comprehensive and attempts to explain why some societies have higher crime rates than others. Many countries much poorer than the United States have low rates of crime. Poverty alone does not account for crime, especially where everyone is poor and getting ahead is not even considered a possibility; but where poverty and wealth exist side by side, and where there is a social implication that those who are really worth their salt will push ahead economically, deviance rates increase. One could object that not all deviance is really directed toward gaining money, and the objection is quite correct. In Merton's view, though, the double failure of the retreatist is connected with the same problem: Unable to succeed by means fair or foul, he gives up and drops out. So far as the rebel is concerned, if the category is extended to include many people with smoldering resentments, whether or not they have any revolutionary ideologies, many acts of vandalism and violence and destruction can be explained.

As with much of the work of Merton, his deviance theory points toward at least partial solutions through greater equalization of opportunity to success by legal means or through a reduction in the intensity of the drive for monetary success. Such goals would be compatible with, although not quite the same as, the recommendations for a greater sense of community suggested by both Durkheim and Thomas. They would run counter to the extremely competitive struggle advocated by Sumner.

Robin M. Williams, Jr.: Overconformity Williams gives us yet another perspective from the school of structural-functionalism, or the idea that problems flow naturally from the structure of society itself. He points out that strict adherence to the norms of society may, itself, produce a type of deviance. Such deviance is illustrated by certain heroic individuals who so strongly follow the official codes of society that, under certain circumstances, they may be regarded as saints but, under different circumstances, may be classified as fanatics or subversives. Williams' example is the person who so literally interprets religious proscriptions against killing that he refuses military service. During the Vietnam conflict, many of these "deviates" protested, were jailed, or fled to neutral countries like Canada or Sweden. In the opinion of some they were honored martyrs to our professed belief in peace; to others they were seen as virtual traitors.

Williams' comments are discussed to indicate the true intent of the neoclassic theorists, which is that the structure of a social system may be such that its very existence can produce functions (consequences) that may be evaluated as "deviant" by a given category of people, according to the values of the time and place. Williams succinctly makes this point: " . . . established institutions may thrive upon a relatively large amount of *passive* conformity and discreet deviation, but are often allergic to full and energetic conformity to their more 'utopian' norms."[7] [Italics added]

Perhaps this explains why zealots are often viewed with suspicion in our society. We accept the "model" individual, the person who adheres to most of the norms most of the time. We think of such a person as "normal" and pattern our institutions around his needs, but the changing institutions often no longer meet the needs or conform to the expectations of the zealots. Hence, while some people view the family as adjusting to new social values, others see it as deteriorating; while some think R and X rated movies are a step toward honesty in films, others see them as a reflection of moral decline. Similarly, while some people note the quiet college campuses of the early seventies as a sign of return to normalcy, others worry about an educational structure that is not producing sufficient intellectual rebelliousness.

CONTEMPORARY EXPLANATIONS OF DEVIANCE

Beginning in the 1960s and continuing into the current decade, sociological theories have examined deviance from three points of view: the deviate's social environment, the deviate himself, and deviance as a

---

[7]Robin M. Williams, Jr., *American Society: A Sociological Interpretation*, Alfred A. Knopf, Inc., New York, 1960, p. 360.

process. Social deviance as viewed from the social environment is probably best understood from the writings of Howard S. Becker and a system of theory known as "labeling."

Howard Becker: Labeling   Labeling theory is not primarily concerned with who is deviant or how far from the norm a deviant act may be but concentrates on how the social group comes to view other people or groups as deviant. In *Outsiders: Studies in the Sociology of Deviance,* Becker shows that deviance involves an interaction between "those who commit (or are said to have committed) a deviant act and the rest of society, perhaps divided into several groups itself."[8]

However, the nature of the relationship between the individual and society puts the deviant into the position of being labeled by the social group. The label depends upon the ideas of right and wrong of the society itself, or even of subgroups within the society. Becker would seem in agreement with the fairly common observation that "Laws make criminals." In the days of the Eighteenth Amendment (which prohibited alcoholic drinks), people who sold whiskey were committing crimes; now they are not, provided they have licenses. People who now oppose laws against marijuana use are also vehement in their opinion that laws make criminals. These are cases in which not all elements of society agree; nevertheless, the drinker in the 1920s and the marijuana smoker in later years received the label of deviate. A reputation is made that is hard to change. Often the label is basically false, as when juveniles are assigned temporarily to juvenile hall for no other reason than that their parents have run off and left them without means of support. Sometimes such youths are labeled in the public mind as delinquents, and the label can affect them adversely. As Becker says, by labeling a person as deviant, the social group seems to assign to that person a new identity and a new role, a new set of expectations. The social group then responds to the individual according to those expectations, thus reinforcing the label and affecting all future interactions.

Erving Goffman: Stigma and the Social Theater   Goffman raises the question of what happens to the person who is labeled. How does this affect one's image of the self, and how does it affect one's performance of social roles? In other words, how does the deviate see himself? The basis for Goffman's later studies appears in his famous work *The Presentation of Self in Everyday Life,* which defines the world as a theater in which we act out the expectations that others have of us.[9] In a subsequent work,

[8]Howard S. Becker, *Outsiders: Studies in the Sociology of Deviance,* The Free Press, New York, 1963, p. 2.
[9]Erving Goffman, *The Presentation of Self in Everyday Life,* Doubleday & Company, Inc., Garden City, N.Y., 1959.

Asylums, he discusses "total institutions," for example, mental hospitals and prisons, as areas that limit behaviors through a series of rules and regulations to which all those classified in a certain category must adhere. Such systems depend upon a type of overconformity as a safeguard against or as a cure for deviance.[10] The finest application of Goffman's theories to the subject of deviance, however, is found in his book, *Stigma: Notes on the Management of a Spoiled Identity.*

In *Stigma,* Goffman tries to analyze the problem of managing a damaged (stigmatized) identity that results from labeling. This management problem may be complex—Marcello Truzzi's study of the dwarf in a land of "giants" provides an excellent example.[11] Or it may be relatively simple: disguising a black eye, innocently acquired, which may be misinterpreted by everyone we meet. Therefore most people have some feeling of being stigmatized at some point in life, and some have the burden constantly. As Goffman says, the only completely unstigmatized person in America is a "young, married, white, urban, northern, heterosexual, Protestant father of college education, fully employed, of good complexion, weight, and height, and with a recent record in sports."[12] Obviously race is a stigma for all who must endure discriminatory practices and prejudiced attitudes. The same is true of female sex in most businesses and professions and of male sex in the role of nurse.

The people who suffer severely from the processes of stigmatization endure extreme psychological strain. Besides struggling with their own identity problems, the stigmatized people must adjust their behavior to interact with others in society. They must learn to make others feel at ease yet also learn to ignore accidental—or even intended—insults. The man or woman who is stigmatized must always be on guard, must always be putting on some kind of act, except when alone. This brings us back to Goffman's initial premise that society is like a theater stage.

By acting we try to hide weaknesses and improve our competitive position in the search for status and acceptance. The child with a father in prison invents another father to describe. The youth with doubts as to his manhood tells tales of his exploits with women. In older days the black American often found clowning to be the only means to acceptance. The illiterate explains away his need for help in looking up a phone number by saying he forgot his glasses.

Often, though, there is no hiding the stigma, and the only way to manage one's identity is to look for companionship in secret societies or

---

[10]Erving Goffman, *Asylums,* Doubleday & Company, Inc., Garden City, N.Y., 1961.

[11]Marcello Truzzi, "Lilliputians in Gulliver's Land: The Social Role of the Dwarf," in Marcello Truzzi, *Sociology and Everyday Life,* Prentice-Hall, Inc., Englewood Cliffs, N.J., 1968.

[12]Erving Goffman, *Stigma: Notes on the Management of a Spoiled Identity,* Prentice-Hall, Inc., Englewood Cliffs, N.J., 1963, p. 128.

subcultures with others of one's kind. There are societies of dwarfs, drug addicts and ex-addicts, alcoholics and ex-alcoholics, ex-convicts, homosexuals, unwed mothers, the blind, and the hard-of-hearing. Recently a man started a society of ugly people, demanding that they be treated as considerately as the good-looking. Acceptability in employment and in social life is strongly influenced by appearance. Little societies for the stigmatized help people to hide for certain periods, to interrelate with others who share the stigma, and sometimes to register protests or to publish information of value to themselves. In such an off-stage setting they can compare notes and discuss the rules of existence in the onstage theater of life.

David Matza, some of whose ideas are similar to those of Becker and Goffman, reminds us that part of the role of being deviant is being devious. The deviant who is engaged in illegal acts or whose behavior would come under severe social scrutiny must cover up his true activities or at least disguise them in such a manner as to be not overly offensive.[13] Therefore investigators of deviance may never get the whole story about the feelings of those whom society labels deviant. Matza, like the other contemporary theorists, recognizes that we all—deviates and non-deviates—play roles and that these roles are designed to fit an occasion.

Stigma, Self-image, and Crime At first glance one might object that stress on the "social theater" or on stigma and labeling tends to make deviance interesting to investigate and describe but ignores much of the serious worry of the general public. Most of us are not overly concerned with small subcultures or deviant groups "doing their own thing" in such matters as sex behavior, alcohol, marijuana, or strange cults, as long as they do not impinge upon us. More frequently the layman is worried about deviant behavior that is threatening: robberies and muggings, assault, rape, and murder. Nevertheless, investigations by those who stress labeling have much to tell us. The usual procedure in such investigations is to study deviant groups by careful observation so that the roots of the deviance can be understood.

A better understanding of deviance shows the seriousness of many kinds of stigma. Stigma and resulting social ostracism can drive people in the direction of deviance, sometimes very serious deviance. The idea of labeling is also important in the development of the deviant life, making it very difficult for the offender to relate to, or to return to, the normative world. The label often works as a self-fulfilling prophecy, as does the

[13]David Matza, *Becoming Deviant*, Prentice-Hall, Inc., Englewood Cliffs, N.J., 1969, p. 39.

famous old expression "Once a con, always a con." At this point we are reminded of Cooley and the looking-glass process, which can create either a favorable or unfavorable self-image, beginning with childhood. If a child is praised whenever possible, the self-image becomes wholesome. Even when a child is corrected, the self-image can be preserved with such a phrase as "A nice boy like you shouldn't do such things." If, instead, the correction consists of "You're just thoroughly bad, incorrigible, vicious, and someday you're going to end up in jail," the self-image becomes negative. The labeling theorists and Cooley would agree on this point.

A surprising confirmation of the importance of early labeling is contained in a book by Stuart Palmer, titled *The Psychology of Murder*.[14] In his investigations of fifty murderers compared with their own brothers who had been in little or no trouble, Palmer found that in nearly all cases the murderers had been the stigmatized children of the family. Sometimes they were battered children and sometimes not, but in nearly all cases they were the least favored, the ones labeled early in life as "foul balls."

Such social theorists as Durkheim, Thomas, and Merton have had much to say about societal trends in deviance; the ideas of stigmatization and labeling say more about the individual who becomes a statistic in social deviance. There are many more threads to the fabric of deviance, though, and more must be examined in the area of subcultures, opportunities to commit crime, and the contrasts between upper- and lower-class crime.

DEVIANT SUBCULTURES

A focus on the idea of subcultural differences and deviance had begun well before Becker, Goffman, and Matza became prominent in sociology. Edwin H. Sutherland realized what the classicists had known: Deviance rates differ in different societies and at different times. He also noted, as others had, that some segments of society have higher crime rates than others. He believed, as all sociologists do, that deviance and crime are types of learned behavior with environmental causes. (The only possible exception would be results of such pathologies as brain damage.) Sutherland reasoned that the main answer to the question of what causes criminal behavior is a matter of environments which teach deviant attitudes and behaviors and give little or no support to normative behavior.

[14]Stuart Palmer, *The Psychology of Murder*, Apollo Editions, Thomas Y. Crowell Company, New York, 1962.

**Variation by age in
type of offense**

**Percent committed by
juveniles under 18**

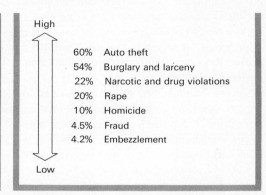

Highest juvenile
rates are in
behavior to which
juveniles have
ready access;
lowest rates are
in offenses
generally
unavailable to
juveniles

High

60%	Auto theft
54%	Burglary and larceny
22%	Narcotic and drug violations
20%	Rape
10%	Homicide
4.5%	Fraud
4.2%	Embezzlement

Low

Other variations. Higher rates are for persons or areas
with best opportunities for learning deviant ways
(Sutherland's theory of differential association).

High: Male   Urban   Inner city   Unstable home
                                                  and community

Low: Female   Rural   Suburb   Stable home
                                                  and community

*For statistics see Albert K. Cohen and James F. Short, Jr.,
"Crime and Juvenile Delinquency," in Robert K. Merton and
Robert Nisbet (eds.), *Contemporary Social Problems*, 3d ed.,
Harcourt, Brace & Jovanovich, Inc., New York, 1971, pp. 105–113.

Edwin H. Sutherland: Differential Association Working during the
latter part of the 1930s, Sutherland developed the theory of differential
association. He claimed that, through the processes of socialization,
certain people are more predisposed to commit crimes than are others.[15]
Those people who are predisposed to criminal conduct have internalized

[15]Albert K. Cohen, Alfred Lindesmith, and Karl Schuessler (eds.), *The Sutherland Papers*, Indiana
University Press, Bloomington, 1956.

a criminal orientation from the groups with which they have interacted. These groups might include the family, childhood play groups, adult friendship groups, or neighborhood, but they would all be of a nature primary enough to be of value to the person in forming his opinions about right and wrong.

Actually, all environments are a little ambivalent about the rights and wrongs of society. Although very few parents actually attempt to teach their children careers of crime, some, especially in impoverished and alienated groups, show very little respect for property rights and regard the police with hostility. Similarly, in a well-to-do family the father might, by example, show that he has little respect for certain other kinds of laws, such as speed laws, income tax regulations, or fair labor practices. Parental attitudes, then, can be negative, even though the official pronouncement is to obey the law and stay out of trouble.

Outside the experience range of the average citizen are subcultures in which it is possible to learn the ways of crime and in which the admonition to "Stay out of trouble" is not taken very seriously. If so, statistics should show a relationship between areas and circumstances of little normative support and the occurrence of crime and delinquency.

The Statistics of Differential Association   A whole series of statistical variations in crime rates supports Sutherland's theory of differential association. A unified, supportive family has much less difficulty with delinquency than a disorganized home. Normative supports are stronger; opportunities to learn deviance are less. A stable community and neighborhood is likely to have a lower crime rate than one with more transient members. Big cities, especially the inner cores, are often scenes of organized crime, with opportunities for the young to learn the ways of the successful criminal. Crime rates are much higher than in rural areas or suburbs. Girls are generally guarded more than boys and kept from frequenting street and alley gangs, which helps to account for only about one-fourth as many juvenile arrests among girls as boys. Young men in their teens and until the usual age of marriage in their twenties are relatively free from controls, able to get out on their own, join gangs, and, if not strongly committed to the norms, break laws. For many of them such violations are transitory—mere matters of drinking and disorderly parties. Later on, jobs, marriage, and responsibilities cause them to settle down, break up their old crowds, and enter the respectable world. For those whose lives have combined many of the deviance factors just listed, however, the chances of abandoning deviance are less.

Another variable commented upon by Sutherland and many others is race or ethnic group. But both racial and ethnic differences in crime and delinquency are purely the result of the factors already listed, not race or ethnicity as such. The reason for high crime and delinquency rates in the poor ghetto is simply that it is a ghetto—usually a place of crowding, poverty, and lack of opportunity. This point is well-illustrated in a classic study conducted by Clifford Shaw and Henry D. McKay. Their investigation of certain areas in Chicago demonstrated that "bad" sections of the city (as measured by lack of opportunity, dilapidated houses, and presence of vice) had by far the highest rates of juvenile delinquency, in some cases twenty times as much as best areas. The high delinquency rate persisted over the thirty-year period investigated, despite the fact that five different ethnic groups had moved into and out of the area during those years. The nationality of the people involved is irrelevant; similar conditions produce similar results.[16]

A final variable that tends to support Sutherland's theory that crime can be measured by differential association with deviant forces is demonstrated by rates of fraud and embezzlement. The accompanying illustration (page 108) shows that whereas auto theft and burglary rates are high among the young, fraud and embezzlement are very low. The reason seems to be that only after years of experience in the business world does one have an opportunity to learn the ways of fraud, graft, kickbacks, illegal pricing, false advertising, and other shady business deals. These latter types of offences, referred to by Sutherland as "white-collar crime," are learned in a particular environment just as surely as other types of deviance are commonly learned in urban slums.

Illegitimate Means   In the 1960s Richard A. Cloward and Lloyd E. Ohlin made important additions to the idea of differential association. Whereas Sutherland stressed a lack of support for the norms, Cloward and Ohlin stress variations in access to illegitimate means.[17] Some run-down urban areas produce much less delinquency than others. Cloward and Ohlin find that an important difference is whether there is an organized underworld in the area in which the youths grow up. Obviously, subcultures of organized crime give both opportunities for deviance and models to follow.

The presence of other deviant subcultures could lead to types of behavior profitable to organized crime, but not the type the initiate into organized crime would follow. The most obvious example is the use of drugs. Drug use is probably counterproductive to valuable service to the underworld, as well as to any successful adjustments for the addict. The

[16]Clifford R. Shaw and Henry D. McKay, *Juvenile Delinquency and Urban Areas*, The University of Chicago Press, Chicago, 1942.
[17]Richard A. Cloward and Lloyd E. Ohlin, *Delinquency and Opportunity*, The Free Press of Glencoe, Inc., New York, 1961, p. 168.

addict, then, becomes a double failure, failing in both the legitimate world and the world of crime.

Anomie and Delinquent Subcultures   Albert K. Cohen combined the subcultural explanations of Sutherland with the anomie theory of Merton in his study of delinquent gangs. Cohen says that lower-class delinquent boys are striving for success in the eyes of their own crowd and that success is measured by ability to circumvent the school authorities, harass policemen and neighborhoods, and do malicious damage. The goals of career achievement and monetary success do not apply here. The hoodlumism of such gangs is difficult for the public to countenance; people can understand stealing for practical reasons but do not understand the motivation for delinquency that is malicious and nonutilitarian. The motive behind much lower-class delinquency is an expression of the resentment against a society whose norms seem impossible to achieve.[18]

Along with James F. Short, Jr.,[19] Cohen makes a similar point regarding middle-class juvenile delinquency. The middle-class parents unwittingly teach a way of life that is fun-loving and hedonistic. The resultant behavior of their offspring is a delinquency pattern centering around sex, automobiles, and liquor. More recently, the behavior of the middle-class delinquent has also included the use of drugs, especially marijuana. But because the eventual achievement of success goals for this group is likely, the delinquency is not apt to lead to adult crime. In fact, attempts are made to prevent labeling them as incorrigibles; instead there is a half-tolerant boys-will-be-boys attitude.

A variation on the theme of lower-class delinquent subculture is that of the violent gang in the city. As Cohen sees it, the origin of such delinquent gangs is similar to the other lower-class subcultures he has described. A more thorough study by Lewis Yablonsky adds to Cohen's theory. The conflict-centered gang helps to overcome a feeling of inadequacy on the part of boys seemingly "born to fail," and it also gives the members a sense of power. It appears that these gangs are not as well-organized as was previously believed and much of their aggressive or violent behavior is turned toward the gang's own members.[20] Such a condition would certainly be a symptom of anomie.

The Deviant Career   Membership in a deviant subculture does not just happen and does not occur quickly. There must be a progressive

---

[18]Albert K. Cohen, *Delinquent Boys,* The Free Press of Glencoe, Ill., Chicago, 1955.
[19]Albert K. Cohen and James F. Short, Jr., "Research in Delinquent Subcultures," *Journal of Social Issues,* vol. 14, March 1958, pp. 20–27.
[20]Lewis Yablonsky, *The Violent Gang,* Penguin Books, Inc., Baltimore, 1967.

involvement with the activities of the group, whether it be composed of Bohemians, homosexuals, or delinquents. The progress from the initial act to full participation has been labeled the "deviant career" by Howard Becker.[21] The initial act may not be undertaken with the intention of joining a certain subculture but may be accidental and unintended. For example, many young boys engage in one or more acts that might be labeled homosexual, but these same boys grow up to be heterosexuals and never in adult life commit another homosexual act. Some of these boys may follow the first acts with others and gradually become committed to that style of life. At this point the sexually deviant career is underway. The same pattern of commitment may come about for people who commit their first crime on a dare, or their first act of prostitution or drug use for "the experience."

As the individual commits more and more deviant acts he gradually is drawn into closer association with others who live by the same rules. This association becomes supportive of the original behavior and provides sufficient rationalization and justification so the individual can assume an identity typified by the deviant subculture rather than the identity he once had in the conventional culture. According to Becker, "The deviant identity becomes the controlling one."[22] Some people become career deviates because of the supportive structure of the subculture and because they enjoy or feel comfortable with the associations they have found there. Other people may be forced into the position of being career deviates because they have been labeled "deviant" by the community and suffer the pains of stigmatization when living with the conventional culture.

David Matza: Components of the Deviant Career   Matza has been highly praised for further insights into the process of becoming deviant. Matza contends that to understand deviance we must first approach the subject from a subjective viewpoint. In other words, we must be able to see the situation from the deviate's position and not from our own set of values. Second, we must recognize the fact that deviance occurs within a complex system of meanings and values. Third, we must become aware of the intentions and responsibilities of the deviate as he follows the process of deviation. Finally, we must not neglect societal reactions to the deviate. These orientations are pulled together in Matza's three "master conceptions" of the process of becoming deviant: affinity, affiliation, and signification.

[21]Becker, *loc. cit.*
[22]*Ibid.*, p. 125.

The deviant process

A
F
F
I
N
I
T
Y

Differential association

Few normative supports
Access to illegitimate means

A
F
F
I
L
I
A
T
I
O
N

Deviant subcultures

Contacting the subculture
Rejection ----------->
or
Commitment to deviant subculture

Societal origins of deviance

Changing norms and anomie

The clash of values

New definitions of the
situation

Loss of community

Uneven access to goals

Conflict of goals and
means

Insincerity: rejection
of the overconformist

Tolerance of white-collar
crime

S
I
G
N
I
F
I
C
A
T
I
O
N

Rejection from normative society

Stigma and labeling
New role of the "social theater"

Affinity refers to anything that can place a person at a disadvantage in a society which gives high prestige to economic success. Poverty, racial discrimination, and mental retardation fit into this category of contributory causes for deviance. *Affiliation* refers to association with a deviant subculture. Here Matza recognizes that proximity to deviant acts may instigate further deviance. *Signification* refers to the significance of the act in the eyes of society, including the idea of labeling. Signification may be the reasonable reaction of society, or, as in the words of one of Matza's admirers, it may be "the arbitrary and ironic nature of the state's involvement in the lives of those who stray, designating them as criminal

113

or whatever. . . ."[23] Each of these master conceptions taken separately is too simplistic to explain the occurrence of deviance, but Matza argues that taken together they give us a more complete picture of the deviate and the process of becoming deviant. These conceptions combine differential association theory, subcultural theory, and labeling theory into a unified approach.

Deviance and Neutrality   Note that nearly all the writers on deviance so far considered have taken a rather neutral position, being more interested in explanation than in condemnation. Matza carries the idea of neutrality to the point of a definite philosophy in what he calls the phenomenological approach—an approach that analyzes phenomena without any biases, presuppositions, or values.[24] Instead, to observe the phenomena without any distortion this approach calls for "immediate intuition" as the means by which one can see the situation clearly. The conclusions must be based purely upon observation, not preconception.

As admitted before, it is much easier to be neutral about some kinds of deviance than about others. Where organized crime and racketeering are concerned, there is always a strong temptation to moralize. In fact, one who has been victimized can hardly do anything else. Why, then, do many sociologists persist in trying to study deviance from a neutral point of view?

There are several answers to the question. Many offenses are so clearly determined by changing public attitudes that even the average layman can take a neutral position. Examples are laws, now definitely on the wane, that try to regulate one's sex life ("invade the bedroom") or laws regarding what we can read or view in motion pictures. Such laws may someday be as obsolete as Sunday closing laws or the admonition to "Suffer not a witch to live."

But what about murder, rape, and vandalism? Certainly one who tries to be neutral in these subjects can be accused of insensitivity to the victims of crime. Nevertheless, there are strong arguments for the neutral position. The analysis of cause is a necessary step in the solution of any problem, and careful analysis can take place only in an atmosphere of calm. Just as the psychiatrist tries to probe the emotional components of the dangerous psychopath, so must the sociologist explore the more usual types of deviates—their character, associates, and interaction with the rest of society.

[23]Peter K. Manning, "On Deviance," (survey essay), *Contemporary Sociology,* vol. 2, no. 2, March 1973, p. 124.
    [24]David Matza, *op. cit.*

In the final two sections we shall look at the more traditional and emotionally involved ways of viewing deviance and, finally, at types of deviance that take enormous monetary toll but receive relatively little condemnation, that is, "respectable crime," or as mentioned, what Sutherland termed white-collar crime.

IMAGES OF DEVIANCE

A person who is judged deviant, by whatever means and from whatever cause, is also judged different from the rest of society. Such differentiation in society is frightening to some and disgusting to others; thus the deviant is often pictured in uncomplimentary—and often incorrect—ways. An excellent summary of this phenomenon is presented by Simon Dinitz, Russell R. Dynes, and Alfred C. Clark, who discuss deviance from five vantage points: (1) the deviant as freak; (2) the deviant as "sinful"; (3) the deviant as criminal; (4) the deviant as "sick"; and (5) the deviant as alienated.[25]

The deviant as freak is a "freak" in a statistical sense; that is, he represents a deviation from the norm. If all behavior in society is plotted along a "normal curve," then the deviant's behavior will be found at the extremes. Unfortunately, this view of the deviant does not focus solely on behavioral patterns but rather on physical attributes. Using this system of classification, not only would the mentally retarded person be classified but also the 7 foot tall basketball player and the genius.

The deviant as sinful relies on the religious-ideological definition of deviance and includes such terminology as sinner, heretic, and apostate. According to this system, the individual is judged not by statistical inference but by commandments, codes, and doctrines. The deviant as sinner violates certain rules that he accepts; the deviant as heretic rejects certain dogma which his society accepts; and the deviant as apostate not only rejects the existing dogma but also accepts some alternative belief system. In this case the ex-Communist or the ex-John Bircher is "guilty" of "ideological treason."

The deviant as criminal is defined according to the legal framework of a society. All societies devise laws to protect themselves from internal destruction. Therefore certain people who represent threats to that society may be labeled deviant. At one level of the legal framework there is apparently good cause to place a stigma on the label applied to the

[25]Simon Dinitz, Russell R. Dynes, and Alfred C. Clark, *Deviance: Studies in the Process of Stigmatization and Societal Reaction*, Oxford University Press, New York, 1969.

transgressor, at least from the viewpoint of the society. For example, felony offenses including murder, theft, incest, and treason are all designed to protect the way of life as Americans prefer to see it. Also, acts that are not judged immoral or necessarily harmful are likewise condemned if they interfere with the public good. Misdemeanors such as traffic violations or breaking of curfew restrictions fall into this category. A third set of laws—those applying to "crimes without victims"—is of less obvious value to a society, although they may be ardently enforced. Drug addiction and homosexuality are common examples. The final set of laws is of even more dubious value to society: crimes with willing victims. In our society abortion, prostitution, and illegal gambling carry severe penalties and significant levels of stigmatization.

The deviant as "sick" is defined pathologically as not being responsible for his conduct. Dinitz and his collaborators inform us that the words deviant and sick or crazy become almost synonymous under this classification category. People seen in this light are "observed" as abnormal and "comparable to disease." Although this is a poor basis by which to classify people, it is largely responsible for changing societal responses to certain deviations from a punitive standpoint to a "treatment" orientation. A recurring and significant problem is that in our society sometimes the "wrong people" are "treated." The decision as to who is "sick" and who is not is often arbitrary, and sociocultural factors enter into decision-making processes. For example, let us hypothesize that two people have identical symptoms, but subject A is upper-middle-class and subject B is upper-lower-class. It is highly probable that subject A will be diagnosed neurotic, but subject B will be judged psychotic.

The deviant as alienated is viewed as "separated from" the mainstream of the society. A consequence of this is a sense of powerlessness affecting one's hold on his environment and his ability to determine his own fate. Personal meaning may become lost as modern life becomes increasingly segmented. Bohemians, hippies, and social dropouts of other natures are recurring examples of this category.[26]

We hasten to add that Dinitz and his associates do not advocate classification according to these systems but merely point out that, in the past, these have constituted definitions of deviance. There are few contemporary sociologists who would attempt to create such a massive scheme of categorization, and the current trend is away from universal application of classification systems.

---

[26]All information, including several examples in this section, are freely adapted from Dinitz et al., *ibid.*

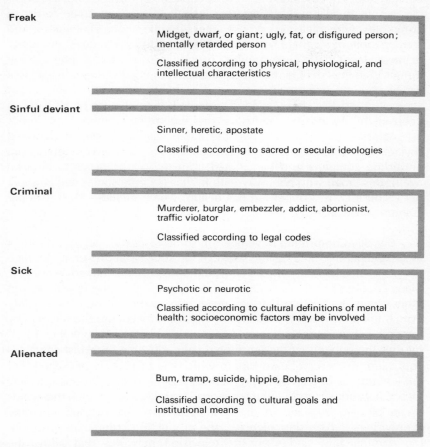

Freak

Midget, dwarf, or giant; ugly, fat, or disfigured person; mentally retarded person

Classified according to physical, physiological, and intellectual characteristics

Sinful deviant

Sinner, heretic, apostate

Classified according to sacred or secular ideologies

Criminal

Murderer, burglar, embezzler, addict, abortionist, traffic violator

Classified according to legal codes

Sick

Psychotic or neurotic

Classified according to cultural definitions of mental health; socioeconomic factors may be involved

Alienated

Bum, tramp, suicide, hippie, Bohemian

Classified according to cultural goals and institutional means

Source: Simon Dinitz et al., Deviance: *Studies in the Process of Stigmatization and Societal Reaction*, Oxford University Press, New York, 1969, p. 13.

THE RESPECTABLE DEVIANT

Much that has been written in this chapter has concerned the deviant subculture and people who are labeled deviant—conditions and individuals that are undesirable to the community at large. However, deviant behavior does not include only those actions and processes that are overt, observable to all, and subject to stigmatization. Even some forms of criminality, when detected, do not suffer from the stigma of deviance, and some people of a certain social standing seem to have a quasi-immunity to the deviant label. Two examples illustrate the point sufficiently: (1) The former Vice-President of the United States who pleaded "no contest" to a list of criminal charges was assessed a small fine, given a suspended sentence, and has received (and accepted at least one) offers to be a "consultant" for business industries and enterprises at more than "modest" salaries; (2) D. B. Cooper, the name used by a yet unidentified skyjacker, demanded and received a considerable amount of money from an airline company and parachuted from the plane, never to be seen again; this "man who got away with it" has become something of a folk hero, and a D. B. Cooper fad has begun, which includes D. B. Cooper T-shirts and watches.

Socially Conforming Deviance   In some cases the social structure or the expectations of a given segment of society allow or encourage people to engage in activities that would otherwise be defined as deviant. Many people are actively engaged in stealing, lying, misrepresenting, and other criminal activities, but they never refer to themselves—or possibly even think of themselves—as liars or crooks. A recent pronouncement by the office of the Surgeon General of the United States (November 1973) informs the public that the nutritional value of some breakfast cereals is equivalent to the cardboard box in which the product is packaged. Yet daily hundreds of televised commercials assure us that we ought to buy these "nutritious" foods. If the Surgeon General is correct, then thousands of people are engaged in an attempt at mass deception, including scriptwriters, advertising agencies, the production companies who film the commercials, and even the television networks that allow the commercial to be shown. Not to mention, of course, the company that produced the cereal in the first place!

Such activities are labeled white-collar crimes because the participants are usually from the upper socioeconomic levels of society and do not think of themselves as criminals. These people perceive of themselves as law-abiding, peace-loving people who are simply doing a day's work for a day's pay. But not only do these people engage in illegalities, they do so often willfully and willingly. Many times these activities are judged by society as unethical but technically not illegal, for example, the sale of a pair of odd-lot shoes too small or too large for the customer. In this case the shoe salesman is aware of the ethics involved but completes the sale for the sake of the company and his own commission.

Marshall B. Clinard informs us that certain activities "in the medical profession are not only unethical but illegal. They include giving illegal prescriptions for narcotics, performing illegal abortions, making fraudulent reports and giving false testimony in accident cases, and fee splitting."[27] Of course, we do not expect medical practitioners to behave in this fashion, but there are few restrictions against such practices. Lawyers and company officials also have been found to be engaged in practices both unethical and illegal. Perhaps most astounding and newsworthy of contemporary examples are the cases of the Watergate Plumbers and the Dirty Tricks Squad: The offenders were not committing crimes *against* their employers, they were committing crimes *for* their employers. Their activities included illegal surveillance, breaking and entering, procurement, entrapment, and others. Several lower echelon people have already been imprisoned, and, at the time of this writing, many higher echelon individuals are under indictment. As of the beginning of 1974, we do not know at how high a level of the hierarchy the blame is to be fixed or who, precisely, is responsible for the initiation of these illegal activities.

Socially Nonconforming Deviance Several activities just mentioned are not expected within our societal pattern, but they "seemed right" or "correct" at the time. Other patterns do not seem right at the moment of commission, and the offender does not see himself as an upholder of law-and-order principles at the time of the activity. However, both before and after the deviant act is committed the individual still conceives of himself as basically a law-abiding citizen. The medical doctor who performs an illegal abortion or euthanasia (mercy killing) is well-aware that he is acting against the ethics of his profession and in violation of the laws of his state, but, usually, he can justify his behavior by reasoning that he did "what he thought best" under the existing circumstances. Such individuals may not think of themselves as immoral, but, using the classification system outlined by Dinitz and his associates, they would certainly fall into the group labeled "criminal deviates."

In corporate society there have been many examples of companies that have deliberately acted against society's norms, federal laws, and public interests. There have been violations concerning wages, public contracts, and labor relations. Sutherland's classic study showed that 70 of the top 200 largest nonfinancial corporations in this country had 980 decisions rendered against them for violations of federal regulations.[28]

[27]Marshall B. Clinard, *Sociology of Deviant Behavior,* Holt, Rinehart and Winston, Inc., New York, 1968, p. 271.
[28]Edwin H. Sutherland, *White-Collar Crime,* Holt, Rinehart and Winston, Inc., New York, 1949, reissued 1960.

However, the corporate executives who organized these violations do not suffer the stigmatization process that persistently afflicts those in the lower strata of society. In white-collar crime the self-image, as well as one's image among his peers, is protected. Clinard gives an excellent summary of Sutherland's conclusions:

> (1) The criminality of corporations is persistent; (2) there is generally no loss of status by an offender among his business associates; (3) in those areas which immediately affect white-collar offenders there is apt to be fairly general contempt for the government as a whole, the law, and the personnel who administer it; and (4) most white-collar business crimes are organized in the sense that the violation is a corporation affair or may extend to several corporations or subsidiaries.[29]

There are other reasons why the respectable white-collar criminal is dealt with more leniently than the common burglar. A rather cynical but perfectly valid reason is that he has more money to hire lawyers and is likely to have friends and protectors in high places. Another difference is that many cases of graft involve dipping into public or corporate treasuries in such a way that each taxpayer or stockholder is robbed of only a few dollars. No one is hurt in the same way as the owner of a house that is burglarized, nor are people terrorized, injured, or killed by gunmen. At first glance the crime seems much less important. In the long run, however, if such practices become virtually the rule rather than the exception, insurance rates, prices, and taxes must go higher to support white-collar crime, and the public pays dearly. Worse yet, a general cynicism regarding business and government can undermine national morale, and corruption can escalate.

Embezzling   The definitive work on this "respectable crime" that fits the classic pattern of white-collar crime was done by Donald Cressey. Cressey began his studies where Sutherland left off, but he gave credit to Sutherland for initiating the research and influencing his field of examination. Embezzlers are special criminals because they generally occupy positions of solemn trust within the company or corporation. If the position of solemn trust were to be eliminated, many business transactions would be hampered, so many accountants are put in a situation where stealing or "borrowing" money is relatively simple. The training required to produce a good accountant is identical to the training required of the "complete embezzler."

[29]Clinard, op. cit., p. 273.

Cressey emphasizes that there are three "essential kinds of psychological process" involved in the act of embezzlement: "(1) the feeling that a personal financial problem is unshareable; (2) the knowledge of how to solve the problem in secret, by violating a position of financial trust; and (3) the ability to find a formula which describes the act of embezzling in words which do not conflict with the image of oneself as a trusted person."[30] Points 1 and 3 concern Cressey most because all accountants must maintain the knowledge necessary for embezzlement. However, he believes that embezzlement could be curtailed if we could devise a way for employees to share their financial problems with some official of the corporation. But often pride or the fear of overscrutinization obstruct this channel; for example, if the accountant tells his employer that he (the accountant) is in financial difficulty, the employer may become suspicious of all bookkeeping procedures henceforth.

The third point is referred to by Cressey as the point of *verbalization*. The potential embezzler convinces himself that he is only "borrowing" the money or that the money he takes is absolutely essential for the well-being of his family. In other words, verbalization refers to the process by which the embezzler talks himself into a conviction that he is still a good person. Cressey believes that the act of embezzlement can be stopped at this level or at the point of sharing the problem.

Cressey's writings predated the age of "computer proliferation," and this era ushered in a new type of "professional crime" that may cause some sociologists to change their thinking about the subject of embezzlement because "computer criminals" do not steal large sums of money from individuals or corporations. These computer programmers may steal only 10 or 20 cents from thousands of people employed by giant companies by making slight adjustments in computer-printed paychecks. The average employee will not miss a few cents, and the company account sheet can be adjusted to show a "correct" figure for payroll. However, the difference between the correct payroll of the company and the actual gross salary of each employee may total hundreds or thousands of dollars each month. The difference, of course, goes into the programmer's pocket. As of this writing a few such cases have been reported, and some research has begun regarding this phenomenon. We hasten to point out that not all computer programmers or other technicians engage in "professional deviance," but the fact that a few have been caught indicates the possibility that others may participate in such crime.

[30]Donald Cressey, "The Respectable Criminal," *Transaction*, March–April 1965.

Once again, Cressey's points seem appropriate. If one is in a position of trust (operation or programming of a computer) and cannot share a financial problem and can verbalize a rationalization ("I'm not hurting anyone by taking a few cents from each check."), then embezzlement is possible. This new type of crime may cause us to change our image of the embezzler, but it does not change the fact that professional deviance exists in our society, and such deviance does not carry the same stigma and labeling as do other acts. Therefore computer crime—like other forms of criminal activity described by Sutherland—qualifies as a white-collar crime.

Cressey's final example is of a rather individualized crime, but it has much in common with many other types of white-collar crime; attempts are made to disguise it by calling it something besides what it is. Probably Cressey's idea of being sure to label such offenses "crime" is exactly the right approach. In the world of white-collar crime we are dealing with people who generally maintain a reputation for respectability and to whom such a self-image is important. A strong threat to the respectable self-image might have exactly the right effect. On the other hand, in the case of the young person growing up in society, the authorities previously cited have been very critical of early labeling, fearing it alienates and can be a self-fulfilling prophecy.

Obviously the problem of deviance is extremely complex, running as it does from top to bottom of society, thriving on alienation and anomie, sometimes fed by our very attempts to label and condemn it, and at other times successfully disguising itself as legitimate enterprise. We can see deviance written into the structure of society, as an outgrowth of social change, as a consequence of impossible goals, of stigma, of unwise labeling, and as a continuing social problem for all members of society.

SUMMARY

Social deviance is a variation from the norms of society that represents some form of undesirable difference. A review of classical theories (including those of Émile Durkheim, Willam Graham Sumner, and William I. Thomas), neoclassical theories that emphasize the school of sociological inquiry known as structural-functionalism (including those of Talcott Parsons, Robert K. Merton, and Robin M. Williams, Jr., and contemporary theories (including those of Howard S. Becker, Erving Goffman, and David Matza) leads us to three conclusions: (1) Deviance is a culturally relative concept, depending upon time, place, and audience; (2) the commission of a deviant act is significant according to the "definition of the situation"; (3) there is no totally adequate definition of deviance.

From the time of the earliest sociological theorists it has been clear that deviance must be studied in a context parallel to conformity. However, conformity is not always adaptive, and nonconformity is not always maladaptive. Neoclassical theorists deemphasized the difference between conformity and deviance and concentrated on the consequences of a given social structure on the behavior of individuals. And contemporary theories have been concerned mainly with the process of labeling, the assignment of stigma to a person or an act, and the acceptance of a position of neutrality in the study of deviance.

Research by Richard A. Cloward and Lloyd E. Ohlin suggested that a "deviant subculture" exists not only because of a gap between cultural goals and institutional means (suggested by Merton), but also that certain individuals become "double failures" because they do not succeed at either legitimate or illegitimate means. Edwin H. Sutherland explained that deviant subcultures come into existence because of "differential association" caused by segregation. According to this theory, the primary associations of some people predispose them to criminal careers. Albert K. Cohen shows that these subcultures may have values different from the conventional culture and hypothesizes that some of the same mechanisms affecting lower-class youth may now be affecting middle-class youth. Lewis Yablonsky applies many of the same principles of the concept of a deviant subculture to the formation of violent gangs.

Becker sees the process of labeling as leading to "deviant careers," wherein a person once labeled deviant is drawn into closer associations with persons sharing the same label. Matza, taking a phenomenological approach, argues that there are three "master conceptions" that when combined contribute to the creation of a "subculture of deviance": (1) affinity, such as poverty or discrimination; (2) affiliation, the subculture itself; and (3) signification, the labeling of the deviant by authorities.

Simon Dinitz and his associates claim that society "pictures" deviants as (1) freaks, (2) sinful, (3) criminal, (4) sick, and (5) alienated. The researchers do not necessarily agree with such categorization but simply point out that historically the community has had these reactions to deviance. Not all results have been negative. The image of the deviant as "sick," for instance, has been a significant factor in turning society's attention from punitive measures to treatment orientations.

"Respectable deviants" generally fall into the category of white-collar crime. They are labeled respectable because they are from the middle or upper stratum of society and they do not think of themselves as criminals. Some are merely conforming to existing norms, for example, dishonest shoe salesmen or advertising executives who know that their product is inferior. Others are nonconformists who know that they are engaging in unethical and illegal practices, such as medical doctors who perform euthanasia. And, finally, some are placed in a position of solemn trust, but find the temptation to embezzle their employers insurmountable. Such employees usually convince themselves that they are really "good people" and are only borrowing the money for a specific period of time. Respectable deviants generally do not carry the stigma of other deviants who come from less fortunate socioeconomic backgrounds.

Chapter 6

Differentiation in Societies: Status, Class, and Caste

Then let us pray that come it may,
As come it will for a' that . . .

That man to man the world o'er
Shall brithers be, for a' that.

Robert Burns
"For A'That and A'That"

For thousands of years it has been the dream of prophet and sage that men could live together as brothers, not differentiated by social class, free of the arrogance of wealth and of the grubbing misery of poverty. Why is it that this seems to be the impossible dream, even in states dedicated to equality? Only a handful of preliterate hunting and gathering societies remain in a state of complete person-to-person equality. In many societies poverty becomes less acute, but the gulf between poverty and riches is wide enough to create resentment and political and social movements of an equalitarian nature. Yet, ironically, even the communistic societies whose philosophy is most dedicated to classlessness find new class divisions arising, based on power and privilege. Henry George (1839–1897), an interesting and unusual American economic theorist, wrote a book titled *Progress and Poverty* in which he indicated that the two are related. Is there such a connection between progress and poverty or, at least, between progress and the differentiation of social classes? To investigate such a question it will be necessary to attempt a definition of social class, a very difficult task in mobile industrial societies, as will become apparent in the following discussion.

STATUS, ROLE, AND CLASS

In the discussion of culture and socialization the concepts of status and role were defined. They have a strong bearing on stratification as well as on the previously mentioned normative and socialization processes. "All the world's a stage," said Shakespeare in "As You Like It," "And all the men and women merely players. They have their exits and their entrances; and one man in his time plays many parts." The many parts that all people play are the ones we mentioned previously: roles of kinship, childhood, adulthood and old age, roles of male or female, citizen or noncitizen and the like. However, there are roles involving wealth and power and roles for the impoverished and outcast that are exclusive to certain segments of society. In some societies there are such statuses as king or nobleman, demanding the role behavior of aristocratic manners, bearing, and taste, exclusive to an extremely small segment of the population.

Status as an Overall Measurement   When we discuss the status and role of king or nobleman we are really using a somewhat different concept from that of age or kinship status in that the former is an overall measurement of a person's position in society. Nearly anyone can be a husband or wife, but society permits only a few to be of the aristocracy. In societies without aristocracies there are also statuses that more or less summarize a person's position in life. A supreme court justice has a very high status, and when we think of his status we mean only his occupational status. Few are interested in whether he has a large number of children, is adept at cards or golf, or has special ability as an amateur artist or poet. His occupational status is the one by which he is classified, just as the king or nobleman is classified by his hereditary status. An occupational status is called an *achieved* status as opposed to the ascribed status already mentioned. The words "achieved status" are self-explanatory and obviously can have other applications besides occupational status: for example, athletic competence, college graduation, and skill in art, music, and writing.

Complications in Status So far it seems that a simple definition of class is about to be reached, equating class simply with inherited title in an aristocratic society or with occupational status in a society without titled aristocracy. However, the problem is not that simple. What positions are equivalent to each other in the two systems? Is supreme court justice the equal of an earl? The same person can hold inconsistent statuses, having great wealth and influence but having such boorish manners as to be unacceptable in elite society. A young man might have high status on the school football team but otherwise be a person of little ability or promise. Another man can finish graduate school, proudly grasp his master's degree, and then be drafted into the Armed Forces as a buck private. What is the overall status of these men? An attempt to define social class in terms of occupational status is helpful but not adequate. Although occupation is a very important measure of class status, it is not the only measure.

Other measures of status include education, income, inherited wealth, family background, reputation, and political power. Some of these measures are difficult to gauge with any precision, so occupation is often used as the one measure of social class. Despite the complications, occupation *does* have the advantage of being fairly easy to determine, and it generally correlates with education and income. However, Weber contended that social-class position must be measured by the criteria of wealth, power, and esteem, with esteem including many areas of acceptability within the higher circles of one's society.

One further complication in the whole attempt to measure social class by standards of occupation, income, and education is that certain ascribed statuses rate differently in prestige and esteem, even in a society that claims to judge people in terms of achievement. Women, for example, often fail to rate as high in prestige in a particular occupation as do men and are much more likely to be passed up for promotion. The junior partner of a law firm does not rank with the senior partners, even though he has the same law degree, because, up to a certain point, age has status. The new college graduate starting business in town will have the advantage of ready-made prestige if he comes from one of the town's distinguished families; otherwise he will have to build his reputation on his own.

Definition of Class   With all these reservations in mind, we can define a *social class* as a collectivity of people sharing similar status or as "a stratum of people who are roughly equal with regard to such factors as family prestige, and occupational-educational-income status, and . . . are accepted by their stratum members as equals."[1] Such a definition may bring to mind a stairstep arrangement of social classes, whereas the American model actually more closely resembles an inclined plane, with one class grading into another almost imperceptibly. Such is by no means always the case with social classes. Social classes can vary from the loose structuring of American society to very great rigidity.

VARIATIONS IN SOCIAL-CLASS SYSTEMS

Social-class systems can be described along a continuum from open class at one extreme to closed class, or caste, at the other. Open class is the ideal type of class system, in which movement from one class to another is completely unencumbered. It fulfills the goal of perfect equality of opportunity but exists as an ideal rather than as a reality.

No True "Meritocracy"   The British sociologist Michael Young wrote a description of a perfect open-class system, which he called the "meritocracy,"[2] the idea being that each individual could rise purely on the basis of merit, and no other way. In this novel about the future he pictured all the changes that England had to make to become a perfect meritocracy. Not only was it necessary to do away with all the titles and estates of the nobility, but all inherited wealth had to be confiscated, and no family could give special help to its children. The family, in fact, was depicted as a reactionary institution whose power had to be broken. The school system had to be revised to give special consideration to children from culturally handicapped backgrounds to ensure them equality of opportunity. Systems of seniority were eliminated so the young man could challenge the middle-aged man for his job. Eventually full equality of opportunity was guaranteed. At last the person who failed could no longer blame his failure on "bad breaks"; he had to blame it on his own incompetence. In the last pages of the book Young boasted that a system had finally been devised that was immune to overthrow because the people at the bottom of the class system were too stupid for any possible effective organization. A footnote at the end of the book adds that the manuscript was found among the author's possessions after his death in the revolution!

[1]Thomas Ford Hoult, *Dictionary of Modern Sociology,* Littlefield, Adams, and Company, Totowa, N.J., 1969.

[2]Michael Young, *The Rise of the Meritocracy, 1870–2033,* Penguin Books, Inc., Baltimore, 1961.

Young is telling us how extremely difficult it would be to establish absolute equality of opportunity. He also implies that no system could make everyone happy and contented. In applying his conclusions to the United States, we could say that our society approaches, but does not achieve, complete open class.

Class Preliterate Societies   There are, as suggested in the opening paragraph of this chapter, societies without class—some, but not all, hunting and gathering societies. If the level of productivity is so low that there is no surplus of goods beyond the minimum for keeping the people alive, there is little chance for class differentiation.[3] In more advanced agrarian societies, social class always comes into existence. Early civilizations had very marked superior classes—military, religious, and governmental—and often very depressed slave and outcast groups. A glance at the progress from simple hunting and gathering societies through the development of agriculture and early urban civilizations would lead to full agreement with the discouraging link between "progress and poverty."

Although many historical systems have become extremely stratified and quite rigid, few have made any upward mobility completely impossible. Vilfredo Pareto, an Italian sociologist, contended that societies have always had a "circulation of elites," either as a result of overthrow or invasion, or as a result of natural changes within.[4] His analysis of circulation within societies was that the clever people (the "foxes") gradually supplement or replace the original conquerors (the "lions") and are eventually themselves replaced by other "lions." Because Pareto had an elitist and antidemocratic bias, he was inclined to exaggerate the lion-fox analogy. Probably the closest approximation of the types of constant changes he had in mind were those of the class system of China.

The Chinese System of Class   The ancient class sytem of China had at least one characteristic of mobility: The scholarly bureaucracy attained position by achievement in competitive examinations, not by heredity. Even in the Chinese system, though, there were advantages to wealth because the studies for the examinations were long and expensive. In theory at least, China, through many centuries, had an interesting class structure headed by the scholarly bureaucrats, with the farmers in the middle and the artisans and traders in lower positions.[5] The scholars held

[3]Gerhard Lenski, *Power and Privilege: A Theory of Social Stratification,* McGraw-Hill Book Company, New York, 1966, chap. 4.

[4]T. B. Bottomore, *Elites and Society,* Penguin Books, Inc., Balitmore, 1968, pp. 7–12.

[5]Egon Ernest Bergel, *Social Stratification,* McGraw-Hill Book Company, New York, 1962, pp. 213–221.

all the important government jobs and helped to centralize the administration and strengthen the hand of the emperor relative to the warlords. The system was very persistent. Although invaders conquered China and new dynasties overthrew the old, the scholarly bureaucracy remained, changing little through 2,000 years of history. There were, however, gaps between real and ideal culture. The number of Manchu officials during the Manchu Dynasty (the last dynasty of China) vastly overrepresented their proportion of the population. Despite Pareto's circulation theory, there always seem to be ways to cheat on the system.

Class in Medieval Europe   The system of stratification of medieval Europe had less "circulation of elites" than China, if it can be said to have had any at all. Europe had an *estate system,* a system in which classes had carefully defined legal rights and duties. Most of the rights went to the aristocracy and clergy, and most of the duties went to the peasants, although even the peasants had the right of inalienability from the land. Although they could not legally be driven off the land, the peasants could be sold along with the land. Peasants, or serfs, existed at several levels, all owing labor to a lord; but some were in a state of virtual slavery, and others owed the lord only about one-third of their labor.[6]

The estate system was more rigid than that of ancient China because it lacked a scholarly route to mobility. Occasionally, however, a sturdy peasant's son would be chosen for military training, and occasionally there was an upward route through the clergy. The European system was not the same as caste, although it approached it closely. The estate system waned with the passing of the Middle Ages, but the old upward-mobility routes through military and clergy still seemed at times to be the most promising ones. Stendhal's famous novel *Le Rouge et le Noir* (1831) presents two possible paths to upward mobility for the poor man: *le rouge* (red), the path of the soldier, or *le noir* (black), the robes of the priest. The central character in the novel chooses the priesthood because military opportunities had declined after the time of Napoleon?

The Modern Change   Comments on such older systems of stratification as those of China and medieval Europe may seem at first to be only of historical interest, but they have another importance to sociological study. They illustrate the worldwide societal trait of separating people into classes with different styles of life, but even more starkly they show the contrast between ancient systems and the types of stratification coming about in modern societies. Whether we speak of

[6]*Ibid.,* p. 129.

Europe, Asia, Africa, or the Americas, wherever modern industrialization takes place the changes are drastic. Societies break their ties with sacred tradition, and instead of having simply one or two heaven-blessed upper classes and a vast, undifferentiated lower class, social differences grow more complex and are based increasingly upon wealth, regardless of heredity, family name, or long tradition.[7] A competitive struggle for status takes place even in societies in which status was once completely determined at birth. The contrast between modernity and traditional caste systems illustrates the point.

Caste   Caste is a system of social class that precludes any possible upward mobility. Caste is rare in the world, but it is not confined to India. A few characteristics of caste have spread to Ceylon, Burma, parts of Indonesia, and other places in contact with Indian civilization. Caste also has developed in areas remote from India, usually in conquest states. In Africa, one illustration of caste is the relationship between the pastoral Bahima and the gardening Bairu in the old kingdom of Ankole in Uganda. The Hamitic Bahima came from the north, probably southern Ethiopia, and conquered the gardening Bantu people, who they call the Bairu. The characteristics of the caste system include occupational differences, the prohibition of intermarriage, the paying of tribute by the Bairu, no military service or right to bear arms by the Bairu, and no holding of public office. There is a denial of any possibility of social equality, as is typical of caste. The total system is complicated by an even lower caste of slaves whose position is also hereditary and precludes any mobility.[8]

The most famous case of caste is in India of course. The system is too complex to describe in detail, but basically there are four castes: Brahmins (priestly caste), Kshatriya (warriors), Vaisya (merchants and artisans), and Sudra (servants). Caste was imposed, or at least strengthened, in India by the Aryan conquest of about 1400 B.C. A system as rigid as caste has also depended upon the internalization of feelings of inequality, the learning of unequal roles, and the development of self-concepts of inferior or superior beings, as the case may be. No system has accomplished this task as thoroughly as the caste system of India because there the progress of the soul depends upon living out one's appointed destiny in a caste position. The progress of one's soul from one earthly incarnation to the next and its ultimate achievement of freedom from the wheel of life by merging with the Eternal depends upon the

[7]S. N. Eisenstadt, *Social Differentiation and Stratification*, Scott Foresman & Company, Glenview, Ill., 1971, pp. 121–148.

[8]E. Adamson Hoebel, *Anthropology: The Study of Man*, McGraw-Hill Book Company, New York, 1966, pp. 408–409.

proper maintenance of caste rules. Modern laws have done away with many of the legal disabilities of caste and have granted the right to vote and the right to an education, but social inequality remains, reinforced by many crippling rules of etiquette and the fear of spiritual pollution.[9]

American Caste   Ever since Gunnar Myrdal wrote *An American Dilemma*, containing an analysis of "the white man's theory of color caste," the word "caste" has been used to describe black-white relationships in the United States. Dollard's *Class and Caste in a Southern Town* uses the same definition of the system. Certainly as long as slavery existed an immobile, endogamous caste existed, supported by law, and even rationalized by religion to some degree. However, the religious underpinnings of caste have been weak in America compared with India. Most of its followers in recent history have thought of Christianity as a religion of equality of man before God. For this reason it took great effort to rationalize the institution of slavery in American society. Strange and conflicting stereotypes had to be created. In one version of racial stereotyping, the black was pictured as complacent, accepting his status, and loving his white master. In the opposite version he was seen as a savage who must be carefully watched lest he tarnish and defile white womanhood.

There were, however, stirrings of discontent over slavery. The slave image was never completely accepted by the blacks or by all whites. Nevertheless, it cannot be denied that many of the earmarks of caste were present and remained a century after the abolition of slavery: the dread of intermarriage; segregated schools, restaurants, restrooms, neighborhoods, and sections of town; and inferior images in entertainment, popular jokes, and the often-repeated phrase "I have nothing against blacks so long as they know their place." Although there are differences between Indian and American caste, it is hard to argue too strongly with those who apply the word "caste" to America's racial history.

There are resemblances to caste in any society in which racial and ethnic groups are so differently treated that being born into any one of them is a distinct advantage or disadvantage. The status of the American Indian has proved a distinct handicap in the United States. In Latin America, especially in colonial times, the status of the American Indian was much lower than that of the mestizo (mixed Spanish-Indian), and the mestizo ranked well below the Spaniard.

The phenomena of class and caste have been widespread throughout the world and throughout history. Class distinctions have existed between

[9]Bergel, *op. cit.*, pp. 35–48.

men in spite of protests, equalitarian ideas, and even revolutions. It is time to look for explanations of social class and ask whether it is functional or dysfunctional to a society.

THEORIES OF SOCIAL CLASS

There have been many theories, some of which have already been mentioned, to support social-class distinctions. Indian caste has been supported on religious grounds as a necessity for the progress of the human soul. A social myth from the Hindu laws of Manu explained that from the mouth of the Resplendent One came forth the Brahmin. The Kshatryia sprang from his arms, the Vaisya from his thighs, and the Sudra from his feet.[10] Slavery in America was rationalized on grounds of "the happiness of the slave with his lot" and of his "need for direction" and sometimes even on religious grounds as God's manifest will.

Modern scholars differ in their interpretations of social class. Lenski[11] shows that for centuries there has been a tendency for conservatives to interpret social class as a functional necessity for the survival of societies. Liberals and radicals, on the other hand, have attacked social-class inequality either as totally unnecessary or as unjustifiably great.

A little reflection on man's inhumanity to man, as seen in the extremes of class, caste, and slavery, is enough to put one's sympathies on the side of the challengers of class. Often rigidly stratified societies have so oppressed the lower classes as to almost exclude them from humanity, thinking of them as beasts of the field, "stolid and stunned, a brother to the ox." "Swine!" Frederick the Great called his Prussian peasants. Thomas Carlyle wrote that so great was the gulf between aristocracy and peasantry at one time in France that returning noblemen, if disappointed in the hunt for game, were allowed to shoot as many as two peasants instead, just for the sport of it.[12] Although much has been made of the idea of *noblesse oblige* (the obligation of the rich and well-born to be good to the "simple folk"), it has often had no impact whatever.

The Views of the Challengers of Class There have been many challengers to the idea of social class, including some of the early Christians, the heretical Waldensians, the leaders of peasant uprisings in the sixteenth century, and the Levellers of seventeeth-century England. Such early socialistic idealists as Fourrier in France and Owen in Wales

---

[10]*Laws of Manu,* Book 1, lines 87–89, in G. Bühler (ed.), *Sacred Books of the East,* Oxford University Press, London, 1886, vol. 25.

[11]Lenski, *op. cit.,* chap. 1.

[12]Thomas Carlyle, *The French Revolution,* A. L. Burt, Publisher, New York, 1900, vol. 1, p. 11.

were strong equalitarians, and there were many anticlass sentiments in the romantic period of English and European literature. Marx, of course, is usually thought of first as the opponent of social class and the prophet of a revolutionary movement aimed at ushering in the classless society, but it is to be emphasized that many others have also called for an end to class distinctions.

The challengers to social class have generally placed a higher value on equality than on stability. They have also supported a number of assumptions about human ability, human societies, and human nature that contrast sharply with the views of conservatives.[13] The challengers' view of essential human nature is optimistic, holding that a just social system can free people from most of their greed for power and wealth. They see societies as generally unjust and, therefore, as centers of struggle, rather than as smooth-running systems that should not be fundamentally shaken. They generally see leadership and high class position as having been attained originally through conquest and main-tained, to a great degree, through inheritance, fraud, and coercion. Laws are generally seen as exploitive, favoring the rich. They may seem to be fair but really are not. As Anatole France said in *Le Lys Rouge,* "The law, in its majestic equality, forbids the rich as well as the poor to sleep under bridges, to beg in the streets, and to steal bread." The opponents of social class believe inequalities are unnecessary and can be ended, that "Man to man the world o'er/Shall brithers be for a'that."

There is little doubt that the constant challenge to gross inequalities has helped to promote more equitable systems than in the past. In nearly all the Western world poverty has been greatly alleviated, but the gulf between rich and poor is still wide. The leading country that claims to have followed the marxian road to classlessness is the Soviet Union, but the reality is a long way from the ideal. The present Russian system can be described as a highly structured class system based more upon power and privilege than upon wealth. At the top of the structure are those in political power. Below them are the military leaders, scientists, recog-nized intellectuals, managers, and leading professionals. Next are leaders at various levels: white-collar, skilled, semiskilled, and unskilled laborers, in layers fairly similar to those of Western Europe or the United States. Peasants rank lower than most industrial workers. The upper classes have marked differences in income, live in separate neighborhoods, are socially segregated, and tend to be endogamous (marrying within their own class or social grouping).[14] Upper classes also get such favors as tax

[13]Lenski, *op. cit.,* pp. 441–443.
[14]Bergel, *op. cit.,* pp. 230–242.

Supporters of social class say:	Challengers of social class systems reply:
Human nature is in need of strong social control.	Human nature is good; bad social systems corrupt.
Stability is more important than equality.	Equality is more important than stability.
Any system is better than chaos.	Better no system than an unjust system.
Unequal abilities call for unequal rewards.	Abilities are not as unequal as laws and rewards.
High position is usually the reward of hard work.	High position is often based on conquest, fraud, or inheritance.
Class inequality makes societies function.	Inequalities are much greater than needed.

(Adapted from G. H. Lenski, *Power and Privilege: A Theory of Social Stratification*, McGraw-Hill Book Company, New York, 1966.)

breaks and better placement of their children in school. Inequalities of wealth have declined because there is no private ownership of estates, mills, mines, and banks; but social class persists in pay, power, and prestige. The more conservative social theorists are not surprised; their position is that social class is necessary and inevitable.

Modern Defenders of Social Class   The supporters of social-class systems no longer rely on mythology for an explanation. Social class now is seen as a functional necessity. Lenski sums up a set of conservative views, the converse of those held by the challengers, that support the concept of social class as a necessity.[15] The conservative view is much less trustful of human nature, seeing the need for a strong social system and legal controls. Stability is more important than equality, for stable systems are necessary to keep up the flow of goods and services on which life depends. Even the poorer members of society are much better off than they would be under conditions of anarchy, the view holds, and they generally realize that fact. Leadership is based to a great extent upon merit, not primarily upon conquest or fraud.

[15]Lenski, *op. cit.*, pp. 441–443.

135

Mosca and Pareto, two prominent Italian social theorists, went further than simply trying to prove the necessity for social class. They (especially Pareto) tried to show how in modern industrial systems there is enough circulation of elites so that there is no really permanent ruling class. Both theorists were elitists and distrustful of democracy.[16]

Robert Michels also criticized the classless dream, advancing an idea that he called "the iron law of oligarchy." After studying European labor movements, he came to the conclusion that a small clique of leaders was sure to emerge eventually. Because of differences in ability and experience, because of the indifference of the followers, and because men like to exert power, Michels concluded that there could never be real equality.[17]

In the United States a long argument has been waged over the idea that social class functions to "instill in proper individuals the desire to fill certain positions" and that it rewards with highest rank those positions that "have the greatest importance for society and require the greatest training or talent."[18] Davis and Moore argue that the above statements apply both to achieving societies and to societies with position based upon ascription. In the former societies the major task is to recruit the right people; in ascription-type societies motivation to perform the duties is given greater stress. The authors wisely avoid a pitfall in their theory by stressing that the theory applies to positions, not necessarily to all persons holding those positions.

In reply to Davis and Moore, Tumin[19] shows that some extremely important jobs are poorly rewarded, that the magnitude of difference in pay is much more than is necessary for motivation, and that inherited ownership alone—not talent—is the opening to many positions. He also shows that class-structured societies and societies with racial or religious discrimination cut out potential talent rather than promote it. It should also be added that explaining class distinctions as a functional necessity runs into the danger of justifying poverty, social snobbery, and arrogance.

Neither the radical theories calling for the abolition of social class nor the functional theories explaining its necessity seem entirely satisfactory. Maybe the real question is one of degree of social class, rather than of its existence or nonexistence. Are there characteristics of social class in modern industrial societies that make it seem less exploitive than Marx would have expected? Is there a constant circulation of elites?

[16]Bottomore, *op. cit.*, pp. 16–20.

[17]*Ibid.*, pp. 18–20.

[18]Kingsley Davis and Wilbert E. Moore, "Some Principles of Stratification," *American Sociological Review*, vol. 10, February 1945, pp. 242–249.

[19]Melvin M. Tumin, "Some Principles of Stratification: A Critical Analysis," *American Sociological Review*, vol. 18, August 1953, pp. 387–393.

SOCIAL CLASS IN INDUSTRIAL SOCIETIES

In the historical development of societies, the general trend has been toward a strengthening of class as higher levels of productivity are reached. Even the advance from hunting to simple slash-and-burn agriculture increases stratification of society. The advance to plow agriculture increases class differences even more and correlates closely with the institution of slavery.[20]

It would seem rather natural that the trend toward greater differentiation of class, fed by the increase of surplus production, would continue. However, in industrial societies the first reversal of the trend is encountered.[21] Slavery becomes an inefficient system of labor in societies calling for industrial skills, and so does serfdom. The amount of mechanical power increases overwhelmingly, so that many jobs calling for backbreaking manual labor are replaced by machinery. Education becomes a job requirement of the new society, and there is no longer an upper-class monopoly on learning, as was once the case. The self-image of the common people improves, and equalitarian pressures grow. Labor movements work in the direction of a larger share of production for the worker, and political parties representing the common people work for other benefits. No longer is the worker a cowed and submissive peasant, "the emptiness of ages in his eyes, and on his back the burden of the world." His demands increase, and he is able to make them heard.

Great inequalities still exist, and so does poverty, but the poor become a minority rather than a majority. When Lincoln said, "God must have loved the poor; He made so many of them," he was talking about the common majority of people, not the minority poor of today. The problem of poverty is not to be glossed over because in some ways it is more agonizing than ever to those who remain behind in an affluent age, but the change from majority to minority status is, nevertheless, characteristic of advanced industrial systems.

Warner's Description of Class   Various attempts have been made to describe the social-class system of the modern United States. The studies of W. Lloyd Warner should be mentioned briefly because they have become a part of our social-class terminology.[22] In community studies Warner identified six classes: upper-upper, lower-upper, upper-middle, lower-middle, upper-lower, and lower-lower. The upper-uppers are the old-money class, high in wealth, influence, and esteem. The lower-

[20]Hoebel, *op. cit.*, pp. 402–410.
[21]Lenski, *op. cit.*, p. 308.
[22]W. Lloyd Warner, Marcia Meeker, and Kenneth Eells, *Social Class in America*, Harper & Row, Publishers, Incorporated, Torchbooks, New York, 1960, pp. 3–33, chap. 1.

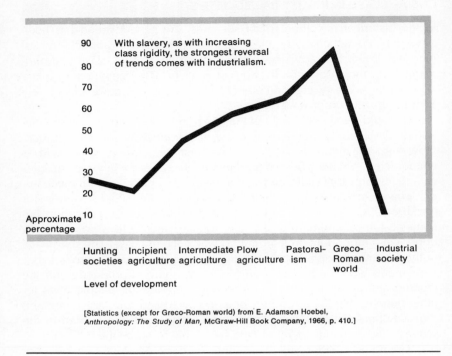

90
80
70
60
50
40
30
20

Approximate 10
percentage

With slavery, as with increasing
class rigidity, the strongest reversal
of trends comes with industrialism.

| Hunting societies | Incipient agriculture | Intermediate agriculture | Plow agriculture | Pastoral-ism | Greco-Roman world | Industrial society |

Level of development

[Statistics (except for Greco-Roman world) from E. Adamson Hoebel,
Anthropology: The Study of Man, McGraw-Hill Book Company, 1966, p. 410.]

uppers are the newly rich. Below them are layers of business and professional people and technical and scientific experts, classified as upper- or lower-middle, depending upon how successful their businesses, jobs, or areas of expertise happen to be. The lower-middle also includes large numbers of white-collar workers. The upper-lowers are the respectable poor, employed most of the time at poorly paying jobs. Below them are the people described by many of the middle class as "shiftless and lazy." Warner's descriptions are interesting, especially for describing the community elite, but modern Americans are so geographically mobile that many do not stay in communities long enough to gain the community reputations Warner describes. He admits this is true of the newer areas of the West, especially for the attempt to identify an upper-upper class.

Self-evaluation Another way of studying class in modern America is by self-evaluation. Richard Centers argues that people are very much aware of social class and that self-rating is of great psychological importance. Hodges shows that self-evaluation is quite inaccurate by any objective standard, but he also argues that some types of class awareness are stronger now than in the past.[23] As some types of ethnic, religious, and rural-urban distinctions disappear, we become more concerned with such distinctions as those between upper-middle and lower-middle class. One other rather important point about self-rating is that the majority of people like to rate themselves as middle class. Whether this is objectively sound or not, it is an interesting refutation of earlier marxian predictions that the middle class would disappear in capitalistic societies.

Objective Classifications　An objective classification of people on an income basis is easily obtainable from the Census Bureau. Income distribution is by no means a perfect measure of social class, for reasons we have already mentioned, but it has the advantage of objectivity and of application on a national scale. Table 6-1 shows a steady increase in the number of people in the higher income brackets and a decline of those in the less-than-$3,000 income bracket, even when the value of the dollar is kept constant. In total income, real progress is being made, but Table 6-2 shows that the poorest fifth of the population has changed very little in relative position, even though its cash earnings have improved. The absolute gap between highest and lowest incomes has increased.

Diagrammatic Representations of Class　On the basis of the income statistics just presented, social class could be shown as a simple stairstep arrangement, but such an illustration fails to account for gradations between steps. Warner's community descriptions could be shown in the same way, but the steps would have very different widths. In Warner's analysis, the upper-lower and lower-middle classes make up a majority, "the common-man level." Another possibility is to represent class distribution as an inclined plane, suggesting that classes grade into each other almost imperceptibly.

Another way to represent social class graphically is by a type of panoramic view. Such a scheme has the advantage of showing that people strive for success in their own areas of life and that there are elites in various fields of striving. Our panoramic view shows the highest peaks as those of the leaders of government, industry, and the military; in this respect it places an emphasis on power. There are few completely flat lands because there are differences in individual prestige at all levels. The submerged area represents people who are really outside the system of competition and of regular employment. The "badlands" remind us that there are levels of prestige and success in the world of crime and that its upper reaches are not too far from the towering heights of power.

[23]Harold M. Hodges, Jr., *Social Stratification: Class in America*, Schenkman Publishing Co., Inc., Cambridge, Mass., 1964, pp. 14–15, 85–89.

Table 6-1 Money Income—Percent Distribution of Families by Income Level in Constant (1970) Dollars, by Regions: 1955 to 1970 (1955 excludes Alaska and Hawaii)

Region and income level	1955	1960	1965	1970
Northeast	100.0	100.0	100.0	100.0
Under $3,000	11.7	9.5	7.9	6.5
$3,000-$4,999	15.9	12.0	10.4	8.9
$5,000-$6,999	24.3	18.0	13.1	10.5
$7,000-$9,999	26.7	27.0	24.4	19.5
$10,000-$14,999	15.8	22.0	27.4	20.1
$15,000 and over	5.7	11.4	16.8	25.7
Median income	$6,849	$7,952	$9,342	$10,696
North Central	100.0	100.0	100.0	100.0
Under $3,000	15.7	14.5	9.6	7.3
$3,000-$4,999	15.8	13.6	10.9	9.6
$5,000-$6,999	19.8	16.1	13.4	10.9
$7,000-$9,999	25.7	26.5	24.4	20.0
$10,000-$14,999	16.6	20.9	26.7	28.8
$15,000 and over	6.4	8.5	15.1	23.5
Median income	$6,876	$7,596	$8,989	$10,327
South	100.0	100.0	100.0	100.0
Under $3,000	27.8	25.2	19.7	12.9
$3,000-$4,999	20.1	18.3	15.6	12.1
$5,000-$6,999	19.0	17.2	15.3	14.3
$7,000-$9,999	18.3	20.8	21.6	20.3
$10,000-$14,999	10.2	12.5	18.1	22.8
$15,000 and over	4.3	5.9	9.5	17.6
Median income	$5,201	$5,753	$6,903	$8,552
West	100.0	100.0	100.0	100.0
Under $3,000	14.8	9.5	7.6	7.5
$3,000-$4,999	14.0	10.9	11.4	10.1
$5,000-$6,999	21.3	15.0	12.5	10.9
$7,000-$9,999	26.1	25.4	22.4	19.8
$10,000-$14,999	17.0	25.2	26.5	27.6
$15,000 and over	6.7	14.0	19.6	24.2
Median income	$6,982	$8,581	$9,490	$10,273

Source: U. S. Bureau of the Census, *Current Population Reports,* ser. P-60, no. 80, 1970 and unpublished data.

Mobility Although the panoramic view of social class depicts various levels and areas of upward striving, it does not tell how much upward mobiliy there is. *Upward mobility* is the movement to a higher position. *Career mobility* refers to an upward or downward class status change during one's own life; *generational mobility* is the measurement

Table 6-2 Percent of Aggregate Income Received by Each Fifth and Top 5 Percent of Families and Unrelated Individuals: 1950 to 1970

Item and income rank	1950	1955	1960	1965	1967	1968	1969	1970
Families	100.0	100.0	100.0	100.0	100.0	100.0	100.0	100.0
Lowest fifth	4.5	4.8	4.9	5.3	5.4	5.7	5.6	5.5
Second fifth	12.0	12.2	12.0	12.1	12.2	12.4	12.3	12.0
Middle fifth	17.4	17.7	17.6	17.7	17.5	17.7	17.6	17.4
Fourth fifth	23.5	23.7	23.6	23.7	23.7	23.7	23.5	23.5
Highest fifth	42.6	41.6	42.0	41.3	41.2	40.6	41.0	41.6
Top 5 percent	17.0	16.8	16.8	15.8	15.3	14.0	14.7	14.4
Unrelated individuals	100.0	100.0	100.0	100.0	100.0	100.0	100.0	100.0
Lowest fifth	2.3	2.5	2.6	2.6	3.0	3.2	3.2	3.3
Second fifth	7.0	7.3	7.1	7.6	7.5	7.8	7.8	7.9
Middle fifth	13.8	13.4	13.6	13.5	13.3	13.8	13.8	13.8
Fourth fifth	26.5	25.0	25.7	25.1	24.4	24.4	24.3	24.5
Highest fifth	50.4	51.9	50.9	51.2	51.8	50.8	51.0	50.5
Top 5 percent	19.3	21.7	20.0	20.2	22.0	20.4	21.1	20.5

Source: U. S. Bureau of the Census, *Current Population Reports,* ser. P-60, no. 80, 1970 and unpublished data.

of a person's achievement in comparison with his parental generation. It is fairly obvious that people are moving up and down the peaks of success and from the lower plains to the higher plains. The real question is whether there is more upward than downward mobility and whether there is as much upward mobility as in the past. America has been a land of opportunity. Is it as much so now as ever?

The occupational demands of industrial systems make it obvious that many of the most rapidly increasing areas of employment are in fields calling for the highly skilled and highly educated, as shown by the educational statistics from the Department of Labor on page 144. These demands have created much upward mobility in many industrial countries, especially in the United States. A comparison of the United States, Great Britain, the Netherlands, and Japan shows considerable upward mobility in all cases, but the movement into the elite classes (approximately the same as Warner's upper-middle and lower-upper) is greater in the United States than in any of the other countries.[24]

Other evidence of mobility is the disappearance, or near disappearance, of some of the most ill-paying and low-status jobs. Household servants are almost nonexistent. Mining and nonfarm labor show no

[24]Thomas Fox and S. M. Miller, ''Intra-Country Variations in Occupational Stratification and Mobility,'' in Reinhard Bendix and Seymour Martin Lipset (eds.), *Class, Status, and Power,* The Free Press, New York, 1966, pp. 74–87.

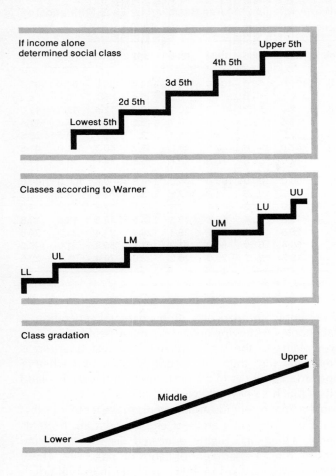

employment gains. While population and labor supply continue to increase, farm labor declines drastically. Pick-and-shovel crews on highways are replaced by mechanized equipment. Small marginal farms are a rapidly diminishing part of the economy, as indicated in the table in the following figure. In 1940, 23 percent of the people lived on farms; by 1968 the figure had declined to 6 percent. The remaining farms are of much higher value, as indicated by the amount of investment per farm

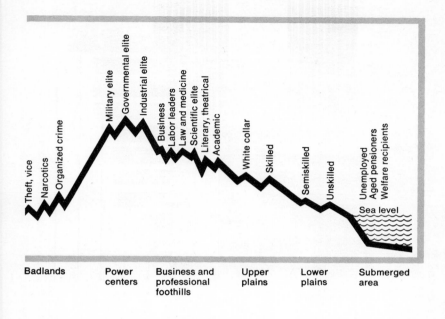

worker—a mere $3,500 in 1940 as compared to $36,000 by 1968.[25] Farming is usually an inherited occupation and has shown less mobility than jobs required in an urban society.[26]

A comparison of occupational distributions over the period 1932 to 1962 shows increasing movement into professional, technical, and managerial jobs and less movement into manual occupations with the passing of each decade. Much of the mobility has been among people moving away from the farms, a process that must necessarily slow down in the future because so few people remain on farms.[27]

Because different ethnic groups have had different experiences in America, it is interesting to see to what extent they have found it to be the promised land of opportunity. The picture differs considerably depending upon which ethnic group is under consideration. The Anglo-Saxons and Scandinavians seem to have a preferred position in job competition.

[25]*Occupational Outlook Handbook,* U.S. Department of Labor Bulletin 1550, 1968, p. 624.
[26]Bergel, *op. cit.,* p. 351.

[27]Otis Dudley Duncan, "The Trend of Occupational Mobility in the United States," *American Sociological Review,* vol. 30, August 1965, pp. 491–498.

143

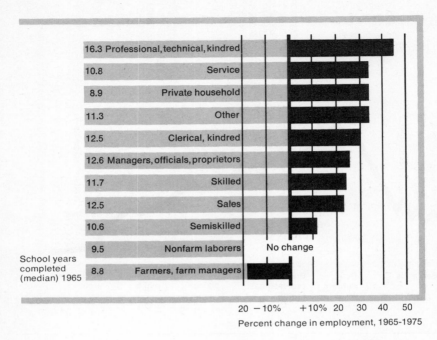

20 −10%   +10% 20   30   40   50

Percent change in employment, 1965-1975

(Adapted from *Occupational Outlook Handbook*,
U.S. Dept. of Labor Bulletin 1550, 1968.)

Russians and Czechs have done better than average, Irish and Poles about average, and Italians a little below average. All have shown more upward than downward mobility and, on an occupational basis, have not been the victims of discrimination to the same degree as blacks, Mexican-Americans, or American Indians. "The notion of equal opportunity irrespective of national origin is a near reality," but not when Latin-American and black minorities are considered.[28] Even when educational level is held constant, the socioeconomic status of the latter two groups falls short of that of the others, especially for black Americans.

It would seem, then, that there is much mobility in American life from lower to middle and from middle to upper-middle class and that this mobility holds for most but not all ethnic groups. What about the top? Is there less "circulation of elites," more stability at the top?

[28]Beverly Duncan and Otis Dudley Duncan, "Minorities and the Process of Stratification," *American Sociological Review*, vol. 33, no. 3, June 1968, pp. 356–364.

144

Stability at the Top   The upper-upper class families of Boston, New York, Philadelphia, and Virginia remain the same over the years. "As for our time, it is safe to say that the upper-upper class is in a state of stability."[29] The tendency for much of the business of the families of old wealth to be handled by expert managers gives a road to upward mobility for the management group, but at the same time it ensures that no foolish heir can destroy the accumulated fortunes of one of the old families. We worry little about the possible fall of the Rockefellers, Mellons, or DuPonts into poverty. There is considerable evidence that the concentration of wealth in the hands of the very rich is increasing (see Chapter 14).

Despite considerable stability at the top, the future is never certain. Sometimes new industrial developments can have a profound effect, lifting people rather suddenly to great wealth.

The question of mobility is not one on which all authorities agree. Some are more certain than others that there is more permanence at the top now than in the past. Some also question the degree of upward mobility at middle levels or have doubts about the future. Porter, for example, warns that we may be developing such a complex system, calling for such long and difficult periods of education, that motivation will not be enough to get people to prepare for some of the top scientific, medical, and technical positions.[30] For example, he cites figures indicating that we have had to import from abroad about 1,500 physicians/year and a total of 63,500 natural scientists, social scientists, and engineers between 1949 and 1964. A more likely explanation for the need to import experts is simply that our educational system could not train the needed personnel fast enough. At present we seem to be overcoming such shortages (see Chapter 13), with college graduates finding more competition for good jobs.

In summary, it can be said that for the majority groups the upward-mobility rate has been highly favorable in recent years, but problems remain for certain minorities, and there may be more stability at the top than in the past. There is also the possibility that rapidly changing demands might upset the future of mobility in some such way as Porter suggests. There is also another problem very much in the minds of people today because of so much recent comment on poverty in America. Is there an *underclass* that is unaffected by the social mobility we have just discussed?

[29]Bergel, *op. cit.,* p. 348.
[30]John Porter, "The Future of Upward Mobility," *American Sociological Review,* vol. 33, no. 1, February 1968, pp. 5–19.

SOCIAL CLASS AS SUBCULTURE

Elsewhere in this book, considerable comment is made on social-class differences in prospects for education, political attitudes, marital stability, and religious orientation because it is impossible to discuss family, religion, government, education, and racial and ethnic problems without also discussing class differences. In this section contrasts in class patterns of living will be discussed largely in terms of a lower-class subculture. Let us first sum up what has already been said or implied in previous chapters about class differences and give a brief preview of how social class relates to topics that follow.

To quite a degree, social classes can be thought of as subcultures with differences in values, points of view, and expectations. Children are socialized into the various social-class subcultures by home experience and interaction, mainly with people of their own class. The lower class is apt to be more severe in physical punishment of children and less likely to emphasize training for independence and upward mobility than is the middle class.[31] The lower-class child has a greater chance of coming from a broken or unhappy home and of being exposed to attitudes out of keeping with the ethic of success-striving. If he comes from a religious family, he is more apt to experience strong emotionalism in religious services and attitudes somewhat hostile to the leaders of the society around him. He is now likely to see that higher education is desirable, but he may find many obstacles in his way to its attainment. Politically, he will probably learn attitudes that are liberal in the sense of wanting to support labor, graduated income taxes, and welfare measures but are illiberal toward the foreigner and the nonconformist.

Other types of life prospects are quite uneven, including the chance of survival itself. The poor have more children than the middle class or well-to-do, and the children are less likely to be planned. They are more likely to be born when the mother is too young or too old for healthy delivery. Although only 6 percent of the deaths in the United States are among infants, in the poorest county of the nation 24 percent of the deaths are among infants. Three times as many people are out of work, with more chronic ailments among people of incomes of $4,000/year or less than among those with incomes of more than $4,000.[32]

What is true of physical health is also true of mental health. Hollingshead and Redlich, using a five-class analysis, found that the lowest class made up 12.8 percent of the normal population but 36.8

[31]Urie Bronfenbrenner, "Socialization and Social Class through Space and Time," in Reinhard Bendix and Seymour Martin Lipset (eds.), *Class, Status, and Power,* The Free Press, New York, 1966, pp. 362–377.
[32]Robert L. Eichorn and Edward G. Ludwig, "Poverty and Health" in Hanna H. Meissner (ed.), *Poverty in the Affluent Society,* Harper & Row, Publishers, Incorporated, New York, 1966, p. 173.

percent of the psychotic population.[33] The more recent Midtown Manhattan Study revealed similar findings. The higher-income groups showed that 9.9 percent were "impaired" in mental health; the lowest-income group showed that 19.8 percent were "impaired."[34]

The poor are less able to exert influence in the community and in organizational life. The "joiners" in American society are overrepresented by the middle and upper-middle classes and are underrepresented among the poor. The same is true for those who rate themselves high in community leadership.[35]

Work satisfaction differs considerably. In one study, 68 percent of the professionals said that they would continue the same kind of work, even if they had no economic need to work; only 16 percent of the unskilled expressed the same attitude. In another study, from 82 to 91 percent of various professional people stated that they would choose the same line of work if beginning their careers again; only 16 percent of the unskilled workers said the same.[36]

In a number of different success beliefs, the poor contrast sharply with the middle class. More of the middle class believe there is a good chance to succeed and that quality of work is more important than "pull" or "politicking" to succeed. More middle class than lower class think well of an occupation that requires a certain amount of risk but has high potential.[37]

Culture of Poverty   The term "culture of poverty" has been used to describe the very poor: the unemployed and those in the urban ghettos and in such depressed areas as parts of Appalachia. Some of the contrasts between middle and lower class used in this chapter have applied to regularly employed people, above the poverty line. The poverty level is hard to define, but there is certainly merit in Coser's description: "In modern societies the deprived are assigned to the core category of the poor only when they receive assistance . . . ." Poorly paid occupations are not stigmatized, but public assistance is.

[33]August B. Hollingshead and Frederick C. Redlich, "Social Stratification and Psychiatric Disorders," *American Sociological Review*, vol. 18, April 1953, pp. 163–169.

[34]Leo Srole, Thomas S. Langer, Stanley T. Michael, Marvin K. Opler, and Thomas A. C. Rennie, *Mental Health in the Metropolis: The Midtown Manhattan Study*, McGraw-Hill Book Company, New York, 1962, p. 217.

[35]Robert Hagedorn and Sanford Labovitz, "Participation in Community Associations by Occupation: A Test of Three Theories," *American Sociological Review*, vol. 33, no. 2, April 1968, pp. 267–283.

[36]Both surveys in Robert Blauner, "Work Satisfaction and Industrial Trends in Modern Society," in Reinhard Bendix and Seymour Martin Lipset (eds.), *Class, Status, and Power*, The Free Press, New York, 1966, pp. 473–477.

[37]Herbert H. Hyman, "A Social Psychological Contribution to the Analysis of Stratification," in Reinhard Bendix and Seymour Martin Lipset (eds.), *Class, Status, and Power*, The Free Press, New York, 1966, p. 488–499.

Oscar Lewis has described a "culture of poverty" as something existing in fairly similar conditions in many urban societies and most extreme in societies just entering industrialization. He has spoken of the culture as characterized by gregariousness, "lack of privacy, high incidence of alcoholism, early initiation into sex . . . a trend toward mother-centered families.[38]

Elizabeth Herzog reviews this concept with some very interesting and significant reservations.[39] Some of the psychological traits mentioned are simply the necessary adjustments to poverty but not part of a culture. She does not contradict the facts presented by Lewis but simply the use of the word "culture" because culture implies values. Although the incidence of illegitimacy is high, it is not culturally approved. The mothers of teenage daughters hope that premature experience with sex and early pregnancies will not occur and that their daughters can make a good marriage. Similarly, many drink heavily, but drunkenness is not really approved. Herzog also points out that some traits attributed to a culture of poverty are really the result of malnutrition: depression, fatigue, lack of ambition, weakness, and difficulty in concentrating. Similarly, poor school achievement is not advocated by parents; it is simply unavoidable under the circumstances. Herzog and Lewis both agree that a mother-centered family is a phenomenon of extreme poverty and is by no means limited to poverty-stricken black families. In many areas of high employment, adult males fail to function as household heads, regardless of their race.

Decline in Poverty   During most of the world's history, poverty for many has been inevitable because of shortages of economic goods. In parts of the modern world that have high productivity and relatively low birth rates there is no longer any crucial economic scarcity. In such welfare-oriented states as Sweden, poverty is virtually nonexistent. In the United States it seems safe to predict a continuing decline in the amount of poverty, in spite of a hard core of impoverishment and more literature about poverty than usual. A reason for so much discussion of poverty is that it constitutes an increasing normative strain in a society that claims equalitarian values and produces enough goods to make poverty unnecessary. For this reason college youth take an active interest in social work and Head Start programs, and politicians find it necessary to at least promise abundance for all.

[38]Oscar Lewis, Introduction to *The Children of Sanchez*, Random House, Inc., New York, 1961 (copyright by Oscar Lewis).
[39]Elizabeth Herzog, "Facts and Fictions about the Poor," *Monthly Labor Review*, February 1969, pp. 42–49 (U.S. Department of Labor, Reprint, *Perspectives on Poverty*).

Poverty was once thought of not only as inevitable but as a necessary goal to force people to work at some of the most dangerous, undesirable, and backbreaking tasks of society. Such jobs are less common than formerly, often having been replaced by machinery. It also appears that there is no shortage of people willing to take whatever jobs are available, provided pay rates are satisfactory. We are not suggesting a disappearance of social class, but it may be that one of the features of social-class systems, grinding poverty for those at the bottom of the heap, will no longer accompany the class systems of prosperous industrial nations. It is regrettable to note, though, that to date the United States has been less successful in eliminating extreme poverty than many countries in Western Europe. There are still cases of extreme malnutrition and death among children on Indian reservations, in poor rural counties of the South, and in Appalachia. Many children of migratory farm laborers are phsyically and mentally impaired by malnutrition.[40] By definition, a class system must have a lowest class, but it is now physically possible to provide the necessities of life for even the most impoverished class.

SUMMARY

Although the desire for a classless society has been expressed frequently in literature and social philosophy, it seems to be an unattainable goal. Societies call for different statuses, some of which have different rank and prestige. Social classes are made up of people of similar status who are conscious of their similarities. Social class is difficult to measure precisely in modern industrial societies, but education, income, wealth, power, and esteem are all suggested as important social-class criteria.

There are great variations in social-class systems. Simple hunting and gathering societies tend to be classless, or nearly so, and the degree of class distinction increases as the development of agriculture makes a leisure class possible. Advanced agricultural societies often form very rigid social systems, such as that of medieval Europe. The most rigid social-class system of all—caste—has developed in a number of conquest states and in India. Although the distinction between position of white and black races in the United States is often compared with caste, there are differences in the amount of mobility and the degree to which the two systems are supported by religious norms.

There are theoretical conflicts over the function of class in societies; conservative writers are a little more inclined to emphasize its functional

---

[40]Robert Coles in testimony before the Senate Subcommittee on Labor and Public Welfare, Migrant and Seasonal Farmworker Powerlessness, part 2, U.S. Government Printing Office, Washington, D.C., 1970, pp. 334–335.

necessity than liberals or radicals. Among modern social theorists, the argument is more a matter of how great a social-class differentiation is necessary than whether one should exist at all.

Industrial societies show less social-class rigidity than advanced agricultural societies. Because they require many trained people in favorable positions and do not allow an elitist monopoly on learning, industrial societies permit considerable upward mobility. Social class continues to exist, but the lines between social classes are not always clear. W. Lloyd Warner describes six social classes in a number of towns in which reputational studies were made. Self-evaluation studies show that a great majority of Americans consider themselves middle class. The objective criteria of education and income are used more easily than self-evaluation or reputational studies, although they are not perfect descriptions of class. A discussion of social-class position also merges into a discussion of elites, people of highest status in various fields. Elites constitute leadership groups but not necessarily classes.

Studies of mobility in the United States and other industrial nations show more upward than downward mobility. Reasons for upward mobility include the appearance of a larger number of high-status jobs and a disappearance of some of the jobs of lowest status and income, for example, farm labor. Although there continues to be much upward mobility, there is some evidence of a stable class of great wealth at the top.

Social classes can be thought of as subcultures, socializing their children into their own customs and values. Viewed this way, lower-class position has the disadvantage of shorter life expectancy, poorer physical and mental health, and less work satisfaction. The various classes have different rationalizations for their position in the system. Wealthy people usually attribute success to effort and ability; lower-class people are more likely to attribute success to luck or pull.

Oscar Lewis has used the expression "culture of poverty" to characterize the way of life of the extremely poor, but there is some objection to the word "culture" in this respect. Many of the life styles of poor people are forced upon them by economic necessity, not by any particular cultural norms that they have developed.

Scarcity of goods once made an impoverished class inevitable, but there is no longer a crucial scarcity in prosperous industrial nations. In spite of the persistence of a "hard core of poverty" there are indications that poverty is on the decline and can be alleviated. Prosperous industrial societies continue to display strong social-class differences, but the tendency is for the condition of those at the bottom of the heap to be less deprived than in the past. Parts of western Europe have made more progress than the United States in eliminating poverty.

Chapter 7

Racial and Ethnic Groups

Hath not a Jew eyes? Hath not a Jew hands, organs, dimensions, senses, affections, passions? Fed by the same food, hurt with the same weapons, subject to the same diseases, healed by the same means, warmed and cooled by the same winter and summer as a Christian is? If you wound us, do we not bleed? If you poison us, do we not die? And if you wrong us, shall we not revenge?

Shakespeare
Merchant of Venice

People living in different parts of the world constitute separate breeding stocks, with characteristic physical traits setting them off from other breeding stocks or gene pools. These separate types are called *races*. Races display average differences in such physical traits as skin color, eye form and color, and body build, but no known differences in mental or cultural capacity. There are many variations in how experts classify race, but always they describe race on the basis of physical type, not cultural type, and always they find much overlap in racial traits. Not all members of tall races are really tall; not all members of black races are purely black, and not all Caucasoids are as white as snow. There must be, however, average hereditary differences in physical type before any segment of humanity can be called a race.

Ethnic groups, on the other hand, consist of people who are different culturally from the majority of those among whom they live. The cultural differences may be in language, religion, or political loyalty, or they may be in such minor traits as food habits, dress, manners, and local accents. People can be both racially and ethnically different from the majority group. For example, American Indians living on reservations and following their old customs are different from most other Americans in both race and culture. Indian people living in town and following the customs of the majority of Americans are racially different but have a similar culture and can be considered a separate ethnic group only if they perceive themselves as such. Jewish people, on the other hand, belong to the white majority race, but if they are orthodox followers of their religious tradition they are somewhat different culturally and can be called an ethnic group.

Both racial and ethnic minorities have suffered persecution in many times and lands. Sometimes they have been treated with inhuman cruelty and nearly exterminated, as was the case of the Jews in Hitler's time, the Armenians in earlier times in Turkey, and many American Indian tribes in American history. Frequently they have been more or less tolerated but not treated as equals; they have been joked about, shut out of social clubs and activities, and even denied desirable jobs, schools, and housing. There are various reasons for the unequal treatment of minorities, but the first one we shall study is that of racial and ethnic myth. Unequal treatment has been upheld by various strange beliefs about racial and ethnic groups, often supporting the idea of naturally and divinely intended inequality.

RACIAL AND ETHNIC MYTHS

Many primitives have had myths of an ethnocentric type about themselves and about other people. Often their name for their own tribe means *ourselves,* or *the people,* or *the knowing people,* as opposed to the outsiders, who are thought of as not quite the same as people. Sometimes the myth explains that a great god made *the people,* but a lesser god, some kind of devil, made the foreigners. More often there is a myth of some great bringer of gifts to *the people* so that they could have a better way of life and be superior to the outsiders.

Modern Mythology Such ideas as these are obviously pure mythology of a primitive type, but the modern civilized world can also hold mythological beliefs about race for the same ethnocentric reasons. Hitler and his followers believed in the superiority of the "Aryan race," although there is no such race, nor is there any such thing as a superior race. The word "Aryan" properly refers to a group of languages, not to a race of people. Americans who believed in slavery made up myths about how God had intended some people to be masters and other slaves. Long after slavery was legally ended in this country, more myths were created to prove that the two races should be kept segregated and unequal. On the opposite side of the racial argument, Elijah Mohammed and his followers propounded a myth explaining how Allah created the black race, and the Devil made the white race, a good example of "reverse snobbery."

Turning to myths about ethnic groups rather than races, one of the best examples is that of medieval mythology about Jews. Jews were accused of worshipping the Devil and of stealing and killing Christian children to use their blood at their secret, Satanic rites. Trachenberg[1] tells of the prevailing Christian belief that all Jews, being very clever, could not help but know that the Christian religion was true. The only reason they refused to accept Christianity was that they had sold their souls to the Devil and joined his side. Consequently, the opinion was that no punishment was too severe for Jews, and many cases of torture, murder, and mass exile resulted.

Racial Myths and Colonialism   Racial myths were used by people of Europe or of European descent to defend colonialism. The non-European world, even including great and ancient civilizations, was pictured as seriously in need of the white man's leadership. "Take up the white man's burden," said Rudyard Kipling, British author and supporter of the Empire. In his famous poem "Recessional" the words "lesser breeds without the law" appear, referring to colonial people whose destiny, as he saw it, was to be led by the British and other Europeans. Jean Paul Sartre summed up the attitude of the white race very neatly in a single sentence: "Not so very long ago, the earth numbered two thousand million inhabitants—five hundred million *men* and one thousand five hundred million *natives*."[2] One of the greatest changes between the present and the recent past is that "natives" now insist on being men and women.

[1]Joshua Trachenberg, *The Devil and the Jews,* Harper & Row, Publishers, Incorporated, Torchbooks, New York, 1966, pp. 124–139.

[2]From Jean Paul Sartre's introduction to Frantz Fanon, *The Wretched of the Earth,* Grove Press, Inc., New York, 1963.

The Rise of the Nordic Myth　　One of the racial myths with the most devastating consequences had a curious beginning. Writing mainly out of resentment against the autocracy of the Roman Empire, the ancient Roman Tacitus praised the Germanic people as the repository of virtue and bravery and as lovers of freedom.[3] Many centuries later the French writer de Boulainvillier, protesting the autocracy of Louis XIV, created the myth that the Latin civilization had always stood for tyranny and the Germanic ''race'' had stood for freedom. It was in the nineteenth century, however, that the myth of Nordic superiority reached full fruition in the writings of Count Arthur de Gobineau (1816–1882).[4] Although by the end of his life the cosmopolitan and erudite de Gobineau had changed his views considerably, his early writings on race had wide impact. He spoke of the horrors of continuous mixing of races and of the impending decline of the Nordic race by blending with Mediterranean and Eastern types and Jews. This ''bastardization'' would lead inevitably to the degeneracy of the Nordic people, just as it had, in his opinion, led to the decline of the ancient Mediterranean civilizations.

Gobineau's racial mythology eventually entered the diseased mind of a fanatical little Austrian painter named Adolph Hitler, and it reached its culmination in the mass murder of 6 million Jews in gas chambers and other death camps.

Reality Versus Myth　　There has been so much mythology about race that we sometimes wonder whether there are any really dependable facts in existence. Physical anthropologists are the most thorough students of human variability and have made some interesting studies on the subject of race. Their classifications do not always agree with each other, and none would feel absolutely certain of his explanation of racial differences. They would agree completely on two points, however (1) Race is a matter of physical difference, not mental or cultural, and (2) all human beings belong to one single species, Homo sapiens. In the latter sense we are all brothers, and anthropological science finds itself in agreement with such teachers as Confucius, Buddha, and Jesus.

RACIAL THEORY AND CLASSIFICATION

Few theories are more widely accepted in the scientific world, or more thoroughly substantiated by an impressive alignment of evidence, than the theory of evolution. As more and more bones of ancient man are unearthed, it becomes increasingly clear that he has gradually developed

[3]Jacques Barzun, *Race: A Study in Superstition,* Harper & Row, Publishers, Incorporated, Torchbooks, New York, 1965, pp. 17–18.
[4]*Ibid.,* pp. 54–77.

from a small-brained animal of approximately 2 or 3 million years ago, generally known as *Australopithecus africanus* (Southern ape-man from Africa), to the large-brained type known as *Homo sapiens* (knowing man).[5] Although there are a few extremely ancient remains from Java, the fossil evidence from Africa is so overwhelming that it seems fairly safe to say that Africa was the place of human origin. At the present state of anthropological knowledge one can tell the white racial bigot, "But you, too, are of African descent!"

Special Adaptation to Climate   Regardless of where human beings originated, they have always had a way of getting around. Hundreds of thousands of years before the age of jet airplanes they were migrating from Africa to all parts of Europe and Asia. At least 30,000 years ago they reached the remote continents of North and South America and Australia. Evolutionary theory would assume that during this long period of time certain physical changes came about to help adapt the species to different physical environments. Most people assume that variation in color was one of these adaptive traits, and there is a certain amount of evidence to support this opinion. Studies of American military personnel under varied conditions of heat indicate that the black soldier has greater endurance for hot, moist climates than has the white.[6] Neither do particularly well in hot, dry climates; black skin absorbs too much heat, and white skin burns. The preferred type for the great deserts of the world is one with considerable brown or yellowish pigmentation in the skin: for example, the Mongol, Tartar, Tuareg, American Indian, or Mexican.

There are a number of other interesting indications of adaptation to environment. Some people have much greater resistance to the cold than do most members of the human race, and this seems to be especially true of certain variants of the Mongoloid race. There is evidence that Eskimo have a greater blood supply to face and hands than do most people, helping to protect them against the bitter cold of their environment. Down at the tip of South America, in the frigid land first discovered by Magellan, live the Alacaluf Indians, who in the past wore almost no clothing. Their children have been known to swim in the cold water among the icebergs. Coon[7] reports tests that indicate a much higher rate of basal metabolism for these people than for most other human beings; thus they are able to maintain body temperatures even under Antarctican conditions.

[5]John Beuttner-Janusch, *Origins of Man*, John Wiley & Sons, Inc., New York, 1966, p. 146.
[6]Paul T. Baker, "Racial Differences in Heat Tolerance," *American Journal of Physical Anthropology*, vol. 16, September 1958, pp. 287–305.
[7]Carleton Coon, *The Origin of Races*, Alfred A. Knopf, Inc., New York, 1962, p. 64.

Another case of racial difference is that of the Indians of the high Andes Mountains. Their lung capacities are unusually large, and their red-corpuscle count is enough to keep them well-supplied with oxygen in the rarefied atmosphere in which they live. Other people build up a larger red-corpuscle supply as they adapt to high mountains, but a prominent anthropologist concludes that the natural adaptation of the Andean Indian is greater than it is for other people and that the trait is hereditary.[8]

Body Build and Adaptation   A kind of general rule about body build known as *Bergman's rule*, has been suggested: Stocky builds are better for cold climates, and long, slender builds are better adapted to hot climates. The Eskimo fit the description for the cold-climate type, and so do many Siberian tribes and Central Asians; they all have short arms and legs in proportion to total body size. There are many exceptions to the rule regarding tall, slender people in hot climates (the Nordic, for example), so that the rule remains in some doubt. There are more cases to support Bergman's rule, however, than there are to refute it,[9] most notably the tall slender people of East Africa.

Anthropologists have sought explanations for other racial differences. The Mongoloid eye form is generally believed to represent special adaptation to extreme cold and strong winds, and, as this theory would suggest, the eye form is more pronounced among northern Asians than among southern Asians.

Mentality as Adaptation   Regardless of climate or altitude, one physical trait has had survival value for the entire human race in all parts of the world: the development of a superior brain. The evolutionary processes that have led to this development have gone on in all parts of the world. The size of the brain has increased with each successive stage of human evolution.[10] It would seem highly illogical to assume that in some parts of the world mental growth has been a favorable and adaptive trait and that in other parts it has been a detriment. The anthropological evidence argues for a great degree of similarity in human capacities, regardless of race or climatic zone.

Perhaps the time will come when we will simply refer to "the human race" without breaking it down into subdivisions. Because we are still strongly race conscious, however, it seems that some type of racial classification should be described.

[8]*Ibid.*, pp. 70–71.
[9]Carleton Coon, "Climate and Race," in Harlow Shapley (ed.), *Climatic Change,* Harvard University Press, Cambridge, Mass., 1954, pp. 13–34.
[10]C. Loring Brace, *The Stages of Human Evolution,* Prentice-Hall, Inc., Englewood Cliffs, N.J., 1967, pp. 59–70.

Racial Classification   The human species was once conveniently divided into precisely three races: Caucasoid (white), Mongoloid (yellow), and Negroid (black). A slight straining of the system included the American Indians as Mongoloid and the Australian aborigines as Negroid. The words "Caucasoid," "Mongoloid," and "Negroid" are still so much a part of common speech that they are hard to drop, but there are suggestions for better systems of classification that have been made by such prominent phsyical anthropologists as Dobzhansky, Washburn, and Garn. Garn and Coon use the concept of *geographical races*—the races that have developed in major geographical areas of the world.[11] These races include European, Indian, Asian, American Indian, Australian aborigine, Polynesian, Melanesian, and Micronesian. Implied in the classification is the idea that when people have been geographically separated long enough, distinctive types develop. To the list of major races Garn adds local races, such as the subdivision of the European race into Northwestern (formerly Nordic), Alpine, and Mediterranean. He also adds a few *microraces,* small groups hard to classify, such as the Ainu of Hokkaido (northern Japan), often classified as white. This type of classification has the advantage of not trying to force all people into three or four basic types. Garn also notes that the blending of races is gradually producing new types, as in the case of the blending of American Indian and European to create a new Latin-American type.

RACIAL AND ETHNIC PREJUDICE

What has been said of physical difference in races is of theoretical interest but is no longer important. In an age of good housing and clothing, climate does not prevent people of any race from living where they choose, even if there are slight differences in resistance to cold or heat. Millions of people of African descent live in the United States, and quite a few are in Canada, experiencing no physical difficulty. Members of the white race live in the hot desert of central Australia and manage to survive. Not only do races learn to cope with different climates, but they learn to adopt different cultures. The black American belongs to the culture of America and is as much a stranger to the land of his ancestors as is the member of any other ethnic minority enculturated into his society.

In spite of the above arguments that racial differences are of little importance, they loom large in the thinking of many people. It is the *belief* that race differences are important that *makes* them important.

[11]Stanley M. Garn and Carleton S. Coon, "On the Number of Races of Mankind," *American Anthropologist,* vol. 57, October 1955, pp. 996–1001.

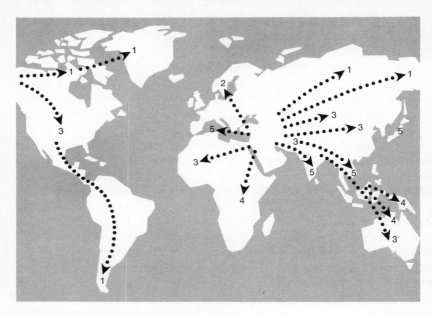

1 Types adapted to the cold; stocky build
2 Blond types in cool, cloudy climates
3 Brown, yellow-brown, reddish-brown in deserts
4 Hot tropics; black
5 Intermediate coloration

Sociology must deal with the beliefs of people, whether they are true or not, because such beliefs are the basis of action. There are strong beliefs that some races are better than others. Many people become the victims of *racial prejudice,* unfavorable attitudes imposed on entire categories of people.

The Origin and Maintenance of Prejudice The explanation of prejudice is very complex, but the phenomenon can be explained, in part, as the result of ethnocentric attitudes about one's own group. To achieve group solidarity and morale, the in-group has to insist that its cultural ways and even its appearance are better than others. The attitude is usually acceptable to the individual member of the group because his ego is inflated through group identification, and group belonging also gives him a sense of security. Out-groups are thought to be a threat to the security of the culture, especially when its members have a superior status that they would hate to lose. Often one or two foreigners are received as a source of interest and curiosity, but large numbers are perceived as a threat. This was the case with the first Chinese immigrants to California. They were treated as heroes; after large numbers arrived there were anti-Chinese demonstrations. The same principle of the feeling of threat to folkways and status probably accounts, in part, for the fact that school integration in recent years has been slowest in areas where the black population is most nearly equal to the white population. The very expression "white supremacy" implies that whites are under threat unless they keep the upper hand.

Stereotyping—the creation of carelessly formed images of what entire races or nations are like—also helps to perpetuate prejudice. We can stereotype other people as well as racial and ethnic groups, but group stereotyping often bears the most cruel results.

Scapegoating is another method by which prejudices can be created and spread, and often it has become the policy of ruling groups. The word "scapegoating" comes from the ancient practice, described in the Bible, of sacrificing a goat to pay for the sins of the people. It is used in modern times to describe a national policy of finding someone to blame for the nation's ills. For example, in the early days of communist rule in Russia the economic system was not working, and millions of people were going hungry. The government made scapegoats of the more prosperous peasants, the Kulaks, accusing them of hoarding food and causing famine. Hitler blamed the Jews for the Great Depression in Germany and even for Germany's loss of World War I. During the period of heavy immigration into the United States, zenophobic people blamed all the ills of our society on the bad influence of foreigners. Many groups have been scapegoats in many parts of the world.

Prejudice often is strongest in groups that are in declining social or economic status. There are also cases where extremes of prejudice are associated with particular personality types. Some seem to feel more threatened by outsiders than others, and some seem to have a great need to lord it over others.

Prejudice as Cultural Transmission In most cases, though, prejudice is more a cultural habit than a symptom of psychological illness. Usually prejudice is simply taught as part of the socialization process. Generations of Englishmen and Irishmen were taught prejudice against each other. Greeks and Turks were long taught by their parents the interminable record of atrocities the out-group had committed. In the United States prejudice against blacks has been taught generation after generation, sometimes deliberately and sometimes unthinkingly by patronizing actions and attitudes.

Prejudice and Discrimination *Prejudice,* as we have seen, is an attitude. *Discrimination* is a practice, a practice of unequal treatment of groups of people, especially racial, ethnic, or religious groups. It seems clear that prejudice leads to discrimination. It is also true that discrimination leads to prejudice, but the second case is not as clear and so needs a little explaining.

As a general rule, black Americans have been discriminated against in education. At the time of the Supreme Court ruling that schools should be integrated (1954), many school districts spent only about half as much per pupil for black schools as for white schools. The result for the blacks was ignorance, poorly paying jobs, and poverty. Whites, then, could see that blacks were generally ignorant, lived in shacks and hovels, and followed only the most lowly occupational pursuits, and this led to prejudice against them. The fact that they were poor and ignorant became a reason for keeping them poor and ignorant.

The same type of connection between discrimination and prejudice has occurred for many other people as well. For centuries the Irish were poorly educated and poverty-stricken. This condition caused the English to look upon them as stupid. The attitude of Germans toward Poles was very similar, as was that of the Japanese toward the Koreans. People can be backward and ignorant as a result of discrimination, and their backwardness and ignorance can result in prejudice, which leads to further discrimination. The situation can be compared with the old controversy over which came first, the hen or the egg. Myrdal[12] has spoken of the relationship as *cumulative causation,* or a vicious circle, with discrimination barring job opportunities and education, and these shortcomings creating prejudice and renewed discrimination.

Breaking the Vicious Circle If prejudice leads to discrimination, then it would seem that a good way to improve conditions would be to educate people out of their prejudices. If, on the other hand, discrimination leads to prejudice, it would seem that making rules and regulations to prevent discrimination would cause prejudice to disappear gradually. Both approaches are helpful, but the second one must be stressed because it produces more rapid results. In an area where everyone is prejudiced, it would be hard to find schools and teachers willing or able to educate people out of their prejudices, but it might be possible to stop the worst forms of discrimination.

One example of officially ending discrimination was the integrating of major-league baseball teams, with Jackie Robinson being the first black

[12]Gunnar Myrdal, *An American Dilemma,* vol. 1, McGraw-Hill Book Company, New York, 1964, pp. 75–78.

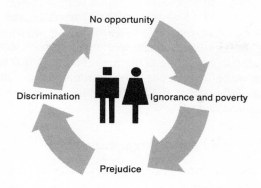

player accepted. There were predictions that the baseball fans would boycott the games, but no such thing happened. Once discrimination was ended, people began to accept integrated baseball as a part of the natural order of things. Many members of the present younger generation assume that baseball has always been integrated.

Throughout American history our armed services have usually been segregated into black and white units. At the end of World War II the Armed Forces were desegregated, as was noted in Chapter 2. The results have generally been favorable, and there has been an improvement in morale of the black troops. There are still complaints regarding privileges and promotions, but integration is generally regarded as the natural order of things, and great progress toward racial justice has resulted.

In 1954 the Supreme Court ruled that public schools should be integrated. Later decisions allowed for "deliberate speed," which some districts interpreted to mean "with deliberate delay." In 1969 the Supreme Court ruled unanimously that integration of the remaining schools should proceed "at once," and integration began in Mississippi in the spring of 1970, against stubborn resistance. Communities in other states have also been resistant, but thousands of schools are now integrated. Resistance tends to be greatest where the percentage of minority students is very large and where strong traditions of inequality exist.

The Jim Crow laws that called for separate buses, trains, waiting rooms, and eating facilities are being abolished. Whites see blacks being treated more nearly equal than in the past, and the result is to think of them as equal; the decline of discrimination is accompanied by a decline of prejudice. There are some members of the older generation whose minds will never change, but the young are much less prejudiced than the old, and even some of the older people change their views. Sometimes there is only a shift in the nature of the prejudice. Whereas nearly four out of five whites now believe blacks to be as intelligent as whites, less than one out of five believe that the black economic distress is mainly the result of discrimination.[13]

REACTIONS TO PREJUDICE AND DISCRIMINATION

Many people feel the sting of prejudice occasionally for such dubious offenses as being too young, too old, coming from the wrong part of the country, or belonging to the wrong church or political party. These kinds of prejudice are annoying, but we are generally able to brush them off. What happens to the individual whose whole life is surrounded by prejudice?

Black children become aware of negative attitudes toward their race at a very early age. By the time they are ready to start school many find communication with whites more difficult than with their own people.[14] In later years even the good student shows heightened tensity, anxiety, and sensitivity to insult. Because all people—black, brown, or white, Christian, Moslem, or Jew—have feelings, some type of emotional reaction is inevitable. The feeling might be stated as in the quotation from Shakespeare's *The Merchant of Venice,* " . . . and if you wrong us, shall we not revenge?" but, in spite of city riots in the 1960s, revenge has not been the usual response. Responses have ranged all the way from a destructive self-image and apathy to smoldering rage and rational protest.

The Negative Self-image A common adjustment to prejudice and discrimination results in a negative self-image and the loss of confidence. If people are always treated as inferior, they have difficulty seeing themselves as bright and capable. When everything about one's position and experiences—miserable homes, poorly paying jobs, frequent resort to welfare, the glances of hostility from others—combine to destroy pride and hope, people often settle into a state of apathy. *Apathy* is the appearance of not caring. Sometimes apathy becomes so much a part of life that it becomes real and not just pretense, at least until some dramatic event changes it into hope or rage.

---

[13]Howard Schuman, "Sociological Racism," *Transaction,* vol. 7, December 1969, pp. 46–47.

[14]Thomas F. Pettigrew, *A Profile of the Negro American,* D. Van Nostrand Company, Inc., Princeton, N.J., 1964, pp. 28–29.

The negative self-image
Failure to communicate
Apathetic attitude
Playing the clown
Hatred of self and others

Adjustments
Finding a place (marginal adaptation)
Excusing all failures
Sullen acceptance

WE SHALL
OVERCOME

Protesting discrimination
Legalistic approach to integration
Mass movements and demonstrations
Political power approach
Violence
Separatism

Adjusting to Discrimination   Sometimes an adjustment to discrimination is made by finding a place that is open in society. In old European cities, Jews often were not allowed to own land or to follow the majority of occupations, but they were allowed to be pawnbrokers and moneylenders. American Indians have been able to weave blankets and make jewelry for tourists, but such occupations fill the needs of only a few. The black people of America have usually had no such possibilities. They have had to compete for the poorest paying jobs and always seemed to be the last hired and the first fired when times became bad, but protests have increased. Urbanization, geographical mobility, military experience, and increased education are among the social changes that have made minority groups much more openly critical of their lot than in the past. The path of the future will not be smooth, but it seems highly unlikely that second-class citizenship will ever again be the accepted pattern of life.

163

Table 7-1 Family Income by Race or Latin-American Origin

Race and ethnic group	Median income, 1971		% of families with incomes below low-income threshold
	Dollars	% of white income	
All families	10,285	96	10.7
White	10,672	100	8.6
Negro	6,440	60	29.8
Spanish sur- named, total	7,548	71	20.4
Mexican descent	7,486	70	21.2
Puerto Rican	6,185	59	29.0
Cuban	9,371	89	13.8
Other	8,494	80	(1)

(1) Not available.

Source: Paul M. Ryscavage and Earl F. Mellor, "The Economic Situation of Spanish Americans," *Monthly Labor Review,* April 1973.

Protesting Discrimination In the 1960s there were large numbers of riots in American cities and protest movements on the part of the Black Students' Union on many American campuses. These were the most widely noticed forms of protest, but more peaceful movements had started among black Americans long before.

One of the most important movements for the improvement of conditions for the black American is the organization called the *National Association for the Advancement of Colored People (NAACP).* For more than a half a century the NAACP has worked to try to improve opportunities in education and employment. Its methods have always been peaceful, and it has attracted most of the professional leaders of the black community. Lawyers working for the NAACP won the case for desegregation of the schools in 1954, and the legal actions they have pursued in the ensuing years have resulted in declaring large numbers of racial laws unconstitutional—laws for segregated buses and trains, segregated restaurants, and all forms of compulsory segregation.

The efforts to end segregation were aided greatly by the *Southern Christian Leadership Conference,* headed by the late Dr. Martin Luther King. A dramatic strike against segregated buses in Montgomery was one of the most important events in the protest movement. It attracted wide attention, caused many white liberals to join the civil rights movement, and started a series of attempts (many of them successful) to end segregation.

Some of the more militant blacks have felt that the new laws are not enough. The fact remains that unemployment among blacks, especially in the city ghetto areas, is much higher than among whites. Housing conditions are extremely bad, and regardless of the law, segregation remains. These conditions gave the words "black power" strong appeal, and such radical leaders as Eldridge Cleaver and Rap Brown attracted wide attention.

For a considerable segment of the black population income has been improving, although the average still lags far behind white income (see Table 7-1). Even a college education does not pay as well for blacks as for whites. Borland and Yett estimated that the average college graduate of 1949 would receive $86,000 more in lifetime income than would a high school graduate, but a nonwhite college graduate would receive only $27,000 more. Ten years later, the corresponding figures were $120,000 and $67,000, respectively. College was paying better returns for black graduates, but a gap still existed. In the authors' admittedly risky projected figures (assuming present rates of improvement for both whites and nonwhites), the differential would not disappear until 2021.[15] Similar income gaps exist for people of Latin-American background, especially Puerto Ricans (see Table 7-1).

A LABOR THEORY OF ETHNIC ANTAGONISM

Although the cultural-tradition approach to prejudice and discrimination is valid in explaining why people easily adopt discriminatory patterns, it is less successful in explaining how racial and ethnic antagonisms came about in the first place. Another problem not explained is why the means of dealing with minority people has fallen along two very different patterns, one being that of exclusion and the other of placing the minorities in a lower-caste position. Edna Bonacich[16] advances a theory that helps to explain both the origins of ethnic antagonisms and why such antagonisms sometimes lead to exclusion and in other cases to a type of caste. She theorizes that characteristics of the labor market are the most important key to both problems and describes what she terms "the split-labor market."

The Meaning of a Split-labor Market A labor market can be called "split" when it contains "at least two groups of workers whose price of labor differs for the same work, or would differ if they did the same

[15]Melvin Borland and Donald E. Yett, "The Cash Value of College for Negroes and Whites," *Transaction,* vol. 5, November 1967, pp. 44–49.

[16]Edna Bonacich, "A Theory of Ethnic Antagonism: The Split Labor Market," *American Sociological Review,* vol. 37, no. 5, October 1972, pp. 547–559.

work.''[17] For example, in the days of slavery in the United States, African slaves and white indentured servants were cheaper than free labor. Antagonisms against both groups arose among native free laborers. In the old South slavery tended to drive out free labor, as it has done in other slave societies of historic times.

During the period of heavy immigration to the United States, especially during the so-called New Immigration of roughly the period 1880 to 1920, the poor immigrants formed the bottom layer of a split-labor market. The New Immigrants were those people who came from the Far East or from Eastern and Southern Europe: Chinese and Japanese, Italians, Greeks, Poles, Czechs, Russians, and many others. They were desperate for jobs, they were unorganized, and they were ignorant of what prevailing wages should be. They were loved by sweatshop employers and hated by native American workers. Some fared better than others, but the antagonism toward the immigrants mounted, resulting in discriminatory legislation against Orientals beginning in the 1880s and against all the New Immigrants by 1921.

Exclusion Versus Caste   As a general rule, impoverished minorities are excluded from countries that have an adequate and well-organized supply of labor. Professor Bonacich finds that in Australia careful calculations were made in the 1840s to show the advantage of importing labor from India at about half the cost of native white Australian labor, but labor unionism became strong at an early date and forced the exclusion of Asian workers. In the United States, as we have seen, the same policy was adopted much more slowly and less totally. When, however, a society needs workers and is dominated by the employer group, ethnic and racial minorities are allowed to enter; in fact, they are sometimes even brought in chains. Even when they are not enslaved, a number of factors come into play to force the minorities into a castelike position. First is the low level of pay along with a de facto exclusion from all but the least desirable jobs. Low pay and inferior jobs are followed by a stereotyping of the minority group as incapable of anything better and, in some cases, a mobilization of the majority to prevent the breach of these aspects of caste.

Split-labor Market and Black America   A castelike situation develops when a minority ethnic group is considered necessary and lives in a symbiotic relationship with other classes of the society, that is, a relationship in which each supplies needs for the other, but the groups remain apart. In the slave systems of the United States, the Caribbean, and

[17]*Ibid.*, p. 549.

Brazil, the most typical job of the slave was that of field hand, a position not entered by whites. In the freedom period of the American South, occupational positions for blacks and whites remained much as they had been in slave days. Blacks continued to be mainly household servants, plantation laborers, road workers, and sharecroppers. In occupations followed by both races, the black people worked for lower pay than the whites, a situation that still exists to a surprising degree.

The Commerce Department reported in 1973 that the average black family income was only 59 percent of the average white family income, no doubt partly a reflection of continuing differences in occupations pursued. Young black college graduates were receiving 78 percent of the income of their white counterparts, but among older college graduates black income was only 64 percent of white income.[18] Apparently men of high training were still encountering the lingering effects of a split-labor market and the castelike system it had produced. It appeared that chances for later promotion were even more unequal than early hiring practices.

The Chicano Position   A strong and vocal Chicano movement is acquainting us with the fact that people of Mexican, Puerto Rican, and other Latin-American backgrounds have also occupied a caste position in the society of the United States. People of Mexican descent, both those who were here before the United States acquired the Southwest and the later arrivals, have experienced a long record of low pay and inferior jobs. For many years their entry was encouraged by agricultural interests desiring a source of cheap labor. Their position has been similar to that of many other immigrants of an earlier period in that they have been so desperately in need of work they have had to accept whatever was offered, with little protection from labor laws or unions. Various explanations have been given for the plight of the Chicanos: language problems, conflicting cultural values, peasant background, and a fatalistic philosophy; but none of these explanations is really central to the problem, and they are by no means always true. The overwhelming problem is that most Chicanos have entered at the bottom of a split-labor market and have been welcomed on no other terms. There is nothing about Chicanos that is sufficiently different from the character of other immigrants to account for their generally depressed economic situation, but their past experience *does* account for it. Agricultural labor, road work, and, in earlier days, mine work and railroading have been isolating occupations, both geographically and socially. It is interesting to note, as Bonacich does, that in the depression days of the 1930s, when Oklahoma people moved to California under similar circumstances and looked

[18]Reuters Dispatch, July 23, 1973, *Los Angeles Times*, part 1, p. 17.

desperately for similar jobs, they met the same types of opposition, antagonism, and stereotyping as that given to the Mexicans, although they were "old stock" Americans—white, Anglo-Saxon Protestant. A split-labor market can even distort views of who is and is not ethnic, and it can cause similar stereotypes of "indolent, fatalistic, and backward" to fall on any group.

Just as the image of Oklahomans suddenly changed from good to bad when they entered a state in which their labor was not wanted, the same has frequently happened to both Chicanos and Mexican nationals. In the labor-short years of World War II, Mexican nationals were imported for labor and praised for their great contribution to the cause of the United States. In the 1970s the situation was so completely reversed that the Immigration and Naturalization Service was excessive in its zeal to exclude them. A suit filed by the American Civil Liberties Union and the Mexican-American Defense and Education Fund accuses the immigration service of arresting and deporting a number of United States citizens along with Mexican nationals, forcibly removing them without due process of law, and of using forcible entry, brutality, harassment, intimidation, and physical assault.[19]

Women in the Split-labor Market   The position of women in the employment field is also explained to a great extent by Bonacich's concept of the split-labor market. Women generally work for lower pay than men and are concentrated in jobs of low prestige. During the Depression years there was a strong feeling that women should not be employed at jobs that could be held by men because they would be putting men out of work. To some extent the same idea continues. We could hardly go so far as to define women as an ethnic group, but many of the same characteristics of antagonism apply. Women are stereotyped as having "their rightful place," either at home or in certain traditional jobs such as waitress, housekeeper, teacher, or nurse. Otherwise they are characterized as "pushy" and unwilling to stay in their places. Psychological stereotypes are drawn up to show why women should fit in traditional roles.[20] As of 1969, average annual pay for women in nonprofessional occupations was $4,457; for men, $7,664.[21] In the years since, the pay has increased considerably, but the ratio has remained about the same. In the higher paid professional and scientific occupations

---

[19]Ron Ridenour, "Deportation Suit Filed," *ACLU Open Forum,* vol. 50, no. 7, July 1973, p. 2.

[20]See, for example, Jo Freeman, "Growing Up Girlish," *Transaction,* vol. 8, no. 1–2, November–December 1970, pp. 36–43.

[21]Marijean Suelzle, "Women in Labor," *Transaction,* vol. 8, no. 1–2, November–December 1970, p. 53.

the income gap between men and women remains just as great as between men and women factory workers. In fact, the woman with a four-year college degree very often earns the same pay as a male high school dropout. To a degree, then, we can say that women fit into an occupational caste system; in other respects attempts are made to exclude them by an overemphasis on traditional mother-housewife roles.

Another segment of the population that has a much more conventionally defined position of ethnic (and even racial) minority is that of the American Indian, who economically is at the very bottom rung of the class system.

The American Indian Native people whose territory has been appropriated by invaders are not discussed in detail in Bonacich's writing, but they form a special case of her theory of ethnic antagonism. In the early phase of conquest a conflict not too different from that of the split-labor market develops over means of livelihood. In the immigrant situation the conflict is over jobs; in the conquest situation the struggle is over another means of livelihood—land. Two solutions are commonly followed: (1) exclusion of the native people by driving them off the land or exterminating them; or (2) creating what could logically be called a "territorial caste" system by assigning them to the least desirable land and to acreage that can support them only meagerly, if at all. Both policies have been used in respect to the American Indians, the latter being the more recent policy.

Occasionally the Indian *does* enter the labor market. In the case of the Navajo reservation, by far the largest of all Indian reservations both in area and in population, all the characteristics of the split-labor market are apparent. Although unemployment on the reservation runs to approximately 50 percent, there are occasional opportunities for work on roads or railroads or in fire fighting. The owner of the trading post has influence in recommending who will be hired. He gives preference to those who have credit accounts at his trading post, but always for a job that only an impoverished Indian would accept. Recently the Navajo legal department has insisted that some Navajo be hired at trading posts, but

> Although half of trading post employees are now Navajo, most are employed in menial positions. Some employers do not hire Navajos at all. Those few that enjoy positions of responsibility are compensated at a lower rate than comparable white employees.[22]

[22]*The Trading Post System on the Navajo Reservation: Report to the Federal Trade Commission,* Los Angeles Regional Office, June 1971, p. 54.

Not only are the Navajo victims of a split-labor market, but they are victims of a trading-post system that underpays them for their handicrafts, charges them "some of the highest prices encountered in the continental United States"[23] for their supplies, and charges usurious rates of interest on their credit accounts. What is true of exploitation of the Navajo is true in varying degrees of many other Indian tribes.[24] Small wonder that it takes the Indians a long time to get over their antagonisms toward whites, when that antagonism is constantly fed! It seems justifiable to add yet another means of handling ethnic minorities besides excluding them or fitting them into a caste system. The other solution is to rob them!

Oriental Caste and Exclusion   Of all the New Immigrants, none worked harder for lower wages than the Chinese, and none received greater animosity. The first Chinese arrived in 1848, before the period generally thought of as the New Immigration. They worked at hard labor in the mines and later on the railroads. Having no property or home base, they moved about wherever needed. They were a "free but controlled and mobile work force . . . a model that encompassed a racial labor caste system together with rigid segregation for a non-slave but racially distinct people."[25] Labor unionists, especially Samuel Gompers, founder of the American Federation of Labor (AFL), saw the Chinese as underhanded allies of the capitalists in a plot to suppress free native labor. Denis Kearney, leader of the Workingman's Party of California, was even more vehement in his anti-Chinese attitude, calling for their exclusion. For many years there were attacks against the Chinese. Many were killed by miners; several California towns burned down their settlements to drive them out. Chinese were unable to obtain legal rights because they were not allowed to testify against whites. In 1882 a Chinese Exclusion Act was passed, barring further Chinese immigration. Already the Chinese were barred from many jobs, not allowed to own property, and their children were excluded from public schools. Even after 1882, white labor unionists continued the struggle to drive out those Chinese who had already entered the United States, some 100,000. Boycotts and threats were used against any employers who hired them, and special taxes were levied against the Chinese when they tried to enter the laundry business or peddle fruits and vegetables. For example, in San Francisco a fee of $8

[23]*Ibid.*, p. 29.

[24]See, for example, A. D. Fisher, "White Rites versus Indian Rights, *Transaction,* vol. 7, no. 1, November 1969, pp. 29–33, and Joseph J. Westermeyer, "Indian Powerlessness in Minnesota," *Society,* vol. 10, no. 3, March–April 1973, pp. 45–47, 50–53.

[25]Herbert Hill, "Anti-Oriental Agitation and the Rise of Working-Class Racism," *Society,* vol. 10, no. 2, January–February, 1973, p. 44.

was charged for laundrymen, mainly white, with horses and wagons, but for those laundrymen who were too poor to have horses and had to deliver laundry by foot (entirely Chinese), the fee was $60.

The Japanese entered the country later than the Chinese. Many people remember that the Japanese in California, including many who were natural-born citizens of the United States, were removed to guarded camps during World War II. They were moved out on very short notice so that they had to sell their possessions rapidly and at heavy losses, for which they were finally compensated very inadequately in 1972, after thirty-one years of litigation. What is not generally known is that the Japanese had previously faced the same problem of a split-labor market as had the Chinese, and that this had something to do with rousing the animosities that were so easily released during the war years. In the first decade of the century, Chinese, Japanese, and Mexicans were excluded from AFL unions. When Japanese and Mexicans waged a successful strike to organize the sugar beet industry in California, they appealed to the AFL for a charter. Samuel Gompers told them, "Your union must guarantee that it will under no circumstances accept membership of any Chinese or Japanese."[26] Such was the fate of ethnic groups in a split-labor market for which there was no properly defined caste position.

Some of the events described in the last few pages are things of the past, but the details of unequal opportunities for many ethnic groups are not. All the above-described events are warnings of the unreasonable results of ethnic and racial antagonisms. Some of the ethnic groups that made up the New Immigration have lost their ethnic identity to a considerable degree; others have not. Will the United States eventually blend all immigrant people into a common culture, or will cultural diversity continue?

AMERICAN CULTURAL PLURALISM

For years the United States has been referred to as a great *melting pot,* with the implication that people from every national background are blending together through intermarriage and cultural assimilation. Blending of this type has taken place with the people of Northwestern Europe and to a lesser degree with the people of Southern and Eastern Europe. Nevertheless, there are many types of Americans who have not "melted." Laws used to prevent, and custom still prevents, many marriages between whites and blacks. Although there are no laws dealing with the subject, it

[26]*Ibid.,* p. 53.

is obvious that Chinese usually marry within their own ethnic group, and the same is usually true of Mexican-Americans. Amalgamation of races is not bringing our racial and ethnic problems to a sudden and happy solution, nor is it necessarily the goal to be sought.

Assimilation   The next possible solution to all racial and ethnic problems would be that of complete assimilation. *Assimilation* refers to a complete blending of cultural traits, but not necessarily intermarriage and racial blending. America has long been noted for her ability to assimilate foreigners who come to her shores, but there is some question as to how total the assimilation should be. Is there not room for continued cultural diversity in America—the ideal of cultural pluralism?

Pluralism   *Pluralism* is the policy of allowing distinct cultural differences to continue on a basis of equality. For example, in Switzerland, French, German, and Italian Swiss all have equal status, with official documents printed in all three languages. Few Americans would advocate carrying pluralism to the extent of using several languages, if for no other reason than the great inconvenience of such a system. Many Americans, however, always have liked a certain amount of cultural diversity. The presence of Chinatown, Jewish delicatessens, Italian bakeries, Mexican restaurants, Greek coffee shops, and Far Eastern import stores add variety to life. New ideas of all types are introduced by people from all parts of the world, and the United States has long profited from this type of cultural diffusion.

The idea of cultural pluralism has never been liked by all people. The most ethnocentric are inclined to say, "Why can't they be more like us?" Nevertheless, it has never been a dominant cultural value of the United States to try to force people to be culturally identical, and there are many minority groups who seek a sense of identity and supportive self-concept by looking to their diverse cultural origins. Many American Indians wish to continue to be identifiably Indian. Many Mexican-Americans not only wish to retain some of their customs but even take a measure of interest in Mexico. The people who are presently most interested in a cultural identity are the young black Americans, as evidenced by a growing interest in college courses in black literature, black history, and other phases of Afro-American culture. Recent statements, organizations, literature, and movements among black Americans, Mexican-Americans, and American Indians make it seem likely that we can look forward to demands for a degree of cultural pluralism well into the future. For some minority groups, the insistence on at least minor cultural distinctions is important for the maintenance of morale and identity.

SUMMARY

Racial and ethnic divisions are prominent in many parts of the world, especially in such a heterogeneous society as the United States. Race is a matter of hereditary physical difference; it is not a determinant of culture. Ethnic groups are groups that are culturally distinct in such respects as values, customs, religion, and language.

Man has invented many racial and ethnic myths aimed at protecting his ethnocentric feelings about the rightness of his own group. Not only have primitive tribes made such myths, but medieval man made up myths about the Jews, and more modern men have believed in myths about Nordic superiority and white supremacy.

There is much that is difficult to explain about the origin of races, but most promising theories view racial traits as special adaptations to various geographical conditions. There are probably advantages to black skin color in hot, moist climates and to brown or yellow-brown skin color in hot, dry climates. There are also probably slight variations in the ability of different racial and subracial types to withstand extreme cold. In all cases, however, human mentality has advanced through the 2 million or more years of man's existence on earth and has been an equally adaptive trait in all climates. Regardless of the slight physical differences of race, all mankind belongs to a single species, Homo sapiens.

Modern racial classifications emphasize such geographical races as European, Indian, Asian, American Indian, and Australian. The implication is that distinctive racial types have arisen in parts of the world that have been isolated from each other. Raciation is also seen as a continuing process, with new types resulting from the process of amalgamation, as in Latin America.

Racial and ethnic prejudices are a common feature of intergroup relations. Prejudice can be explained partly as a result of ethnocentric feelings about the superiority of the in-group and the often imaginary threat of the out-group. Prejudice can also be explained in terms of stereotyping and as a defense mechanism for the person with psychological problems. Often prejudice is reinforced by popular or official policies of scapegoating, blaming misfortunes on the out-group. Prejudice is also very much a matter of cultural tradition. Where particular groups have always been observed in an inferior position, they are thought of as inferior; custom is accepted without reflection.

Prejudice is a matter of unfavorable attitudes; discrimination is uneven treatment. It is commonly stated that people discriminate because of their prejudices. It is equally true that people develop prejudices because they discriminate. For example, long discrimination against blacks in education equipped them only for inferior jobs, prevented their intellectual development, and led to further prejudice against them.

The vicious circle of prejudice and discrimination is not easily broken, but the best results are accomplished through institutional change. Integration of major-league baseball and other sports has been accepted and has probably also decreased unfavorable feelings. Similar results have been accomplished in the Armed Forces—not that racial strife never develops, but racial integration is successful enough to have become the recognized pattern. Considerable progress has also been made in school integration and in the elimination of Jim Crow laws, although not without a struggle. It is particularly in areas where racial distribution of blacks and whites is fairly even and long traditions of great inequality exist that whites feel most threatened and are most resistant to change.

Minority groups react to prejudice and discrimination in various ways. Treatment as an inferior can result in an unfavorable self-image and/or great hostility. Sometimes minority groups adjust by finding special occupations that are open to them. Sometimes they display the symptoms of retreating from life. In recent years various factors, including urbanization and more education, have made protest movements common.

Among the explanations of antagonisms between racial and ethnic groups, one that has great applicability to many groups in American history is the idea of the split-labor market, defined as a situation in which a minority group works for lower pay or exclusively at inferior jobs, or both. Wherever such a situation exists ethnic antagonisms increase, and the minority group faces either exclusion or treatment as a lower caste. This has proved to be the case during much of American history for blacks and Chicanos, American Indians, and sometimes southern Europeans and Orientals. The theory is also applicable to women in that they have traditionally worked for lower wages than men and usually at less desirable jobs.

The old assumption that all minority groups wish complete assimilation is open to considerable doubt. For some groups a degree of cultural pluralism seems to be strongly desired and much needed as a means of identity and group morale.

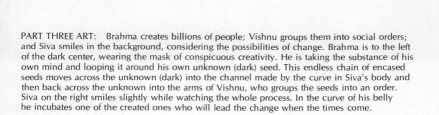

PART THREE ART: Brahma creates billions of people; Vishnu groups them into social orders;
and Siva smiles in the background, considering the possibilities of change. Brahma is to the left
of the dark center, wearing the mask of conspicuous creativity. He is taking the substance of his
own mind and looping it around his own unknown (dark) seed. This endless chain of encased
seeds moves across the unknown (dark) into the channel made by the curve in Siva's body and
then back across the unknown into the arms of Vishnu, who groups the seeds into an order.
Siva on the right smiles slightly while watching the whole process. In the curve of his belly
he incubates one of the created ones who will lead the change when the times come.

Part Three

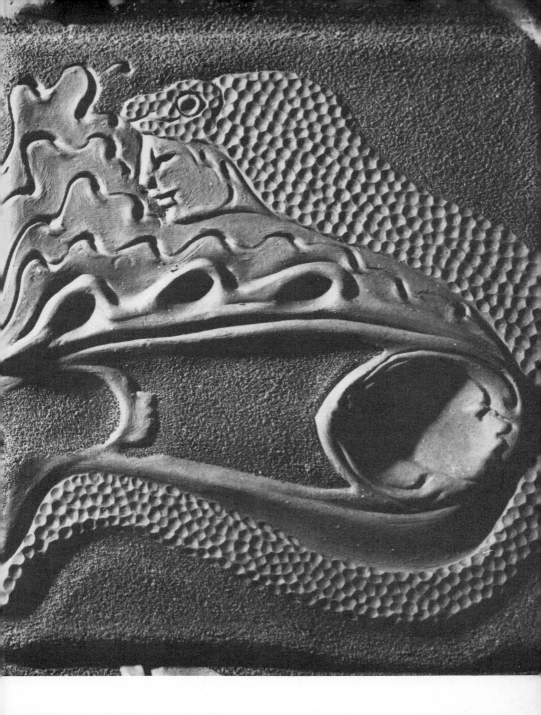

Trends in Societies

Through the millennia of time, Brahma has fulfilled his task of creation with increasing vigor. Starting with a mere handful of people, he has increased their numbers into the billions. Vishnu, in his attempt at preservation, once grouped those people into little protective bands of hunters and gatherers. Then he saw the need for more production and moved most of them into farms and villages and finally to factories and cities. However, the same productive methods needed to preserve the people physically altered them socially and psychologically. Siva smiled as he saw how the very attempts at preservation raised unlimited possibilities for disrupting the ways of the past.

Through much of today's world the pressure of population is such that we are not sure the Preserver will always be able to fulfill his task. Occasionally droughts occur and a few million people perish, but determined efforts are made to increase production and distribution and preserve more human life. Is the preservation problem being solved, or are we merely staving off a catastrophe that will break with greater fury as a result of its long postponement?

The preservation of the modern world depends upon great human nerve centers known as cities, where trade and finance, research and experimentation, exchange of ideas, and all the tasks of political and economic management of huge populations can take place. While Vishnu structures such centers for the preservation of the social order, Siva seizes opportunities for change and even subversion. The types of people are not the same as those who tilled the soil in centuries past.

They relate to each other in new ways, if at all. The primary controls of village gossip are nearly absent. The individuals are freer, but perhaps lonelier in the new crowds. The jobs people do become so varied that each person is little aware of the occupational world of the other. Divisions between rich and poor are as stark as sheer cliffs, and they are often divisions of race as well as of social class. At the same time, gains are made in education and social awareness. The cities are alive and ever-changing, tearing down, rebuilding, displacing old neighborhoods, shifting the poor for the sake of redevelopment, spreading out into new suburbs, devouring the surrounding countryside. Creator and Destroyer are constantly at work; the role of the Preserver is minimal.

Although there are divisions within the cities and the urban society in general, communications from place to place are rapid. Shocks felt in one part of the society set off temblors in other parts, more rapidly than ever before. Often the shocks are minor ones, mere fads and novel interests: new comedians, new shows, new games. At times, though, the shock waves are of a different type, bringing forth riots and disorders, making new demands on governments, countering semiofficial propaganda with new movements and causes. Groups and interests long ignored have to be heeded. A hundred social movements, often tugging in opposite directions, struggle to change the society in its details if not in its basic substance. The very composition of society that Vishnu has seen as necessary for its physical preservation plays into the hands of the God of Change.

Chapter 8

The Growth of the Human Group: Population

A settlement of the moon may be of some military advantage to the nation that does the settling. But it will do nothing whatever to make life more tolerable, during the fifty years that it will take our present population to double, for the earth's undernourished and proliferating billions.[1]

Aldous Huxley
Brave New World Revisited

When Aldous Huxley issued the above statement there were about 3 billion people living in the world. He predicted that there would be a world population of 6 billion around the year 2010 and warned that we could not survive if we did not curb the growth of the human group. Today the prospect of an overpopulated world in the near future is accepted by even the most optimistic sociologists. In fact, most population experts are inclined to trim ten years more from Huxley's prediction.

[1]Aldous Huxley, *Brave New World Revisited*, Bantam Books, Inc., New York, 1958, pp. 7–8.

The overriding question asked by people concerned about the future of humanity is "Do we still have enough time to save ourselves from the effects of population explosion?"

THE DEMOGRAPHIC TRANSITION AND THE POPULATION EXPLOSION

If we could turn our clocks backward about 50,000 years, we would find a rather sparsely populated world. People would be gathering food or hunting other animals to provide themselves with enough nutrition to survive their rather short life-spans. Population density might be as low as 200 square miles/person, and the possibilities of overpopulation would be extremely remote. What then has happened to humanity to bring us to our present predicament?

One fact is certain: Population increase is intricately bound with the availability of food and the state of technology within a society. In his "Essay on the Principles of Population," the Reverend Thomas Malthus, an early nineteenth-century economist, stated that population tends to increase more rapidly than food supply and is held in check mainly by famine, war, and epidemic. Increases in population can be maintained only when new technologies increase food supply. The hunters or food gatherers of an earlier era followed a migratory way of life. They were nomads who traveled the land in a constant search for food, usually moving in a circuit over a wide territory. As their population grew at a slow and probably unsteady rate, it eventually became apparent in many places that hunting bands were competing for a supply of game that was becoming insufficient for their needs.

About 10,000 years ago, in at least a few parts of the world, the life style of the human species began a gradual metamorphosis. Increasing amounts of wild grain were gathered, then a certain amount of planting began to supplement the way of life of the hunter. Next came permanent settlement in farming villages. These early villages continued to grow until they took on the shape and characteristics of a city. This urban revolution probably began about 4000 B.C. in the fertile valleys of the Tigris-Euphrates, the Nile, the Hwang-Ho, and the Indus Rivers, and possibly at an equally early date in Thailand and Burma.

The formation of these early cities was as important as the invention of agriculture in determining the future of human development. In terms of population and food production, the character of the city is important because it dictates that some people become farmers to supply the food while others become nonagricultural consumers to "keep the farmers in business." As agricultural technology advanced, greater surpluses of food enabled an increasing number of people to free themselves from the land.

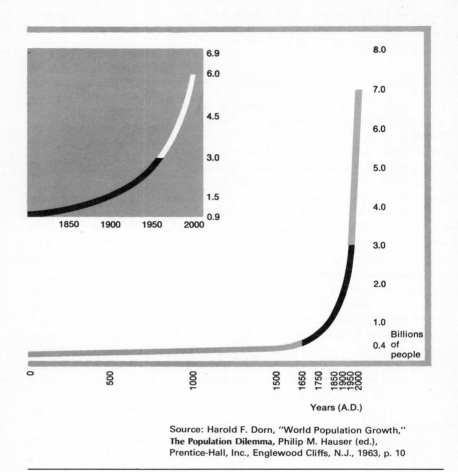

Source: Harold F. Dorn, "World Population Growth,"
The Population Dilemma, Philip M. Hauser (ed.),
Prentice-Hall, Inc., Englewood Cliffs, N.J., 1963, p. 10

Once this trend was set it continued to perpetuate itself. Throughout modern history we have witnessed an accelerated exodus from rural to urban areas.

The urban trend was hastened by the Industrial Revolution—the third great technological advancement in human history. The net effect of industrialization has been to increase the density of population in the cities. Mass production and rapid transportation have transformed the Western world into an urban world. But the comforts of the modern city have not developed without demanding the cost of growing and congested population, with all their attendant impact on nature and ecological balance.

Davis notes that " . . . the growth of the earth's population has been like a long, thin powder fuse that burns slowly and haltingly until it finally reaches the charge and then explodes."[2] It is becoming increasingly evident that, viewed in world perspective, we are now reaching the charge. About 1830, after hundreds of centuries of rather slow growth, our species reached the point at which 1 billion persons were living. It took only 100 years to add a second billion. This was realized about 1930; and, as we have mentioned, in 1960 there were 3 billion people living in the world and by 1970, 3.7 billion. This fantastic spurt in our growth rate is graphically illustrated by Harold F. Dorn.[3] It is interesting to note that his projection of future population is significantly higher than that predicted by Huxley (see page 182).

The peoples of the nineteenth and twentieth centuries are certainly no more prolific than those of the preceding eras. The great change in the complexion of the world's population, therefore, cannot be explained in terms of natural reproduction. Again, we must turn our attention to the relationship between population growth and food production and technology. In remote and isolated parts of the world we find that birthrates are quite high, but so are death rates. The people who inhabit these regions enjoy only the lowest level of technology and live on a bare subsistence level. Until recently their population has not grown appreciably because a lack of food and modern medicine (a technological advance) caused the people to be susceptible to the spread of morbid diseases. If the birthrate was unusually high (50 births/1,000 population/year), it was counterbalanced by an equally high death rate. Industrialized nations introduced the people of these areas to new methods of agricultural production and the use of modern medicine. Several outcomes resulted: Death rates fell drastically, life-spans increased significantly, and unless the birthrate is arrested, population will explode. In a less dramatic sense, this is basically what has accounted for the rise in world population.

POPULATION CHARACTERISTICS

Population characteristics are studied by a specialized field of sociology known as *demography*. A demographer is one who attempts to describe and analyze living groups of people. The major reason demography falls within the realm of sociology, rather than some other science, is that the main causes of population trends are social. In pursuing knowledge of these social trends the demographer has employed three basic concepts

---

[2]Kingsley Davis, *Human Society*, The Macmillan Company, New York, 1949, p. 595.

[3]Harold F. Dorn, "World Population Growth," in Philip M. Hauser (ed.), *The Population Dilemma*, Prentice-Hall, Inc., Englewood Cliffs, N.J., 1963, p. 10.

known as the *demographic processes*: fertility, mortality, and migration. By analyzing each of these processes he can obtain a fundamental knowledge of the nature of the group.

Fertility refers to the actual number of children born within a given population. Usually this is expressed as a birthrate. There are many different ways of determining the birthrate of a group, but the simplest is called the *crude birthrate,* which is obtained by dividing the total number of births per year by the total population (according to midyear estimate) and multiplying the quotient by 1,000.

$$\text{Crude birthrate} = \frac{\text{total number of births/year}}{\text{total population}} \times 1,000$$

Often fertility is expressed in terms of the number of births per year per thousand of population; but whether expressed as a percentage or as a mathematical ratio, fertility should not be confused with fecundity. *Fecundity,* a concept related to but not synonymous with fertility, refers to the reproductive potential of a population. Social factors always keep the fertility rate well below the biological capacity for reproduction in all groups.

A few examples will illustrate the difference between fecundity and fertility. If a woman with high reproductive potential could produce as many as twenty children, the twenty children would represent her *fecundity.* Yet in most societies, particularly in the Western world, the woman who bears twenty children is far above the norm. She is more likely to have two or three children, which will be her actual *fertility.* The basic values of people often dictate the ultimate family size, regardless of fecundity or the fertility rates desired by national policy. For example, in 1944 the Supreme Soviet passed legislation designed to stimulate the birthrate in Russia, partly because of heavy Russian casualties in World War II. Beginning with her third child, the Russian mother was paid a lump sum of 200 rubles/child. Additionally, she received 40 rubles/month for each child, beginning with her fourth offspring. With the arrival of her eleventh child, and for all subsequent children, she received an initial payment of 2,500 rubles plus 150 rubles/month. These economic rewards seem more than sufficient when we consider that the average monthly income in Russia at the time was about 650 rubles.[4]

---

[4]All statistics are cited in E. W. Burgess, H. J. Locke, and M. M. Thomas, *The Family,* American Book Company, New York, 1963, chap. 6. Also see Gerald R. Leslie, *The Family in Social Context,* Oxford University Press, New York, 1967, chap. 5

However, a study conducted by Strumilin published in 1961 points out that the average size of the Russian family was nearly identical to that of the United States at the same time, approximately 3.7 members.[5]

Mortality or death rates are calculated the same way as birthrates and are also influenced by social factors. Recently the question has been posed as to how much we value life and to what extent we shall go to preserve it. In Western society we have transplanted vital organs to individuals who most certainly would have died without such operations. Artificial hearts and kidneys have been devised to prolong life, and even after death a person's body may be preserved through the new methods of cryonics, or "freezing," to await the day when the course of the terminal disease that ended his life may be reversed. Among certain other cultures, the attitude might be such that death is more readily accepted as a natural occurrence that must take its normal course. Man's interference with the "plan of cosmos" may not be permitted. A strong belief in reincarnation may not be conducive to an excessive or artificial lengthening of one's present life.

The third demographic process is *migration*. Although this process refers to the movement of people into or out of a given geographic area, demographers often prefer to specify the direction of the movement. *Immigration* signifies the movement of people *into* a geographical location from some external source; *emigration* denotes the movement of population *out of* a given area. The choice of which concept is used depends upon one's point of reference. If a native of Great Britain moves to the United States, she is an immigrant in this country and an emigrant according to Great Britain.

Sociologists tend to emphasize the importance of birth and death rates in determining the course of population growth because migration does not affect the statistics if we take a world perspective. This, of course, would not be true if we were colonizing the moon or other planets. However, migration has been a very important factor in the growth of many regional populations. Its effect on the United States is obvious: We have received 30 million immigrants since 1800. What is not nearly so obvious is the effect that the Great Irish Emigration, starting with the "Potato Famine" of the 1840s, had on Ireland, reducing its population from 8 million to 4 million. Likewise, the significance and repercussions of the forced immigration of Africans to the New World has been overlooked by the white American population until recently.

---

[5]S. Strumilin, "Family and Community in the Society of the Future," *The Soviet Review: A Journal of Translations,* vol. 2, no. 2, 1961, p. 7, cited in Burgess et al., *loc. cit.*

Effects of Age and Sex   All three demographic processes are profoundly influenced by two fundamental factors: age and sex. Dennis Wrong points out that age and sex "are the most important population characteristics from the formal demographic standpoint, because they are directly related to fertility and mortality."[6] We must add that they are also highly correlated with migration patterns. Wrong goes on to explain that only women "within a certain age span are capable of producing children, and people die more frequently at some ages than at others."[7] The relationship of age and sex to migration is not as clear. Yet we can devise some reasonably accurate generalizations based upon past observations. First, people on the move are likely to be young. Petersen notes that over two-thirds of the immigrants to the United States in the nineteenth century were between fifteen and forty years old.[8] Sometimes areas have been partially depopulated of their young until they have begun to look like colonies for the aged. During the period of heavy migration out of Ireland, some rural villages looked as though an evil pied piper had lured away their young. The pied piper, of course, was the hope for economic opportunity in the New World. Within the United States migrants are also likely to be young. It seems that as we get older we are less likely to search for new horizons, and we are less apt to adjust to new demographic conditions.

Sex is not as highly correlated with migration as is age, but some significant findings have been reported. Generally, we have observed that "Internal migrants are predominantly female and international ones predominantly male. . . . "[9] Although this has certainly been true in the past, it would seem that the continuing emancipation of women, increased opportunities for female employment, and weakened parental bonds are gradually changing the composition of international movement. Moreover, within the United States the pattern of internal migration has undergone a change. It is now common for a family to move its permanent residence across state boundaries. The farm boy who once lacked the skills appropriate for city life is now gaining these skills through our expanding system of public education, thus enabling him to move to the city. The net effect of these changes might well bring about a leveling of the significance of sex in internal and international migration. Nevertheless, as late as the 1970 census, Washington, D. C. had an excess of females, and Alaska had an equally great excess of males.

---

[6]Dennis H. Wrong, *Population and Society,* Random House Inc., New York, 1967, p. 6.
[7]*Ibid.,* p. 6.
[8]William Petersen, *Population,* The Macmillan Company, New York, 1961, p. 593.
[9]*Ibid.,* p. 593.

Actually, an uneven sex ratio can develop regardless of any migration. In countries where medical care is good, women have a lower mortality rate than men, and there are considerably more women in the population, especially in the later years of life. Occasionally this ratio is reversed, but mainly in countries where medical care is almost nonexistent and many women die in childbirth. People often attribute the greater number of women in the population to the effects of war on the fighting men, but this accounts for only a fraction of the difference in most cases. The main difference is a higher male death rate from heart disease, accidents, and many other aspects of ordinary civilian life.

ECONOMIC AND SOCIAL EFFECTS OF DEMOGRAPHIC CHANGE

Changes in fertility rates have a profound effect on many aspects of society. The baby boom of the 1940s and 1950s resulted in shortages of school classrooms and teachers and higher educational expenses to make up the shortages. The downturn in births beginning in the 1960s is now having a reverse effect on grammar schools and high schools, making it difficult for new teachers to find jobs. The 1970 census revealed a 51.6 percent increase over the 1960 figures for the age group 20 to 24, and a 44.3 percent increase in the 15- to 19-year-old group. The consequence is a very large number of young people entering the labor force in the 1970s, helping to make the employment picture less bright than before.[10]

Demography and Juvenile Crime Through the 1960s and early 1970s there was much comment upon the increase in juvenile crime, with figures indicating that the crime rate had risen much more rapidly than population. What most of the figures failed to show was that the number of juveniles in the 15- to 19-year-old group had risen nearly 45 percent, although the total population had increased only 13.3 percent during the 1960s. Much of the increase in juvenile crime was simply the reflection of a disproportionate increase in the number of juveniles.

Demography and Housing The 1970s are witnessing a very large increase in new families because the products of the baby boom of the late 1940s and 1950s are marrying and starting families, although generally small ones. The economic result has been a very active housing market that will probably slow down as the generation born in the 1960s comes of age. Another demographic factor that also results in demands for housing is the continued migration of people to heavily populated areas.

[10]Philip M. Hauser, "The Census of 1970," *Scientific American,* vol. 225, no. 1, July 1971, p. 25.

Despite large increases in population in both the last two decades, nearly half the counties of the United States have lost population as people move toward the cities and suburbs and to the sunshine states of the Southwest and Florida.

For the last two decades the number of elderly people has been increasing rapidly, very slightly as a percentage of the total, but markedly in absolute numbers, making gerontology an expanding field. People of 65 years and over now number just over 20 million, or 10 percent of the total population. The percentage is due to increase considerably as the birthrate falls. The increase in numbers of aged, combined with a disinclination of families to take care of the old and increasing aid from the federal government, has resulted in a booming rest home industry and has made services for the aged an increasing occupational field.

Population and the Economy Demographic changes then can obviously have effects on segments of the economy, increasing occupational opportunities in some areas and restricting them in others as well as increasing or decreasing the tax burdens of education. A much more vital question is whether a declining birthrate, such as the United States at present considers desirable, can have a depressant effect on the economy. John G. Wells, head of the Industrial Economics Division of the University of Denver Research Institute, gives convincing arguments that the answer is "No."[11] His conclusion is that by the twenty-first century we would have a 20 percent higher standard of living if our population stabilizes than if it continues to increase. One reason is that smaller families would be able to save more money, resulting in higher investment, which economic theory equates with higher productivity in years to come. Secondly, there would be no repetition of the population distribution of the 1960s, with a disproportionate number of children demanding heavier educational and other expenses.

The President's Commission on Population Growth and the American Future reached the same conclusion about the favorable economic impact of a lower birthrate and also emphasized that continued population increase would eventually be a primary cause of environmental deterioration.[12] The Commission recommended that birth control information and devices should be made available to all women, including sexually active teenage girls, and that laws against abortion should be greatly liberalized or repealed. Although President Nixon rejected the

[11]John G. Wells, "The Economy Doesn't Need More People," *The Wall Street Journal,* Apr. 22, 1970.

[12]Charles F. Westoff, "Commission on Population Growth and the American Future," a paper read at the American Sociological Association Convention, New York, Aug. 28, 1973.

Commission's report, the Supreme Court in 1973 made a decision virtually ending strict state laws against abortion, and the ideas contained in the report are having an impact on thinking about population both in the United States and abroad.

The effects of population change on educational problems, the care of the aged, and employment in certain segments of the economy, however, are problems of minor concern compared with the effects of population explosion in many parts of the world, especially in the less industrialized countries.

INDUSTRIALIZED AND DEVELOPING NATIONS

The statistics on population growth for selected countries (Table 8-1) tell a significant story. Certain European countries kept their population increase down from 5 to 7 percent for the decade of 1960 to 1970 and have an even lower birthrate now. At the same time, India and Indonesia increased their populations by approximately one-third, while Brazil and Mexico added nearly one-half to their populations. Certain historical characteristics of demographic change help to account for the difference.

European Populations A rapid upturn in population began in Europe and in areas of European settlement by about 1650, and later the same rapid increase in population began in other parts of the world. There were several reasons for the increasing numbers of Europeans, many of them following the theory of Malthus. The introduction of new food crops, especially potatoes, from the New World, along with improvements in farming techniques, made larger populations possible. The Thirty Years War ended in 1648, and although European nations continued periodically to tear each other apart, no later wars ever exterminated as large a percentage of the population as had the Thirty Years War. Bubonic plague, which three times brought death to nearly one-third the people of Europe, became less virulent. In short, death from famine, war, and pestilence was being checked to a considerable degree. By the nineteenth and twentieth centuries remarkable breakthroughs in medicine and sanitation (including modern plumbing and the flush toilet) resulted in even greater progress against death.

The early consequences of the changes were that people of European stock increased from 24 percent of the world's population in 1650 to 34.5 percent by 1900.[13] What had happened was that the demographic transition of modern history occurred first in Europe, where death rates

[13]Warren S. Thompson, *Population and Progress in the Far East,* The University of Chicago Press, Chicago, 1959, p. 12.

Table 8-1 Population Increase for Selected Countries, 1960 to 1970*

Country	1960	1970	% gain
Austria	7,049,000	7,420,000	5
United Kingdom	52,383,000	55,702,000	6
Sweden	7,471,000	8,046,000	7
Japan	93,600,000	103,540,000	11
United States	179,660,000	203,185,000	13
USSR	214,400,000	242,758,000	13
China†	679,232,000	759,620,000	12
Indonesia	92,600,000	121,200,000	31
India	408,250,000	550,376,000	35
Brazil	65,743,000	95,305,000	46
Mexico	34,626,000	50,670,000	47

*From *Information Please Almanac,* Simon and Schuster, New York, 1962, 1972.

†Statistics from China are generally regarded as unreliable; most estimates placed her population at about 800 million by 1970, with a percentage gain of nearly 18.

fell rapidly and birthrates fell much more slowly. The same general change eventually was to take place in most parts of the world. In fact, by the twentieth century the population increase was becoming much more rapid in Asia, Africa, and Latin America than in Europe. The transition in population has generally followed the trend shown in the diagram on the next page.

The first phase of demographic transition represents the historic and prehistoric past, when life-spans were short and only high birthrates ensured the survival of humankind. Phase II shows the transition to a low death rate combined with a continuing high birthrate—the situation that developed first in Europe but is now much more pronounced in other parts of the world. Phase III illustrates a development noted in all urban-industrial countries: a tendency for birthrates to decline. Phase IV shows a decline in birthrates continuing until zero population is reached, which by 1970 was approximately the case in Sweden, Austria, and West Germany. There are indications that much of Europe and even the United States are rapidly approaching Phase IV.

Declining birthrates in many industrialized countries, however, do not mean that their population problems are over. Many environmentalists would argue that even present populations of Europe, the United States, and Japan are too great because they are prosperous populations that use far more than their share of the world's resources and spew out more than their share of contaminants into water and air. One environ-

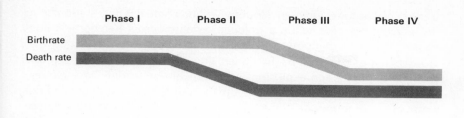

	Phase I	Phase II	Phase III	Phase IV
Birthrate				
Death rate				

mentalist states the problem succinctly: "I define as most seriously overpopulated that nation whose people by virtue of their numbers and activities are most rapidly decreasing the ability of the land to support life."[14] Backward countries may face famine, but it is the most highly developed nations that may eventually do the most harm to the earth, even without any large increase in their population.

The Underdeveloped Countries One of the bitter ironies of the population problem is that many of the world's poorest countries now have the highest birthrates. Their death rates are still high, but not nearly as high as they used to be. There are still many countries in which average life expectancy is only about forty years and nearly half the people die before the age of twenty; but even this represents real progress in death control. Time was when life expectancy for most human beings averaged about twenty-seven years.[15]

Often, even within the same country, poorer and more backward areas have high birthrates while urban areas have low birthrates. Even in the United States there is still a grain of truth to the old saying, "The rich get richer and the poor get babies," although the statement is not nearly as true as in the past. A more startling example of differences within the same country appears in the Soviet Union. The birthrate of European Russia is now so low as to be a subject of concern to leaders of the Kremlin—a birthrate of only about 11/1,000. Meantime, the predominantly rural Moslems of Central Asia have birthrates of about 42 to 46/1,000. There is some concern that as a consequence Russia may try to encourage larger families among her European subjects.[16] There is

[14]Wayne H. Davis, "Overpopulated America," *New Republic,* vol. 162, Jan. 10, 1970, p. 13.

[15]Thomas Frejka, "The Prospects for a Stationary World Population," *Scientific American,* vol. 228, no. 3, March 1973, p. 19.

[16]David M. Hier, cited in "The Population of the USSR," *Scientific American,* vol. 228, no. 1, January 1973, p. 46. See also "Russian Birth Decline; More Babies Urged," Associated Press report, Nov. 20, 1972, *Bakersfield Californian,* p. 44.

some doubt as to whether any country will be content with a stationary or declining population while a potential enemy across her borders continues to grow in manpower.

For many years China has been thought of as the world's prime example of population explosion. At times Chinese leaders have expressed the opinion that a society with a marxist distribution system need not worry about its multitude of people and have even spoken of the Chinese population as their atomic weapon. Recent reports, though, indicate that China is very much aware of the population problem. Birthrates are declining. Contraceptives, abortions, and voluntary sterilizations are being used, especially in the cities. In all cities family planning is part of the general health program, and couples with too many children are regarded as showing disrespect for the party.[17] However, there are divided opinions and shifts in leadership in China, and the peasants do not respond very well to birth control propaganda. Although the official 1970 estimate of the Chinese population was 756 million, most experts believe it to be at least 800 million. Despite progress in birth control, the population is still growing.

In many parts of the less industrialized world birthrates are considerably higher than in China. India has made attempts at population control, but progress is so slow that her population is now growing faster than ever. Rural parts of Latin America are perfect illustrations of Phase II of demographic transition, with death rates declining sharply but birthrates as high as ever. Mexico has made remarkable economic and educational progress in recent decades, but her population explosion is enough of a problem to eat up much of the gain. Mexico City, located in one of the most beautiful valleys in the world, is one of the world's fastest growing and most polluted cities, with an annual population increase of nearly 6 percent. Alarmed, President Echevarría has finally ordered a nationwide birth control program with free clinics in all areas, especially rural ones.[18]

Growing populations are characteristic of Africa as well as of Latin America. Kofi Sefa-Boakye, a student from Ghana in West Africa, explains why the pill has little effect in his part of the world.[19] The points he makes have been noted by American sociologists: As a general rule people voluntarily limit family size only when they are prosperous enough to develop many interests outside the family. The poorest people have little else to be concerned about except family and kinship. As Sefa-Boakye states,

[17]"Family Planning in China," *Scientific American,* vol. 227, no. 5, November 1972, p. 50.
[18]"The Cities: Darkness at Noon," *Newsweek,* Aug. 27, 1973, p. 88.
[19]Kofi Sefa-Boakye, "Why the Pill Won't Work in the Third World," *Los Angeles Times,* Jan. 7, 1973, sect. G, p. 1.

> Children in underdeveloped countries are economic assets rather than economic burdens—and in the struggle to wrest a living from the soil, the bigger the family the better. Also, parents are dependent upon their children in old age. Since many children die before reaching reproductive age, many must be born to close the gap.[20]

Numerous children are also interpreted as a sign of the father's manhood, and there are strong feelings about the preservation of the family. These are the attitudes of the underdeveloped world that are most difficult for the urban-industrial world to understand or to persuade against. The mere availability of birth control pills does not guarantee they will be used.

Religious attitudes also often have a bearing on population increase. The Catholic Church has not yet approved the use of contraceptive devices or abortion, so it would seem likely that Catholic countries would have very high birthrates. Oddly enough, this is sometimes true and yet sometimes very far from the truth. Catholic France was one of the very few countries to have achieved zero population growth in the period between World Wars I and II. Poland, a staunchly Catholic country, now has such a low birthrate that she fears a drastic decline in population in the next fifty years.[21] The great majority of Catholics in the United States practice some kind of birth control. On the other hand, rural areas of Catholic Latin America generally have extremely high birthrates. The difference is more a matter of old-fashioned rural values than of church strictures. Even Hindus, who have always placed a high religious value on fertility, are often willing to practice birth control, but mainly if they belong to the urban, educated segment of India's population.

POPULATION FUTURES

The problem of predicting the future is very difficult, partly because wars, famines, and natural disasters cannot be foretold but mainly because fertility rates change. In the 1950s the United States was having a baby boom. In 1973 the U.S. Census Bureau reported for the first time that the birthrate had fallen to a level that could eventually mean zero population growth. However, the zero growth would not take place immediately. The population of the United States at present includes a disproportionate percentage of young people in the reproductive years of life. If each young married couple limited itself to only two children, the population would increase from its present 205 million to 233 million by 2050. It is

---

[20] With permission of Kofi Sefa-Boakye, *ibid.*
[21] Thomas Frejka, *op. cit.,* p, 20. See also "Poland Suffers from Decline in Birth Rates," *Los Angeles Times,* Feb. 16, 1972, part 1B, p. 3.

Present

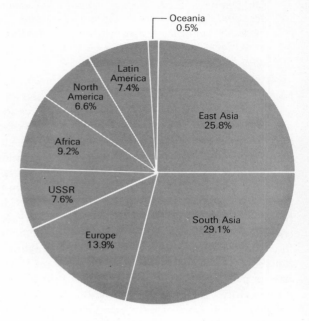

Year 2100

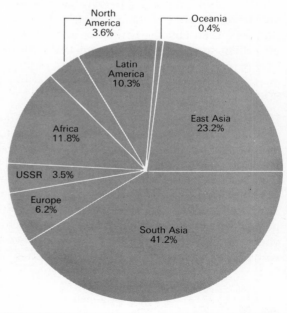

easy to imagine how much greater the population increase will be for countries whose birthrates continue to be high. Even if a two-child family suddenly became the average throughout the world, the world's population would reach 8 billion by 2050. If such a change in family size were to come about gradually between now and 2050 (the best that could possibly be hoped for), the world's population would reach 13 billion by then.[22]

Even if world birthrates gradually declined to an average two-child family by the mid-twenty-first century, the present balance of world's population would change drastically, reflecting the enormous numbers of young people in the present populations of underdeveloped countries. The figures in the table on page 194 show how population balance will continue to shift until 64 percent of the world's population will be living in Asia, compared with 55 percent now. The figures assume that low birthrates will continue in Japan and that present progress in birth control in China and Korea will continue. The assumption is that in parts of southern Asia, such as India, Bangladesh, and Indonesia, a reduction in birthrates will come much more slowly. The table, based upon eight major areas of the world, portrays shifts in population that would be expected under a projection which assumes a net reproduction rate of 1 by the period 2020 to 2025. (The eight areas are used by the U.N. for socioeconomic classifications.) Such a prediction of a world, with 13 billion people by 2050, is a rather conservative estimate, yet even this estimate calls for more than three people for every one now in existence—and the date is only one average lifetime away. Some authorities hope the family-planning trend noticeable even in many underdeveloped countries will prevent this rapid an increase in population. Kingsley Davis, on the other hand, is rather pessimistic about the family-planning prospect.

The Family-planning Panacea   Davis, a leading expert on population, questions the idea that present-day family planning is having much effect except in urban-industrial areas of the world.[23] His studies in the 1960s found that the birthrate was upward in twenty-seven out of thirty-four underdeveloped countries investigated, the reasons generally being better health, successful pregnancies, and fewer stillbirths. To such countries the Western world arrives with a message of family planning stated simply: "We can show you how to have only as many children as you want." What is most discouraging to Davis is the very point cited

[22]Thomas Frejka, *op. cit.,* p. 21.
[23]Kingsley Davis, "Population Policy: Will Current Programs Succeed?", *Science,* vol. 158, Nov. 10, 1967, pp. 730–739.

previously from an African informant, that the number of children *wanted* is far too many. He found that in Taiwan, generally cited as an excellent example of sudden interest in birth control, intrauterine devices were frequently requested only by women who already had four or more children. In a number of underdeveloped countries he found the family ideal to be about 4.3 children. Another demographer reports that even in the United States the poorest segment of the population considered 3.7 children to be the ideal family size.[24]

Davis' answer to the dilemma is that more must be done than simply telling people to have the number of children they want. Economic incentives should be used for limiting family size, such as special tax breaks for unmarried people or for couples with only one or two children, and economic penalties for more. Educational systems should teach strongly against the old familial ideas of numerous offspring. Women must be given high status, equal pay, and equal chances for promotion when they choose careers other than that of mother and housewife. Encourage all factors that tend to delay marriage, such as education, career preparation, and the idea that young people should have a number of free years before undertaking marriage. Many of these ideas can be recognized as those that are already taking hold in much of the industrialized world. A few of these ideas, such as the attempt to postpone marriage, are prominent in China, along with a slight downgrading of the almost sacred position the family once held.

One of the most serious difficulties with Davis' proposals—and one that he has himself commented on previously—is that many of these changes in family attitude seem to come about naturally only after a fairly high standard of living has been achieved. It is then that women are most likely to desire new careers. A high standard of living calls for industrialization, but industrialization can be retarded by the extreme poverty caused in part by high birthrates and correspondingly high percentages of young children. There is, then, a kind of vicious circle at work in many underdeveloped countries, with overpopulation and its attendant poverty slowing down industrialization and therefore perpetuating overpopulation and poverty.

The Threat to Freedom   One means of coping with large, poverty-stricken populations in underdeveloped countries is by the massive mobilization of the people that has been achieved in recent years in China. To the Western observer such a society is too regimented, too much of a human beehive. Whatever its accomplishments, it is a system

[24]Judith Blake, "Population Policy for Americans: Is the Government Being Misled?", *Science*, vol. 164, May 2, 1969, pp. 522–529.

that severely limits individual liberty. Yet such a social system will become increasingly attractive to the underdeveloped world if population pressures make it impossible to bring people the rising standard of living that all the world now demands. In this sense, one of the consequences of population pressures could be a decline of freedom. To hungry people, food is more important than constitutional rights of which they have never heard, and they will accept regimentation as the price of survival. It is doubtful that any wars waged by the United States or other Western powers can prevent such a trend if the population pressures continue to increase.

The War Threat   In the days of Hitler and Mussolini there was much talk about population pressure and its threat to peace. Japan had seized Manchuria, with the rationalization that she needed a source of food and a place for her people to settle. Italy seized Ethiopia for the same stated reasons. Hitler spoke endlessly of *lebensraum* (living space) for his people and looked hungrily at the plains of Russia, and both he and Mussolini advocated larger families. In retrospect it can be seen that these were cases of rationalization of aggression rather than valid reasons. Each of the three countries mentioned now lives in greater prosperity on its own territory than it did before World War II. However, the world has seen a precedent for using the idea of living space as an excuse for aggression. The situation of the future could easily play into the hands of demagogues similar to Hitler and Mussolini.

Crowding and Social Pathology   Much has been written in recent years about crowding and social pathology. John B. Calhoun,[25] in his experiments with crowded rats, found that populations stabilized at a particular level of crowding because of the pathological behavior that set in at that level. After crowding reached a particular level, infant mortality climbed to almost 100 percent, with mother rats often neglecting their young and even failing to build nests for them. Males fought more for territory than before and sometimes went berserk, biting females and the young and occasionally even becoming cannibals. Some males became completely passive and somnolent; others grew "pansexual," not discriminating proper sex partners as rats ordinarily do. They made homosexual advances and sometimes attacked juveniles and females not in estrus.

Later studies have also found pathological behavior to be associated with extreme crowding of animal populations. Desmond Morris believes

[25]John B. Calhoun, "Population Density and Social Pathology," *Scientific American*, vol. 206, Februrary 1962, pp. 139–148.

the same to be true of the human species—a theme very prominent in his book *The Human Zoo*.[26] The anthropologist Colin Turnbull, in *The Mountain People*,[27] notes the pathological behavior of a primitive people whose territory is inadequate to support them. In the case of Turnbull's study of the Ik of northern Uganda, the problem is not increased population but merely decreased territory, with crowding, malnutrition, the breakdown of social norms, and everyman's hand against his neighbor's.

Food, Environment, and Resources   People of the poorer countries of the world (for that matter, some of the poorest people of such a wealthy country as the United States) have long suffered from a protein deficiency that stunts growth, shortens the life-span, and can even result in brain damage. Until recent times the protein problem has hardly entered the consciousness of well-fed people in prosperous countries. Now it is suddenly looming as a problem for all people, as the fisheries of the world decline in their yield and as the properous countries bid up the price of meat until it becomes unavailable to the poor. Even with wheat and other grain resources the world no longer has its old-time surpluses. In the 1950s the United States worried about how to dispose of an oversupply of agricultural commodities; now the problem could exist only in a year of unusual bumper crops. Most of the world has no surplus on which to draw, and the specter of simultaneous crop shortages in many areas of the world is terrible to contemplate. Already drought and accompanying starvation have struck felling blows at the people of the Sahel region of Africa, just south of the Sahara. Millions of people and cattle have died. Millions more will grow up "blighted in their infancy by malnutrition, retarded in mind and body,"[28] and the desert encroaches into the green areas to the south as the vegetation is eaten away by starving cattle and goats. Demographers have long warned of future shortages. Now they are here. The battle is joined. While the world contemplates a threefold increase in its population in the next seventy-five years, it wastes its resources, watches its lands erode, poisons its streams, rivers, and seas, and hopes somehow it will not have to pay the consequences. Admittedly the first steps are now being taken to save the environment, to slow down the population explosion, and even to reach international agreements on the oceans and fisheries of the world, but social norms and institutions move slowly and cumbersomely while the future rushes upon us.

[26] Desmond Morris, *The Human Zoo*, McGraw-Hill Book Company, New York, 1968.
[27] Colin Turnbull, *The Mountain People*, Simon and Schuster, Inc., New York, 1972.
[28] "Future is Famine for Ten Million South of Sahara," *Smithsonian*, vol. 4, no. 6, September 1973, pp. 73–77.

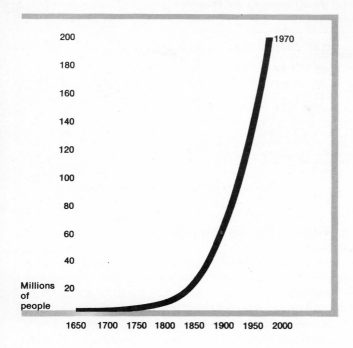

SUMMARY

Fifty thousand years ago the world was rather sparsely populated when hunting and food gathering societies predominated. However, as surpluses of food were built up in early villages (and later in the first cities), population began to increase. By 1970, an overpopulated world of 3.7 billion people existed.

The study of population is known as demography, a field of sociology that describes and analyzes living groups of people. The major demographic processes are (1) fertility, the actual number of children born within a given population; (2) mortality, the actual number of deaths that occur within a society or region; and (3) migration, the physical movement of people into or out of a given geographic area.

Because of a decrease in mortality rates, many areas of the world are undergoing a period of tremendous population increase. Nonindustrialized countries seem to be growing faster than industrialized nations.

199

Table 8-2 Falling Death Rates in the Hungry
World (Per Thousand)

	1935	1950	1965	1980 *
World	25	19	16	12.7
Asia	33	23	20	13
Africa	33	27	23	18
Latin America	22	19	12	8.2

Source: Population Bulletin of the United Nations, no. 5, 1962, p.
17, and Population Reference Bureau, World Population Data Sheet,
December 1965, in William Paddock and Paul Paddock (eds.), Famine:
1975! America's Decision: Who Will Survive, Little, Brown and
Company, Boston, 1967, p. 16.
    *Projected

However, even industrial nations are now facing the problems caused by
too large a population.

Population control has benefited several countries whose methods of
birth limitation, legalized abortion, and voluntary sterilization have been
observed. Some nonindustrialized or industrilizing countries, such as
Korea, have already instigated massive programs to limit the size of their
populations. As birthrates continue to decline, the population as a whole
ages. The field of social gerontology is becoming increasingly important
because it is concerned with the problems of the aged. Other economic
effects of demographic change include rises or declines in educational
expenses, housing needs, availability of jobs, and increased or lessened
strain on the environment and resources. Expert opinion, including that of
the President's Commission on Population, holds that continuing
economic well-being depends upon keeping birthrates down to a zero
population growth level, even for prosperous countries.

Although population growth is a problem for the entire world, the
strains are most severe for much of the underdeveloped and generally
poorer of the world's nations, which are now registering the highest gains
in population. Efforts to spread the idea of birth control in the world's
rural areas are often defeated by traditional values calling for large
families. There is even fear that some countries might engage in a
population race, such as was attempted by Hitler and Mussolini.

Besides presenting the obvious threat of resource and food shortages,
the booming population of the world may also present threats to freedom
and peace. There is even speculation that excess crowding can result in
pathological behavior, as has happened in a number of animal experiments.

Chapter 9

Congestion of the Human Group: The Urban Trend

The houses were never high enough to satisfy them; they kept on making them still higher and built them thirty or forty storeys with offices, shops, banks, . . . one above another; they dug cellars and tunnels ever deeper downwards. . . .
No light of heaven pierced through the smoke of the factories with which the town was girt, but sometimes the red disk of a rayless sun might be seen riding in the black firmament through which iron bridges plowed their way, and from which there descended a continual shower of soot and cinders.[1]

Anatole France
Penguin Island

Mankind has gathered into communities not only to protect life and ensure its propagation but to enrich life through meaningful contacts with other human beings. People come together to exchange ideologies, to stimulate the process of innovation, to stabilize a set of values, and to

---

[1]Anatole France, *Penguin Island,* Modern Library, Inc., New York, 1933, p. 279.

201

establish an orderly pattern of existence. Yet when we look at the sprawling cities of our modern industrial nations we find that the congestion of the human group may often interfere with the attainment of those goals for which we have adopted the city as our habitat. Exactly what has happened to bring about the crises of urbanism is not easily explained, but a consideration of the trend that has led to the contemporary condition can shed some light on the development of our urban predicament.

URBAN GROWTH AND URBAN CRISES

The growth of cities was not rapid in the early periods of urban development. Large numbers of peasant and pastoral people had to supply the food and other commodities needed by urbanites, and the yields of farmland were not great enough to support more than a small minority of nonfarming people.

Ancient Cities   The ancient cities faced many problems that would be with man in one form or another throughout the remainder of history. Not only was the problem of the production of an agricultural surplus with which to feed the town a formidable task, but the problems of transportation of goods to the city created another barrier to urban growth. The great cities of antiquity had to be small compared with the metropolis of today because of the problems of food production and supply. Ur of the Chaldees attained a population of about only 34,000 during its first 2,000 years of existence, but eventually it numbered over 200,000. The latter estimate however, included populations living outside the city walls.[2]

In ancient times, as well as in modern, there was normative conflict between city and countryside, as recorded in Biblical maledictions upon Sodom and Gomorrah, Babylon, Nineveh, and Tyre. The ancient city also had its problems of sanitation. Many cities were located along rivers that acted as open sewers and garbage disposals, and fluctuations in the population of imperial Rome may have been caused in part by problems of sanitation.

The word "polis," applied to the cities of the Greeks, is related to the word "politics," implying that the city was the center of government. In this respect many cities had a greater importance than do modern cities in spite of the smaller size of earlier cities. They developed as independent entities, dominated a hinterland around them, and occasionally became

---

[2]Lewis Mumford, *The City in History*, Harcourt, Brace & World, Inc., New York, 1961, p. 62.

the centers of empires. The city of antiquity was thus a place of pride and power, demanding a loyalty of its citizens that is now claimed by the nation-state.

The Medieval City Many of the cities of Southern Europe in the medieval period were the shrunken remains of the cities of the Roman Empire, but they often had much of the independence of the ancient polis. They maintained garrisons and carried on diplomacy. The Hanseatic cities of Northern Europe were formed more exclusively for trade and commerce and, in this respect, resembled the twentieth-century cities. They also attained a degree of independence and allowed much greater freedom for their citizens than was permitted the serfs of the medieval estates.[3] There was a saying, "City air is free air"—in the city, one could shed the shackles of serfdom. In a sense the statement remains true throughout history, not in relation to serfdom but in relation to the crippling bonds of traditionalism and provincialism that are common in small towns and villages.

The problems of health and sanitation were met only in very crude ways during that period. Sometimes open streams carried off the sewage of the city, but often there were virtually no disposal facilities. Mumford points out that in Cambridge piles of dung were allowed to accumulate in public places for a week, and in many towns corpses were buried in the city centers where, by decay and seepage, they contaminated the water supply.[4] In spite of this, he concludes that the medieval town or city was not as bad as it is sometimes pictured. It had the advantage of little crowding so that people could usually dispose of their wastes in the ample garden plots behind their houses. The problem of wastes was to become worse in some respects in the modern world.

The Modern City The modern city is an industrial city. Much more than the ancient or medieval city, the modern city is an outgrowth of trade and industry. As it grew in size and affluence it also became more enmeshed in both the economy and polity of the larger society. Sjoberg has made a study of the preindustrial city, including modern cities of a nonindustrial type, as well as cities of the past. Although such cities differ from case to case, a generalized summary shows both contrast and similarities when compared with the industrial city.[5]

---

[3]Max Weber, *The City*, Don Martindale and Gertude Neuwirth (trans. and eds.), The Free Press of Glencoe, Inc., New York, 1958, p. 182.

[4]Mumford, *op. cit.*, p. 288.

[5]Gideon Sjoberb, *The Preindustrial City*, The Free Press, New York, 1964, pp. 323–332.

The contrasts

The preindustrial city
   Small, usually 10,000-100,000

   Politically independent

   Extended (consanguineal) family

   Education upper class

   Religious unity,
   approaches "sacred society"

   Sanitation problems:
   mainly human and animal wastes

   City walls, limited suburbs

The contrasts

The industrial city
   Large, usually 100,000-8,000,000

   Subordinate to nation

   Restricted (conjugal) family

   General education

   Religious diversity, and secular

   Sanitation problems:
   industrial waste, air contamination

   "Exploding metropolis," suburbs

The similarities

The growth of class differences

Segregation of minorities

Economic and ecological segregation

Heterogeneity: all walks of life, many kinds of people

Mass entertainment

Development of intellectual life, arts and sciences

Contrasts   By comparison with the modern industrial city, the preindustrial city is small, numbering only 10,000 in population in most cases, and numbering 100,000 only rarely. The extended family tends to dominate the way of life in some respects, although the city, in general, is characterized by habitation of smaller nuclear families. The city itself, as previously noted, tends to be an independent political entity with a centralized and oligarchic government. Education is only for the privileged class in the preindustrial setting; under conditions of industrialization, it is provided for all classes.

The preindustrial city was more sacred than secular because it was often the center of religious life. Religious norms were enforced by custom and sometimes even by law. Political and religious unity, along with the influence of the extended family system, gave it more a sense of community than is generally observed in the industrial city of this era.

The production of an agricultural surplus has always been a requirement of city life, but here again a contrast in life styles can be noted. In the preindustrial city a majority had to till the soil so a minority could live in the city. Today, a majority live in the city. Even by the time of the Civil War only one-third of the people in the United States had to work the land. By the end of World War II only one person in twelve farmed for a living. By 1970, the agricultural product of the United States was increasing more rapidly than ever before. This observation takes on special significance when we consider the fact that now only one man in forty-three is occupied with farming![6]

Similarities Although a number of contrasts have been cited, many similarities appear to exist when industrial and preindustrial cities are compared. For example, class differentiation is very much in evidence in both types of city. Minority groups are segregated into particular quarters today, as they were in preindustrial cities. The modern industrial city also is segregated into various economic categories in much the same way as the ancient city was segregated into specialized areas for various crafts, shops, and types of labor. New forms of entertainment exist today, but they are reminiscent of the Roman circus maximus, the Byzantine hippodrome, the Olympic Games, or the Greek theater.

Urban Crises As the industrial era proceeded, cities began to expand by extending their boundaries and crowding more and more people within the urban complex. Factory systems were developed to provide for the increasing numbers of people, and the rudiments of mass production came into existence. To operate effectively, the city needed an ever-growing labor force. For some time the mutual dependency established between population and cities worked well. However, the saturation point has been reached. Manhattan has an average population density of 75,000 persons/square mile, and more than 23,550,000 inhabitants live within a 10-mile radius of the city.[7] This is just part of a larger urban complex, Megalopolis, that will be discussed shortly.

Arensberg and Kimball point out that the human community is a minimal unit of population whose members must coexist to ensure the continuance of the species.[8] As communities continued to grow in size and population they became cities. In the United States, when the first

[6]Jules B. Billard, "The Revolution in American Agriculture," *National Geographic,* vol. 137, February 1970, pp. 147–151.

[7]Estimated population statistics based on Philip M. Hauser and Leo F. Schnore, *The Study of Urbanization,* John Wiley & Sons, Inc., New York, 1965, p. 11.

[8]Conrad M. Arensberg and Solon T. Kimball, *Culture and Community,* Harcourt, Brace & World, Inc., New York, 1965, pp. 16–17.

Table 9-1   The World's Largest Cities

City	Population
Shanghai	10,800,000
Tokyo	9,012,000
New York	7,895,000
London	7,763,000
Moscow	6,942,000
São Paulo	5,685,000
Bombay	5,534,000
Cairo	4,266,000
Rio de Janeiro	4,207,000
Peking	4,010,000

Source: *Information Please Almanac,* Simon and Schuster, New York, 1972, except for Shanghai, first reported in *U. N. Demographic Yearbook,* Office of Public Information, United Nations, New York, 1973, as world's largest city. The U. N. also calls New York City plus suburbs the "world's largest urban conglomerate, with 11,572,000."

national census was taken in 1790,[9] there were twenty-four urban places, only two of which had populations in excess of 25,000. By 1960, 5,400 urban areas had absorbed 92 percent of the total population growth,[10] and the 1970 census showed the same trend. In time, and with further expansion, some of these urban places began to merge so that one could not tell where one city ended and the next began. On the northeastern seaboard of this nation, such an area is described by Jean Gottmann as *Megalopolis.* It is "an almost continuous stretch of urban and suburban areas from southern New Hampshire to northern Virginia and from the Atlantic shore to the Appalachian foothills."[11] Over 40 million people live in this rather small land space. Some experts, including Lewis Mumford, believe that under such conditions community may become anticommunity, contributing not to the enhancement of human life but, perhaps, to its demise.

This statement may seem somewhat alarmist; however, there is some evidence to justify its inclusion in a sociology text. It is not the intent of the authors to predict the doom of urban areas, but rather to point out that such conditions may not be beneficial to the inhabitants of these supercities. Aside from the economic and psychological needs that draw

[9]Hauser and Schnore, *op. cit.,* p. 7.
[10]*Ibid.,* pp. 7–8.
[11]Jean Gottmann, *Megalopolis,* The Twentieth Century Fund, New York, 1961, p. 3.

people into close association, such as the need to identify with a group and the need for security which comes from acceptance by others, human beings also have physical needs. Water and air are the most basic of these.

Laurence M. Gould reports that at least sixty underdeveloped nations already face water-shortage problems, and in America, New York City dumps 200 million gallons of raw sewage into the Hudson River every day, thus threatening the water supply.[12] On the other side of the continent, San Francisco is facing the problem of losing its famous bay to land-fill operations, most of which have been caused indirectly or directly by covering former garbage dumps. In November 1969, reacting to the cries of the citizenry to "Save our bay," the San Francisco Board of Supervisors' Health Committee recommended that the city ship its garbage by rail to Lassen County. Although this increases the economic problems of San Francisco, it is an economic boon to Lassen County, which hopes to become the "garbage dump of America."[13]

The problem of clean air was nearly nonexistent so long as most of the people lived at "home on the range . . . ," where the skies were not only free of clouds but free of smog and pollutants. As living patterns changed, so did the condition of the atmosphere. In 1900, only 40 percent of this country's 75 million population lived in urban areas. By 1970, with a population of 203 million, 73.5 percent of the people were urban dwellers. Edward Edelson points out that now "More than half the American people live on just 1 percent of the nation's land mass. It is in these relatively small and crowded areas where most of the country's air pollution is created."[14]

When people mass together in great numbers extensive services must be devised to meet their needs. In the process other problems may be caused. Operating industrial plants and heating houses and apartments through the use of fossil fuels adds pollutants to the environment. Every day, chimneys in the United States pour out 100,000 tons of sulfur dioxide, and motor vehicles add 230,000 tons of carbon monoxide.[15] It is no mere coincidence that the growth of urban areas has been accompanied by problems of air and water pollution; the pattern has been continuous throughout history. It is only the technology of the industrial city that adds to the problems started in medieval times.

[12]Laurence M. Gould, "While There Is Still Time," *Bell Telephone Magazine*, American Telephone and Telegraph Company, New York, January–February 1969, p. 6.

[13]Charles Hillinger, "The Garbage Dump of America," *Los Angeles Times*, July 4, 1969, p. 3.

[14]Edward Edelson, "The Battle for Clean Air," *Public Affairs Pamphlet No. 403*, Public Affairs Committee, Newark, N.J., 1968, p. 3.

[15]Gould, *loc. cit.*

SOCIAL AND ECOLOGICAL CHARACTERISTICS OF THE CITY

In a sociological sense, *ecology* refers to the relationship between people and their natural and social environment. The ecological pattern of a neolithic village was quite different from that of the modern metropolis. Such a village was relatively uncomplicated; it was composed of people from like backgrounds who had similar interests, a condition known as *homogeneity*. The members of the village enjoyed a primary relationship with each other and a strong feeling of community. Tönnies described such a social organization as one that was oriented toward the achievement of group goals. Each individual took part in the activities of the community. His actions were prescribed by tradition, and his attitudes were based upon sentiment. Tönnies called this pattern of group life *gemeinschaft,* a community in which the relationships among members were valuable in and of themselves.[16]

However, as population increased the need for a different kind of living arrangement developed. The gemeinschaft type of society did not have the distinct authoritative body that is necessary to govern large numbers of people. Because it was tradition-oriented, it lacked the cultural perspective necessary for change; its emphasis on close personal relationships hampered its ability to expedite matters. As a result, early communities, villages, and tribes began to take on the shape and characteristics of the modern city, which had some undesirable side effects.

To administer a large population is to divest individuals of some of their autonomy; to maintain the population is to mass produce; to specialize parts of the population for the performance of different activities is to separate individuals from other parts of the total culture. As the city developed and grew it needed greater centralization of power and mass production (and eventually automation), and it produced increasing alienation among its members. In Tönnies' terminology, this represents a movement away from gemeinschaft toward gesellschaft. The *gesellschaft* pattern is more impersonal, and the goals of the individual take precedence over the goals of the group. Rather than depend upon tradition and custom for guidance, people are controlled through a formalized system of laws. This is an *associational society,* with superficial and transitory relationships based upon the rational pursuit of self-interest through business and commerce. Although gesellschaft society exists only in the imagination, many sectors of the modern world are rapidly approaching its realization.

[16]Ferdinand Tönnies, *Community and Society,* The Michigan State University Press, East Lansing, 1957.

Gemeinschaft

Homogeneity: sameness, likeness

Group-oriented

Tradition dominates patterns

Individual guided by sentiment

Each man part of
the overall culture

Each man a jack-of-all-trades

Relationships among people
valuable in and of themselves

Gesellschaft

Heterogeneity: mixed
background and interests

Individual-oriented

Business and commerce dominate

Man guided by rational pursuit
of his own interests

Specialization

Relationships transitory
and superficial

Models of Urban Growth In industrialized countries, the trend toward gesellschaft orientation is exemplified in the cities. The characteristics of gesellschaft have resulted in the segregation of cities into special-interest areas. In 1925 Ernest Burgess attempted to describe this pattern by introducing a model of city development known as the *Concentric Zone Theory*. His idea was that at the core of a city, using Chicago as a specific example, a central business district would be located. As one journeyed toward the outer band of the circle he would encounter a deteriorating area called the "zone in transition," a workingman's residential area, a middle-class residential area, and finally, the commuter's zone. The Burgess hypothesis regarding the dispersal of white-collar workers to suburban areas has been confirmed in

209

**Urban growth
as seen by Burgess**

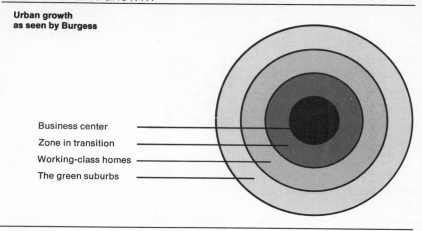

Business center

Zone in transition

Working-class homes

The green suburbs

**Sector development
according to Hoyt**

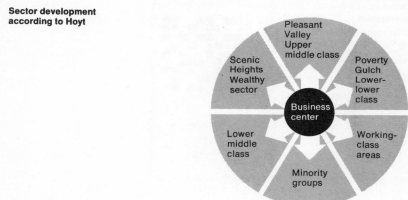

Pleasant
Valley
Upper
middle class

Scenic
Heights
Wealthy
sector

Poverty
Gulch
Lower-
lower
class

Business
center

Lower
middle
class

Working-
class
areas

Minority
groups

**Recent view:
exploding metropolis**

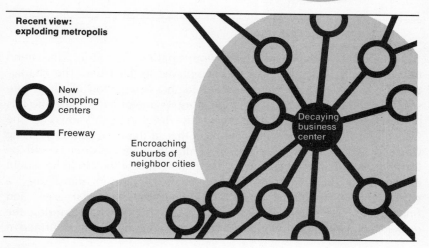

New
shopping
centers

Freeway

Encroaching
suburbs of
neighbor cities

Decaying
business
center

a recent study in twelve out of seventeen metropolitan areas.[17] Nevertheless, because the Concentric Zone Theory shows only a slight applicability to some of the cities and completely fails to describe a few, other theorists have devised other models. One of the alternate theories, Hoyt's Sector Theory, is illustrated on page 210.

The sector of the city that was once the highest priced residential area eventually declines, but high-value areas extend beyond it in the same part of town. There are many areas where this is true, especially if natural beauty or other advantages give particular areas of the city a high residential value. Often, though, other factors also affect the pattern of growth—railroads, industrial developments, hills, or other natural barriers. Often in rapidly growing Western communities the most impoverished area is a rural-urban fringe at the outskirts of the town (usually stretching out along railroad tracks) rather than the zone in transition near city hall.

Other new patterns are emerging, the major one being an outward explosion in all directions, resulting in urban areas with many centers. Some cities, notably Los Angeles, originally grew by combining several communities. Other cities, once compact, now resemble Los Angeles, reaching out tentacles in all directions and establishing new suburban centers at the ends of each.

Natural Areas   The nature of the city and people's attraction to urban living can be summed up by reviewing the theory of Robert E. Park, a leading University of Chicago sociologist. "In the freedom of the city," he wrote, "every individual, no matter how eccentric, finds somewhere an environment in which he can expand and bring what is peculiar in his nature to some sort of expression."[18] Basing his ideas on this premise, Park concluded that each city was made up of "natural areas," subcommunities which have characteristics attractive to those whose special needs or interests are matched to the ecological conditions of the areas. Therefore, in some unplanned fashion every city will evolve a central business district, exclusive residential areas or suburbs, areas of light or heavy industry, a labor mart, slums, ghettos, bohemias, and hobohemias. As the appeal of cities began to spread to wider and wider factions of the population, the city per se became indistinguishable from contiguous areas outside its political boundaries. The *metropolis* had been formed!

Cities and the Census Bureau   Today, metropolitan areas spill beyond their central cities, embracing smaller cities and towns and

[17]Avery M. Guest, "Retesting the Burgess Zonal Hypothesis: "The Location of White Collar Workers," *American Journal of Sociology,* vol. 76, May 1971, pp. 1096–1108.

[18]Robert E. Park, *Human Communities,* The Free Press, Glencoe, Ill, 1952, p. 86.

surrounding numerous semirural patches."[19] Within the metropolitan area the central city politically, socially, and economically dominates most areas outside its own politicogeographic boundaries. To classify properly the residential patterns of the United States' population, a new concept was devised by the Census Bureau and put into effect in 1950. As of that date, much of the nation's population was counted as inhabitants of *Standard Metropolitan Statistical Areas* (SMSA). The SMSA is a largely nonagricultural area containing a "mother city" or a pair of twin cities of at least 50,000 population. In the SMSA, unincorporated areas are strongly influenced by the general characteristics of the central city or cities. The 1970 census showed that there were 247 SMSAs, 148 of which had a combined population of over 139 million, showing an increase of 13.9 percent in ten years.

However, by 1960 a new category was needed. Some metropolitan areas had continued to grow to the extent that the end of one SMSA could not be distinguished from the beginning of another. To eliminate an artificial separation of residential areas, the concept of the *Standard Consolidated Area* was added to the list of classifications used by the Census Bureau. The Standard Consolidated Areas (SCA) are contiguous Standard Metropolitan Statistical Areas. At the introduction of this new classification only two SCAs were reported: New York—northeastern New Jersey (the largest) and Chicago—northwestern Indiana. The first is only part of Megalopolis.

THE GHETTO IN AMERICAN CITIES

As the problems of the city began to enter the consciousness of the American public, a new word was added to its vocabulary: "ghetto." However, the word is not a new one, nor is the ghetto a phenomenon in recent American history. A *ghetto* is a segregated area (or neighborhood) within a city whose inhabitants are largely confined to a single ethnic or racial category. This ecological pattern may well be as old as the city itself. Certainly it was a principal living arrangement for Jewish people in the medieval cities of Europe, and it has been a consistent pattern in America. Usually it emerges in the oldest parts of the city and houses the most recent group of immigrants. As any specific group becomes more "acceptable" to the dominant group of society, it usually experiences gains in prestige, economics, and power. When an immigrant group becomes economically successful it is likely to move out of the ghetto, leaving the neighborhood to less successful or more recent arrivals. Peter

[19]Edgar M. Hoover and Raymond Vernon, *Anatomy of a Metropolis*, Doubleday & Company, Inc., Garden City, N.Y., 1959, p. 2.

Ecological segregation:
natural areas

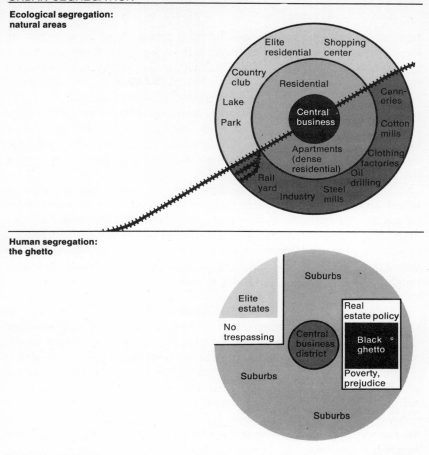

Human segregation:
the ghetto

I. Rose gives the following description: "In the metropolitan centers of the North the pattern was often repeated: the areas of original settlement successively became the ghetto-communities of the older settlers, the Irish and Germans, East Europeans, Jews, Italians and most recently, Negroes from the South, and Puerto Ricans."[20]

However, after World War II the nature of the urban ghetto began to change. Immigrants still came to the shores of the New World but not in massive ethnic or national units. The migration of greatest significance was an internal migration. Southern and rural blacks came in increasing numbers to the northern cities and settled in the deteriorated neighborhoods vacated by former Jewish and Italian immigrants. Of course, black

[20]Peter I. Rose, *They and We,* .Random House, Inc., New York, 1964, p. 33.

213

Americans were here long before the other groups, but they were among the last to urbanize. Once the process started, however, it moved rapidly. Broom and Glenn observed that by 1960, in the twelve most populous metropolitan areas, only 19 percent of the blacks lived outside the central city, whereas 55 percent of the whites lived outside the central city.[21] The same black urbanization continues. Between 1960 and 1970, white population in SMSAs increased 13.9 percent, while black population increased 31.6 percent.[22] This phenomenon has completely erased the old rural stereotype of black America and has changed popular usage of the word ghetto.

Traditionally, the ghetto communities of large cities represented urban areas distinct from one another in terms of cultural heritage, language, and customs. For example, in traversing New York City one might have passed through a neighborhood where Italian and English languages were used interchangeably, and end in an area where Chinese characters identified the different businesses. Such foreign language neighborhoods still exist, but today the word ghetto means "black."

Financial Problems   It is quite significant that the inflow of blacks to the cities has been paralleled by an outflow of whites. In a real sense, the development of suburban areas has been a major contributor to the growth of urban ghettos and major cause of the decay of core cities. It is no secret that the majority of urban blacks are poor and that the majority of suburban whites are at least economically comfortable according to national standards. As whites leave the city they take most of their taxable income with them, but still whites tend to control the power structure of the metropolis. The meaning of this chain of events is aptly conveyed by Kenneth E. Boulding:

> *The reason why cities are ugly and sad*
> *Is not that the people who live there are bad;*
> *It's that most of the people who really decide*
> *What goes on in the city live somewhere outside.*[23]

The suburb is intricately linked to the city. Were it not for the city's business and merchandising districts, it is unlikely that the suburb could support itself. Most of the suburban dwellers work in the city; it is their primary source of subsistence. It would seem that the suburban people

---

[21]Leonard Broom and Norval D. Glenn, *Transformation of the American Negro,* Harper & Row, Publishers, Incorporated, New York, 1965, p. 163.
[22]U.S. Dept. of Commerce, Bureau of the Census, *Statistical Abstract of the United States, 1972,* p. 16.
[23]Kenneth E. Boulding, "Ecology & Environment," *Transaction,* vol. 7, no. 5, March 1970, p. 40.

would become deeply concerned with its problems as the city's costs of transportation, street repair, police protection, fire protection, sewage and garbage removal, and urban redevelopment rise, but such is not always the case.

As analyzed by Norman Hill, in many states the rural and suburban vote tends to ignore the problems of the city.[24] Somehow the ghetto becomes unreal; ghetto life becomes a horror story intended to scare people in the same fashion as did Frankenstein's monster. Pure fiction! However, if it is not fiction, if such things do exist, it is better not to talk about them. The suburbanite is likely to go to the polls, vote "No" on state aid to the cities because it will increase his property tax, return home, turn on his television, and watch stories about crime, which he is sure can only happen to other people.

Urban Renewal   It would give an unfair and overly pessimistic view of American cities to deny that much has been done by way of urban renewal in many metropolitan areas. The numerous renewal projects of the 1950s removed deteriorated sections and made urban centers much more attractive for business than they had been. In many cases, though, urban renewal was spoken of by impoverished groups as "removal of the poor," or even as "black removal," because many projects cleared out housing that, however wretched, at least had the attraction of being cheap. Often no provisions were made for the people removed from urban slums. In 1966 a Model Cities program was initiated, aiming at spreading urban-renewal benefits to the poor by insisting that such projects use labor from within the renewal areas, make provision for housing for those who might be removed, and provide a balance between housing, business, and social service. The Model Cities program has brought a measure of improvement in some cases but has rarely done anything to prevent continued racial segregation and social-class segregation. The new housing continues to be out of the financial reach of the poor.[25] Amendments to housing and development acts have provided financial help to poor families toward home purchase or rental of apartments. Although of some help, the acts have been poorly funded in recent years, and they also fail to help the very poorest because the aid is usually extended to people above the defined level of poverty.

In recent years a New Towns program has been launched, drawing federal support from a housing bill of 1970. The idea is to promote the building of new, uncrowded towns, with a balance of housing, business, schools, and shopping facilities in an attempt to create real communities,

[24]Norman Hill, "The Crisis in the Cities," *Agenda,* vol. 4, no. 5, May 1968, p. 6.
[25]Jonathan H. Turner, *American Society: Problems of Structure,* Harper & Row, Publishers, Incorporated, New York, 1972, pp. 30–31.

rather than mere sprawling suburbs. After making a national survey of New Towns, Leonard Downie concludes that only a few have accomplished their multiple aim. Columbia, Maryland, has done rather well with racial integration; Cedar-Riverside, near Mineapolis, is congratulated for having mixed-income areas, multiple facilities, and more sense of an integrated community than is usual. In a majority of cases, though, the old problems remain. The New Towns attract only prosperous people, do nothing to promote racial desegregation, and often even miss their aim of reducing congestion and traffic problems. In crowded Orange County, California, especially, the New Towns are rapidly engulfed by the old towns in the familiar type of urban sprawl that rapidly fills up all green areas.[26] Downie and many other critics feel that some of the New Town projects of Europe show better planning, much more even benefits to various income groups, and far more concern for an overall development that leaves green belts to prevent the endless monotony of concrete. Progress has been made in many American cities too, but the nagging problems of slums and the deteriorated inner core are still with us.

MENTAL LIFE AND THE CITY

The city has been the focus of much criticism in American history, long before our current worries over water and air, traffic congestion, and racial segregation. Some of the criticism was merely that of a romantic love for nature, nostalgia for an old way of life close to the good earth, or the old man's warning against the temptations of the city. Rural life was seen as better than city life, closer to nature and to God. The Populists and followers of other farm movements argued against the interests of the urban East, not merely in economic terms, but in moralistic terms. The Eastern interests that William Jennings Bryan saw "pressing down upon the brow of labor this crown of thorns" were represented by city men—for the most part, New Yorkers and bankers.

Criticism by the American Intellectual More intellectual men than Bryan were also unhappy about the city. Jefferson worried about urban mobs and hoped for a nation that would forever preserve a rural orientation. Emerson echoed a similar theme. Morton and Lucia White[27] did a study of the anticity bias of large numbers of American intellectuals—Jefferson, Emerson, Melville, Hawthorne, Henry James, William James, Dreiser, Dewey, Park, and many more. We shall return to the views of Dewey and Park after first studying the perspectives of Georg Simmel, a German sociologist and a teacher of Robert Park.

[26]Leonard Downie, "The New Town Mirage," *Nation*, vol. 214, May 15, 1972, pp. 617–621.
[27]Morton White and Lucia White, *The Intellectual Versus the City*, Mentor Books, New American Library, Inc., New York, 1964.

Georg Simmel   Although Simmel (1858–1918) did not belong to the modern period of Megalopolis, his writings on the subject of interaction in the city and the effects of city life on intellectual and emotional life sound contemporary and have influenced sociological thinking up to the present day.

According to Simmel, the city calls for increased alertness on the part of the individual. More stimuli impinge upon the senses and nerves at all times, intensifying awareness and stimulating the mentality of the individual. At the same time, the emotional side of life begins to decline. People do not relate to each other as closely as in the less crowded areas of the country and village. People are seen more as competitors than as friends: `` . . . city life has transformed the struggle with nature for livelihood into an interhuman struggle for gain. . . . ''[28]

Simmel calls the essence of the city personality the *blasé attitude,* the feeling that one can take anything in his stride without becoming ruffled. The contrast is clear in the reaction to the tragedies that constantly occur in life. If a fatal accident occurs in a small town, everyone is concerned, there is common grief, and the incident lingers as a subject of conversation. In the big city, fatalities attract almost no notice. One listens to a recitation of traffic accidents on the local radio station, becomes bored with it, and turns to the latest hit songs.

The big-city dwellers must dismiss many things from their minds or face constant neurotic worry. The field of perception is narrowed to that part of the cityscape that concerns us—that and no more. This causes us to wall out other people. In apartment living it is not unusual to wall out the next-door neighbors. They are so close physically that social distance must be maintained for the sake of preservation of privacy. The walling-out process becomes a habit of mind and emotion. We do not see people whom we prefer not to see, nor do we see ``the other side of the tracks.'' Our view is limited and exclusive.

Robert Park and John Dewey   Simmel's point of view is similar to that of Park.[29] Because of a background in journalism, Park was particularly interested in the city from the viewpoint of communication. In the great city, he observed, communication between regions, social classes, and ethnic groups tends to break down. The major human problem of the city becomes that of preservation of a sense of community through mutual understanding and awareness of common interests and issues. Dewey[30] saw the problem in a similar way. He feared that the reduction

---

[28]Georg Simmel, ``The Metropolis and Mental Life,'' in Eric Josephson and Mary Josephson (eds.), *Man Alone,* Dell Publishing Co., Inc., New York, 1962, p. 162.

[29]White and White, *op. cit.,* pp. 160–170.

[30]*Ibid.,* pp. 171–180.

in primary-group interaction was a threat to democracy and that the city was too cold and impersonal for the interchange of opinions and ideas so necessary to the democratic process.

The Evidence Pro and Con   The criticisms of the city's effect on the mental and emotional life of people cannot be dismissed lightly. There is much evidence that tends to support the critics. Crime rates are higher in the city and so are rates of narcotics addiction, alcoholism, mental disorders, and suicide. The most deteriorated areas of our cities abound with people who seem to have been crushed by the urban struggle. The city is also the scene of riots and disorders (to be discussed in the next chapter). Such facts seem to argue strongly against the city, but some reservations must be made. Are these unfavorable traits characteristic of all urban areas or only of certain urban areas? Do they exist of necessity just because of the urban way of life, or are they amenable to improvement even under urban conditions?

Leo Srole and his colleagues, in their study of mental health in midtown Manhattan,[31] use descriptions reminiscent of Simmel—"city of strangers," "anomic," "loneliness in the crowd." They are describing a city of high competition, rapid pace, and considerable opportunity for the striver. They quote various people who like the area because it does not intrude on privacy or interest itself in small-town gossip. But the mental-health statistics are not encouraging; they show a rate of psychological impairment about three times higher than those found in a similar study of the smaller city of New Haven. There are, however, differences within midtown Manhattan, with the poor having considerably higher rates of psychological impairment than the middle class. It is also interesting to note that impairment rates were not as high in other parts of Manhattan as in its central section. Three areas in Manhattan were found that were almost perfect models of community concern, with self-help associations, recreational facilties, a jobs-for-youth service, and even open-air art shows and concerts. It seems that alienation is not an inevitability of the big city.

Whatever its psychological problems, the city environment is not as insistent upon tradition and conformity as the rural area. It is the city that protects and encourages the unusual artists or musicians; there they find kindred spirits to encourage them, people who form little subcultural groups interested in the very things that interest them. It is in the city that they will find the schools and libraries and art galleries and museums that

---

[31]Leo Srole et al., *Mental Health in the Metropolis: The Midtown Manhattan Study*, McGraw-Hill Book Company, New York, 1962, chaps. 7–8.

help to liberate the human mind. (The very word "civilization" derives from the Latin word for city.)

THE FUTURE OF THE CITY

Lewis Mumford asks, "If the places where we live and work were really fit for permanent human habitation, why should we spend so much of our time getting away from them?"[32] The dream of nearly every urban person is to have someplace—a cabin in the mountains, a bungalow at the beach, a cottage in the countryside—to "get away from it all." Of course, we like to go to the city for cultural activities and to do our shopping, but the truth is that few people really want to live there. This is the real urban crisis: When the city can no longer satisfy its inhabitants, the people no longer care about the maintenance of the city.

The cities will survive, but the question we now are asking ourselves, both public citizens and elected officials, is how shall they survive and in what condition shall we find them twenty years from now. Will the cities continue to deteriorate, or can they be revitalized? The answer lies in the extent and types of fiscal policy, political action, and social reform that develop. Hill[33] has proposed a threefold plan:

1. Creation of a national job pool. This first strategy for easing the frustration and decay of the cities would involve organization and planning by the federal government to move people to where jobs are available. It would mean moving people out of the inner city. People would have to be relocated near new employment centers, and they would have to be provided with integrated housing units, services of every nature, and schooling.

2. A national land policy. The creation of a national land policy would enable the federal government to buy up idle land held by speculators or to utilize land now in its possession in order to build new towns and communities. Such communities might be developed as "satellite cities"—smaller, self-sustaining cities located near large metropolitan areas. Such communities would draw their populations from presently overcrowded urban areas, thereby not only contributing attractive living space but easing the population pressure of the metropolis.

3. A national migration policy. In America, people are free to migrate wherever they desire, but some cities seem to repel migration

---

[32]Lewis Mumford, *The Urban Prospect,* Harcourt, Brace & World, Inc., New York, 1968, p. 9.
[33]Norman Hill, *loc. cit.*

because they do not match the expectations of potential immigrants. There are wide disparities, for example, in health and welfare facilties from city to city and state to state. Eliminating such disparities might serve to level off population densities by redistributing the people who now crowd into some cities and shy away from others.

The future of the ghetto within the city may well be as complex a problem as the future of the city itself. Jane Jacobs has reported that the slum ghetto is as much an organized way of life for its residents as is the suburb.[34] In some cases attempts at urban renewal may break down the cohesiveness and "sense of community" that separate the ghetto from the total culture of the city. Even though life in this part of the city may look bleak to the outside observer, it may well be meaningful and important to the inhabitant. Ghetto dwellers often resist the relocation programs that sometimes accompany urban-renewal projects because these programs destroy a way of life that is familiar.

Stanley Milgram concludes that people respond adaptively to the city and its patterns.[35] If this is the case, we may assume that such an adaptation might occur in such specialized areas of the metropolis as the ghetto and suburbia. These characteristics only complicate the matter of trying to understand the future of the city.

SUMMARY

Although the city is relatively new in history, it has gone through a number of interesting transformations. The ancient cities were independent entities that sometimes became centers of empires. Medieval cities also attained a degree of independence but usually encountered many of the same problems faced by the modern metropolis. The modern city is industrialized, larger in scope, and more involved in the economy and polity of the larger society.

Cities and population generally have been mutually dependent upon one another. Some cities have expanded, incorporating more territory and larger populations. Megalopolis now represents hundreds of cities and tens of millions of people merged together on the Northeast coast of the United States. Under such conditions, problems of air and water pollution (among others) are magnified.

In a sociological sense, ecology refers to the relationship of people to their social environment. In an ecological sense, humanity's history has been the history of progression from gemeinschaft (village commun-

---

[34]Jane Jacobs, *The Death and Life of Great American Cities*, Random House, Inc., New York, 1961.
[35]Stanley Milgram, "The Experience of Living in Cities," *Science*, vol. 167, no. 3924, March 1970, pp. 1461–1468.

ity) to gesellschaft (closely represented by Megalopolis). As cities' influences began to spread beyond their geopolitical boundaries, populations had to be counted in units referred to as Standard Metropolitan Statistical Areas, and in 1960 two Standard Consolidated Areas were delineated by the Census Bureau.

The ghetto is part of a city's ecological pattern. It is a segregated area within a city whose inhabitants are largely confined to a single ethnic or racial category. Although the ghetto may be a ''normal'' development within cities, and ghetto life may be meaningful to its residents, it is generally viewed by outsiders as a substandard part of the city.

According to Georg Simmel, the city has a dual effect on the mind of man, increasing his mental perception but interfering with emotional response. Whatever its faults, the city provides a mental freedom unknown in the small town.

Today the city faces many problems, and a number of proposals have been examined as possible solutions. Among them is a threefold proposal to create a national job pool, establish a national land policy, and institute a national migration policy. Despite the proposals, the problems remain with us, and the future of the city is unclear.

Chapter 10

Collective Behavior

. . . (T)he great waves of enthusiasm, indignation, or pity which sweep through a crowd do not originate in any one particular mind. They come to each of us from without and are liable to carry us away in spite of ourselves.

Émile Durkheim
The Rules of the Sociological Method

If all societal rules, roles, and procedures were perfectly patterned, there would be no need for a chapter on collective behavior. However, especially in modern societies, new developments and ideas constantly arise, calling forth mass actions in situations that display little social structuring. Collective behavior is the term applied to such actions, including fads and crazes, spontaneous audiences and crowds, many types of social movements, demonstrations and riots—in short, all the collective phenomena that sweep people into contagions of enthusiasm, fear, anger, or reforming zeal. The United States, with its restless and heterogeneous population, its freedom of expression and rapid communication, and its conflicts between ideal and social reality, has long been characterized by collective behavior of many kinds. Examples of such behavior range all the way from such inane frivolities as marathon dancing, flagpole sitting, goldfish swallowing, and, "streaking," to sincere and devout movements to wipe out alcohol, pornography, and sin, and to the horrors of lynch mobs and burning cities. What are the situations that erupt in spontaneous crowd behavior, demonstrations, and emotionalized attempts to affect public policy? What is the distinction between collective behavior and more structured types of group interaction?

COLLECTIVE BEHAVIOR IN EVERYDAY LIFE

Group life and group activity are inextricably bound to the human condition. Although it is true that each individual may have some influence on the group of which he is a member, it is incontrovertible that the group exercises a somewhat greater influence on the behavior of its members. In the study of collective behavior we are interested not only in the nature of the collectivity but also in the feelings and actions of the individual. People in an auditorium, quietly listening to a formal lecture, applauding politely at the conclusion, and then dispersing illustrate a structured situation.

On the other hand, audiences can reach a state of excitement in which members stimulate responses from each other, as in emotionally charged political rallies or old-fashioned revival meetings. Under other circumstances an audience may become so emotionally charged that, en masse, it may rampage through the streets, breaking store windows, hurling bricks, and injuring people.

An illustration of the type of collectivity, familiar to nearly everyone, that is often on the borderline between *structured* and *unstructured* behavior is the college football crowd. Much of the activity in this case is conventional: bands, cheer leaders, song leaders, half time entertainment, colors, flags, pompons, and all the paraphernalia of the football complex. However, the situation is such that unusual behavior arises; even the quiet person shouts and yells, jumps up and down, throws confetti, and acts in ways which would be difficult to predict from his otherwise constrained behavioral patterns.

To analyze the extremes of collective behavior, sociologists often use a tool known as the *idea-type continuum,* a model or theoretical construct that may or may not exist in reality. This model is composed of polar extremes or theoretical opposites separated by a continuum or line of variation from one extreme to the other. For example, if one extreme were white and the other black, the continuum would include all the possible shades of gray separating the polar opposites. In the case of collective behavior the polar extremes are represented by the type of collectivities that influence the feelings and activities of the individual.

The Crowd and the Public The *crowd* occupies one polar extreme on the continuum of collective behavior; the *public* occupies the other. The activities of the crowd include a number of patterns found in otherwise normal, everyday life. For one thing, as a member of a crowd, one does not cease to be a member of society, bound by many of the general norms of social interaction. For another, even in everyday social interaction one is strongly influenced by group activities, opinions, and norms. In the crowd there is *heightened suggestibility,* the feeling that one must go along with the action suggested by the entire group, whether it be laughter, exuberant shouting, or a destructive act of hostility. There is a sense of *loss of individual responsibility,* a feeling of *anonymity.* If the activities in which one participates are those suggested by the crowd as a whole, then how can one be held individually responsible for the outcome of that action? As a member of the crowd, one is also unidentifiable, simply a part of the audience, rally, or mob. *Lessened judgment and reflection* are apparent; one engages in collective behavior not because reflection leads him to think it is wise but because the collectivity has decided it for him. There is a sense of *invulnerability:* "No one can get the whole crowd of us!" In some cases there is a *moral ambivalence* to the crowd. In one sense, the crowd feels a "lofty morality," wrecking vengeance on the wicked and upholding equity and righteousness; but at the same time the crowd can commit every conceivable outrage and atrocity—stoning, hanging, burning, castrating, and otherwise killing or mutilating its victims.

The activities of the public are, at least theoretically, more rational. As a member of a public, one is not usually in close physical contact with others, and this greatly reduces the possiblity of engaging in activities such as those enumerated above. The *public* is a dispersed collectivity. It may think alike or feel alike, but it is not likely, except under extraordinary conditions, to act together, as does the crowd. The *lessened suggestibility* of the public is a function of the fact that a public is composed of individuals who make individual decisions. These decisions, of course, may be influenced by covert or subliminal propaganda, such as is used often through the mass media in advertising, or it may be overtly influenced by a skilled propagandist who openly attempts to convince individuals to accept his viewpoint.

Crowd
Heightened suggestibility
Loss of individual responsibility
Anonymity
Lessened judgment and reflection
Sense of invulnerability
Moral ambivalence

Public
Lessened suggestibility
Individual responsibility
Perceived individuality
Increased sense of individual judgment
Vulnerability
Accountability for one's actions

In either case the individual must accept sole *responsibility* for the decision. He is *not* an *anonymous* part of the crowd; he is a person who can be held accountable for his decision. As an individual, he is *vulnerable* to the philosophical or political attacks of others with whom he disagrees.

Classification of Crowds Even though crowds and publics occupy the polar extremes of the ideal-type continuum of collective behavior, they are not as distinctly oppositional as are black and white. Nor, for that matter, do all crowds occupy the polar extreme; some may approach or approximate the extreme, others may be only barely identifiable as crowds. Therefore, for the purpose of analysis we present the following typology of crowds, adapted in part from the work of Herbert Blumer.[1]

1. Casual crowds. A collectivity of people watching a demonstration in a department-store window may be classified as a *casual crowd*. Much of their behavior will not fit the characteristics of the crowd previously presented, but, under certain circumstances some of the characteristics might emerge. To a certain extent, people who are

[1]Herbert Blumer, "Collective Behavior," in Alfred M. Lee (ed.), *New Outline of the Principles of Sociology*, Barnes & Noble, Inc., New York, 1951, pp. 178–185.

225

physically together are also socially together because there is always a degree of social interaction. If, for example, a department-store employee is demonstrating a high-speed food blender in the store window, people may congregate on the street to observe the effectiveness of the product. If the demonstrator forgets to place the cover on top of the blender, turns the machine to high, and is then inundated by the contents of the receptacle, the casual crowd is likely to burst into laughter. A lone individual is not likely to stand in the street laughing aloud, although he may find the situation funny.

2. Conventional crowds. *Conventional crowds* are popularly called *audiences,* but, sociologically, their behavior is conventional in that most of their behavior is defined by the existing norms of the social system. Attenders of political conventions or collegiate dramatic presentations and spectators at football or basketball games typify the conventional crowd. Their behavior generally conforms to norm-role expectations, but circumstances may arise whereby extraordinary demonstrations may occur. If the home team is involved in a crucial game, the applause of the fans may be disproportionate to the achievements of the players. If by playing only a mediocre game the home team wins, the spectators are likely to tear down goal posts or carry the coach off the field. This unstructured behavior is built into the system so that each spectator will be sensitive to the emotions of fellow spectators and equally sensitive to the importance of the event.

3. Expressive crowds. The *expressive crowd* is generally organized in such a way as to permit personal gratification for each of its members. Generally its activity is viewed as an end in itself, with no objective other than the expression of group emotion. Some expressive crowds are fairly well-structured—a college dance; others are less structured—a religious revival meeting; and some are fairly unstructured—a campus demonstration. Although it may be argued that a campus demonstration may have objectives other than personal gratification (influencing public opinion or changing administrative decisions), it is true that while the demonstration is in effect the members are congregated for the purpose of expressing their inner emotions.

4. Orgiastic crowds. Although some sociologists may classify the *orgiastic crowd* as one form of expressive crowd, and others would place it in the category of the active crowd, this text will treat it as an aggregate different from either because it displays characteristics of both. In its structure and dynamics the orgiastic crowd is much like the expressive crowd, but there is a heightened suggestibility, anonymity, sense of invulnerability and moral ambivalence, and a lessened sense of individual judgment, responsibility, and reflection. Under such conditions the norm-role definitions that are generally maintained may be greatly modified or completely abandoned. New Year's Eve parties and Mardi Gras typify this behavior on a wide scale; on a smaller scale the orgiastic crowd may take the form of wife-swapping clubs or marijuana smokers.

5.   Active crowds. The *active crowd* is self-explanatory: The crowd is in action. Its behavior may be observed as an intergroup fight, act of destruction, or prolonged riot. In any case, the identity of the individual increasingly becomes transformed to an overall identity with the group. When this occurs, all the characteristics of crowd behavior are observable in the most extreme form. For analytical purposes we shall examine two manifestations of the active crowd: the mob and the rioting crowd.

The *mob* is a unified crowd with a single objective. Generally, it ignores norm-role definitions and the usual societal restraints. However, group control of the individual is quite strong because mob membership requires absolute conformity from its constituency. The lynch mob is a good example. The individual member shifts his sense of moral responsibility to the group and thus achieves a strange combination of sadism and righteousness. When "respectable" members of the community participate in a lynching without interference by local authorities, the situation could be described as *sponsored* by the local mores. The anti-Jewish *pogroms* of czarist Russia were deliberately promoted by the government, as were the attacks on the kulaks in leninist Russia. Long before the program of total extermination developed in Nazi Germany, destructive popular outbursts against the Jews had been promoted.

The United States, as a whole, has deplored such policies, but among local authorities there has been a parallel. A great majority of the lynchings of blacks (3,408 between 1900 and 1947) that have taken place in this country have been carried out by spontaneous mobs or Klan organizations, with little or no opposition from local officialdom. Erskine Caldwell has characterized the situation in his book *Trouble in July* in which the sheriff always manages to be away fishing when a lynch mob forms, even if he has to get up in the middle of the night to be "accidentally" gone.

A *rioting crowd* need not be unified; it may involve several groups of people in different locations. However, these groups will evolve almost simultaneously and engage in almost identical behavior. Riots have been common in the United States, and some of the historical cases should be mentioned so selective memories do not make us think that the urban disorders of today are entirely new. Antidraft riots in New York City during the Civil War period resulted in over 1,000 deaths. Fights between various immigrant groups and the old Americans have been common, as were fights between Catholics and Protestants. Radical labor organizations such as the Molly Maguires and the IWW have been involved in many acts of violence and have been falsely accused of many more. The Haymarket Riots of Chicago in 1886, culminating in a bombing, resulted in seven deaths. One of the most destructive riots of all time occurred in Chicago in 1919.

The rioting crowd is particularly characteristic of urban societies with pronounced religious, racial, or national divisions. Many riots occurred in North Africa before the end of French occupancy. Northern Ireland has been a scene of riots and bloodshed because of the deep religious hostility between Protestants and Catholics and the national hostility of both groups against the British. Riots involving minority groups have occurred frequently in the cities of the United States. The most widespread riots were those that broke out in the 1960s, especially in the spring and summer of 1967. Altogether eighty-three deaths were reported that year in forty-one riots listed by the President's Commission on Civil Disorders and designated serious or major.[2] The pattern of development of the riots was fairly consistent with sociological theory, although no sociologist was astute enough to predict the coming of the riots at the particular time they occurred, nor was anyone sure when they would end or whether they would recur.

Neil J. Smelser, a sociologist, provides a most enlightened analysis. He sees the city riot as the product of six conditions which, taken together, constitute "necessary and sufficient" cause for riots. That is, they must be present, or the city riot will not occur; if all six conditions are present, a riot is inevitable. These background conditions for what Smelser calls the *hostile outburst* are as follows:[3]

Structural conduciveness refers to the characteristics of a society that make crowd actions possible—a society of conflicting interests, with some groups unable to make themselves heard through legitimate means but with easy communication and accessibility to objects of attack. This idea of structural conduciveness is applicable to the labor riots of earlier times and to antiforeign riots and demonstrations. As applied to the city race riots, all the elements of structural conduciveness are present. The dilapidated ghetto dwellings of so many urban black neighborhoods lead to demands for new areas of settlement; whites oppose the gradual spread

[2]*Report of the National Advisory Committee on Civil Disorders*, Bantam Books, Inc., New York; 1968, pp. 6–7.

[3]Neil J. Smelser, *The Theory of Collective Behavior*, The Free Press, New York, 1962, pp. 222–269.

to new areas. The ghetto has its problems that are not handled by officialdom, and traditionally the group has not been heard very loudly at city hall. There is ready accessibility to the symbols of the power structure: business, rental properties, police and firemen.

Structural strains are the next ingredient in the explosive situation. On the physical side, these strains consist of such problems as inadequate housing, unemployment, and various forms of discrimination. On the normative level, strains have become especially intense in recent years because of an increasing acceptance of the ideal of equality and a lingering gap between the ideal and the practice. At the same time, greater awareness of the gulf between poverty and wealth heightens the feeling of relative deprivation—a condition whereby the gains of the poor fall further and further behind the greater gains of the middle class.

The spread of generalized beliefs is the next step toward a hostile outburst. Such beliefs spread through rumor, scapegoating, or knowledge of a specific incident. In many riots, these beliefs have centered upon the issue of police brutality and/or the economic exploitation of the poor. The ghetto creates an unenviable situation both for its residents and for the police who, because of public sentiment, should be well-trained men, sober in judgment, and cool in performance. No police force completely meets the requirements, and harassment takes place against both black and white lower-class people.[4] Whether such beliefs are true or greatly exaggerated is irrelevant as a background for riot; the important point is that people act on what they believe to be true.

Next, precipitating factors come into play. Sometimes the precipitating cause is more rumor than actual event, or it may be an insignificant event exaggerated by rumor. For example, in the Los Angeles area Watts riot the precipitating event was "the arrest of a drunken black youth about whose dangerous driving another black had complained."[5] While the motorcycle officer who made the arrest waited for a patrol car, an angry crowd began to form, and various versions of what had happened began to spread. A suspicious hate-laden atmosphere needs little to bring on an explosion of emotion. One need only remember that World War I was triggered by a single assassination.

Mobilization for action is also necessary. There is no implication of a vast plot on a national scale in either Smelser's theory or in the Report of the National Advisory Committee on Civil Disorders (known as the Kerner Report). However, there must be at least small organizations and violent

---

[4]Albert J. Reiss, Jr., "Police Brutality: Answers to Key Questions," *Transaction*, July–August 1968, pp. 10–19.

[5]Report by the Governor's Commission on the Los Angeles Riots, *Violence in the City: An End or a Beginning?*, State Printing Office, Sacramento, Calif., 1965.

leaders to harangue the crowd and spread leaflets. In the big city, mere physical proximity creates a situation in which organization is possible. Earlier in the history of this country, fear—induced by the dominant white group—was so strong in the South that mobilization of the black minority was made impossible.

Finally, there must be a *failure of social control*. If norms of nonviolence are strongly internalized, they will act as a factor for self-control. Although there were large numbers of counterrioters in all the disturbances of the summer of 1967 urging people to "cool it," there were obviously many who had no such feelings about nonviolence, especially among the more hostile ghetto dwellers. Attitudes toward community leadership were negative. If other agencies of control are adequate, the use of police as a controlling force is unnecessary; when social control breaks down, external controls (police or National Guard) are often brought to the scene.

This, very briefly, is Smelser's theory, with some supportive examples of our own. How does it align with the facts as ascertained by the President's Commission on Civil Disorders?

The terminology is different, but the conclusions are the same. On the subject of structural conduciveness and structural strains, we read "This is our basic conclusion: our nation is moving toward two societies, one black, one white—separate and unequal."[6] In the area of generalized belief, the commission concludes, "The police have come to symbolize white power, white racism, and white repression. And the fact is that many police do reflect and express these white attitudes."[7]

On the subject of precipitating causes, the commission reveals case after case in which there were a series of incidents, each intensifying a hostile situation. On the subject of mobilization for action, the conclusion is that the riots of 1967 were "not the consequence of any organized plan or 'conspiracy,' . . . but militant organizations, local and national, and individual agitators, who repeatedly forecast and called for violence, were active in the spring and summer of 1967."[8] Finally, the commission notes the ineffectiveness of social control in several ways: the complaints of inadequate protection for the nonrioters; the hostility of the rioters toward the police; the alienation of rioters from the normative structure; and the lack of training of police, especially National Guard troops, for coping with such emergencies. One of the tragic stories from Detroit illustrates the difficulty in the latter respect:

[6]*Report of the National Advisory Commission on Civil Disorders*, p. 1.
[7]*Ibid.*, p. 11.
[8]*Ibid.*, p. 9.

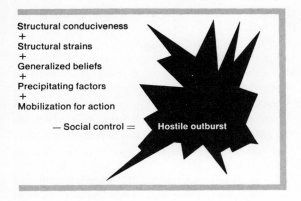

Structural conduciveness
+
Structural strains
+
Generalized beliefs
+
Precipitating factors
+
Mobilization for action

— Social control = **Hostile outburst**

Employed as a private guard, 55 year old Julius L. Dorsey, a Negro, was standing in front of a market when accosted by two Negro men and a woman. They demanded he permit them to loot the market. He ignored their demands. They began to berate him. He asked a neighbor to call the police. As the argument grew more heated, Dorsey fired three shots from his pistol into the air.

The police radio reported: "Looters, they have rifles." A patrol car driven by a police officer and carrying three National Guardsmen arrived. As the looters fled, the law enforcement personnel opened fire. When the firing ceased, one person lay dead.

He was Julius L. Dorsey.[9]

Looking back on the events of the 1960s, one can see that the President's Commission and a number of sociologists had much of importance to say about the causes of riots, although there is obviously much more to be known about the level of tensions and precipitating events. In a number of cities the President's Commission recommendations, calling for integration and training of police forces both in riot prevention and in intercultural understanding, have been attempted with fair success. The views expressed by the President's Commission and implied in Smelser's work, though, call for more integration of neighborhoods and sweeping improvements in slum areas. The source of the riots

[9]Ibid., p. 98.

was seen to lie in the internal conditions of the cities themselves. Yet many of the conditions described by Smelser are still present, but they do not always seem to lead to riots.

Seymour Spilerman[10] contends that one more ingredient figured in the riots of the 1960s: National events were necessary to set the stage for rioting—frustration over blockage of black upward mobility in the late 1960s, the civil rights movement, and the assassination of Dr. Martin Luther King. The rapid spread of the news by the mass media helped cause rioting to spread by imitation. On one point Spilerman's conclusions agree with Smelser's: Heavy crowding of the black population (part of Smelser's "structural conduciveness") correlated almost perfectly with areas of rioting. At present, though, sociologists do not really know enough to predict when such outbreaks will occur, if, indeed, it will ever be possible to know. Spilerman suggests that to find the answer we must look to national events, social movements, and general unease, not just to localized events in particular cities.

VARIETIES OF COLLECTIVE BEHAVIOR

The above examples of mobs and riots by no means exhaust the field of collective behavior. Such phenomena as mass hysteria and rumor often accompany riot situations but need a brief description of their own. There are also the interesting and often entertaining phenomena of fashions and fads. How do these diverse phenomena occur and how do they happen to fit under the general label of "collective behavior?"

Mass Hysteria   Mass hysteria is a widespread feeling of fear and threat, often brought on by panic situations. The hysteria that accompanied a 1938 radio drama of "War of the Worlds" proved harmless and amusing, but such cases are rare. In the late Middle Ages, mass hysteria developed when Christendom failed in its Crusades and later when it was rocked with dissension in the Protestant Reformation. Troublesome times led to increasing worry about the Devil and to a search for the witches who were acting as his agents. Hundreds of people were burned in a mass hysteria that lasted for centuries and finally found its way to Salem, Massachusetts. The term "witch hunt" has more recently entered our vocabulary to describe a situation in which subversive agents are being sought by an inflamed public, or people falsely believed to be subversive agents. In the 1920s America was obsessed with the idea that foreigners were trying to import communism into the United States, and as a result a

---

[10]Seymour Spilerman, "What We Know and What We Can't Know about Racial Disorders," paper presented at the American Sociological Association Convention, New York, Aug. 27–30, 1973.

wave of antiforeignism swept the country. The Ku Klux Klan was revived, this time even more hostile to foreigners and Catholics than to blacks.

Following World War II a similar wave of hysteria developed, led by Senator Joseph McCarthy, who claimed the State Department was literally swarming with communist agents. Suspicion fell on more and more people, with some extremists even accusing such conservative and respected Americans as General Marshall and President Eisenhower of being involved in the communist plot. By that time the charges were becoming so absurd as to cause a reaction, with lampooning of the witch hunters. Some college students were singing, to the tune of Battle Hymn of the Republic;

> Mine eyes have seen the horror of the coming of the reds;
> They are hiding in our closets; they are underneath our beds;
> They are tearing up Old Glory in a hundred million shreds;
> They'll get us one and all!

The song is amusing, but the hysteria was not. State Department career men were fired, and all the people most knowledgeable of China were discredited. Uncontroversial mediocrity was all that remained in many sections of the foreign service. Professors were frightened of "getting the axe," and the intellectual world no longer dared be bold and outspoken. Apparently, because major wars bring widespread dislocation and suffering and they fail to result in the happy and peaceful new world promised, they leave the public particularly prone to mass hysteria.

Rumors   It is very fashionable to castigate the rumormonger, and yet almost all people spread rumors to some extent. On the neighborhood level, rumors can be cruel almost beyond belief, destroying reputations and leaving people afraid to meet their neighbors. On the national scale, rumors can also be harmful. Rumors were deliberately spread in France by Germany to undermine confidence in the government of France during World War II. Occasionally "whispering campaigns" are deliberately started to ruin someone's business or political reputation, for example, the "dirty tricks" for which Donald Segretti was sent to prison for a short term in 1973.

There are also public situations that are almost sure to bring forth rumors. When there is little access to information, when things are being hidden from the public, and when officialdom conducts itself in a way to arouse suspicion, rumors are inevitable. Rumors are spread if they fit the preconception of the rumormonger. Democrats most easily spread rumors about Republicans, and Republicans about Democrats. Not only are rumors spread, but they grow, and in the direction of the preconceptions of the people who pass them along. Probably the best antidote to political rumors is honest, open information. Although the press is sometimes accused of spreading rumors, and is sometimes guilty, the level of rumor spreading is much greater when there is no open access to the news. Anyone who has had experience on a military base during times of great secrecy can easily attest to the prevalence of rumors.

Fads and Fashions   Fads and fashions are both included as part of collective behavior because both spread contagiously, but fads fit better the description of unstructured behavior. Fashions are usually promoted by designers and industry; in older times they were set by upper classes, often the nobility, and became almost a matter of mores. Woe unto the girl who wore short hair or a short skirt or the man who wore long pants instead of knee breeches! Even now fashions come much closer to formalized and regulated behavior than do fads. Fads arise spontaneously among the people and are usually of short duration. Like many forms of collective behavior, fads imply a dissatisfaction with things as they are. New fads in music can be interpreted as a revolt against the music of the previous generation, which now seems dull and repetitious. Fads are most prominent among "marginal people," those who do not feel a sense of full belonging to the system—the young, ethnic minorities, and lower classes. Adherence to fads is a means to an identity. Certain styles of dress, hair, slang, music, and entertainment give group identity.

It must be admitted, though, that fads are by no means exclusive to the young or to ethnic groups. In the 1950s, when hula hoops became a fad, many middle-aged people attempted swinging them around their middles to lose weight, and a number of them ended up with dislocated vertebrae or hips. In earlier decades, people of mature years suffered heart attacks during the marathon dance fad. There are special kinds of fads in business, musical, literary, and academic circles. This year one must read a particular author, see a particular play, or watch a series on TV or he can hardly keep up with the conversation of his or her peers. The individual follows the interests of the group in order to belong to it, whether the group is young, middle-aged, or old. We shall agree with most analysts that the compulsive nature of fads is usually stronger for the young than for the middle-aged, but it is by no means exclusive to them. As with so much collective behavior, there is a social contagion about fads and a compulsion to do what others are doing. The next area of collective behavior to be considered—public opinion—is in many respects more rational and reflective than fad behavior, but it too is influenced by social contagion.

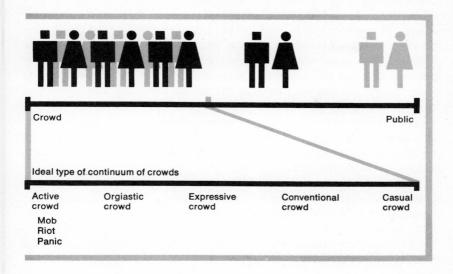

Crowd   Public

Ideal type of continuum of crowds

| Active crowd | Orgiastic crowd | Expressive crowd | Conventional crowd | Casual crowd |

Mob
Riot
Panic

THE PUBLIC AND PUBLIC OPINION

The public, unlike the crowd, is a dispersed collectivity. The individual member of the public is less likely to see himself as a member of a group and is therefore more likely to maintain his own sense of identity. He is interested in making decisions about matters of importance to him, and he tries to make them in a way that seems rational. The summation of all the decisions of individual members of a public is known as *public opinion*.

In some ways public opinion seems more organized than some of the types of crowds we have been discussing, but it also has a large element of spontaneity and unpredictability about it. Some communities allow urban deterioration to proceed to the point of no return before public opinion becomes aroused. Local graft and corruption become important issues sometimes, but sometimes they are bypassed. Nearly everyone is familiar with contemporary attempts to sound out public opinion relative to elections, and although methods have been carefully developed over many years, there is still an element of guesswork involved in predicting the winner.

There is even some difference in point of view as to the degree to which public opinion is spontaneous and the degree to which it is manipulated. Often the words "mass society" and "mass media" conjure up pictures of a public that is ruled and regulated by forces behind the scenes. In this case public opinion becomes only that which the leaders desire it to be. C. Wright Mills was prone to this type of analysis. He believed that contemporary public opinion is formed by a flow of information from the leadership downward to the people, whereas at some previous time opinion was formed at the grass-roots level and communicated upward.[11] However, he admitted that in our present society there are countervailing powers in the leadership, but he feared that countervailing forces were on the decline in a world in which major decisions must be made in areas where the public is in a poor position to judge—for example, military affairs.

Whatever the merits of Mills' view, public opinion is still important enough for tremendous sums of money to be spent on its maniuplation, whether for sales promotion or for winning elections. Public relations firms become increasingly prominent in building favorable images of products and corporations, candidates, parties, and officeholders. Some of the techniques used are argument and debate, presenting evidence, and giving reasons. Many methods of winning the public, however, are such well-worn techniques of propaganda as catchy slogans, name calling, card stacking, or the transfer technique of throwing the luster of the "Party of Lincoln" or the "Party of Jefferson" on a collection of lackluster candidates for local office. If the success or failure of such techniques depended entirely upon the intelligence of the audience, then public opinion could be considered purely rational, deliberate, and hardly connected with the rest of what has been described as collective behavior.

The difficulty is that public opinion can be manipulated in subtle ways, ways difficult to argue with: sheer volume of publicity, good photography, the well-selected clothes and practiced mannerisms of the candidate, the right colors, effective "spots" on television, and all other techniques of image making. If the opposition lacks the money or the shrewdness to fight back just as effectively, a bandwagon effect can be created. The bandwagon technique is a manipulative device that brings public opinion into line with much of the rest of collective behavior. Much of the compulsive power of fad and fashion and crowd interstimulation is brought to bear. Everyone is said to be switching over to Candidate A; there is a ground swell of enthusiasm for him, and enthusiasm is contagious. The time comes when only the most committed people will risk the stares of their neighbors by posting signs for the rival

[11]C. Wright Mills, "The Mass Society," in Eric Josephson and Mary Josephson (eds.), *Man Alone: Alienation in Modern Society*, Dell Publishing Co., Inc., New York, 1962, pp. 505–516.

candidate. This is not to say the bandwagon technique is so effective as to wipe out the opposition entirely, but the efforts of political parties to create (or even to fake) the so-called ground swell is evidence enough that the shrewdest politicians feel that nothing succeeds like the image of success. The ground swell of enthusiasm is the very factor that changes rational public decision making into something fairly close to crowd behavior. The growth of public relations firms and the merchandising of candidates leads many to fear that even a fairly well-educated society might lose much of its ability to make rational decisions.

This very brief discussion is enough to demonstrate the complexities of public-opinion formation and public-opinion research. It is an oversimplification to say at the end of each election campaign, "The public has spoken clearly." It is also erroneous to assume that the public is always putty in the hands of the mass media, the establishment, or whatever term is used to designate the supposed controller of opinion.

SOCIAL MOVEMENTS

Social movements are usually attempts to influence the future of society by means of popular action rather than merely leaving policy decisions to elective legislative bodies. A few movements are of a utopian communal type, and a few others partake of the nature of expressive crowds, more concerned with reaffirmations of faith and resolutions for righteousness than with actual influence on policy. Such has been the case with many evangelistic movements in American history. Most movements, though, attempt to influence public policy, whether to move it toward a brighter future or to try to restore some of the practices and values of the past.

As with other types of collective behavior, social movements differ in type from the completely spontaneous and unpredictable to the relatively organized and controlled. John D. McCarthy and Mayer Zald[12] suggest that the trend is toward well-organized, controlled, and even "professionalized" social movements, promoted by trained leaders and contributed to by people who send their dues to Common Cause, Zero Population Growth, the American Civil Liberties Union, Nader's Raiders, and various war-on-poverty and minority-rights groups. Some of the organizations are almost identical to voluntary associations, the only difference being that they are working for the types of social change usually advanced by social movements. Such movements have received funding from churches, national foundations, or even the federal government.

[12]John D. McCarthy and Mayer N. Zald, *The Trend of Social Movements in America*, General Learning Press, Morristown, N.J., 1973.

On the other hand, traditional social movements have involved a social situation calling forth feelings of discontent expressed by many ill-organized people who do not know how to proceed with remedial actions. After protests spread widely, leaders emerge who define the problem clearly, develop an ideology, gain financial support from their followers, and apply pressure to the proper areas of government or other institutions. Such a description would apply fairly well to early labor movements, the nineteenth-century women's rights movement, the Prohibition movement, and, at an earlier period, the antislavery movement.

The position of McCarthy and Zald is perfectly valid for many modern professionalized movements in which leaders of established organizations focus attention on social problems rather than waiting for a spontaneous wave of popular protest. There are, however, modern movements that follow the traditional model: the civil rights movement, long led, but by no means started by, Dr. Martin Luther King; the new women's rights movement; anti-Vietnam war movements of a few years ago; an agricultural labor movement led by Cesar Chavez; an environmentalist movement encouraged by such organizations as Sierra Club, but not started by them; and a commune movement (already on the wane) without a national leader. Most of these movements have leadership, but there is no doubt that the leaders are simply organizing and effectively vocalizing widely felt grievances. These are what we call "classical-type" social movements as opposed to what McCarthy and Zald have termed "professionalized" movements. Obviously the professionalized movements are the ones that come close to the previous description of public opinion, whereas the classical type of social movement comes a little closer to spontaneous crowd behavior.

Another and more common way to classify movements is to ask whether their aim is to set an idealized model for the world to follow, to try to restore an older order, to reform certain aspects of the social order, or to make a total revolutionary change. These types of movements are called, respectively, utopian, reactionary, reform, and revolutionary.

The Genesis of a Utopian Movement   Throughout the decade of the 1960s there was a rising tide of discontent about the trend of modern industrial society that probably helped to generate environmentalist as well as antiwar movements during the Vietnam conflict. Other fallouts from the same feeling of discontent included student movements and campus demonstrations as well as a reaction against rational-scientific thought in favor of increasing interest in astrology, drug-induced states of mind and vision, a fascination with witchcraft, and imitation of Eastern mysticism, and other forms of world rejection. An interesting development arising out of negative attitudes toward urban-industrial society was a rise in the number of experimental communes in the country —something by no means new in American history, but maintained by a new rationale. Older American communes had been formed either as religious utopias or as attempts on a small scale to make cooperative commonwealths a way of life. The new communes often developed from a feeling that modern-industrial society is doomed.

Bennet M. Berger[13] investigated a large number of hippie-type communes. He admittedly started with a negative attitude toward them but eventually developed a real admiration for at least some. In his analysis, the new communes are not too divergent from some of the older communes of historical America, with their religious and utopian motivations. Early religious communes sought to save the few faithful from a satanic world. Modern communes seek salvation from an urban-industrial society whose collapse is believed to be imminent. The communal life is a hard life, and it is not surprising that many communes fail. What is more surprising is that in the early 1970s a number were still alive and flourishing, despite their countering the economic trend of the modern world and the immaturity and inexperience of their members.

In general, the communes exhibit four features that help to hold them together: (1) The collective learning of survival skills (farming, building, repair) to maintain life when industrial society collapses; (2) an equalitarian ethos extending to men and women, children, and racial minorities; (3) group belongingness developed into something resembling close kinship ties; and (4) a new sanctification of life and a sense of purpose. Children are reared in an easygoing manner without the tension displayed by middle-class parents in trying to make their children "amount to something." Children, Berger says, are looked upon as "healthy plants" that will grow at their own rate with only a little encouragement, able to adapt to a world whose old order is in a state of collapse. As is the case in a number of religious communes, a belief in the falsity of the world's values is a necessary ingredient for holding the communes together and giving them purpose. The other kinds of social movements to be discussed all assume the urban-industrial world is here to stay, but they wish to redirect it in one way or another.

Reactionary Movements   Like all social movements, the reactionary type has a background in structural strain. Those who join a reactionary movement see the ills of modern society as a consequence of recent changes. To them the way to improve society is to return to the "good old

[13]Bennet M. Berger, "American Pastoralism and the Commune Movement," paper presented at the American Sociological Association Convention, New York, Aug. 27–30, 1973.

days.'' The Ku Klux Klan after the Civil War attempted to restore a sizable remnant of the old order, and later white supremacy movements have aimed at similar goals. Antiforeign movements have occurred several times in American history, attempting to keep the racial and ethnic composition of American society the same as it was in earlier times. The America First Movement before World War II attempted to return the United States to its traditional policy of isolation and avoid involvement in the war against Hitler. In recent years, the John Birch Society has been known for its attempt to restore what its members think of as traditional American values and resist what they see as a communist plot to take over America.

Often local movements to reduce tax spending draw more support than most of the movements just mentioned. Their members would not necessarily be reactionary in many respects, but they would nevertheless aim at reducing government services to the level of previous years. Movements with such limited objectives are obviously different from the more thoroughgoing reactionary movements mentioned above.

Reform Movements In general, reform movements are aimed at accomplishing the announced values and ideals of the society that, according to the members, have not yet been realized. In the past we have witnessed the antislavery movement, labor movements, the suffragette movement, and the Prohibition movement. More recent years have seen a rash of movements. The civil rights movement, working for equal rights for black Americans, has been followed by an equally militant Chicano movement and the American Indian movement, as well as a new women's liberation movement, and even a gay liberation movement. All such movements aim at granting rights to people regardless of race, ethnic group, or sex. Other prominent movements of a reform nature include the movement to organize farm labor, environmentalist movements, antipoverty movements, population-control movements, and consumers' movements.

Some of the reform movements are newer versions of ones that first occurred long ago. The civil rights movement was necessary because the freedom movement stopped far short of equality for black Americans. The new women's liberation movement has arisen because the mere granting of the right to vote did not solve the women's problems of employment, promotion, and social equality. Other movements, such as Zero Population Growth, are entirely new because new types of problems are now facing the society.

Revolutionary Movements Revolutionary movements usually aim at achieving an ideal society, just as the utopian commune movement

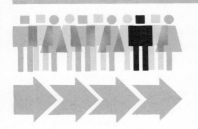

Crowd

Short-range group goals

Individual sees himself
as member of group

Physical proximity necessary

Public

Short- or long-range
individual goals

Individual does not see
himself as member of group

Physical proximity unlikely
and unnecessary

Social movement

Long-range group goals

Individual sees
himself as member of group

Physical proximity unnecessary

discussed above attempts to do. The difference is that the revolutionary movement wishes to reorganize the total society rather than merely to set up a little model society of its own. The word "revolutionary" can be applied to a movement that aims at total change, even if it does not aim at accomplishing the change by violent methods. In this sense the communist movement is revolutionary, even though in some countries the communists have cooperated with more moderate parties and agreed to constitutional means of working toward their goals. The Black Muslim movement in the United States can also be included as revolutionary in that it aims at a total change. At one time Muslim advocates of black nationalism proposed that a separate black state be set up within the United States and that this state be inhabited and administered solely by members and sympathizers of the movement.

The Third World movement is one that involves certain groups within the United States, but it also has a strong international appeal and following. The movement is aimed at all oppressed peoples or people who feel they are being oppressed. It has a strong bent toward socialist philosophy and a real, but unsystematized, goal of social revolution.

SUMMARY

Collective behavior is the behavior of an aggregate of people. It may take the form of a crowd, wherein one might observe physical proximity, loss of individual responsibility, anonymity, lessened sense of judgment and reflection, a sense of invulnerability, heightened suggestibility, moral ambivalence, and increasing group identity. An aggregate of people may take the form of a public—a dispersed collectivity representing the polar extreme opposite that of the crowd and displaying all the opposite characteristics. Finally, it may take the form of a social movement, with long-range goals and elaborate organization.

Crowds may be analyzed according to where they "fit" on a continuum. The continuum is a line of variation, but along the line we may observe certain points that are descriptive of distinct types of crowds—casual, conventional, expressive, orgiastic, and active. Active crowds may also be classified according to the patterns they display and the structure they assume—mobs, riots, or panics.

As a member of a public, one is interested in making private decisions, although his decisions may be subject to manipulation by others. The collective product of all private decisions is called public opinion, and the manipulation of public opinion is referred to as propaganda. Although propaganda is effective in some situations, it may also have a boomerang effect and achieve the opposite results in other situations.

Public opinion that is favorable to a particular social movement may help to further the cause of that movement. All social movements have a background in structural strain, but different movements react differently in attempting to relieve the strain. Reactionary movements generally aim at returning to a previous and more "sane" social order. Reform movements try to improve the existing system. Revolutionary movements would like to change the system to one that is more ideal or utopian.

PART FOUR ART: Siva subtly works his will in the traditional realm of formalized institutions. All the social institutions are interlaced in agreement. All are together in the attitude of maintaining their position. However, Siva, appearing to be part of these structures, infiltrates and works his influence on them.

Part Four

Changing Institutions

Institutions are defined in sociology as the formalized, socially approved methods of carrying out the requirements of the folkways and mores. Such a definition places institutions firmly in the realm of Vishnu, the God of Preservation, because they are not only connected with normative values but are bound up in habit, formality, and tradition. Because institutions are necessary for the survival of society, they draw the devotion of its members. To the United States citizen, not only is religion sacred, but so are the family, the school, the free-enterprise system, and constitutional government. Families provide for the protection and care of the young, for intimacy and affection, for a refuge from the impersonalized world. Religion fills the gap between observable reality and desire; it reassures; it lends support to the normative order, and on occasion is a tremendously strong unifying force.

Education acquaints the younger generation with the cultural tradition and prepares the next generation for taking its place in society. The economic system is thought of as more than a mundane matter of money and livelihood; it is glorified into a system of economic freedom. Government is a means of making and enforcing laws and protecting from enemies, but it is much more than that. Government is the institution that symbolizes the society more than any other and sets the societal tone as democratic, aristocratic, oligarchic, or dictatorial. People feel very emotional about their system of government and are sure it is better than the governmental systems of rival states.

All the major institutions, then, have about them an aura of the sacred, the traditional, and the eternal. Siva, Destroyer of the Old, entered into each of the previous topics we studied. One would think he could be excluded from a study of the sacred institutions, but alas for the old order, he intrudes into the traditional realm as well as everywhere else!

The family has changed. It lacks the old-time cohesion and forcefulness, and more alternative patterns of life become possible. Paternal authority weakens in a society that calls for increasing degrees of freedom and equality and gives decreasing heed to status. Religion remains strong in some social classes but has lost most of its influence in education, government, and the formation of laws. Religion too has become more varied in form, with many people following what strictly orthodox members of older generations would have called heathen gods. Education has become more necessary, longer, less exclusive, but in so doing it has had to become more innovative, less traditional. The greatly vaunted free-enterprise system of economics has had its freedom encroached upon by gigantic corporations, the rise of managerial enterprise and multinational enterprise, and an increasing concordance with government. Government too has grown vast and bureaucratic, entering into areas once denied it. The old rule book which once said, "That government is best which governs least," has been completely discarded. Thus we find that the discussion of institutions, like all previous sociological discussions, must be constantly related to the God of Change. In the following chapters we shall see in more detail what these changes are and in what subtle ways Siva works his will.

Chapter 11

The Family in the Modern World

A man must be with his family to amount to anything with us. . . . In the white ways of doing things the family is not so important. The police and soldiers take care of protecting you, the courts give you justice, the post office carries messages for you, the school teaches you. Everything is taken care of, even your children if you die; but with us the family must do all of that.[1]

Pomo Indian quoted by permission of Burt Aginsky
"An Indian's Soliloquy"

As the above quotation suggests, there are societies in which the family embraces all modern institutions—government, law, economics, religion. In ancient China the sage Confucius spoke of the family as the foundation of the state. Comte said that the family, not the individual, should be thought of as the social unit for study in the developing science of society. Cooley called the family the first and most ideal example of

[1]Burt Aginsky, "An Indian's Soliloquy," *American Journal of Sociology*, vol. 46, 1940, pp. 43–44.

primary groups, those groups that are a "nursery of human nature" and the creators of the finest sentiments known to man. Every politican running for office keeps up the family image with a smiling picture of himself, his wife, and his children. The family would seem to be the most secure of all institutions.

Yet there is much concern about the family in modern society because of slowly rising divorce rates, the "generation gap," difficult children and harassed parents, and the gradual absorption of more family duties by the school and other institutions. Has something suddenly gone wrong in the "nursery of human nature," or have there always been problems? In the midst of our troubles, do we sometimes look upon family life of older societies with a nostalgia that it does not entirely deserve?

CONTRASTING FAMILY AND MARITAL TYPES

A comparative view of family types may help to answer these questions. The types of families found in the world are interesting and greatly varied. Some are based upon polygynous marriage, with one man to several wives; a few are polyandrous, with one wife for several husbands. In a few cases marriage ties are of minimal importance, and the real care of the children is vested in the mother and her brother. This has been true of some of the Pueblo Indians of the Southwest and of the Nayars of the Malabar Coast of India. Sometimes the married couple moves to the man's village (*patrilocal residence*) and sometimes to the woman's village (*matrilocal residence*). Lineage is sometimes traced through the mother's line but more frequently through the father's line. All these and many other variations are of interest and theoretical importance in the development of social systems but are of less importance for the present study than another underlying difference in family arrangements. Does the family include large numbers of relatives, held closely together by the kinship bond, or is it a small, isolated unit? How powerful an institution a family is depends to quite an extent upon the answer. We shall describe two contrasting family models to illustrate the difference in structure and function and the consequent differences in the strength of the family organization.

The Consanguineal Family   The first family model, the one particularly typical of China in the days before the Communist Revolution, consists of a large number of kinsmen living under one roof or in close proximity to one another—often the grandparents, their sons, their sons' wives and children, and even their sons' children's children. The word "consanguineal" is applied to this type of family, meaning literally "of one blood," but in this case applied only to relatives of the father's line. There is a strong allegiance to the family elders, and even deceased ancestors are held in high respect. Rules of status and etiquette make the family a well-regulated system in which each member knows his proper place. The family as an entity is far more important than the individual; consequently marriages are usually arranged by "wise old parents" rather than depending upon the whims of young lovers. Males are dominant, and the young bride is responsible to her husband and his parents. A famous statement in the writings of the ancient Chinese philosopher Mencius gives an interesting idea of the length to which female inequality was carried:

> It does not belong to a woman to determine anything of herself, but she is subject to the rule of the three obediences. When young she has to obey her parents; when married she has to obey her husband; when a widow she has to obey her son.[2]

The basic link in the consanguineal family is between father and son, and it takes precedence over the husband-wife bond. This family has an eternal quality about it: Members die but are replaced by other members, and the family as an entity goes on forever. There is a well-defined division of labor between man and woman. Although the formal rules give the advantage to men, women often gain status and prestige with the passing of years. The young are subordinated to the old so that the family has a conservative, unchanging character about it. This family is well-adapted to an agricultural society where tradition is strong and change is slow and where all members must work together to survive. It gives a sense of belonging and security, although the individuals must subordinate their desires to the good of the family group. Even before the Communist Revolution the old type of family was gradually changing, especially in the urban parts of China under the impact of modern technology.[3] In rural areas, family structure is still strong.

The Nuclear Family   The opposite type of family can be called the *nuclear* or *restricted conjugal family,* consisting of a married couple and their children. It is typical of the middle class but by no means the only type of family found in America. This family is fairly well-separated from

[2]Will Durant, *Our Oriental Heritage, Story of Civilization,* vol. I, Simon & Schuster, Inc., New York, 1954, p. 683.

[3]Ch'ing-k'un Yang, *The Chinese Family in the Communist Revolution,* The M.I.T. Press, Cambridge, Mass., 1959. For description of consanguineal family, see also Francis L. K. Hsu, *Under the Ancestors' Shadow: Chinese Culture and Personality,* Columbia University Press, New York, 1948. See also David Mace and Vera Mace, *Marriage East and West,* Doubleday & Company, Inc., Garden City, N.Y., 1959.

Consanguineal family

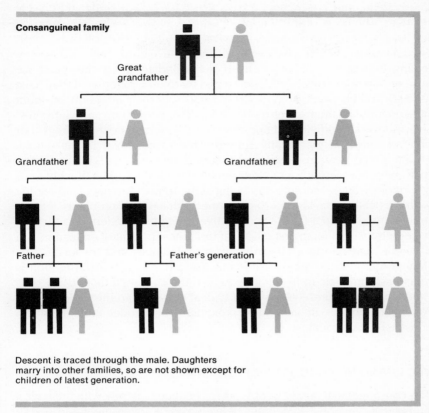

Great grandfather

Grandfather

Grandfather

Father

Father's generation

Descent is traced through the male. Daughters marry into other families, so are not shown except for children of latest generation.

Nuclear family

other relatives, visiting only occasionally if at all. "Conjugal" refers to the marriage tie, and "restricted" means that the family includes no outside relatives. The basic unit is that of a husband and wife who have married for love, with or without the approval of anyone else, often on short acquaintance. As parents, the man and wife do not have the secure feeling that goes with well-defined status and role, but they read the current literature on care of children and try to remember what they have learned in their psychology classes. They have their moments of doubt but congratulate themselves on being modern, democratic, and unrepressive. Above all, individual happiness is the goal, and neither parents nor children must be too greatly subordinated to the good of the whole. Husband and wife are equal and have the right to equal gratification in marriage; otherwise it is not worthwhile. This family can be thought of as a temporary entity, coming into being at the time of marriage and ending with the death of the last marriage partner. Whatever its problems, it tends to free the individual for the competitive struggle of modern society with its requirement of changing places of residence, pursuit of education and a career, and constant changing of acquaintances and associates. Although many of the family sentiments remain, this type of institution is much less familistic in its orientation than the consanguineal family. The American family presented is most typical of suburban middle class, but American families in general approximate this model more than the consanguineal model.

THE CHANGING FUNCTIONS OF THE FAMILY

The consanguineal family is, obviously, the type of family with the largest number of functions, sometimes being almost a government and social-security system of its own. In modern societies families have tended to lose some of their traditional functions as other social institutions grow iin importance. The family functions that show sufficient change to require discussion are sexual regulation and procreation, status ascription, economic interdependence, education, recreation, and care of the aged.

Sex Regulation and Procreation At first glance the functions of sexual regulation and procreation might seem to be constants in a society. All societies impose certain restraints on sex (an incest taboo as a bare minimum), although few have attempted to impose the absolute rule that no sexual relations can be tolerated outside of marriage. This puritanical standard has long been thought of as the ideal norm in America, although it has been violated by a large part of the male population. Violation of the sexual norms by many males, but only a few females, was once made possible by prostitution. In recent decades more women also have sexual relations outside of marriage, although usually with men they love and hope to marry. The change is gradual, however, and not the sudden "sex revolution" played up in the popular press. A collection of statistical surveys, in spite of a few inconsistencies, generally indicates the gradual nature of the change in sexual behavior.[4] A poll of college students in late 1969 found 61 percent of the men and 35 percent of the women students reporting premarital or extramarital relations.[5] It is noteworthy that those majoring in business—in many respects a conservative group—rated highest in premarital affairs. Apparently political and sexual conservativism do not go hand in hand. The uneven rates reported by the two sexes indicate that at least a few of the women must have a permissive philosophy.

Statistics on premarital relations do not imply that pressure for marriage has declined, but they do indicate that the romantic ideal of the "woman on the pedestal" has declined. Men and women are more nearly equal in "sin" as well as in politics. This so-called new morality is by no means universal, and its impact on marital success is not clear, but the point is that sexual relations are less restricted to marriage than in the past, and the modern family is less able to teach strict sexual norms to its children. It is also much more common for a trial marriage to take place, with young couples simply living together, eventually marrying if compatible, but otherwise breaking up and trying new partners.

Procreation is still considered legitimate only within the context of marriage and family, but it is estimated that one-fourth of all brides are pregnant at the time of marriage.[6] This means that many couples start marriage with a child on the way, which is only an extreme case of a very important trend regarding procreation: the tendency for nearly all children to be born while the parents are still young. In 1890 the average age of the father at the time of birth of his last child was 36; by 1959 the age was 27.9. For the mother the corresponding ages were 32 and 25.8. Since life expectancy for the wife had increased by ten years in the same length of time, and for the husband by more than five years, the conclusion can be drawn that the responsibilities of parenthood occupy a small portion of the total lifetime of the family. Much of the work of the family is completed while the parents are still fairly youthful; the dependence of member upon member does not last as long as it once did.

[4]Erwin O. Smigel and Rita Seiden, "Decline and Fall of the Double Standard," *The Annals of the American Academy of Political and Social Science,* vol. 376, March 1968, pp. 7–17.

[5]"The New Mood on Campus," *Newsweek,* vol. 74, December 1969, pp. 42–45.

[6]"Middle-Class Litters," *Nation,* vol. 200, June 28, 1965, p. 687.

Table 11-1 Median Age at First Marriage, 1890 to 1970.

Year	Male	Female
1890	26.1	22.0
1920	24.6	21.2
1930	24.3	21.3
1940	24.3	21.5
1950	22.9	20.3
1955	22.6	20.2
1960	22.8	20.3
1965	22.8	20.6
1967	23.1	20.6
1970	23.2	20.8

Source: U. S. Dept. of Commerce, Bureau of the Census, *Statistical Abstract of the United States,* 1968, p. 61, and 1972, p. 62.

Family Status   Looking next at the concept of *ascribed status,* it can be shown that awareness of family status is less acute than in the past. Admittedly the family still tries to give the children all the advantages it can (in this respect it is one of our antiequalitarian institutions), and in the case of "old money" families these advantages are very considerable and persistent. For the average middle-class family there is a strong contrast. Formerly such a family lived in a small town and was well-known by reputation. Everyone knew about the Van Bluebloods in their mansion and about the Joads in their shack. Family status persisted. Now, on the other hand, the children of each family go to a large, anonymous school in a big, anonymous city and will eventually hold positions working for an equally anonymous corporation. Also, the achieved status of the individual is no longer expected to be that of his parents. In the days of an agricultural society occupations were much more apt to be inherited than they are now. All these changes weaken the family's ability to give the children a permanent ascribed status.

Economic Change   By far the most important area of function change for family is in the field of economics. This applies to economic interdependence of family members and to family cooperation in economic production. The eminent French anthropologist Claude Lévi-Strauss[7] provides an interesting insight into the first of these economic factors in family. He concludes that the institution of marriage

[7]Claude Lévi-Strauss, "The Family," in Harry Shapiro (ed.), *Man, Culture, and Society,* Oxford University Press, New York, 1960, pp. 261–285.

is most compulsive in a society in which the division of labor between men and women is so clear cut and absolute that the single or divorced person finds existence almost unbearable. This, he goes on to say, is much more important than sexual attraction in many societies where extramarital relations are easily tolerated. Shaw's famous witticism that the popularity of marriage derives from its combining the maximum temptation with the maximum opportunity hardly applies in such cases. The dependence of man and woman upon each other for survival does apply. In modern Western societies, with women achieving greater and greater economic equality and independence, this reason for remaining married is far less compelling than in the past.

The other economic change, which is even more important, is in the role of the family as a unit. Once the average family was a collective enterprise, running a farm, blacksmith shop, grocery store, or other small business. Boys learned their occupational roles from their fathers and girls from their mothers. Children were in constant contact with the parents, absorbing their knowledge, their views, their mores, and also their old wives' tales, superstitions, and prejudices. Now children spend far more time at school, and the father has a job that keeps him away from home. The family no longer earns its living together—a strongly integrative function—but is more inclined to compete in the spending of the income, a somewhat divisive function.

Education, Recreation, and Protection   Education and recreation remain, to some degree, family functions. Certainly the family is concerned with them, but family members learn different specialities in school. The teaching changes with each generation, and increasingly the methods and content of education are thought of as the business of the school. Because families are extremely uneven in their ability to give mental stimulation to young children, there are increasing attempts to get children from slum homes into preschool programs to give them a better start in life. For many other families, including the affluent middle class, there is a slow trend toward more nursery schools to ease the burden of child care for working mothers. Even the old family function of discipline is, to a great degree, turned over to the school. The family carries on certain recreational activities together, especially when the children are young, but commercialized facilities now make an age grading of recreation more and more possible, with family members going their own separate ways.

The family role of protection and care for the aged has almost disappeared. Social security and welfare services represent institutional efforts to care for the aged in other ways, and private enterprise is now opening beautiful retirement communities for those aged who are sufficiently affluent to afford them. Convalescent homes are a booming business, providing for the less affluent and for the senile among the elderly, but often are poorly run and provide only minimal custodial care. Despite much sentimentality over such institutionalized occasions as Mothers' Day, the aged, as a class, tend to be poor and increasingly separated from the main currents of life.

Shortcomings of Families of the Past   Lest the above description sound like nostalgia for the past, it should be pointed out that there were also strains in older types of families. Dire economic necessity undoubtedly forced many women to tolerate mistreatment. Children were often thought of as an economic investment and were overworked. Many times families were rendered miserable taking care of ancient, tyrannical grandparents. We shall examine various possibilities for evaluating changes in family function; the main point until now is that the changes have had the cumulative effect of making the family an institution with fewer functions than it once had and not as strongly compelled by economic or other necessity to remain together.

INTERPRETING CHANGES IN THE FAMILY

The family, once an institution that asserted its primary position in many of the basic tasks of society, now is more limited. It still has the important roles of early socialization into societal customs and values and of providing companionship, affection, and psychological security. However, when people express a desire to "put father back at the helm" or to return to "the good old days," they fail to realize the necessity for a correspondence between family type and societal need. The young must be prepared for the world of today and tomorrow, not for the good old days. The family must produce children capable of adjusting to a rapidly changing society. Does the modern family accomplish this task?

Optimistic Interpretations of the Modern Family   The most encouraging interpretations of the modern American family are from those who see it in terms of adaptive transformation to meet societal and individual needs. A famous essay by Talcott Parsons[8] analyzes the family in terms of function and concludes that the middle-class American family is precisely the kind of family required by an urban, mobile society. The individual is freed from most kinship responsibilities, creates his own

---

[8] Talcott Parsons, "The Social Structure of the Family," in Ruth S. Cavan (ed.), *The Family: Its Function and Destiny,* Harper & Row, Publishers, Incorporated, New York, 1959, pp. 241–274.

The old farm family

Procreation: many children,
long period of childbearing

Status: strong community
awareness of ascribed status

Livelihood: all share
in family work at home

Education: largely a family function

Recreation: largely a family function

Care of aged: family responsibility

The modern urban family

Procreation: few children,
planned, close together in age

Status: less awareness
of family status

Livelihood: father works away
from home, often mother does too

Education: specialized task of the school

Recreation: specialized
and commercialized

Care of aged: public responsibility

achieved status, and is free to form his associations among his status equals. Parents do not stand in the way of children if their best opportunities lie in moving away to a distant city, and hopefully a personality type is created by the new family that makes the continuous adjustment to new places, people, and circumstances relatively easy. Davis expresses a similar view, seeing the reasons for change in the family as basically economic and generally functional to the society. " . . . it (the family) achieves more companionship and democracy than its predecessor. On the whole it is far better than the patriarchal mode of peasant-agricultural countries, far better than the *mariage de convenance* [literally "marriage of convenience," but actually meaning an economically wise marriage] of the European upper classes. . . . "[9] Both Parsons and Davis look upon occasional break-up of marriage and some isolation in old age as simply the price that must be paid for an individual-oriented family in a society placing a high value on freedom and individual happiness. No family system can combine the best of all possibilities.

[9]Kingsley Davis, "The American Family, What It Is and Isn't," *New York Times Magazine*, Sept. 30, 1951, pp. 18, 41–42.

A Pessimistic Evaluation   Not all sociologists are as sanguine as Parsons and Davis about the family. Arnold Green, in his essay "Why Americans Feel Insecure,"[10] pictures an upwardly mobile middle-class family in which parental attitudes toward the children are strongly ambivalent. Children get in the way of parental career ambitions and hedonistic enjoyment of life. A decline in respect for parental status makes the children harder to manage, resulting in the use of love and the threatened wi hdrawal of love as weapons of control. The threat of love wi hdrawal, plus many conflicting expectations on the part of parents and society, make for neurotic tendencies in many. Criticisms of this type appear often in sociological and psychological literature as well as in popular magazines. They may help to explain the phenomenon called generation gap, but changes in family roles undoubtedly also contribute to the gap.

Changing Roles of Family Members: Mothers and Children   Such terms as "matriarchal" (mother rule) and "filiocentric" (child centered) have been used to describe the present American family. The implication is that father has lost much of his role and that "mom" reigns supreme or that the children have taken over. Before making too many hasty judgments about the sudden emergence of dominant wives and uncontrollable children, however, it is well to recall that folk literature is full of tales of nagging wives and undutiful sons. What was really the typical situation in the American past? Furstenberg has researched this question historically with a study of large numbers of commentators on American society in the period 1800 to 1850. For those who blame Dr. Spock for the permissive pattern of rearing our children today, there is a rude shock. "The most significant observation about American children was the permissive child-rearing patterns that were apparently widespread at this time."[11] One of the observers he cites (Harriet Martineau) comments on the connection between this pattern and preparation for democracy:

> Freedom of manners of children of which so much complaint has been made by observers . . . is a necessary fact. Till the American states cease to be republican the children there will continue as free and easy and as important as they are.[12]

Just how permissive the people of earlier America were, compared with today, is a little harder to assess, but it is significant that our ancestors

[10]Arnold W. Green, "Why Americans Feel Insecure," Commentary, vol. 6, July 1948, pp. 18–28.
[11]Frank F. Furstenberg, Jr., "Industrialization and the American Family," American Sociological Review, vol. 31, June 1966, pp. 326–337.
[12]Ibid., p. 332.

also were seen as permissive parents. Such cultural patterns usually develop over a long period.

The Woman's Role   On the subject of woman's role, Furstenberg's studies tend to bear out the popular view of its gradual growth and increasing complexity. Foreign observers of the early eighteenth century expressed surprise that the married woman was so severely restricted by home duties. After marriage her freedom was gone; she was "laid on a shelf," as a woman of the time stated the matter, although in many ways she was treated with great politeness and respect.

What seems to be true now is more or less the opposite. The modern woman might complain that chivalry is gone, but she certainly cannot complain of being put away on a shelf, out of sight of the social world. Today over half the married women work outside the home for at least part of their married years, and the family is interested in educating girls as well as boys for a job. Although pay and opportunities for promotion are grossly unequal for women and are becoming part of the focus of a new women's rights movement, women's social participation has increased greatly, and the "right" type of marriage is a companionate type. Woman has gained status, but her role is a more complicated one than formerly. She must often work both inside and outside the home and face role conflict problems. She is expected to stay youthful in appearance, to be a companion to her husband, to be a good mother, and to supplement the family income with a job that pays less than a similar job held by a man. She also finds, in an age of birth control, that the traditional housewife-mother role lacks the prestige and sentimentality it once had.

The Father's Role   The role of the father has changed as a result of changing job requirements. For several generations more and more fathers have worked away from home; now the pattern is almost universal. This fact has left more of the responsiblity of the children and their disciplining to the mother. Ideally, the father should be in a position to set a role-model in more ways than merely as breadwinner. A good relationship between father and daughter is closely connected with later marital happiness for the daughter. For the son, a good relationship with the father helps the learning of proper masculine roles. This task is rendered difficult when television and motion-picture stories show "true" masculinity as gunning down badmen or bombing enemy cities, while the father is quietly at work as a bank teller. The wild West definition of masculinity is not in keeping with the current period of cultural development and is consequently dysfunctional. Another problem is that too many jobs of the adult world have no appeal for growing boys. This creates many problems for youth and is a major theme of Paul Goodman's book *Growing Up Absurd*. Many fathers find it easier to relate to their sons through the athletic and recreational worlds than through the world of work or intellectual training. Youth advisors would certainly agree that this situation is better than having no common interests whatever and that anything that keeps communications open between parents and offspring is helpful, but is it a little too superficial? The disillusioned youths of today, often coming from families of high socioeducational background, make it seem that something of the kind is amiss. Are fathers and mothers able to convey the kind of message that will make the future of the family secure?

Children and the Family Future   As previously stated, children do not have the role in the economic maintenance of the family that they once had, except occasionally in the impoverished family. They are not needed for tilling the soil, clearing land, or taking care of their parents in their old age. It is in this respect that the family depends more upon affection for its center of being and is closer to the norms of today than many older families would have been. In the typical middle-class family there are from two or three children, they have been wanted and planned for, and there is no intent to exploit them economically. The family has a vested interest in its children, nevertheless, wanting them to be a credit to the family, maintain its status, save the parents from a lonely old age, and possibly even fulfill the dreams that the parents were not able to fulfill. Are the family and other institutions of society socializing the children in a way that will permit them to fulfill this future?

Many writers have dealt with the problem of new socialization patterns for children. Martha Wolfenstein writes about the "fun morality" that requires making fun out of all the duties of parenthood so that infants and children will be joyous and unfettered by guilt feelings.[13] She believes that the attempt at merging work and fun results in diffused impulses and insufficient drive. Riesman wrote in a similar vein, seeing the emerging other-directed personality as a type with less drive and less firm convictions than the older inner-directed type. Years ago Parsons wrote an analysis of the role of youth, especially high-school youth, as primarily an irresponsible one, in no way preparing practically for later duties in society.[14] Goodman perceives the position of youth as one that is ignored and not taken seriously by society and one that has especially ominous problems for the young man who is not academically gifted.[15]

[13]Martha Wolfenstein, "The Emergence of the Fun Morality," *Journal of Social Issues,* vol. 7, no. 4, 1951, pp. 15–25.

[14]Talcott Parsons, "Age and Sex in the Social Structure of the United States," *American Sociological Review,* vol. 7, no. 5, 1942, pp. 604–614.

[15]Paul Goodman, *Growing Up Absurd,* Random House, Inc., New York, 1960.

What worthwhile occupation beckons him? What hope does he have? Goodman sees youth as envied, advertised, and glamorized but not assigned an important role or even treated as though an important role is possible.

One can still question whether any of these studies really demonstrates that youth is not, in the long run, preparing for societal roles and for family roles. In a marital system based on free choice, dating and popularity pursuits in high school (part of the "irresponsible" role) might be precisely the right preparation. In a society calling for more white-collar workers and professionals than businessmen of an aggressive type, the other-directed pattern might be fairly satisfactory. Miller and Swanson did a study of two Detroit family types that they refer to as *entrepreneurial* and *bureaucratic* families. The older entrepreneurial family conditions children to enter the competitive world of business, emphasizing the old virtues of independence, thrift, and agressive approach to life. This type of family is still in evidence but on the wane. The bureaucratic family (so called because it equips a person to take a position in a bureaucracy), the growing type, tends to stress getting along with others but places less emphasis on independence, thrift, and business values.[16] Whether one grieves over the decline of the entrepreneurial family or not is a matter of values, but a functional interpretation of culture would maintain that family training is functioning to create the personality type needed for saleswork, meeting the public, and fitting into the organization.

Independence Training   The foregoing discussion seems to imply an indoctrination into a pattern of either bureaucratic conformity or entrepreneurial success-striving. Actually, many young people seem to turn their backs on the entrepreneurial values and to resist bureaucratic conformity as well. The separation between generations seems to be wider today than previously, but youth's search for independence is, in many ways, a familiar story. A restricted conjugal-family system must allow youth to achieve a measure of independence from the family home. Such freedom, to a degree, is acceptable to parents, but a distinction must be made between sponsored and unsponsored independence.[17] If young people are trained to take care of their own money, hold part-time jobs, assume the care and maintenance of their cars, and so forth, they are attaining an independence sponsored by their parents. If they run off from home to join a commune, they are asserting an unsponsored independence. The type of relationship that exists between generations will help to determine which kind of independence is followed.

[16]Daniel R. Miller and Guy E. Swanson, *The Changing American Parent,* John Wiley & Sons, Inc., New York, 1958.
[17]Bernard Farber, *Family: Organization and Interaction,* Chandler Publishing Company, San Francisco, 1964.

There is a strong correlation between social-class position and the training of children for independence. Bernard Farber says of the social-class contrast:

> Ordinarily, for middle-class children, independence from the family has the meaning of maturing into adulthood while for lower-class children independence from the family means deviance from conventional standards through committing delinquent acts.[18]

The lower-class family pattern aims more at trying to enforce obedience to rules than at training for sponsored independence. Ethnic background too shows considerable influence on the independence-training pattern. Bernard Rosen[19] made a study of independence and achievement training among several ethnic groups in a New England community. He concluded that Jewish and Greek families stressed achievement and independence training more strongly than the other groups in the study: Italian, French Canadian, and black. He sees this difference as part of the reason for the more rapid achievement of middle-class status by the former two groups.

FAMILY STABILITY

It would seem reasonable to suppose that the family which performs a large number of functions and exists in a society that is strongly kinship oriented would tend to have considerable marital stability. Yang and Hsu describe the old Chinese family as having these characteristics and as being a family system in which divorce was very uncommon. The fact that marriage was arranged rather than carried out on a basis of free choice would seem to the Westerner to spell less marital happiness, but Yang concludes that marriage was, generally, at least as happy as in the West.[20] There was a tendency for people to marry and then fall in love; here people fall in love and then marry.

Western Romantic Expectation Western marriage places a high premium on romance, which does not always result in permanence of attachment. The lyrics to such songs as "Some Enchanted Evening," implying eternal attachment at a moment's glance, make beautiful poetry but constitute an unrealistic basis for marriage. The sudden glow of passion and marriage based upon short acquaintance undoubtedly help to explain why our highest divorce rate to date came immediately after

[18]*Ibid.*, p. 370.
[19]Bernard Rosen, "Race, Ethnicity, and the Achievement Syndrome," *American Sociological Review*, vol. 24, February 1959, pp. 47–60.
[20]Yang, *op. cit.*

World War II, when many wartime romances proved not to have the necessary stability.

Success Factors in Marriage Because the American marriage system is not strongly bolstered by ecconomic necessity and because law and public opinion more readily accept divorce, the road to marital stability would seem to lie in the careful selection of compatible mates. As a matter of fact, love is not entirely blind. A large percentage of dates are between people of similar social class and interests, and a large percentage of marriages link people of the same social class, same locality, same race, and same religion.[21] Similarities of background, interests, and value are stressed in college courses in family and marriage as predictive of marriage success, as are long acquaintance and sufficient maturity. Census Bureau statistics indicate that in one recent year 10.6 percent of married couples fourteen to twenty-one years of age obtained divorces, whereas only 5.1 percent of those aged twenty-two to twenty-seven years obtained divorces, and 5.8 percent of those married between ages twenty-eight and sixty.[22]

Divorce Rates In all Western countries the divorce rate has tended to rise in recent decades, but at present the rate is higher in the United States than in any part of Europe.[23] Although it is perfectly true that this rate is partly a reflection of our values of independence and the right to the pursuit of happiness, a high divorce rate creates many problems. The decision to break a marriage is an unhappy one for the marriage partners, often damaging to self-concept and to relationships with old friends of the married couple. In recent years a majority of divorces have occurred in families with children.[24] The shock of divorce is severe for most children, although the problem of living in a family devoid of love is often more severe. One study found that those children who expected a divorce because of the quarrelsomeness of their parents sometimes felt a sense of relief when the break finally came.[25] However, there was always shock, there were attempts to hide the event from friends, and there was a lowering of self-confidence for the children of divorce, especially in their relationships with members of the opposite sex.

[21]William J. Goode, *The Family*, Prentice-Hall, Inc., Englewood Cliffs, N.J., 1964, pp. 33–35.

[22]U. S. Dept. of Commerce, Bureau of the Census, *Statistical Abstract of the United States*, 1971, p. 62.

[23]*Ibid.*, p. 96.

[24]Murray Gendell and Hans L. Zetterberg, *A Sociological Almanac for the United States*, Bedminster Press, New York, 1964, p. 47.

[25]Jack Harrison Pollack, "Are Children of Divorce Different?", in Judson R. Landis (ed.), *Current Perspectives on Social Problems*, Wadsworth Publishing Company, Inc., Belmont, Calif., 1966, pp. 190–193.

Table 11-2   Marriage and Divorce Rates Per Thousand Population

Year	Marriage	Divorce	Children involved per divorce
1910	10.3	0.9	
1915	10.0	1.0	
1920	12.0	1.6	
1925	10.3	1.5	
1930	9.2	1.6	
1935	10.4	1.7	
1940	12.1	2.0	
1945	12.2	3.5	
1950	11.1	2.6	
1955	9.3	2.3	.92
1960	8.5	2.2	1.18
1965	9.2	2.5	1.32
1970	10.7	3.5	1.34

Source: U. S. Dept. of Commerce, Bureau of the Census, *Statistical Abstract of the United States,* 1972, p. 50.

Stability and Social Class   One factor that is positively correlated with marital stability is social class, as mentioned in Chapter 1. Proneness-to-divorce tables show that laborers are about three times as likely to divorce as professional persons and that the higher the income the less likely the couple is to seek divorce.[26] Because larger numbers of people are achieving professional and semiprofessional positions, it would seem that the divorce rate might eventually decline. However, the undermining factors already mentioned—less economic need to stay together, emphasis on the individual's rights, and more permissive attitudes in law and public opinion—seem to more than offset this possibility (see Table 11-2).

FAMILY VARIABILITY

Much of the present discussion of family has been of the typical American middle-class model, the kind most frequently studied by sociologists and discussed in popular magazines. Social workers, psychiatrists, school counselors, and juvenile authorities are well-aware of families of a very different type, with parents unable or unwilling to play the expected roles or with parents completely missing. One does not have to look at the disorganized household, though, to find important variations on the American model. There are many perfectly cohesive, functioning homes that vary from the middle-class type, and even the middle-class type is not the same in rural and urban settings.

[26]See Chapter 1, p. 15 of this text.

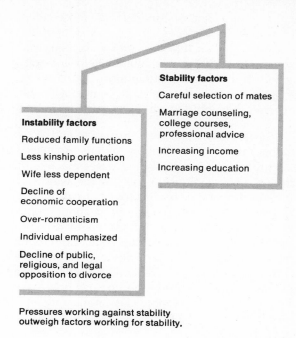

Instability factors

Reduced family functions

Less kinship orientation

Wife less dependent

Decline of
economic cooperation

Over-romanticism

Individual emphasized

Decline of public,
religious, and legal
opposition to divorce

Stability factors

Careful selection of mates

Marriage counseling,
college courses,
professional advice

Increasing income

Increasing education

Pressures working against stability
outweigh factors working for stability.

Urbanization and Family It has been commonly supposed that the city works against kinship cohesion for any except the most immediate members of the family; yet some studies have shown considerable visiting among relatives even in the city. Two studies made in Wisconsin and Michigan showed that other factors as well as urbanism help to explain differences in family cohesion.[27]

The general conclusion was that rural people interact with kinsmen more frequently than do city people, but migration has a strong bearing on the pattern. If an urban family has lived in one city for generations, the interaction between relatives is just as strong as it is in rural districts. When both rural and urban families have moved considerably, urban families are more likely than rural families to lose contact with kinsmen.

Another factor besides urbanism and migration enters the picture, however, and that is ethnicity. In the case of the study in Chicago, the

[27]Robert F. Winch, Scott Greer, and Rae Lesser Blumberg, "Ethnicity and Extended Familism in an Upper-Middle-Class Suburb," *American Sociological Review,* vol. 32, April 1967, pp. 265–272 Also see Robert F. Winch and Scott Greer, "Urbanism, Ethnicity, and Extended Familism," *Journal of Marriage and Family,* vol. 30, February 1968, pp. 40–45.

only "ethnic" contrasts studied were those between Catholics, Jews, and Protestants. Of the three groups, Jewish people kept in contact with the largest number of relatives, met with them most frequently, and were most likely to engage in mutual help and gift giving. Catholics rated second in these forms of familism, and Protestants third. However, all groups maintained at least some contact with and interest in relatives and expected to be able to call upon relatives in an emergency.

Social-class Contrasts: Husbands and Wives　An extensive study among middle-class families of Los Angeles indicated that a large majority of both husbands and wives placed considerable stress on the idea of a companionship role for the wife.[28] Their feeling was that a husband should owe his first loyalty to his wife, and she to her husband. They should consult each other first about problems rather than consulting parents, relatives, or friends. Mirra Komarovsky[29] tested the same ideas in interviews in a blue-collar community to find whether the attitudes were the same. She found contrasting patterns within the blue-collar community. Generally speaking, those who were high school graduates tended to view the companionate marital relationship much the same way as the middle class, frequently replying that the first one to consult about a problem was the husband or wife. The less educated group, however, took far less interest in such a companionate view of marriage. If a woman is in a bad mood or has problems, they contended, she should talk to her mother or some of the other women. A man, similarly, should talk over problems with other men. After all, they reasoned, you could not expect men and women to understand each other's problems.

Other attitudes of the less educated segment of the blue-collar group included the idea that it was all right for the man to go out frequently, but not for the woman, and that the man should not be expected to help in the house. Other studies emphasize for the same class of people the traditional definitions of masculinity in sexual affairs, which restrict mutual sexual enjoyment. "Tenderness and concern for the wife's response will be rare if sexual gratification is viewed as a male prerogative . . . any variation in technique or procedure is viewed as a perversion."[30] A double standard in sexual affairs is in decline throughout modern society, but less so in the working class than in the middle class.

Social-class Contrasts: Children　It is generally assumed that middle-class families are somewhat less likely to use physical punishment

[28]Nathan Hurvitz, "The Components of Marital Roles," *Sociology and Social Research*, vol. 45, April 1945, pp. 301–309.
[29]Mirra Komarovsky, *Blue Collar Marriage*, Random House, Inc., New York, 1967.
[30]Betty Yorburg, *The Changing Family*, Columbia University Press, New York, 1973, p. 165.

in disciplining their children than are lower-class families and that different kinds of pressures are placed upon children in different social-class positions. Several studies have found such differences in the rearing of children.[31] Working class parents are more likely to insist on obedience for its own sake; middle-class parents are generally more concerned with having children who will "be eager to learn, to love and confide in their parents, to share and cooperate. . . . "[32] Consciously or unconsciously, parents are training their children for the type of occupational experiences with which they, the parents, are familiar. Middle-class jobs often stress learning and getting along with others on a give-and-take basis (as in the bureaucratic family discussed previously). Working-class job experience is more likely to be one of obedience. Melvin L. Kohn[33] found in a comparative study of middle- and working-class families that differences in methods of discipline were less pronounced than had been supposed, but there was a striking contrast in the reasons for punishment. Working-class parents were more likely to punish the children simply for wild play, for making a nuisance of themselves, and for doing damage accidentally. Middle-class parents were more likely to take motives into consideration, more likely to overlook accidental damage, but severe in cases of deliberate cruelty and unconcern for others. The mother-father roles also differed on the average in the two family types. Working-class fathers were more likely to be regarded mainly as disciplinarians; middle-class fathers were more likely to share with the mothers in supportive and educational interaction and to have no greater role in discipline than the mothers.

Declining Ethnic Differences   It once seemed more valid than now to describe American family differences in ethnic terms. Increasingly the differences are becoming more a matter of social class and urbanization than ethnicity, although the old ethnic differences have not completely disappeared. No group has been more characteristically familistic than the Chinese, and many of the families still display strong solidarity. Yet in some of America's Chinatowns the authority of the old families has been hard to maintain against a type of youth rebellion, especially where heavy immigration from Hong Kong has resulted in overcrowded and impoverished conditions.[34]

Much has been written about the female-centered black family, but it will be recalled from our discussion of social class in Chapter 6 that Oscar

[31]Helen McGill Hughes, *Life in Families,* Allyn and Bacon, Inc., Boston, 1970, pp. 131–135.
[32]*Ibid.,* p. 133
[33]Melvin L. Kohn, "Social Class and Parent-Child Relationships," *American Journal of Sociology,* vol. 68, January 1963, pp. 471–480.
[34]Ivan Light and Charles Choy Wong, "Dilemmas of the Tourist Industry in America's Chinatowns," paper presented at the American Sociological Association Convention, New York, Aug. 27–30, 1973.

Lewis' "culture of poverty" is characterized by female-headed families wherever poverty and alientation run deep, regardless of race or previous cultural experience. The middle-class black family is generally quite comparable to the middle-class white family, except that the husbands are even more willing to share in household chores and child-rearing than white husbands.[35]

Families of Mexican- and Latin-American descent have often been described as paternalistic and familistic, with family ties extended through the old ritual of *compadrazgo* or coparenthood. Fernando Peñalosa,[36] in a description of the typical Chicano family of California, notes a decline in such traits and a growth in individualistic as opposed to familistic values. He is speaking of a population that is 83 percent urbanized, with 46 percent of employment in skilled or semiskilled blue-collar labor and 22 percent in white-collar jobs.

Manuel Ramírez[37] conducted a study of Mexican-American high school boys, finding striking differences between those he calls the "identifiers" (identifying with the parental culture) and the "Anglicized" group. The former answered in the affirmative to such questions as "Do you consider relatives, even distant ones, more important than friends?" and "Is respect for adults one of your most important values?" The Anglicized boys were much more likely to identify with peer groups and to be critical of parents. Although there is a strong feeling of common cause among most Chicano groups and a desire to retain a cultural identity, the identity is a new one, not traditional, old-country culture. The very presence of large numbers of women students in the major Chicano student organization MECHA is a good indication of the gradual change toward female equality and family modernity.

SUMMARY

Although the family is regarded as a virtually sacred institution, there is considerable worry about its future. The modern family is often compared unfavorably with that of the past, probably partially because of a tendency to idealize the past.

Comparisons of family types show that they must fit the requirements of the societies in which they are found. A contrast between the ancient Oriental family and the modern American family points out the strengths and weaknesses of two of the world's most frequently found family types.

[35]Yorburg, *op. cit.,* p. 143.

[36]Fernando Peñalosa, "The Changing Mexican-American in California," in Edward Simmon (ed.), *Pain and Promise: The Chicano Today*, Mentor Books, New American Library, Inc., New York, 1972, pp. 61–71.

[37]Manuel Ramirez, "Identity Crisis in the Barrios," in Edward Simmon, *op. cit.,* pp. 57–60.

The Oriental family has greater permanence and status security; the modern American family provides greater independence for its members. The two types of family are basically adapted to different types of societies.

An analysis of the functions of the family shows that many traditional functions have undergone change. Sexual relations have never been as strictly limited to matrimony as the Puritan ethic would imply, and norms have gradually grown more permissive. More fundamental in its impact on family relations is the change in economic functions of the family. Because the family farm and other family businesses have virtually disappeared, the family is no longer an organization with the highly integrative task of cooperating for its economic subsistence. The result is that the young learn less of their adult roles from parents than in the past, absorbing less of their information and, probably, less of their misinformation. Status is still provided by the family, but there is less general awareness of family status in urban life than in the older, rural life. Education, recreation, and care of the aged have become more specialized tasks, with less family involvement.

In interpreting the changes in family, it is not to be concluded that they are "bad" or "good," but rather that they are adaptations to a changing way of life. This point of view is stressed by Talcott Parsons and Kingsley Davis. There are, of course, some authorities who argue that the new type of family develops special psychological strains. Arnold Green stresses this theme in his analysis of conflicting pressures in modern societies and families.

Other analyses of the effects of changing family type focus on the roles of family members. Historical evidence casts doubt on the common assumption that we are much more lenient with our children than were our ancestors. The role of the mother in the family relationship seems to have become more dominant, as seen by the children, because job requirements keep the father away from the children more of the time.

Studies of children and their socialization patterns have stressed such ideas as "fun morality" and "other-directedness," but these patterns are not entirely incompatible with many types of societal demands. A study of the bureaucratic family, for example, indicates that family-training patterns are changing to fit the requirements of people who will spend most of their lives working for corporations and who probably need other-directed personalities.

Over the last half century there has been a gradual increase in the divorce rate of Western countries, especially the United States. The divorce rate in the United States reached a peak immediately after World War II, then declined for a while, but by 1970 was at the previous high.

Research in marital stability indicates that similar beliefs and interests are closely associated with successful marriage and that marital stability improves with class position and education, although many divorces now occur in all social classes.

Although the discussion of family has centered mainly on the white middle class, there are many variations in American family types. Rural families, and even urban families that are permanently settled, keep up ties with relatives better than do more mobile families; and Jewish and Catholic families are somewhat more kinship-centered than Protestants. Middle-class and the better educated working-class families give greater equality to women than do the less educated members of the working class. There are also differences in child-rearing patterns, with each social class, consciously or unconsciously, teaching what has seemed valuable to the parents—obedience for working class and learning to get along with others for middle class. There are also typical differences in ethnic groups, although over a period of years, especially among urbanized people, ethnic families tend to take on the characteristics of the social class to which they belong.

Chapter 12

Religion in Society

Comfort ye, comfort ye, O my people,
saith your God,
Speak ye comfortably unto Jerusalem. . . .

Isaiah 40:1–2

Think not that I come to send peace on earth;
I come not to send peace but a sword.

Matthew 10:34

Cultures have come into existence in the company of their gods. Sometimes these gods bring comfort and serenity, and sometimes they fill the heart with terror. Sometimes they fire the imagination with dreams of worlds to conquer; sometimes they are themselves conquered, their temples broken, their statues defaced, and their people dispersed or enslaved. Usually the gods are unseen beings, but sometimes they exist in the flesh, as in the person of the ancient Egyptian pharaohs or as the frenzied leaders of more recent totalitarian states. Sometimes tensions exist between the high priests and the rulers of the state, but more frequently the gods and their state live amicably together, coexistent and inseparable.

Perhaps this description of gods seems a mere flight of fancy in an age of secularization, when science seems to explain all and when the types of gods described are fading from the consciousness of man. This will depend partly upon how we look upon religion. In sociology we study religion mainly in terms of the functions it performs for society for it is not within our competence (nor that of anyone) to evaluate and say whose religion is "best." We ask whether the functions performed by the gods are still called for and whether they are still performed by the religions of contemporary society.

THE CONFLICTING FUNCTIONS OF RELIGION

The functions that religion accomplishes for society are often of opposing types. Seen in the short run, they seem contradictory; in the long range of history they may be complementary, the one supplying stability and the other providing for change. Religion generally supports the societal norms, reassuring the people that their ways are right and their cause is just; but at the same time the great religious prophets have all been critics of their societies. Religion tells us that man has an important place in the universe and that he is made in the image of God; it also emphasizes our insignificance in his awesome presence. Religion tells us that there is an ultimate justice in the divine will, yet it admonishes us to achieve that justice ourselves. Religion says, "Comfort ye, O my people," but for many it brings also anxiety and vexation of spirit. Research has shown that the strongly religious person rates higher in anxiety level than the less religious.[1] The religious leaders of society have generally taken a place in the social system just below that of the leaders of the state, high in prestige and position,[2] yet many religions have spoken out for the poor and humble. Finally, religion unites people into one great community of the faithful, but under some circumstances, it has been one of society's most divisive forces, resorting to the pillory, the rack, and the stake in its zeal to stamp out heretics.

[1]James A. Glynn, "An Investigation of the Relationship between Degree of Religiosity and Degree of Manifest Anxiety among Catholic College Students," unpublished master's thesis, San Jose State College, San Jose, Calif., 1966.

[2]Kingsley Davis and Wilbert E. Moore, "Some Principles of Stratification," *American Sociological Review*, vol. 10, April 1945, pp. 242–249.

Religion as a Unifying Force   The discussion of culture in Chapter 3 presented evidence to show that the primitive tended to conceive of a divine order which bore a striking resemblance to his social order. This tendency relates closely to the function of religion as a unifying force and is what Durkheim had in mind in his statement, "Is it not, then, that God and society are the same thing?" Many religious skeptics have said that "Man creates God in his own image"; Durkheim's view was that man creates God (or gods) in the image of his society. This definition of the sacred is part of the explanation of the social order—social class, laws, legitimate rule, ethnocentric attitudes toward one's own group, and the many folkways and mores. In support of Durkheim's view, it is interesting to note that historically many conquests have resulted in the destruction of the enemy gods, as when the idols of Baal were destroyed by the Israelites. Conquest of the enemy gods, apparently, meant conquest of the enemy people. At the very least, tremendously important "symbols of collective identity" were being destroyed.

What bearing does this have on religion today? Certainly modern man is much too sophisticated to create an ethnocentric God. Or is he? When nation fights nation, each calls upon God for help. In wars between Christian nations each has called on precisely the same God, but have they not thought of God in ethnocentric terms, as a God more interested in their cause than in that of the enemy? The American said "In God we trust," and the German soldier had inscribed on his belt buckle "Gott mit uns" (God with us). In times of emergency there is still the tendency to call upon a deity. Even atheistic Russia had an increase in church attendance during World War II and a more tolerant attitude toward religion than had existed for many years. Some of Hitler's most fanatical followers even wanted to revive the old Nordic gods, but the general policy in Nazi days was simply to require ministers to take the "Aryan oath." Hitler was seen as a messianic character. In countries with more conventional religious attitudes, more people prayed than before, and always with the expectation that God would listen to them and not to the enemy. In America great appeals were made to Catholics, Protestants, and Jews to attend religious services. A broadly tolerant attitude seemed to say "Regardless of which church you go to, you are worshipping a God that will aid our cause; He believes our way."

Will Herberg, in his book *Protestant, Catholic, Jew,* develops the same theme to describe recent American society. In his analysis, the religion underlying all the denominations is "the American way."[3]

[3]Will Herberg, *Protestant, Catholic, Jew*, Doubleday & Company, Inc., Garden City, N.Y., 1960, pp. 75–90.

A plausible argument is also sometimes made that some modern nations have created a new kind of god—a totalitarian state—defining man's place and his rules of conduct in terms of a new ideology. It would be possible to call such an ideology a religion only in a limited sense of the word, but many of the unifying functions of religion were present in the ideology of the Nazi state, and the same is true, to a great degree, of the Communist state. Drawing the analogy even further, a communist hierarchy of secular saints can be named, especially Marx and Lenin (in China, Mao Tse-tung), and their writings have become a communist equivalent to holy writ. Possibly the attitude analogous to religious fanaticism that has existed in Russia is now on the wane, but in an emergency it might be rekindled. Some theorists belief that a loss of traditional ties, including traditional religion, in modern society helps to set the stage for the fiery political movements which are looking for new meanings and new gods. This is part of the explanation that Erich Fromm gives for the rise of Nazi Germany in his *Escape from Freedom*.

Religion as a Divisive Force   Religion becomes a divisive force in history when a society is faced with conflicting and mutually intolerant religions or conflicting and mutually intolerant interpretations of the same religion. Religion also has been divisive at other times, as when a new religion began to spread in a society whose institutions and values were incompatible with its doctrines. The latter occurred when Christianity began to penetrate the Roman Empire and more recently when Christian missionaries introduced new ideas and practices into societies firmly rooted in different beliefs and values. Colin Turnbull, in *The Lonely African*, tells the story of the clash of religious beliefs and practices in a Congolese society and the disorientation of human lives in the process.

The clash between Christians and Moslems in the early days of Moslem penetration into the Circum-Mediterranean world is one of the best examples of societies being torn apart by two distinct and bitterly conflicting religions. Christendom saw the armies of Islam as armies of heathen darkness, trying to destroy all that was good in the world. Later, in the days of the Crusades, the Moslems saw the Christian armies in exactly the same light.

The results of the Protestant Reformation illustrate the divisiveness of conflicting interpretations of the same religion when the two interpretations are regarded as irreconcilable. Fear, wars, executions, and a witchcraft hysteria wracked Europe for centuries. The Thirty Years War depopulated parts of Central Europe as no other war has done, including the Napoleonic Wars or two world wars.

Religious controversy played an important part in early America. Many people migrated for religious liberty, but many were unwilling to grant such liberty to others. It was against this background that the doctrine of religious tolerance grew in the United States, with a fairly complete separation of church and state implicit in the First Amendment to the Constitution. In spite of the doctrine of separation of church and state, problems have arisen over religious rights. Court decisions have gradually eliminated many Sunday closing laws and other blue laws, and the Supreme Court has handed down rulings that try to prevent denominational indoctrination in the public schools. The Court feared that such practices would give preferential treatment to majority views and would tend to make outcasts of the children of non-Christian families. By such decisions, and by the gradual increase in religious tolerance, the problems of denominational divisiveness tend to recede. Probably the most important division remaining is the division between religious liberalism and religious conservativism, which, to some degree, cuts across denominational lines.

STABILITY AND REFORM

Religion has generally tended to act as a conservative force, preserving the social order in which it is found. Today the average American feels that a democratic way of life is implied in Christianity, but this was certainly not the view in the Middle Ages. Then the highly structured social system was seen as the will of God; the doctrine of the divine right of kinds emerged, generally gaining religious sanction. A good indication of this tendency to support the social order was the message of many southern ministers in the days of slavery, approving the institution and even defending it on religious grounds. Two of the recent prime ministers of South Africa, strong supporters of *apartheid* (a doctrine of extreme racial segregation and unequal treatment), have been ministers of the Dutch Reformed Church. In addition, it should be pointed out that conservative points of view regarding morals, changes in fashion and entertainment, and new ideas from the world of science are all more closely associated with the religiously orthodox than with the less religious.

The Radical Criticism of Religion   It is such examples of the conservative nature of religion that have led many liberals to be anticlerical and have made many radicals, most notably Marx, want to throw out the whole of religion. Marx's famous phrase "Religion is the opiate of the

Functions related to stability	Functions related to social change
Supporting the social order	Criticizing the social order
Institutional stability	Charismatic leadership and change
Comfort and reassurance	Anxiety and feelings of guilt
Uniting society	Dividing society
Promising divine justice	Demanding man-made justice
Reassuring the wealthy and prestigious	Providing hope for the poor and humble

masses" implies that religion blinds people to their troubles and makes them ready to accept things as they are. The much less radical but strongly reformist British Prime Minister David Lloyd-George had the same feeling about some of the traditional ideas taught to him as a child, particularly the prayer:

> God bless the squire and his relations
> And keep us in our proper stations.

In America a radical labor unionist wrote in a marxian vein about religion:

> There'll be pie by and by
> In that sweet land beyond the sky;
> Work and pray, live on hay;
> You'll get pie in the sky
> By and by when you die.

Religion as a Reforming Force   The radicals, however, are not the only people who sometimes show resentment against religion. Criticism also comes from the extremely conservative. Spencer had a strong distaste for religion because it usually preached doctrines that mitigated the philosophy of unbridled competition and struggle. In recent years the ultraconservative American writer Ayn Rand has expressed similar views about what she considers are the softening effects of religion. More frequently the conservative criticism is aimed at particular ministers whose activities are seen as "improper" rather than at relgion as an institution, but it is clear that religion can draw the fire of the right wing as well as the left. A brief analysis will show why this is true.

Although the religion of a society tends to be linked to other parts of the social order, and hence to support them, the links are never perfect. Religion upholds the idealized norms, and there is always a gap between idealized norms and actual practice, so normative strains appear. The type of man to whom religion brings more anxiety than comfort is troubled by these imperfections and cries out against the evils of the system, as did the prophets of the Bible:

> *Woe unto them that decree unrighteous decrees . . . to take away the right from the poor of my people, that widows may be their prey, and that they may rob the fatherless!*

Isaiah X:1–2

At times such voices seem to have been raised feebly or not at all. The wretchedness of the medieval peasant seems to have bothered few people of importance. Even Martin Luther, the reformist, was horrified by the peasant uprisings of his day and strongly supported the established political order. In his attempt to end corrupt practices within the church, however, he illustrates the reformist element of religion.

More recently, in spite of the fact that churches often condoned slavery, many ministers were counted in the ranks of the early abolitionists. Many became supporters of the suffragette movement or reform for conditions of labor for women and children, of prison reform, and of reform of mental institutions and orphanages. In recent years a small but dedicated minority of church leaders has been prominent in the civil rights movement; several have given their lives in the cause. Ministers working among the poverty-stricken migratory laborers and in rural and urban slums become highly critical of the unequal opportunities offered by society. Occasionally modern clergymen boldly take part in such unpopular causes as repeal of abortion laws and merciful treatment of drug offenders and homosexuals. Such activities represent only a small minority of religious leaders, but it is enough to illustrate that religion is not, in all its aspects, a conservative, self-righteous supporter of the existing order.

Religion is in a position to perform this function because it represents an important source of norms that, in the eyes of the believer, are stronger than those of the state, law, or tradition. When troubled times and normative strains occur, voices are raised for reform. These voices are by no means always those of religious leaders, and never do all religious leaders join in a reform movement; many remain placid and uninvolved. However, the issues of reform are raised often enough to make this one of the major functions of religion, complementing the function of support for the existing order. The marxian indictment is not always founded in reality; the ultraconservative often fears the inspired religious reformer as much as the radicals fear the religious establishment.

Although many laymen and nonbelievers take part in the same types of reforms, the religious man sometimes approaches the problem with greater zeal and conviction. Bertrand Russell, when he was a boy, met the British Prime Minister Gladstone, whom he described as the most frightening person he had ever met. Gladstone, said Lord Russell, was so full of religious certainty that he seemed always to be speaking with the voice of the Almighty. Many years later the same Lord Russell had the experience of meeting Nickolai Lenin. The same frightening righteousness beamed from the face of the godless radical as it had from the face of the proper and godly British liberal. The religious emotion is apparently the same whether the god is the well-known Jehovah or the pagan god called *dialectical materialism*.

CHARISMA TO INSTITUTION: THE DEVELOPMENT OF THE CHURCH

The word "charisma" denotes a characteristic of a person with strong personal magnetism who attracts devoted followers. To a limited degree the term "charismatic" can be applied to almost anyone with strong qualities of leadership, but by usage it is reserved for the dynamic, irresistible type of leader—the man who has an aura of magic about him, who can make people dream dreams of new worlds to come: the "earth shaker," the "mover of mountains." He comes as an innovator, unsupported by established institutions, but challenging the established order. The word originally referred to religious leaders, but since Max Weber's time also includes leaders of political movements. As an "ideal type" the charismatic leader is the opposite of the bureaucrat; his power is personal, not institutional. He asks for the complete surrender of his followers to him: "Forsake all else and follow me." Zoroaster, Jesus, Mohammed, and Buddha are all early examples of charismatic leaders, but the term also applies to leaders of a very different type—Hitler, Fidel Castro, Lenin, Kemal Ataturk.

The Church in Adversity Eric Hoffer describes the charismatic phase of a religious movement as one that tends to attract the wretched of the earth, the poor, the outcast, and the miserable, giving them cause for hope.[4] "Great is your reward in Heaven" is an exciting promise to those who have known only poverty and oppression. Actually, not all religious movements have started among the poverty-stricken; those of Luther, Calvin, Cromwell, and Henry VIII were among the rich. Nor have new religions in areas outside the Christian world necessarily won their first converts among the poor. But early Christianity and many recent sectarian movements have been of the type Hoffer describes.

Because the message of early Christianity was to the poor and lowly, it is small wonder that it was among such people that the faith spread rapidly throughout the Roman world, coming to be looked upon as a subversive force, not just by such insane tyrants as Nero and Caligula but by such able emperors as Marcus Aurelius and Diocletian. During the reigns of many Roman emperors life was precarious for the Christians, and only the true believers dared stand up for their cause. Gradually the church triumphed, the pagan gods of Rome were overcome. Constantine embraced Christianity, and the time came when it was unsafe not to be a Christian. Julian "Apostate" made a last futile attempt to stem the new order and restore the "ancient virtues," but the old Roman way was gone, and the church was triumphant.

The Church in Triumph The church in its triumph became a different type of social force. No longer was it concerned exclusively with the promised paradise to come. It began to change into an institution. The inspiring, charismatic leader, exciting but unpredictable, an innovator by nature, a disturber of established order, no longer was allowed to trouble the waters; a new order was established, guaranteed by a powerful and "infallible" institution whose leader was seen as God's representative on earth. How different were the problems: negotiations with the mighty of the earth, wars, diplomacy, collecting of funds, establishing new bases of power, settling theological and jurisdictional quarrels, and even humbling the Holy Roman Emperor at Canossa! How different were the leaders, dressed in clerical splendor, supported by the princes of the earth! With the triumph came also corruption. The persecuted church took in only saints; the church triumphant took in also the sinners. One of the great stories in Boccaccio's *Decameron* is of the wise and kindly Jew whose Christian friend feels that he must be converted to Christianity for the sake of his soul. The Jew decides not to accept the faith until he has

[4]Eric Hoffer, *The True Believer,* Harper & Row, Publishers, Incorporated, New York, 1966, pp. 38–48.

Denomination	Sect
Institutionalized, formal, trained ministry	Informal, self-anointed leader
Membership through socialization	Membership through emotional conversion experience
Quiet, reserved service	Emotional service
Appeal to middle and upper classes	Appeal primarily to the poor
"Integral part of existing social order"	"Forget worldly things; the last days are at hand"

traveled to Rome. The Christian is aghast. How can he ever be converted after seeing such a den of iniquity! Nevertheless, the Jew returns from Rome ready to embrace the Christian faith, for, he says, only with the blessing of God could such a church flourish in all its branches when its very roots are rotten with unspeakable corruption.

The irreverent Boccaccio may have exaggerated, but his point is valid: An institution that embraces all elements of society cannot retain its purity. In the conservative phase the god and the state become "coexistent and inseparable."

So far the discussion has centered on Christianity. The process of institutionalization has never been as thorough in the Moslem faith because of less centralization of religious authority and the extreme religious democracy of Islam. Although very different from Islam, Buddhism is the opposite of the Catholic Christian model in some of the same ways, such as not having an equivalent to the Pope and cardinals. Yet both these religions have gone through phases of rapid growth, missionary zeal, and then greater complacency and possibly even decline. Perhaps modern Arabic nationalism will rekindle the zeal of Islam to make it a more dynamic force again, or perhaps the Arabic world will find its new religion in more worldly ideologies.

Denomination and Sect   The contrasts just described in a historical framework reappear in contemporary society in the contrast between denomination and sect. A few definitions are now necessary. The *ecclesia* is the type of religious organization in the strongest position in a society—an established church claiming to represent national religion officially, such as the Catholic Church in Italy, the Lutheran Church in Sweden, and the Orthodox Church in Greece. They are no longer as exclusive as was the Medieval Church (others are tolerated), but they do hold a special position and often have considerable influence in education. The *denomination* is a large and relatively stable group, usually long-established, well-organized, and institutionalized. The *sect* is generally smaller, with less formality, appealing more to the poor, and usually gaining members through the emotional experience of conversion rather than through the slow process of socialization, as in the denomination. The word "cult" also applies to a smaller group and especially to one emphasizing a particular phase of religion that does not appear as strongly in the major denominations—for example, faith healing.[5] For our purposes the major interest is in the distinction between denomination and sect, very well described by the German sociologist Ernst Troeltsch, but note that he uses the word "church" for our word "denomination:"

> ... The fully developed church ... utilizes the State and the ruling classes, and weaves these elements into her own life; she then becomes an integral part of the existing social order; in so doing, however, she becomes dependent upon the upper classes, and upon their development. The sects, on the other hand, are connected with the lower classes, or at least with those elements in Society which are opposed to the State and to Society; they work upwards from below, and not downward from above.[6]

Some denominations fit Troeltsch's description of *church* better than others, and they range in their religious orientation from very conserva-

---

[5]Terminology is not uniform as regards sects and cults. Bryan R. Wilson, in *An Analysis of Sect Development,* describes and categorizes many differences. Our word "cult" is approximately equivalent to his "gnostic sect." Bryan R. Wilson, "An Analysis of Sect Development," in Seymour M. Lipset and Neil J. Smelser (eds.), *Sociology: The Progress of a Decade,* Prentice-Hall, Inc., Englewood Cliffs, N.J., 1961.

[6]Ernst Troeltsch, *The Social Teaching of the Christian Churches,* Oliver Wyon (trans.), The Macmillan Company, New York, 1931, pp. 331–332.

tive to liberal, but they are generally "an integral part of the existing social order." The sects vary considerably too, and it is hard to get a single term to fit every case. Jehovah's Witnesses fit Troeltsch's description almost perfectly in their lack of interest and participation in affairs of the state and the military service and in turning their backs on this world, which they believe is now entering its last days. The Pentecostal Holiness groups are other examples of sectarian development because they are an exclusive brotherhood of the faithful. The sects are apt to be made up of the outsiders—the poor and the disoriented, the people looking for new meanings, for emotional release through religious ectasy, and for a sense of belonging and self-worth. The sect, more than the denomination, is inclined to see itself as a community of the righteous pitted against the outside world.

Liston Pope, in his book *Millhands and Preachers,* tells the story of a series of such sects whose sermons tend to emphasize some of the doctrines of early Christianity—"Blessed are the meek," and "The first shall be last, and the last, first." Contrast such statements of the high religious status of the lowly with the status of labor as seen by industrialist George F. Baer in the great coal strike of 1902:

> The rights and interests of laboring man will be protected and cared for—not by labor agitators, but by the Christian men to whom God in his infinite wisdom has given control of the property interests of the country, and upon the successful management of which so much depends.[7] (Emphasis added)

There was no doubt in the mind of Baer as to who would be first and who last! His statement was considered excessive even then, but it points out in exaggerated form the contrast between the religious views of the rich and the poor. To the rich, religion justifies the established order; to the poor it promises better things to come in the next world or possibly even in this world.

The Serpent Handlers   A good illustration of the impact of faith upon the emotional lives of the poor and needy is contained in a recent study of the serpent-handling religions of West Virginia.[8] The serpent handlers take the following quotation from Mark as a commandment and bravely carry it out, even taking up dangerous snakes:

[7]Mark Sullivan, *Our Times: The United States, 1900–1925,* Charles Scribner's Sons, New York, 1927, p. 425.
[8]Nathan L. Gerrard, "The Serpent Handling Religions of West Virginia," *Transaction,* vol. 5, May 1968, pp. 22–28.

And these signs shall follow them that believe; in my name they shall cast out devils; they shall speak with new tongues; They shall take up serpents; and if they drink any deadly thing, it shall not hurt them; they shall lay hands on the sick, and they shall recover.

Mark 16:17−18

If a member is bitten by a snake and dies, as has happened, he or she has proved the true depth of faith. The recovery of a member proves that the Lord blesses the sect. The location of the church is at Scrabble Creek, West Virginia. The Scrabble Creek people are poor, of the "stationary working class," and do not expect to get anywhere. Many other people in this depressed area are gloomy, and there is much that is depressing for the serpent handlers as well. However, they look forward to their frequent religious meetings with their fervor, emotional outpouring, ecstatic dancing, talking in tongues, feeling the touch of the Holy Ghost upon them, faith healing, and finally the greatest of all: the serpents. The rest of the service is similar to that of many other Pentecostal Holiness churches, but the serpent handling is unique.

Nathan Gerrard, the author of this study, speaks of the serpent cult as one of *religious hedonism,* the gaining of great immediate joy out of the religious experience. Although the result is not hopeful from the point of view of upward mobility in this world, its psychological results, especially for the aged, are remarkable:

While the older members of the conventional church seemed to dwell morbidly on their physical disabilities, the aged serpent handlers seemed able to cheerfully ignore their ailments. . . . Three old serpent handlers we knew in Scrabble Creek were suffering from serious cardiac conditions. But when the Holy Spirit moved them, they danced ecstatically and violently. And they did this without any apparent harm.[9]

Religion makes various promises and serves various needs for different groups. For the mighty of the earth, it supports the established system. For the poor and lowly, it gives reassurance that there is a better world, here or in the future, and promises that they will not always be the wretched of the earth. For these same people the ecstatic side of religion relieves boredom and alienation. The serpent handlers are an extreme and sensational case, but the feeling of being "possessed of the Holy Spirit" is widely known in sect and cult, as it was known by the Apostles at Pentecost. In fact, the emotional appeal is so great and such a strong

9*Ibid.,* p. 24.

bonding force that possession sometimes becomes a vogue in some of the more conservat ve churches. The same feeling has come over large numbers of disturbed youths in great emotional need and far from any of the conventional churches. The so-called children of God have found temporary solace in the same type of emotional outpouring, having found at least for the moment "the tie that binds."

LATENT FUNCTIONS OF RELIGION

Beside the obvious functions of religion previously discussed, there are latent functions, not originally intended and sometimes unobserved. For example, missionary activity has sometimes paved the way for traders, exploiters, and even conquerors. Missionary activities may upset old customs in such a way as to turn younger generation against older. This, too, is an unintended result, but a very common one.

Max Weber's Theory: Latent Function of Protestantism   Weber's famous book *The Protestant Ethic and the Spirit of Capitalism* is the best known sociological work that deals mainly with a latent function of religion. Weber notes that modern industrial capitalism seems to have arisen first in Protestant countries, and he argues that one of the reasons was that certain teachings of the early Protestants, especially those of Calvin created an ethic particularly useful for the development of modern capitalism. Those Protestants most strongly affected by the teachings of Calvin—Puritans, Presbyterians, and German Pietists—were rendered extremely uneasy about the f ture of the soul. Calvin taught that insofar as God is infinite in His wisdom and power, He must know all that has been and all that is to be. This would not be possible if everything was not already predetermined. We are born with or without the grace of God. Some will be saved, and many will be cast into hell.

Such a doctrine is an uncomfortable one to live with. How do we know whether we are the chosen of the Lord? Increasingly, Weber says, the belief began to emerge among the Protestants that "God blesses the works of those He loves." It would seem likely, then, that the blessed would be people who work hard and accomplish much; hence the emergence of the doctrine of hard work. Because extravagance is evil, the products of one's labor could not be squandered idly; rather, they were reinvested. What could possibly be a better ethic for the beginning of one of the most highly competitive systems the world has ever known? The ethic adds honesty because it is impossible for a system of free capitalism to develop unless there is a certain amount of faith in contract.

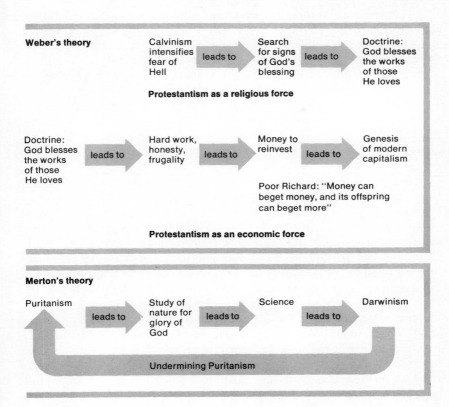

Weber's theory

Calvinism intensifies fear of Hell → leads to → Search for signs of God's blessing → leads to → Doctrine: God blesses the works of those He loves

Protestantism as a religious force

Doctrine: God blesses the works of those He loves → leads to → Hard work, honesty, frugality → leads to → Money to reinvest → leads to → Genesis of modern capitalism

Poor Richard: "Money can beget money, and its offspring can beget more"

Protestantism as an economic force

Merton's theory

Puritanism → leads to → Study of nature for glory of God → leads to → Science → leads to → Darwinism

Undermining Puritanism

However, there is another side to the honesty ethic; it is a matter of policy. The best way to succeed in the world is to be known as an honest person. Virtue and utilitarianism are combined. Of course Weber did not naïvely contend that all early capitalists were honest, but he did say that the system contrasts sharply with many in which the road to wealth is through gathering taxes and cheating the government (as in the latter days of Rome), oppressing the peasant, or military conquest and plunder.

The Protestant ethic was not the only one to teach the importance of work, but it was peculiarly intense in its devotion to the idea. Once such a highly competitive system started, Weber reasoned, it would tend to spread and draw in other members of society to some extent, Catholics as well as Protestants, but some differences might persist.

Gerhard Lenski finds that differences still exist between Catholics and Protestants in some of the respects that Weber's theory would suggest. White, middle-class Protestants are more upwardly mobile in their orientation than are Catholics, and they place a higher amount of faith in the rewards of hard work as compared with family connections as a source of success.[10] An analysis of family life among Catholics and Protestants shows more familism for Catholics and greater individualism for the Protestants. This relative release from family ties makes the Protestant freer to pursue his career, and he is already likely to be more success-oriented.[11]

Puritanism and Science   Another latent function of religion has been suggested by Robert K. Merton, the leading sociologist to develop the concept of latent function. It is his contention that the Protestant point of view had a bearing upon the development of modern science because of its emphasis on the study and glorification of nature as the handiwork of God.[12] He documents this viewpoint with quotations from many leading scientists of Puritan conviction and with interesting statistics on the religious identification of scientists in the Royal Society of the seventeenth century; practically all of them were Puritans. It is ironical that by the time of Darwin science and religion were in sharp conflict. In short, a latent function of Puritanism was the promotion of science, which in turn led to the undermining of many of the beliefs of Puritanism and of fundamentalist Christianity in general. This undermining of the fundamentalist view (the seven-day creation, the Garden of Eden story, and so on) is part of the general process of secularization in modern societies, related to many factors besides the latent functions just mentioned.

THE PROBLEMS OF AN AGE OF SECULARIZATION

There are conflicting points of view about the fate of religion in modern society, but few would deny that one trend of the world is toward secularization and that this tends to place certain limits on religious interpretations. No longer does religion provide a picture of the workings of the universe, with a comfortable, self-assured world around which revolve the sun, the moon, and all the stars. This is part of the contrast between sacred and secular society, but the terms need further definition.

[10]Gerhard Lenski, *The Religious Factor,* Doubleday & Company, Inc., Garden City, N. Y., 1963, p. 321.
[11]*Ibid.,* chap. 5.
[12]Robert K. Merton, *Social Theory and Social Structure,* The Free Press of Glencoe, Inc., New York, 1957, pp. 576–577.

The Sacred Society   A *sacred society* is defined as one that sees all its customs and institutions as being of divine origin. Misfortunes are generally explained as the result of the breaking of divine law, and people are closely responsible to nature and the spirit world. Even the fertility of the soil and the abundance of nature are human responsibilities regulated by ritual observances and conduct. Although people often make a distinction between the things that are sacred and those that are not, the distinction is not too great in the sacred society. Religion is a pervasive, everyday affair that regulates law, marriage, moral obligations, taking of food, planting and harvesting, curing of illness, and all the multitudinous aspects of culture.

The Secular Society   A *secular society,* on the other hand, can have its religious rituals and mores, but most social arrangements are thought of as simply the practical ways of meeting the material problems of life. Laws are rules made by legislatures, not by the divine will of God. Planting and harvesting are arranged on the basis of scientific knowledge, as are all aspects of the economy. Religious views still enter the picture when new social and moral issues are at stake, but in most of the every-day routine of life religion is less evident. Many members of society no longer engage in an type of religious observance, and many others think of religion as strictly a Sunday affair. Today's secular societies hold much greater funds of knowledge than the societies of the past, but sometime a sense of loss is experienced in other respects. Whereas the sacred traditions usually look upon man as the finest handiwork of God, a modern biologist of philosophical bent can say "The human brain, monstrous tumor of the universe, in which questions and agonies proliferate without curb, like malign cells!" and "Man is far from being the creation of a lucid will; he is not even the culmination of a confused and blur ed effort."[13]

Secularization does not always reach this outcry of despair, of course, for the secular society still has its faithful, and the United States actually saw a steady increase in church attendance in the 1940s and 1950s. The explanations given for a renewed interest in religion in those decades vary considerably, but probably the uncertainties of the war period and the unifying function of religion in such emergencies played a hand. There are also conflicting views on how healthy the institution of religion is in the United States today. Yinger criticizes the tendency of some writers to speak of secularization as though it means the abandon-

[13]Jean Rostand, *The Substance of Man,* Doubleday & Company, Inc. Garden City, N.Y., 1962, pp. 58, 65.

ment of religion or false piety.[14] He prefers the words "religious change" to "secularization" for describing the present situation in the United States. He rejects the view of many critics that religiosity of recent times is not "really" religion: If people think of themselves as religious, then let us accept them as such, even though some of their views might be quite different from religious views of the past. Yinger believes that if humanistic and natonalistic themes become a part of religion, it is still religion. The conspicuously churchlike behavior that is often an outward manifestation of middle-class values is definitely religious. The Norman Vincent Peale positive-thinking approach to religion may be philosophically shallow, but has there ever been a time when all people were philosophically profound? Lenski's conclusions are rather similar to Yinger's in some respects because they question the viewpoint that the urban society is so secularized as to make religion irrelevant.[15] Many traditions continue in urban life, including religious identification.

Others are more doubtful about some modern religious trends: " . . . a kind of creeping piety, a false piety and religiosity which has slithered its way to astounding popularity."[16] The writer Eric Goldman gives examples of dial-a-prayer, pray your weight away, and a quotation from a Hollywood actress, "I love God. And when you get to know Him, you'll find He's a livin' doll," as false religiosity. At the present time, people in the Los Angeles area can tune their television sets on a Sunday evening to "The Swingin' Gospel." Recently there has been a development of *scientology*, an amateur approach to a wedding of religion and psychiatry. Even psychedelic drugs have taken on a cultist facade as a dangerous shortcut to the ecstacies of religious mysticism. Traditionalists are not sure whether to applaud or react in horror at the highly ecstatic children of God movement. One should be cautious, however, in giving such developments as evidence of an "unhealthy" state of religion in modern society. Many strange ideas and practices have come and gone—apocalyptic prophecies, strange messiahs, bleeding icons, visions, dancing manias, and flagellation, to name but a few.

The Churches and the College Generation   The vast majority of the religiously committed do not follow strange cults but remain in the major churches—Catholic, Protestant, Jewish, and Orthodox. What are the trends in these churches as far as attendance is concerned? Dr. Gallup's figu es on weekly church attendance show 49 percent in 1955, the high

---

[14]J. Milton Yinger, *Sociology Looks at Religion,* The Macmillan Company, New York, 1963, p. 63.
[15]Lenski, *op. cit.,* pp. 8–12.
[16]Eric F. Goldman, "Goodbye to the Fifties, and Good Riddance!", *Harper's Magazine,* vol. 220, January 1960, pp. 27–29.

point of the century, and a decline to 44 percent in 1966, 45 percent in 1967, and 42 percent in 1969.[17] Much more disturbing for the churches than this minor decline in church attendance are the trends reported by Stark and Glock, who find a sharp distinction between older and younger generations in church attendance, a distinct on that seems to be increasing. Among young adults there was a drop of 11 percent in church attendance in the years 1958 to 1966.[18] In 1957, 69 percent of the people interviewed by Dr. Gallup thought that the influence of the church was increasing; in 1966 only 23 percent thought that its influence was increasing. These figures suggest that for many young Americans the church brings neither the comfort suggested in the opening quotation of this chapter nor the sword of reform. A two-decade study of Williams College students found a 20 percent decline in religious commitment, especially marked among students from religiously conservative families. The authors speculate that the major reason was the growing political commitment of the generation, not sanctioned by the traditional churches.[19]

Declining attendance is only one of several problems that Stark and Glock see for contemporary religion. Although the vast majority of Americans believe in God in some definition or other, orthodoxy of belief is declining. This decline creates a serious problem for church support because it is the strongly orthodox believers who are most likely to attend church and provide its financial support. The dissociation of the unorthodox from the church is a likely explanation of why such a liberal denomination as Unitarianism remains small in membership. Only a few of the unorthodox are committed to the church. Yet another dilemma, according to the same findings, is a contrast between belief in religious ritual, tradition, and doctrine on the one hand, and ethics on the other. In their measurement of "Christian ethics" (defined as agreement with the importance of "loving your neighbor" and "doing good for others"), the unorthodox measured slightly higher than the more conventionally religious. It is this dilemma of the stronger supporters of Christian ethics being little committed to the church that causes Stark and Glock to say "Today the acceptance of a modernized liberal theology is being accompanied by a general corrosion of religious commitment."[20] Those who remain with the churches, however, make more generous donations

---

[17]George Gallup, "Church Going in the United Stated Continues to Decline," *Los Angeles Times,* Dec. 27, 1969, p. 19.

[18]Rodney Stark and Charles Y. Glock, "Will Ethics be the Death of Christianity?", *Transaction,* vol. 6, June 1968, pp. 7–14.

[19]Philip K. Hastings and Dean R. Hoge, "Religious Change among College Students over Two Decades," *Social Forces,* vol. 49, September 1970, pp. 16–28.

[20]Stark and Glock, *op. cit.,* p. 11.

than in previous years. The National Council of Churches reports that in 1972 donations to ten major Protestant denominations had increased 5.2 percent over the 1971 figures, but all denominations showed losses in membership, with totals down from 29.8 million to 28.3 million, a loss of almost 5 percent.[21]

Comparison with Europe   Despite the suggested decline of religious commitment, the United States stands very high in stated religious belief compared with most of Western Europe. The April 1968 issue of *Catholic Digest* reports findings indicating that 92 percent of Americans think religion is important to them. A 1960 study of several Western nations finds the following percentages of people believing in life after death.[22]

United States	74%	Great Britain	56%
Norway	71%	Switzerland	55%
Canada	68%	Sweden	40%
Netherlands	63%	West Germany	38%

Statistics on prayer were given for only two countries; 92 percent of Americans claimed to pray at least occasionally; only 54 percent of Swedes indicated that they ever pray.

Whether Stark and Glock have detected a trend that will eventually make the United States more like Western Europe in skepticism cannot be said for sure. Trends do not always continue. Another certainty is that of defining "religious." The above statistics of 92 percent saying religion is important to them, and the same percent claiming to pray at least occasionally, combine strangely with only 74 percent believing in life after death. It is clear that many people consider themselves religious even though their views are not the traditional ones. The readers must decide for themselves whether religion includes not only commitment to God or the gods but also commitment to causes, to humanitarianism, to unfulfilled searches for meanings, to modern existentialist thought, and even to the "God is dead" philosophy of some of the religious avant garde.

The opening statement that "Cultures have come into existence in the company of their gods" does not mean that no individuals of today live without their gods. There seems to be widespread skepticism in a secular age and in a troubled age looking for new meanings. Neverthe-

[21]George W. Cornell, "Church Contributions Rise; Givers Decline," *Los Angeles Times*, Dec. 8, 1973, p. 34.

[22]Richard F. Tomasson, "Religion Is Irrelevant in Sweden," *Transaction*, vol. 6, December 1968, p. 47.

less, it would be rash to announce the demise of faith, even very fundamentalist faith. Recently, the Southern Baptist Convention, representing over 11 million members, adjourned after giving its overwhelming vote to the belivers in the literal truth of the Bible and dedicating itself to its traditional soul saving.[23] For the foreseeable future we can expect to see large numbers of religious believers. Some will seek inner peace; some will seek emotional excitation. They will argue and debate and sometimes show animosities, but in times of societal adversity they will tend to unite. There will be the traditional churchgoers supporting the conservative norms of society; and there will be lesser numbers of the religiously committed persistently challenging society for its shortcomings. Such are the many faces of the gods of mankind.

SUMMARY

Throughout all known history societies have had their religions. Sociologists approach religion from the point of view of social function; that is, what are its consequences for society? At first glance the functions of religion seem rather contradictory. Religion generally supports the society and proclaims its "rightness" above that of others, but at the same time the great religious prophets have been critics of their societies. Religions assign man an importance in the universe but also stress his insignificance. Religious leadership often is accompanied by high worldly status, but many religions (including Christianity) give sacred status to the poor and lowly. Religion unifies its followers and is sometimes the embodiment of the society itself. Under other circumstances religion can be a divisive force, causing internal conflict, as in the Thirty Years War.

These contradictory functions of religion can also be thought of as complementary, providing for opposite needs of social systems. There are conservative implications of religion, appealing to the well-placed members of society and sharply criticized by the radicals. The reforming zeal of religion, on the other hand, has caused great criticisms from conservatives. In this sense, different aspects of religion can be thought of as supporting and challenging the status quo. Except in time of considerable turbulence, the fearless social critics constitute only a very small minority of religious leadership.

The charismatic leader, with the magnetic, emotional appeal, characterizes the beginning phase of a new religion or of a new movement within an old religion. Often charismatic movement provides a challenge to the old order, as was the case with Christianity in its early history in the Roman Empire. Eventually a successful religion becomes established and

[23]Southern Baptists Reaffirm Traditions," *The Bakersfield Californian,* June 21, 1969, p. 2.

central to the society, as happened with the Roman Catholic Church at the height of its power. Within Protestantism there has been a partial parallel to the development of the Christian church of earlier times: New sects have appeared, largely among the poor. These sects often stress the doctrines of early Christianity—the unimportance of low status in this world, promise of better things to come, and the idea that the first shall be last and the last first.

Religion also has its latent (unintended or unnoticed) functions, for example, the frequent cases of missionaries unintentionally helping to pave the way for imperialism. Max Weber has the most famous thesis on the latent functions of religion. He contends that calvinist doctrine accidentally contributed to the intensely competitive economic system known as capitalism. Robert Merton shows that a latent function of Puritanism was the study of nature as the handiwork of God. The Puritan's study of nature contributed to the development of modern science, which, in turn, undermined many Puritan beliefs.

The present age is generally characterized as an age of secularization—one in which everday life is no longer permeated by religion. Is such a society necessarily in a state of religious decline? Researchers differ to some degree in their conclusions. J. Milton Yinger prefers the term "religious change" to "secularization," noting that churches are well-supported in spite of a decline in religious orthodoxy. It must also be pointed out that interests in new religious philosophies, mysticism, and humanitarianism cannot be dismissed as irrelevant to religion. Rodney Stark and Charles Glock, on the other hand, reviewing statistics on a decline of commitment to the church, speak of a decline in religion, especially on the part of college youth. Others wonder if the much greater decline in church attendance in many parts of Europe will be duplicated here. Presently, however, fundamentalism and evangelism have great popularity among many segments of the American population. Church attendance has declined from a high point in the late 1950s, but the decline is only slight. It would be an overstatement to say that religion has lost its functions in an age of secularization.

Chapter 13

Education

The scholar may not be without breadth of mind and vigorous endurance. His burden is heavy and his course is long.

The Analects of Confucius, Book VII, No. 7

Education has the universal function of contributing to the perpetuation of societies, transmitting their ideas from generation to generation, preparing the young for active roles in culture, and assuring the society its job roles will be filled. Education is therefore a reflection of the culture itself, and in complex and changing societies it displays some of the value conflicts and strains between real and ideal norms that are typical of all cultures. Because social change is an inevitable part of societies, especially modern societies, education does more than merely transmit the accumulated wisdom of the past. It has the function of adding to the knowledge of the past, helping to select what is to be retained, and making critical evaluations of tradition. For this reason, education, like religion, has complementary and sometimes conflicting functions—those of preservation and innovation. Schools can be so rigid in their attempt to instill loyalty to old traditions that they become stifling to the needs of social change, or they may virtually ignore tradition, making their cultures seem rootless and lacking in sense of identity. The latter is more likely to be the fate of ethnic minorities than of the traditions of dominant groups.

Another set of educational functions is that of preserving social status for well-placed families and attempting to achieve upward mobility for those of lower status. Although education serves as a major track for upward mobility, our discussion of both high school and college will show that the lower-class family often finds major barriers in the way of realization of this goal. There are, of course, many other functions of educational systems. Among the most obvious are those of contributing to socialization, providing the manpower resources needed by the society, and training people for the duties of citizenship.

As is the case with other institutions, education has latent, unintended functions. The needs of societies for adjusting to new technologies and ideas can result in demands for higher levels of education, and often the highly educated become the intellectual critics of the very social system that produced them. Education is a vital necessity, but its consequences in periods of change can be disturbing to old ways, not just in tradition-ridden or dictatorial countries, but in all social systems.

CHANGING FUNCTIONS OF EDUCATION

For preliterate people education was not separated from the remainder of life as a specialized institution but was a day-to-day process of imitation of elders, listening to instructions in necessary techniques, and learning the myths and the folk wisdom. Until the last century or two the pattern of education in the Western world had not differed too greatly from this same tradition, except for the upper classes. The common people learned from their parents; they learned how to farm and to care for children and learned the wisdom and the old wives' tales of the culture. There was less to learn than now, but learning was immediate and practical and possessed the self-assurance of long tradition. There was no long gap in years between learning and the application of learning.

Education in Early America   Although the United States was a new nation with new ideas, there were ways in which education in its early history seemed to stress the preservation function more than that of innovation. In Puritan New England, schools had started as a means of giving everyone the ability to read the Bible for the sake of the soul's salvation. Later the jeffersonian ideal of an educated electorate became a major inspiration for the building of schools in America. Along with educating a people to be competent to govern themselves, there was a great emphasis on patriotism and American heroes, the building of national tradition,[1] and devotion to the free enterprise system.

A certain amount of ethnocentrism is part of the instruction of all people, and America was no exception. Immigrants arriving in America learned to adopt its heroes and identify with the country, partly through the public education system. An important part of the school systems of midnineteeth-century America were the McGuffey Readers; they were high in morality and sentimentality and in the idea of inevitable progress. There was a constant emphasis on the good American virtues of morality, sobriety, and diligence. Over long years these readers preached to generations of school children, helping "shape that elusive thing we call the American character."[2] They also emphasized the obvious value of education as a way of getting ahead in the world. Thus education in much of American history has stressed the conservative values of building and romanticizing a cultural tradition. It was seen as the business of the growing public school system to equip individuals in their loyalties and skills to fit into the society, not to become its critics.

The Triumph of Mass Education   Our early schools were small and taught by poorly trained teachers, so it sometimes seemed that the blind were leading the blind. In the early years many curious European visitors scoffed. Others began to take real interest. The first British commission to study the American system arrived in the 1860s.[3] Before the end of the century many European visitors, official and unofficial, came to study and to learn. The idea of mass education was taking root and spreading. In America there was a gradual increase of literacy, with more and more people completing high school. Mass education was obviously becoming increasingly functional for a society moving into the modern age of science, industry, and commerce. Other industrial nations began to move along similar lines in mass education.

By 1970 young adults aged twenty-five to twenty-nine averaged 12.7 years of schooling. More than 75 percent of young adults were high school graduates, and 16 percent had completed four or more years of

[1] J. Merton England, "The Democratic Faith in American Schoolbooks, 1783–1860," *American Quarterly,* vol. 15, no. 2, Summer 1963, pp. 191–199.
[2] Henry Steele Commager, *The Commonwealth of Learning,* Harper & Row, Publishers, Incorporated, New York, 1952, p. 102.
[3] Ruth E. Maguire, *English Commentary on the American Common School 1860 to 1900,* unpublished doctoral dissertation, University of California at Los Angeles, 1961, vol. 1, pp. 19–20.

college. Figures for the total population past age twenty-five reflect lower educational achievements for older people.[4] Only 55 percent of the total of those twenty-five or older had finished high school, and only 11 percent had finished college.[5] As can be seen, the trend of schooling has been rapidly upward.

Mass education seemed to be an overwhelming success, and yet criticisms were growing. Colleges were not the needling critics of society that they are today, and educators aimed their criticisms more at education itself than at the total society; but the implications of the progressive educator, following the philosophy of John Dewey, were to equip people for a more cooperative society. With the passing of time the criticisms have come to cover a much wider range, including the charge of inadequacies in such educational functions as equality of opportunity, upward mobility, training for democracy, and relevance to modern life.

New Educational Demands   As the United States and other technological societies adjust to the modern world they have created, strains are placed on their educational systems. There is a demand for more schooling and more funds for the purpose. Because societies need large numbers of college graduates, they must tap the intellectual resources of a larger segment of the population rather than drawing leadership mainly from a self-perpetuating elite. For upper-class families an extra four or five years of maturing at college has long been traditional, but to many middle- and lower-middle-class people this seems to be an incredible lengthening of the period of youth. Youth is greatly played up to in song and advertisement but has an extremely ambiguous status— "a romantic but surplus commodity," Kvaraceus has called it. A period of ill-defined status is lengthened. The young person once looked upon his high school graduation as a "coming of age" ceremony, almost as definitive as primitive "rites of puberty," changing him from a boy to a man. Now its significance is downgraded in that more schooling lies ahead before full adult status is reached.

THE MODERN HIGH SCHOOL AS A SOCIAL SYSTEM

Although the demands for college education increase, a majority of people only finish high school, and some drop out before completion. The functions of the high school are, of course, generally seen as those of occupational training, citizenship training, furthering socialization, and

---

[4]Francis Keppel, *The Necessary Revolution in American Education,* Harper & Row, Publishers, Incorporated, New York, 1966, pp. 18–19.

[5]Christopher Jencks et al., *Inequality: A Reassessment of the Effect of Family and Schooling in America,* Basic Books, Inc., Publishers, New York, 1972, p. 63.

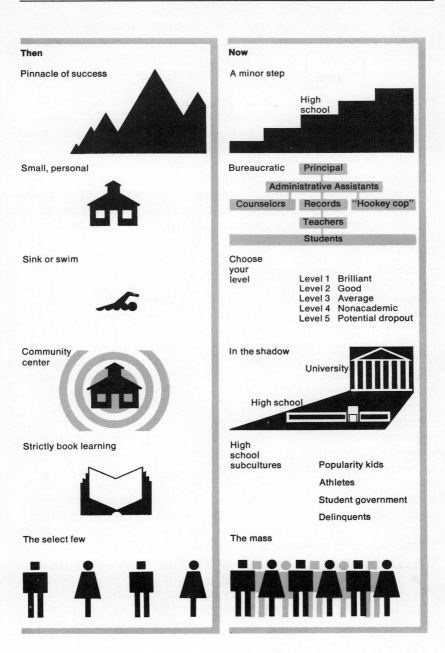

Then

Pinnacle of success

Small, personal

Sink or swim

Community center

Strictly book learning

The select few

Now

A minor step

High school

Bureaucratic — Principal — Administrative Assistants — Counselors — Records — "Hookey cop" — Teachers — Students

Choose your level

Level 1 Brilliant
Level 2 Good
Level 3 Average
Level 4 Nonacademic
Level 5 Potential dropout

In the shadow

University

High school

High school subcultures

Popularity kids

Athletes

Student government

Delinquents

The mass

delaying entry into the labor market. The functions are usually innovative only in the sense of personal preparation for a society that is constantly undergoing change and for the creation of teen-age norms. How does the high school function in the accomplishment of its intended purposes, and what unintended results does it help to bring about?

In some respects the average high school shows the same bureaucratic tendencies as the rest of the society. The student enters a high school in which personal contact with the teacher is very limited. Naturally there are counselors, but they are often kept so busy with the role of disciplinarian that the well-behaved student seldom sees them. From the first day the bureaucratic side of school makes a very strong impression. Individual reputations earned in grammar school are often ignored, and the student is rated, processed, scheduled, assigned and pigeonholed into the right academic level on the basis of a battery of tests. The student is now in a school that is part of a large city system, with its "better" schools, its average schools, and its "Siberian exiles," correlating with the socioeconomic composition in the community.

In an age when college expectations are high, the high school is less a center of community pride than it once was. Its enrollments have grown rapidly, however, and so have its costs. The massive enrollments contribute to high school discipline problems until some schools take on the atmosphere of a reformatory, with rigid and absolute rules. In the opinion of one critic, the rigidity tends to "infantilize adolescence," slowing down maturation in decision making and hampering ability to be heard and taken seriously.[6]

The Popularity Culture   Within the high school many of the characteristics of any social system emerge, with competition for the rewards the system can offer. Although much of the formal structure of the school is geared to recognize academic excellence, status is defined mainly by the informal social structure of the student body itself, not by the outside world. James Coleman, in an intensive study of ten high schools, found none in which status is gained primarily by being a good student. Criteria of status are more apt to be skill in athletics, school politics, dating, entertaining, and going to parties. Coleman speaks of this as an _adolescent subculture,_ "with values and attitudes quite distinct from those of the adult world."[7] In some respects the high school society and the adult world are distinct, and they are certainly treated as distinct by the entertainment and advertisement interests, but the distinction can be

[6]Edgar Z. Friedenberg, "The Modern High School: A Profile," _Commentary,_ vol. 36, November 1963, pp. 9–21.

[7]James S. Coleman, "The Adolescent Subculture and Academic Achievement," _American Journal of Sociology,_ vol. 65, January 1960, pp. 337–346.

overdrawn. Certainly the adult world also spends more time at parties, night clubs, athletic events, and at watching television than it does reading the world's great books.

There are ways in which the popularity culture is functional to the school system. It prevents the total annihilation of those who are not academically gifted and relieves a long four years that many students find boring and not very fruitful. Athletic competition gives a place for some who might otherwise become high school dropouts, but this point can be overemphasized. There is a tendency for students who participate in this type of youth subculture to be those with at least fair academic potential.

Conflicts Within the School   The popularity culture is the nuclear center of high school student bodies, except in cases where the entire school is demoralized, as often happens in the inner city. Sometimes conflict emerges even in schools with generally good morale and student cohesion. A national survey by the National Association of Secondary School Principals found that in such schools the most frequent conflict is over codes of student dress and appearance. Such confrontations often open new avenues of communication between students and administration and are resolved by modifications of restrictive codes.[8]

In schools with mixed ethnic populations and large numbers of students from low socioeconomic areas, arguments over dress codes also occur, but much more important are confrontations over curriculum content, counseling, and other school policies. An extensive study of California schools finds that the most frequent student explanation for low morale, conflict, and crime on the campus could be called the "ethnic-low-income-alienation complex," made up of a set of interrelated causes, including:

1.   *Segregation and isolation of minority and low-income students within the schools, via clubs, enforcement of rules, tracking (to be explained later), and other more subtle mechanisms.*

2.   *Teaching practices and curricula that fail to address the social realities of American society and enhance the self-esteem of minority and low-income students.*

3.   *Increasingly poor employment prospects for those who drop out of school. . . . This factor was reported as having the additional effect of keeping larger numbers of students in school who would prefer not to be there.*[9]

[8]"Student Activism and Conflict," *National Association of Secondary School Principals Bulletin,* vol. 55, January 1971, pp. 70–89.

[9]California State Department of Education, "A Report on Conflict and Violence in California's High Schools," Sacramento, Calif., 1973, p. 13.

There were particularly bitter complaints about schools whose student activities required the purchase of student body cards, excluding the poorest students from most activities. Equally frequent were complaints about the shortage of counseling staff, with a demand for more time to be spent with students, more specialists who understand employment opportunities and requirements, and minority representatives on counseling staffs. Apropos of this need for minority representation on counseling staffs is Report no. 5 of the U. S. Commission on Civil Rights, which concludes

> The basic finding of this report is that the schools of the Southwest are failing to involve Mexican-American children as active participants in the classroom to the same extent as Anglo children. On most of the measures of verbal interaction between teacher and student, there are gross disparities in favor of Anglos.[10]

The conclusions also imply that the problems are more a failure of interethnic understanding than of intent to neglect—a situation that could best be corrected by more Mexican-American members of the staff. The disparities are greatest where students are segregated on the basis of test scores. The same complaints are voiced constantly by black students as well.

Next in importance in high school student complaints is a fact that is gaining increasing recognition: Much of the high school curriculum in a majority of schools is geared strongly toward preparation of students for college, although, especially in the low-income districts, very few students go on to college. Their need is for courses that prepare them for jobs upon termination of high school. In many parts of the country two-year community colleges are available later to help such students, but the ones most prone to drop out are not interested even in two-year colleges.

Vandalism and Other School Crime   The incidence of school crime in the United States increased 36 percent in a four-year period studied by a Senate subcommittee in 1970, with school vandalism costs at that time estimated at $200 million/year.[11] The incidence of vandalism, fighting, and drug-alcohol offenses were directly related to the size of the school. The big, bureaucratic institution seems unsatisfactory for harmonious

---

[10]U.S. Commission on Civil Rights, rept. 5: *Mexican American Education Study; Teachers and Students: Differences in Teacher Interaction with Mexican American and Anglo Students,* U.S. Government Printing Office, Washington, D.C., March 1973, p. 43.

[11]California State Department of Education, *op. cit.,* p. 5.

relations between students. Low socioeconomic status and ethnic conflicts within the city also correlated with higher crime rates. The rates of crime and violence are of such a serious nature as to prompt a National Commission on Reform in Secondary Education, sponsored by the Kettering Foundation, to discuss the possibility of lowering the age of compulsory school attendance to fourteen.[12] Such a recommendation runs counter to a long tradition of trying to educate people to the maximum of their potential, and the Commission concluded that a better alternative is to offer a wider range of programs for high school students. The California Education Department report also avoids a policy of merely giving up on difficult students; it cites two school districts (Pasadena and Riverside, California) that have been able to improve vastly both order and morale in their schools by programs to prevent alienation of the poor and ethnic minorities. The programs are addressed to most of the criticisms already mentioned, and they also succeed in involving parents of ethnic communities in the school programs. Such programs cost time, money, and effort but save greatly in the costs of vandalism, crime, and human wreckage.

Ability Grouping and Social-class Perpetuation   There are many levels of ability among the students in high schools, and something must be done to make the whole heterogeneous mass teachable. One alternative would be to have very small classes so a teacher could give special attention to each student. This policy is too costly for most districts, so there remain two other alternatives: throw them all into the same class to sink or swim, or "ability group" them. Ability grouping makes it possible for bright students to be in competition with and be challenged by other bright students. It just as assuredly weeds out any possibility of much intellectual challenge to those students in the lower groups, and it makes the job of teaching the lower groups appalling to all but the most dedicated teachers. Then there is another problem: children from poverty areas start school under a cloud, and the cloud grows more impenetrable with the passing of years. Lack of good reading habits at home leads such children to a slower start in the first grade, which causes them to be assigned less challenging work. By the time such children are in high school there is no way of knowing whether they ever had academic potential; possibly it once existed but was stultified by miserable self-concept fostered by the ability-segregation system. A disporportionate number of minority students follow the long trail through school on the second, third, or fourth level below the top.

[12]"National Commission on Reform in Secondary Education," *New York Times*, Dec. 1, 1973, p. 2.

Intelligence Tests as Normative Strain   Much of the assignment of students to various academic levels is done on the basis of intelligence tests, which have recently come under heavy attack. The intelligence test scores are, on a general average, a fairly good prediction of academic work, but averages often hide many exceptional cases. Some students perform better than the tests would indicate but have their confidence shaken by unfavorable test scores. More important than a few individual cases is the tendency for the intelligence test to be unfair to students from a subcultural background that differs substantially from that of the white middle-class family. This problem was mentioned previously in Chapter 7 in relation to race and ethnic group, with the general conclusion that intelligence tests do not work except for the culture on which they are standardized.[13]

Zealous attention to intelligence quotients can run into normative dilemmas of other types besides that of unfairness to minority groups. It is easy to use intelligence scores to explain too much and to warrant giving up on some students, although the educational norms call for the highest possible development of each individual. The school system is also charged with the responsibility of producing the kinds of talents needed by today's society. If the testing system discourages capable people from developing their potentials, it adds to social wastage. Robert Faris contends that we set too many aspirational boundaries for both society and individual. By *aspiration boundaries* he means limits beyond which we dare not aspire. Once it is realized that there are no insurmountable barriers to a particular field of achievement, more people try, and many of them succeed.[14] Several studies have shown marked improvement in ability scores among children with improved opportunity and improved self-image. At the same time, one can hardly assume that there are no individual variations in human potentials.

Bruce K. Eckland,[15] in his study "Genetics and Sociology," reviews the literature in the field and comes to two important conclusions: (1) observed intelligence differences between social classes are partly caused by assortative mating and heredity, but this is probably not true of observed differences in races; (2) despite some average differences observable on a social-class basis, many lower-class children have high intelligence and vice versa. Because his first statement sounds a little contradictory, it requires an explanation. Members of the majority race

[13]Carolyn Stern, "The Changing Concept of the Changing I.Q.," *California Teachers' Association Journal,* May 1969, pp. 13–15.

[14]Robert E. L. Faris, "Reflections on the Ability Dimension in Human Society," *American Sociological Review,* vol. 26, December 1961, pp. 835–843.

[15]Bruce K. Eckland, "Genetics and Sociology," *American Sociological Review,* vol. 32, April 1967, pp. 173–194.

have had a reasonable opportunity to better their position, so that some upward mobility among the most able would seem likely. Because the road to upward mobility has been virtually closed for blacks, Chicanos, and Indians, there is no reason for assuming that low class position on their part is necessarily connected with low ability.

If we accept Eckland's conclusions, we shall perceive a society in which abilities are evenly distributed among races but which are distributed with slight inequality across social-class lines. Even granting this, there are very large numbers of children whose potential is wasted for themselves and for society. One-fourth of slum children in northern cities have IQs of 109 or above.[16] Too many of them represent a waste of human resources, partly because of lack of encouragement and partly because of lack of funds to go to school. It seems likely that we can add to this the possibility that ability-grouping systems close doors to many students before they get far enough into high school to be measured for college. The "measuring-for-college" system is another barrier.

THE UNEVEN RACE TO COLLEGE

In most European educational systems examinations are given by the age of sixteen to determine whether people have the academic potential to go on to college. The competition for college is much greater than here, and the pressure is greater. The system effectively excludes those who have not passed their examinations.

The Barriers   In the United States the pressure is not so great, but the trend seems to be in the same direction. Where junior colleges are not available, one can eliminate himself from consideration by a state college or university by doing poorly in high school or on the College Entrance Examinations. Junior colleges generally admit all applicants, but they have to "wash out" a great many along the way. They do, however, serve the function of helping people who are late to mature or to become motivated.

Much of the motivation for college is a matter of family socioeducational background, which is found to be even more predictive of college entrance than is ability.[17] In a study completed in Wisconsin in 1968[18] it was found that high school graduates with high ability eventually

[16]Kenneth Eells, Allison Davis, Robert W. Tyler, and Virgil C. Herrick, *Intelligence and Cultural Differences,* The University of Chicago Press, Chicago, 1951, p. 154.

[17]Burton R. Clark, *Educating the Expert Society,* Chandler Publishing Company, San Francisco, 1962, pp. 61–62.

[18]William H. Sewell and Vidal P. Shah, "Parents' Education and Children's Educational Aspirations and Achievements," *American Sociological Review,* vol. 33, April 1968, pp. 191–209.

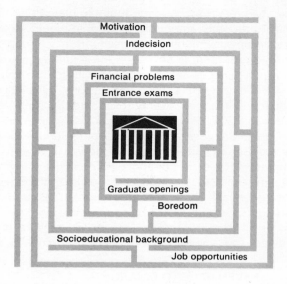

Motivation
Indecision
Financial problems
Entrance exams
Graduate openings
Boredom
Socioeducational background
Job opportunities

graduated from college in 63.4 percent of the cases if their parents had high educational achievement. However, if the parents were low in educational achievement, the rate of college graduation for their offspring was only 21.1 percent, even for high-ability students. This is not just a reflection of economic ability to pay college tuition. Of the sons and daughters of well-educated parents in the study, 95.4 percent reported parental encouragement to go to college. Only 51.9 percent of those whose parents had little education reported such encouragment, even among high-ability students, although the differential in parental encouragement is probably declining.

Lack of parental encouragement is not the only factor, of course, in college plans. Both money and ability are needed. Money is especially important in states that do not have tuition-free junior colleges or low-tuition state colleges. Annual tuition at privately endowed colleges has increased from three to fivefold in the last thirty years, and even state colleges and universities have become increasingly expensive. Vietnam veterans have generally found private colleges completely out of their financial reach. Even where the cost of tuition is held to a minimum, living costs are high, and there is a great economic differential in the ability to enter. Often students have to go to work to help with family expenses, or, at best, they cannot hope for financial aid from home but must earn their own way completely. This can be done with great effort but at a sacrifice of the time needed for reflection and for taking advantage of the cultural opportunities presented by the college.

The road to college is strewn with barriers: insufficient ability or motivation, lack of financial means, or low test scores. The effort is great enough that many do not choose to go even if the means are available. Some majors and graduate programs are virtually closed to women students, although the barriers are beginning to crumble.

One final problem concerning the entering of college is that many students have not yet been able to make up their minds about vocational choice. There is a tendency to be most aware of jobs that are represented by family and acquaintances, and this raises a difficulty for low-income youth who have little knowledge of the types of jobs open to college graduates.

The College Barron's *Profiles of American Colleges* lists over 1,200 regionally accredited four-year colleges and universities in the United States, ranging in size from 200 or 300 students to 35,000 or more. Today the large schools are more typical than are the smaller ones. The major state colleges and universities are impressive in size and academic staff, drawing large research grants from government and industry and hiring many of the world's greatest scientists and experts in all fields of learning. Their presses are busy turning out the books and research papers of their professors. Their diplomas are envied, especially those awarding higher degrees. Certain schools—Berkeley, Harvard, and Columbia, for example—are honored with many Nobel Prize winners and other great names in the academic field.

The trouble is that the undergraduate students are but vaguely aware of the most distinguished members of the staff. They are often taught in classrooms consisting of hundreds of students by young assistants who must publish or get out. Education departments complain that too little attention is given to the techniques of teaching.[19] The impersonal, bureaucratic atmosphere of high school is multiplied manyfold in the large colleges and universities. Even school spirit and involvement are hard to develop. Many students are involved only in small primary groups of their own, and there are also "loners" who seem to need the atmosphere of the small college but cannot afford it.

[19]James B. Conant, *The Education of American Teachers,* McGraw-Hill Book Company, New York, 1964, pp. 1–14.

Attitude Change   Whether the student goes to a small college or a large university, it is generally assumed that his education will broaden his perspectives, removing some of his prejudices and provincialism. Whether as a result of instruction or maturation and being away from home, certain attitude changes usually do take place. Not all surveys agree, but a majority show a slightly greater tolerance of conflicting political opinions on the part of college seniors than of entering freshmen. There is a decline in racial prejudice, an increase in religious tolerance, and less religious fundamentalism. To a slight degree this is the result of a selective function of the college, weeding out some of the more narrow minded, but to a great degree it also shows a change of attitude with increasing education.[20]

Charles Stember's study on education and attitude change is not quite as encouraging as most.[21] The simplest stereotypes, he admits, are seldom found among the educated—such stereotypes as "all Germans are brutal," or "all Orientals are sneaky." Anti-Jewish prejudice declines with every step of the educational ladder, but a decline in anti-black prejudice occurs mainly at college, with earlier schools showing little change. The remaining difficulty, as Stember sees it, is that sometimes prejudices are simply a little more sophisticated in their justifications. Higher-class people usually preserve enough of a pattern of discrimination to maintain considerable social distance from minority groups. Education tends to remove prejudice, but the higher-class position that goes with it does not. The conditions that reinforce the favorable effect of education on racial attitudes are urbanization and personal contact with minority people of equal status. Education widens the gap between the prejudiced and nonprejudiced more in the South than in the North and more among people with foreign-born parents than among those with American-born parents.

In political matters the effects of education seem to foster liberal attitudes. Research at the end of the conservative decade of the 1950s found that a majority of the very vocal conservatives on college campuses came from conservative homes. Although the liberals were less vocal then than later, there were considerably more students rating themselves as "more liberal" than their parents than "more conservative."[22] In a more recent study by Free and Cantril,[23] it was found that 45 percent of

[20]Clark, op. cit., pp. 30–37.

[21]Charles H. Stember, "Education and Attitude Change," in James L. Price (ed.), Social Facts, The Macmillan Co. of Canada, Limited, Toronto, 1969, pp. 287–298.

[22]Russell Middleton and Snell Putney, "Student Rebellion against Parental Political Beliefs," Social Forces, vol. 41, May 1963, pp. 377–383.

[23]Lloyd A. Free and Hadley Cantril, The Political Beliefs of Americans, Rutgers University Press, New Brunswick, N.J., 1967, p. 139.

those offspring who classified their fathers as "very conservative" classified themselves as "very liberal." Only 1 percent of "very liberal" parents had offspring who classified themselves as "very conservative," although a majority (80 percent) moved slightly to the right— "moderately liberal" or "middle of the road." When political activism shows a strong revolt against the parents, it is likely to be a revolt against strong conservativism. Gallup's figures for 1969 showed a liberal trend on the part of college students. In his survey, 21 percent of the students called themselves "conservatives," 24 percent "middle of the road," and 53 percent "liberal."[24] Only time will tell whether the liberal convictions will change with the passing of years and greater vested interest in the status quo. The early 1970s showed a decline in political involvement compared with the 1960s.

Vocational Selection   College education generally shows results in the most practical of respects—occupation and income. The income of the college graduate has long remained about three times that of the grammar school graduate and about twice that of the high school graduate. Professional and technical workers were largely college graduates by 1940, but at that time only 23 percent of managers, officials, and proprietors were college graduates; by 1960 the corresponding figure was 35 percent.[25] Clerical, sales, and kindred workers, and farmers and farm managers had attended college in smaller numbers, but their percentage of graduates was also increasing.

The diploma mills continue to grind out the needed degrees, with a few surpluses and with shortages in medicine and some scientific areas. The student enrollment increases steadily, and the population rises in its average level of formal education. To some educators it seems that the golden age has arrived. For others there is the disturbing thought that thousands of people hardly fitted by temperament or interest for college are being ground through the machine while many able people of depressed social background have been excluded by the hard facts of economics. There is also the worry that a college education is not accomplishing what the academically minded would like to see—graduates with awakened, inquiring minds, interested in the world of ideas, science, and society. The attention to graduation and to vocational preparation in a specialized age can be too narrowly instrumental. The national rivalry attitude toward education, observable espe-

[24]"Gallup Poll: Strong Swing to the Left Noted on Campuses," *Los Angeles Times,* May 27, 1969, part 1, pp. 10–11.

[25]John K. Folger and Charles B. Nam, "Trends in Education in Relation to the Occupational Structure," *Sociology of Education,* vol. 38, Fall 1964, pp. 19–33.

cially in the years immediately after the Russians launched their first Sputnik in 1957, can lead in the same technically specialized direction. Most colleges are aware of this problem and try to avoid the training that Burton Clark characterizes as *technical barbarism* (more fully defined later), but the more narrowly technical training is a trend in much of the world.[26] A glance at the student subcultures within the universities will show many divergencies of opinion and interest but not too strong a concentration on the world of the intellect.

THE COLLEGE SUBCULTURES

Present-day college student bodies are quite different from those of the past, especially if we use the large colleges and universities as models. Clark, using some of Martin Trow's terminology, describes four distinctive college subcultures, showing the gradual change in student type.[27]

The first, the *collegiate subculture*, consisting of the Joe College-Betty Co-ed type, has long been on the decline, although it never completely disappears and may be reviving to some degree at present. The collegiate types were and are loyal supporters of the old alma mater, faithful followers of the team, and likely to join the alumni association in later years. Never intellectuals, they nevertheless identify with the school. When the collegiate subculture was at its height in the days before the Great Depression, the majority of college students came from fairly wealthy homes, and they were the ones who set the tone for the college. The collegiate subculture was not sufficiently dedicated to learning to please the academic professors, but it was functional for the school in that it found outlets for youthful exuberance which supported the school rather than protesting its policies. To a considerable degree the fraternities and sororities served the function of seeing that girls met boys from the "right" social background.[28]

The *academic subculture* has never constituted a majority because not that many people are truly scholarly. There are probably as many members of the academic subculture today as ever, but they are lost in the growing mass of less academic students. The academics are the people devoted to learning and loyal to the school as a place of enlightenment. They are the types of scholars referred to in our opening quotation from Confucius with "breadth of mind" and "vigorous endurance."

[26]Clark, *op. cit.,* p. 288.
[27]Clark, *ibid.*
[28]John Finley Scott, "Sororities and the Husband Game," *Transaction,* September 1965.

A decline in the relative importance of the academic subculture could be dysfunctional to democratic societies. It has long been the viewpoint of liberty-loving nations that their freedom of expression, although sometimes disturbing, provides them with the very self-criticism that is needed. Social criticism is most likely to be given consideration if it comes from men of scholarly training. Autocratic regimes often find it expedient to promote expensive systems of technical and scientific education, but they take precautions against the development of cliques of intellectual critics. A system that supports science and technology, at the same time discouraging the critical capacities of the intellectual, is characterized by Clark as *technical barbarism*.

The majority college subculture is the *vocational subculture* that consists of people attending college to prepare for jobs. This subculture is a serious one but not necessarily in the sense of a love of knowledge for the sake of knowledge. Often the students are married, with home responsibilities, and sometimes make their way through school by slow degrees in night-school. Even the unmarried often do not have enough support from home. The result is that their hours of work interfere with much of the collegiate-subculture type of activity. The vocational subculture is a reflection of the change that has brought larger numbers of aspiring people from lower-middle class and working class into college.

The last of the subcultures described by Clark is the *nonconformist subculture*—a small one once but on many campuses a rapidly growing one. Furthermore, the nature of this subculture has changed as it blends increasingly with student activism. As originally described, the nonconformists were interested in art and music, dressed distinctively to the point of being shocking to the "squares," and generally did not relate to the college in loyalties. Their basic disregard for what they considered false middle-class standards made them ready recruits, or even leaders, for the student activism that became so prominent during the Vietnam war.

Student Activism Colleges and universities have been political storm centers in many countries of the world. During periods of national crisis student groups have been political activists in various countries of Europe, Asia, and Latin America. Even in the United States many college campuses were characterized by active political factions during the Great Depression, but they lacked the ability to mount the massive demonstrations of the 1960s and 1970. Student activism falls clearly into the category of latent functions of education, never intended by college governing boards or political administrations. Student-activist leaders see themselves as performing the critical, reformist, and innovative functions of education.

Although student demonstrations had actually started with a free-speech movement at the University of California, the student activists became much more prominent in lending substantial help to the civil rights movement. Many struggled for the cause of racial equality in the deep South at a time of real danger. A few were killed. Northern liberals were inclined to applaud but were sometimes worried about the safety of the students and their academic future. In the next phase, student activism took up the antiwar cause, not only by opposing the Vietnam war but by opposing recruitment on campuses, campus ROTC, and the acceptance by colleges and universities of large research grants from the military.

Eventually there were violent episodes of the type that occur so easily in conditions of mass excitement. Many colleges and universities were closed by strikes. Public support declined, and students were criticized for emotional volatility, violence, and lack of political experience. The students replied with sociologically important arguments: the only effective opposition has to come from those not old and deeply involved in the system either through lifelong habit or vested interest. Only youth, they maintained, could see clearly the gap between social ideal and social reality. Even critics of the youth subculture have been willing to concede that the older generation was remiss in providing leadership in such causes as civil rights and antimilitarism.[29]

As of the early 1970s the college campuses were rather quiet, with some indications of a reawakened interest in sports and fraternities and an even stronger practical, vocational interest. Colleges must always be thought of, though, as having a critical role that can sometimes become explosive, providing, as they do, a questioning atmosphere, liberal professors, and idealistic youth without too much awareness of a vested interest in things as they are. What the future holds probably depends upon what new issues arise and whether they lead to those elusive types of social contagion previously discussed under collective behavior. At present, the trend of the campus seems to be toward the practical pursuit of careers, "a lessening demand for a traditional college education and a rising demand for career education."[30]

Minority Subcultures The presence of sizable minority groups on the campuses of the large state colleges and universities has been both a

---

[29]For example, see Theodore Roszak, *The Making of a Counter Culture*, Anchor Books, Doubleday & Company, Inc., Garden City, N.Y. 1969, chap. 1.

[30]David S. Bushnell, *Organizing for Change: New Priorities for Community Colleges*, McGraw-Hill Book Company, New York, 1973, p. 116.

reason for and a consequence of the student activism of the 1960s. Although it is obvious that black and Chicano students contribute to both the academic and the athletic subcultures, there are reasons why their interests have tended strongly toward both student activism and the practical, vocational subculture. Professor Harry Edwards, a black sociologist and a militant, in a study based on research of the late 1960s, describes a pattern of campus subcultures within the black minority.[31]

Edwards informs us that the black protest movement of the 1950s was centered largely in southern cities and did not directly involve colleges. Even such "new prophets" of the civil rights movement as Malcom X, Stokely Carmichael, and Rap Brown worked mainly in the streets but eventually began to look toward integrated campuses as a means for mobilizing pressure for major social change. Soon the schools were thought of as "the main battlegrounds in the struggle."[32] Eldridge Cleaver, another militant with strong feelings against the white establishment, saw the only hope for the future of race relations in young black students, joined by large numbers of the young generation of whites with new value patterns.[33]

The black college students described by Edwards can be grouped into two basic types: conformists and various kinds of protesters. The center of the protest subculture numerically is made up of *militants,* generally young students with the primary goal of a college education but also devoted to political activities aimed at improving educational opportunities. A smaller group that provided the original leadership consists of *radical activists,* generally older, academically well-grounded and secure, and politically sophisticated. Both groups are interested in academic progress but are also devoted to improving the position of their race. A much smaller part of the protest subculture consists of *revolutionaries,* not shunning violence if they deem it necessary, identifying strongly with international revolutionary movements, and calling for a complete change in our institutions. Finally, there are the *anomic activists,* products of the "naked and unadulterated black experience in America," ill-educated or miseducated, lacking a clearly formed ideology. Anything that dissipates the hatred and fury of the anomic activists is "relevant"—sit-ins, riots, or other rebellious acts.

At variance with protest groups are the *conformists,* interested totally in degrees and career preparation. In the Edwards description they were second to the militants in numbers. The quiet nature of the campuses at the time of this writing makes it appear that the conformists are now the

[31]Harry Edwards, *Black Students,* The Free Press, New York, 1970.
[32]*Ibid.,* p. 62.
[33]Eldridge Cleaver, *Soul on Ice,* Dell Publishing Co., Inc., New York, 1968, pp. 68–72.

definitive group. There is no doubt, though, that in his investigations Edwards learned much about resentments that continue to smolder under the surface, with a potential for reactivating the protest subcultures.

SOCIAL CHANGE AND THE ACHIEVEMENT FUNCTION OF EDUCATION

Two functions of education mentioned previously are both involved in achievement: the provision of training for jobs and the provision of equal opportunity for the pursuit of those jobs. Neither function is ever performed perfectly. In the 1940s and 1950s the situation differed from the present in that too few teachers, mathematicians, and scientists were produced. Even now there are too few doctors, although other medical training programs are seeing a rapid increase in enrollment. So far as the second function is concerned—providing equality of opportunity—we have already looked at many of the barriers to full equality, especially for college graduation. More must be said about the continuing struggle for educational equality, but first some observations are needed about the inconstancy of societal demand for college graduates.

The Higher Education Market   The 1960s were a decade of extremely rapid expansion of higher education, ranging from 200 percent increase for combined public and private college graduates to nearly 300 percent for graduate level students. The number of Ph.D. degrees awarded rose by over 200 percent and master's degrees by 168 percent in the same decade.[34] Employment for professional and technical workers grew over twice as fast as total employment. The largest increase, one-fourth the total, was in the demand for teachers. There were also very great increases in the demand for scientists and engineers, health services, auditors and accountants, programmers and systems analysts. The total employment of professional and technical workers rose to 11.1 million by 1970 but began to level off by 1971, although the number of college graduates continued to increase.

Shortages of jobs sometimes develop, reflecting a number of changes, one of which is demographic. A declining birthrate is reducing the need for new teachers in elementary schools and even in junior highs and high schools. Government policies are also important in the decline of some kinds of employment opportunities. Federal research grants have declined drastically, especially in engineering fields, but employment

---

[34]These and the following statistics are from Michael F. Crowley, "Professional Manpower: The Job Market Turnaround," *Monthly Labor Review*, October 1972, pp. 9–15.

problems in science and engineering are not entirely a matter of changed government policy. According to Allan M. Carter, Chancellor of New York University, "Even without the topping out of federal support, we would have begun to have an abundance of doctoral scientists in most fields of specialization in the early 1970s, becoming particularly marked later in the decade."[35]

Some of the changes in employment prospects are of a long-range nature and some are temporary. In spite of the problems mentioned, unemployment among college graduates is very low, although many do not find jobs that fully utilize their training. All predictions for the future are subject to error, but the Labor Department foresees, assuming continued prosperity and progress and no major wars or other disasters, that about 13.6 million students will graduate from college in the 1970s. Needs for expansion and replacement will require only about 11 million, so that "a sizable proportion of graduates through the 1970s will enter jobs previously performed by persons without a college degree."[36] Possible areas for absorption of such graduates will be in such fields as government, management, computers, and salesmanship. The Labor Department's prediction does not spell unrelieved gloom, but it does indicate greater competition for the desired jobs. Sociologically, the prediction shows the degree to which such factors as demography, government policy, general prosperity, and technical change can affect individual plans for the future. The other sociological problem raised concerns what segments of the population will complete college most successfully and be given first consideration for the jobs available. This leads us to consideration of the traditional public sentiment that education should give equal opportunity to all.

Education and the Demand for Equality Several comments have been made about barriers to college that are more severe for lower-class than for middle- or upper-class students, especially the barriers of insufficient money and little help from home. In spite of these obvious inequalities, it is a general American belief that people should have equality of educational opportunity. This belief was manifested long ago in the drive for free and compulsory public education, and it was even written into the old "separate but equal" Supreme Court decision of 1896 and greatly strengthened in the desegregation decision of 1954. Veterans' educational benefits and government loans have helped to extend

[35]Allan M. Carter, "Scientific Manpower for 1970–1985," *Science*, vol. 172, p. 132.
[36]Crowley, *op. cit.*, p. 14.

possibilities for equal access to a college education, although America has never gone so far as to support all qualified students in college. Instead, at present, there is a cutback in the government funds that have helped so many students, especially in science. Part of the reason is the obvious one just discussed. There is no longer a critical shortage of personnel. There are also signs of a change that might be more ominous to the old goal of educational equality, a change which stems in part from the difficulties of school financing.

Elementary and secondary schools are victims of elections in a way that many public institutions are not. Their support often depends upon public approval of school bonds, and the voters, tired of rising taxes, often turn them down. Another problem is that school districts are very uneven as to the wealth of their tax base, so that some cannot afford as well-equipped schools as others. A 1973 Supreme Court decision turned down a demand for statewide equalization of funds for school districts; thus district inequality is constitutionally legal. The decision reverses a twenty-year tendency for courts to interfere in favor of equality. Some states make honest attempts to equalize districts regardless of the decision, but those that do not have equalization policies cannot be forced to make them. Probably another difficulty for schools is that segments of the public have been offended by student activism and by much publicity about drug use by students and have developed an unfavorable stereotype of both college and high school students.

Against a background of difficulties for the school have come a series of reports tending to challenge old-time American faith in school as the vehicle for mental development and success in the world. The work of Christopher Jencks and his colleagues at the Harvard Center for Education Research is typical of this viewpoint.[37] Several of their conclusions would make strong propaganda for opponents of school bonds and general school expenditures. On the subject of high-quality staffing and equipment of schools, they conclude that "Differences between high schools contribute almost nothing to the overall level of cognitive inequality (the abilities measured by achievement tests). Differences between elementary schools may be somewhat more important, but evidence for this is still inconclusive."[38] Elsewhere they say "Most differences in adult scores are due to factors that schools do not control."[39] The factors referred to are social class, culture, parental occupation, and genetic differences. They neglect to say that all but one of these factors (genetic differences)

[37]Jencks et al., *op. cit.*
[38]*Ibid.*, p. 93.
[39]*Ibid.*, p. 104.

bear a strong connection to educational achievements of the parental generation.

In defense of Jencks and his colleagues it must be admitted that they advocate good schools for the sake of the happiness and well-being of the young, but not because of a conviction that they make much difference otherwise. To meet the problem of inequality, Jencks advocates much greater equality in pay for jobs, whether they depend upon a great amount of education or very little. This is his alternative to what he sees as a hopeless task of trying to achieve equality through the medium of schooling.

Godfrey Hodgson reviews a series of similar conclusions from Patrick Moynihan, James Coleman, and others. He reminds us that in times past social darwinists used such arguments against educating children of the poor at all and that similar arguments were used against good education for black children after the reformist sentiments of the Civil War period declined. He speaks of the "dangers that this new skepticism, which is eroding the liberal assumptions, could be distorted and used to rationalize a second period of indifference in a nation once again weary of the stress of reform."[40]

Christopher Jencks does not deny that black Americans have made spectacular progress in education in recent years. The average black person one generation ago had two to three years less education than the average white. By 1970, the difference had declined to only one year. By the 1970s black Americans expressed a desire for more schooling than did whites with comparable test scores and economic backgrounds.[41] A California poll taken in 1973 found both blacks and Chicanos more convinced than the average citizen that college is necessary for the young person who wants to get ahead in the world.[42]

It has to be granted that there are certain educational myths in American society. There would not be sufficient openings for college graduates if everyone went through college. There is no certainty that the people who dropped out of high school would have eventually done well in life if they had been somehow compelled to finish. Various psychological problems are being overlooked if such a claim is made. But the important question is whether minority groups are right in assuming that college is really important, especially for groups whose family backgrounds do not provide them with access to the more coveted jobs. Labor

[40]Godfrey Hodgson, "Do Schools Make a Difference?", *Atlantic,* vol. 231, no. 3, March 1973, p. 46.
[41]Jencks et al., *op. cit.,* pp. 142–143.
[42]Mervin D. Field, "Value of College Education Losing Weight with Public," *Los Angeles Times,* July 3, 1973, part 1, pp. 3, 20.

department statistics seem to give an affirmative answer. During the 1960s the ratio of black to white earnings improved slightly for high school graduates, but much more markedly for black college graduates.[43] Our schools are faced with a situation in which previously educationally disadvantaged minorities are accepting the traditional American faith in education. It seems doubtful that the Jencks' solution of better pay for low-prestige jobs would be sufficient, even though it would help. A more typical demand of minority group leaders is that of access to a larger share of the jobs which require high educational achievement and carry a commensurate feeling of status. It would be a cruel irony for public support for education to decline just as America's minorities are seizing upon schooling as the path to the future.

SUMMARY

In all societies education has the function of transmitting the accumulated culture of the past to future generations. In modern societies,especially, it has the additional function of developing new ideas in order to remain abreast of present developments and prepare for the future. Other major functions of education are training needed personnel, promoting citizenship, and maintaining status for some, and encouraging social mobility for others. Educational systems also display such latent functions as the development of adolescent subcultures, violence and vandalism, and various kinds of student activism. In modern societies a gap develops between the time of learning and the time of application of knowledge, making education long and difficult.

Early American education stressed the cultural-transmission function of education and the development of national feelings. As education became increasingly universal, it began to be seen largely as a vehicle for upward mobility, but for many there were barriers in the way.

Because educational systems are a reflection of their societies and influence the growing generation, an examination of high school and college reveals many of the distinguishing traits of the society. In the United States, a fun-and-popularity subculture in high school, although criticized by adults, is a fair reflection of a fun-loving adult world. Ability-grouping in schools reflects the strain between the ideal of equality and the realities of differing starts in life and differing academic possibilities.

The path to and through college can be viewed in some respects as a long, uneven race, with high hurdles to be surmounted by those of

[43]U.S. Department of Labor, *U.S. Manpower in the 1970s: Opportunity and Challenge*, Superintendent of Documents, Government Printing Office, Washington, D.C., 1970, p. 7.

working-class or depressed ethnic-group background—the problems of initial motivation, "knowing the ropes," and raising the money.

Whatever the criticisms of college, it accomplishes the task of training the needed personnel for the job market, with a few exceptions, especially in the field of medicine. The college probably also has the function of liberalizing attitudes toward racial and ethnic groups and increasing tolerance of opinion differences. In spite of these changes, the higher-class position achieved by many college graduates tends to separate them from minority racial groups.

The college subcultures that have been analyzed are the collegiate, academic, vocational, and nonconformist. Burton R. Clark suggests that a decline in the academic subculture and rise in the practical, vocational subculture may lead to a technically expert society, but a society without enough reflection on purpose, direction, and philosophy.

The last of the college subcultures, nonconformist, has merged with student activism, and student-activist movements attract many other students as well. Student activism can be analyzed as a development made possible by a somewhat separated college world developing an antagonism toward what it sees as "the establishment." Other developments are necessary before such attitudes erupt into demonstrations, but these developments have been frequent in recent years. Although antiwar sentiment is a major factor, student activism of recent times started with other causes, such as free speech and civil rights.

Increasing interest in education has developed among depressed minority groups just as job shortages have begun to develop in many fields requiring college degrees. Several recent studies have displayed skepticism as to whether college achievement is possible for many working-class youth or whether the alternative of better pay for noncollege-type jobs is the only solution. It must be emphasized, though, that much of the struggle for racial equality in the United States is a struggle for status and prestige, not just higher pay for menial jobs.

Chapter 14

The Economic System

The new life which has emerged so suddenly has not been able to be completely organized, and, above all, it has not been organized in a way to satisfy the need for justice which has grown more ardent in our hearts.

Émile Durkheim
The Division of Labor in Society

Economic systems are the institutionalized arrangements developed by societies for the production and distribution of goods. These systems differ widely and usually develop through long custom and necessity rather than through consciously stated economic philosophies. Nevertheless, there is a close relationship between economic systems and other aspects of a culture. For example, often in hunting and gathering societies land, hunting and fishing areas, and food-bearing plants are thought of as communal properties that are not parceled out to individuals.[1] Close

[1]E. Adamson Hoebel, *Anthropology: The Study of Man*, McGraw-Hill Book Company, New York, 1966, pp. 415–416.

cooperation and food sharing are so necessary for survival that they become part of the moral order. In later agricultural societies, productivity becomes great enough to support upper classes who often rationalize the uneven division of rewards on the basis of their own superiority or even of God's will. The very need for rationalization, however, indicates that societies have seen something of a moral issue in their systems of production and reward.

In modern societies the concept of "just rewards" is constantly referred to in every labor dispute. The regulation of industry, tendencies toward monopoly, conflicts of interest in economic and political power, and threats to free enterprise are all viewed as issues of right and wrong.

We shall study the historical rise of our modern economic system and then return to the issue posed by our opening quotation from Durkheim: whether the system can "satisfy the need for justice." We shall look also into the problems and prospects of an economy that meets at least some of the requirements of free enterprise but becomes increasingly regulated because the struggle between free enterprise and social control is also seen as a normative issue.

CAPITALISM IN HISTORICAL PERSPECTIVE

The medieval economic systems were very different from those of today. There were a few wandering merchants and a few trade centers, but for the most part the economy was of a subsistence type, with peasants producing their own goods. Most economic arrangements were based upon obligation to the feudal lord whose lands had to be worked by the serf. Lands belonged in feudal estates and were not for sale. To suggest the sale of manorial estates would be as much out of order as to suggest that the United States sell Texas to Mexico.

Emergence of the Competitive Economy　In contrast, a highly competitive exchange economy emerged with the passing of the Middle Ages. The new economy was still somewhat encumbered by fees and obligations and the granting of special monopolies to favorites of the Crown, but it was moving in the direction of control by supply and demand. Adam Smith, the great champion of the new system, wrote in the late eighteenth century that an "invisible hand" would guide a free economy to make sure that the goods needed by society were produced in the quantities called for by a competitive market. Distribution would be fair and just, with the businessman earning his share in repayment for his enterprise, skill, and risk; the laborer would receive a lesser share for his work, which required less planning and risk. Because labor was plentiful, the laborer would be in a poor bargaining position but at the very worst would have to be paid enough to stay alive and to reproduce his kind.[2]

Smith's idea had great appeal to the rising business classes who wanted greater freedom of the economy, a policy called *laissez faire*, meaning literally "to let alone." The government was not to interfere with business. The encumbrances of the mercantile system were broken, especially in the newly independent United States, and the new laissez-faire economy seemed to be off to a good start. Malthus and his friend David Ricardo saw the possibility of an economy that would produce too many laborers. Ricardo especially thought that if the laborer earned too much money he might cease to work, or even more likely he might produce and successfully rear enormous numbers of ragged children. This would mean that in the next generation there would not be enough jobs, and the result would be unemployment and starvation. (Ricardo incorrectly assumed that deep poverty would cause people to practice restraint in their breeding habits.) Therefore the safe policy would be to pay labor only the barest minimum of survival wages, an idea known as "the iron law of wages." Small wonder that Carlyle spoke of economics as "the dismal science."[3]

Conditions of Labor   Descriptions of the conditions of labor in the late eighteenth and early nineteenth centuries indicate that Ricardo was taken seriously in the emergent industrial nations. The English Factory Acts of 1833, in the name of reform, forbade children under nine to work in textile factories and ruled that children less than thirteen could not work more than forty-eight hours/week in factories or mines. Nine years later it was decided that it was improper for women to pull coal carts through the mines, and women and girls and boys under ten were forbidden to work in the mines.[4] Reform was running wild!

As was to be expected, labor agitation was on the rise, and many thoughtful critics questioned whether the "invisible hand" was working in behalf of the people. Heinrich Heine expressed the bitter mood in his "Song of the Weavers": "Old Germany, listen, e'er we disperse; we are weaving your doom with a triple curse!" In England, Elizabeth Barrett Browning pleaded against the conditions of child labor. She wrote in 1843, "Have you heard the children weeping, O my brothers (while) All day long the iron wheels go onward, grinding life down from its mark, (and) A child's sob in the silence curses deeper than a strong man in his

[2]Robert Heilbroner, *The Worldly Philosophers,* Simon & Schuster, Inc., New York, 1958, chap. III.
[3]*Ibid.,* chap. IV.
[4]J. Salwyn Shapiro, *Modern and Contemporary European History,* Houghton Mifflin Company, Boston, 1951, pp. 133–134.

wrath." While reformers pleaded, angry revolutionists called for an end of the system: "Let the ruling classes tremble . . . the proletarians have nothing to lose but their chains. They have the world to win," declared the *Communist Manifesto* in 1848.

Rising Productivity and Reform Actually, revolutions of the type Marx called for were thwarted, and even today such revolutions are much more the phenomena of peasant and "underdeveloped" countries than of the industrial societies in which Marx had expected revolution. Although the capitalistic system did not deserve the rapturous praise given it by Smith, its very productivity began to frustrate its most bitter enemies and to undermine the iron law of wages policy. The "quantum theory"—the idea that there is only so much to go around, and so it would be disastrous to raise wages—became less convincing. The economic system was showing enough growth so that wages could rise slowly without destroying profits. The dogged resistance to labor unionism broke down slowly in several Western capitalistic countries, and in Germany the powerful Chancellor Bismarck attracted worldwide attention by granting sickness insurance, accident insurance, and old-age pensions. This, said Bismarck, makes working men "far more contented and easier to manage. . . . A great price is not too much to pay if the disinherited can be made contented with their lot."[5] What happened in Germany in the 1880s has finally become common practice in all the major capitalistic nations, although not always bringing the worker the contentment Bismarck expected.

THE DIVISION OF LABOR AND THE MORAL ORDER

One of Durkheim's most important works is *The Division of Labor in Society,* in which he speaks of a new moral order resulting from the increasingly complex division of labor in industrial societies. Before industrialization, people were held together by the traditional norms they followed rather blindly because they were all socialized into the same pattern. They were as alike as though they had been "turned out of the same machine," and it was this culturally induced likeness of belief and habit that gave society its cohesion and its moral order. Durkheim goes on to say that in the modern society, with its intricate division of labor, each man is an exchangist, contributing the product of his labor and depending upon the product of the labor of others. In this type of society a new moral order must be worked out based upon the increasing feeling of interdependence. Hence new rules and regulations arise. Each man can

[5]*Ibid.,* p. 396.

be different; there can be a growing amount of individuality, but the society will be cohesive because new norms based on interdependence will determine what is just, although Durkheim did not maintain justice was yet achieved.

New Norms of Industrialism   Following Durkheim's line of thought, we could speak of the new pension and insurance laws as a first step toward the new moral order, alleviating the poor conditions of labor and, hopefully, winning the loyalty of labor to the economic system. Later, recognizing labor unions, negotiating terms and conditions of labor, shortening hours of work, and in some cases even adopting profit-sharing schemes all came as further steps in this new normative adjustment.

Other regulations illustrate the same trend toward a new type of equity: pure food and drug acts, fairness-in-advertising legislation, and laws to curb monopoly in order to keep competition alive. All these are ameliorative traits of the free-enterprise system and have helped to make it a more attractive system than the Marxists foresaw. At the same time, such policies have curbed the purely laissez-faire features of capitalism, often work only part way, and leave many other problems unsolved.

Growing Interdependence   The interdependence produced by the division of labor in society has had its counterpart in world trade. Not only was each man an "exchangist," but so was each nation, and the dynamic industrial systems of the West began to have a sweeping influence on other parts of the world. Marx, the arch enemy of the system, saw clearly what was happening. As usual he placed the blame at the feet of the "bourgeois" class—the leaders of industry, trade, and finance. Note that the words "industrial society" could easily be substituted for his word "bourgeoisie" without changing the aptness of his description.

> *The bourgeoisie, by the rapid improvement of all instruments of production, by the immensely facilitated means of communication, draws all, even the most barbarian nations, into civilization. The cheap prices of its commodities are the artillery with which it batters down all the Chinese walls, with which it forces the barbarians' intensely obstinate hatred of foreigners to capitulate. It compels all nations, on pain of extinction, to adopt the bourgeois mode of production; it compels them to introduce what it calls civilization into their midst, i.e. to become bourgeois themselves. In a sense, it creates a world after its own image.*
>
> *The bourgeoisie has subjected the country to the rule of the towns. It has created enormous cities, has greatly increased the urban population as compared with the rural, and has thus rescued a considerable part of the population from the idiocy of rural life. . . ."*[6]

[6]Karl Marx and Friedrich Engels, *Manifesto of the Communist Party*, Charles H. Kerr, Chicago, 1888, p. 20.

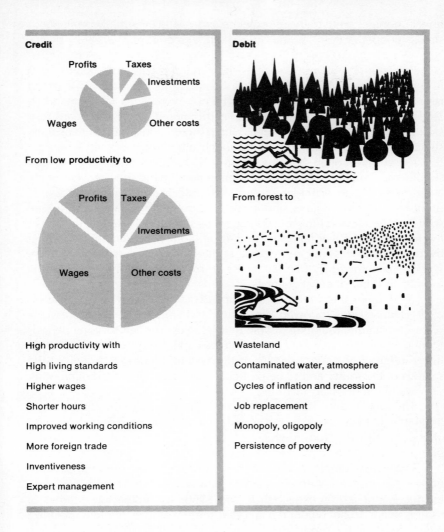

Credit

Profits Taxes

Investments

Wages Other costs

From low productivity to

Profits Taxes

Investments

Wages Other costs

High productivity with

High living standards

Higher wages

Shorter hours

Improved working conditions

More foreign trade

Inventiveness

Expert management

Debit

From forest to

Wasteland

Contaminated water, atmosphere

Cycles of inflation and recession

Job replacement

Monopoly, oligopoly

Persistence of poverty

Whatever else could be said of the economic system, it had achieved a devastating level of productivity, drawing the whole world into its vortex, as Marx predicted. It had also accomplished a higher standard of living than its earlier critics had thought remotely possible, had added many of the rules of Durkheim's "new moral order," had swept agriculture into its system, had found its needed markets and resources, and had displayed great vitality and inventiveness. It also had necessitated international cooperation in trade and science and would eventually bring about similar cooperation in "common-market" agreements.

Persistent Problems   Was the "new moral order" complete? A long list of problems arose. The industrial system, in its rapid development of resources, had often been wasteful. Forests were devastated, marginal lands were eroded, mines scarred the earth, mountainous slag heaps rose skyward, and in petroleum areas sump holes spread their miasmatic stench over the countryside. Not enough attention was paid to waste; rivers and lakes often became cesspools, fish and wildlife died, and supplies of drinking water were contaminated. Living species were being exterminated by insecticides and other chemicals used for the increase of production. Worries grew about the contamination of the atmosphere with automotive and industrial smog. In the summer of 1969 all the fish in the lower Rhine River (an estimated 40 million) were accidentally killed by pesticides. In some respects it seemed that modern industrialism, whether developed by free enterprise or by other systems, was running too fast to think of consequences.

A problem that harassed the capitalistic systems was the business cycle. Depressions followed prosperity, and some of these depressions were devastating, plunging people into hopeless despair for long periods of time and resulting in loud attacks on the capitalist system itself. At other times inflation became a danger to the system, tending to wipe out the savings of the thrifty and to be particularly hard on the elderly and other persons living on fixed incomes.

The system even had a tendency to limit the very competitive motif upon which it was based by the growth of monopoly or, more commonly, *oligopoly*—a condition in which a few producers control practically all of a particular area of production, for example, the automobile industry.

There also remained a number of problems concerning the distribution of wealth. No economic system distributes its wealth with complete evenness, nor is this expected. In the 1960s an increasing number of studies began to document the fact that some elements of the population did not share in the productive prosperity in any way; they remained in a well of poverty, isolated outside the system. This was especially true of aged people and many inhabitants of bypassed rural areas and city slums, as pointed out by Michael Harrington in his book *The Other America* and by Myrdal in *Challenge to Affluence*. The problem became particularly bitter in an age of racial tensions because the largest concentrations of poverty were to be found in the black ghettos, the Mexican-American *barrios*, and the Indian reservations. Congressional committees that investigated the problem of poverty in 1969 were shocked to find malnutrition common in some regions. In some cases the protein shortage was sufficient to show up in cases of *kwashiokor*—an African name for severe protein deficiency characterized by a distended stomach and skinny arms and legs, often resulting in early death.

One problem of the modern economic system is controversial and ill-defined but nevertheless should be mentioned. Was the prosperous economy of the United States getting so involved in war, preparation for war, and the supplying of military equipment that it could rightly be called a *military-industrial complex,* with the implication that pressures would be exerted to keep up military spending because of vested interest in such spending? Left-wing critics consider the answer undoubtedly "Yes." More conservative people hate to accept this view, and yet this is the very possibility that President Eisenhower warned against in his farewell address to the nation.

Obviously, Durkheim's "new moral order" is a long time being born.

THE ORGANIZATIONAL TREND

The trend of the economy has long been in the direction of massive formal organization. Many of the great business enterprises of the nineteenth century were examples of what is termed *family capitalism.* Occasionally the business empires were the work of poor boys who made good, but nearly always they were directed and built into gigantic industries by men from families of at least moderate means. The great fortunes of the Rockefellers, Mellons, Morgans, Du Ponts, Fords, and others were the outcome of energetic entrepreneurs and were managed by the founders and their relatives. With the passing of time and the continued growth of industries, the organizations grew more bureaucratic. Leadership passed increasingly into the hands of managers trained in production, finance, marketing, personnel, and other specialities, and decisions were made by boards of directors. Firms of lobbyists and lawyers were hired to keep the organization on good terms with the government, and public relations men used every wile to give the firm a favorable public image. Such were a few of the trends molding modern giant industries and determining the nature of their organization.

Formal Organization   In an earlier discussion of groups in Chapter 2, considerable attention was paid to the tendency of modern life to be dominated by secondary groups, many of them taking the form of associations or formal organizations. Large universities, police forces, hospitals, and government bureaus are types of formal organizations. In government such organizations are generally spoken of as bureaucracies (discussed in the next chapter), but bureaucratic organization is now just as typical of industry as of government. In the opinion of Peter M. Blau and Richard Scott, authorities on formal organization, "The most pervasive feature that distinguishes contemporary life is that it is dominated by large, complex, and formal organizations."[7]

One need only think of the typical daily routine of life to realize the truth of Blau and Scott's statement—working for a corporation; paying bills to a dozen corporations; using a telephone by the grace of International Telephone and Telegraph Company; making a mortgage payment to a multibillion-dollar insurance company; shopping in a national supermarket; and being entertained in the evening by ABC, NBC, CBS and interrupted by a dozen advertisements of finance companies, drug manufacturers, and a confusion of nationally known products whose hucksters creaselessly jar and grind on the public nerves. All these represent anonymous corporations, not family capitalism. The designation given most corporations in Mexico is fitting to corporations everywhere—*sociedad anónima,* literally, "anonymous society." We have changed enormously since the days of small shop keepers, craftsmen, and farmers. At the top of each corporate organization is a small group of men who rule, not because of ownership, but because of their managerial ability. To this group Galbraith gives the name "technostructure."[8] the technostructure is always a committee of experts, acting jointly to reach decisions. An interfering owner cannot overrule the technostructure for fear of creating tensions that would disrupt the system. If a group is hired to do a study, make itself expert, and reach conclusions, and its conclusions are then overturned, a likely result is demoralization and possibly resignation. Consequently the staff is depended upon completely. It becomes a cohesive group, planning together and drawing in the best advice from each area of expertise. It almost resembles a plot for gaining government contracts, increasing its share of the market, outdistancing competitors, and creating greater consumer demand through advertising. Although small businesses continue to exist, the large corporation of this type has many advantages, gradually making the concentration of industrial power more and more unchallengeable.

The technostructure depends upon a stable economy and therefore is concerned with the fiscal and monetary policies of the government. Social security and other devices that tend to keep buying on an even keel are generally seen as beneficial to such organizations because they help

[7]Peter M. Blau and Richard Scott, *Formal Organization,* Chandler Publishing Company, San Francisco, 1961, p. ix.

[8]John Kenneth Galbraith, *The New Industrial State,* Houghton Mifflin Company, Boston, 1967, pp. 60–71.

to give the stability needed for long-range planning. In other respects the industrial order becomes more enmeshed with and dependent upon the state, and the situation is mutual. The industrial system serves the purposes of the state, doing the research work necessary for weapons development, space programs, and other new advances in science. "The state, through military and other technical procurement, underwrites the corporation's largest capital commitments in its areas of most advanced technology."[9] State and industry merge in ends and methods.

The corporation that supplies equipment for the Navy begins to identify with the Navy. It takes the Navy point of view, and customer and industry pull together for larger appropriations. The interrelationship of corporation and state is not apt to be based upon old-fashioned bribery for special favors (as when railroads virtually owned state legislatures) but is based upon commonality of interest. In a broader sphere, both are dependent upon a stable economy, a well-supported educational system, expansion and growth, scientific advancement—in short, national goals.[10] The military-industrial complex is at hand especially where military, industry, and government develop a mutual involvement and vested interests in weapons development. The real question is whether this is a complex that rightfully prepares the defenses of the United States against possible foreign aggression or whether it is a complex with a dynamic of its own, leading to more and more arms expenditure regardless of need and constituting a threat to peace.[11]

The Organization Man Members of the corporation, especially those at the top of the structure, learn to identity with the organization. The organization is the source of salary and promotion, and it becomes also a source of identify. William H. Whyte made the term "organization man" famous by a book of that title written in the 1950s. So great is the dependence of the organization man upon committee work that Whyte suggests many of our leaders are losing the capacity for independent judgment. Like Riesman's other-directed personalities, they allow their lives to be dominated by others and must dress properly, move to the right neighborhood, drive the right car, make the right friends, and even marry wives who fit in with the group. In the final chapter of Whyte's book, "How to Cheat on a Personality Test," he suggests that the best organization man must be very sharp but must always stop short of being really outstanding or original for fear of appearing somehow different—and different is bad.

[9]*Ibid.*, p. 308.

[10]*Ibid.*, p. 309.

[11]Marc Pilisuk and Thomas Hayden have an excellent discussion of this problem in "Is There a Military-Industrial Complex Which Prevents Peace?", *The Journal of Social Issues*, vol. 21, July 1965, pp. 67–117.

In recent years we have seen many examples of the type of "group think" that is thus promoted. Company or political policies are rigidly followed even if they are unethical or illegal. Loyalty to the organization prevents too much protest. Individual judgment is not needed and therefore withers. The organization has the further trait of being highly protective. It is extremely difficult to pin blame on a particular person within a corporation. Often a corporation is fined for infractions of rules, which means, in the final analysis, that a large number of stockholders get a very tiny reduction in their profits, but no one is really hurt, certainly not the organization man.

The Concentration of Wealth and Power   The late C. Wright Mills wrote a book titled *The Power Elite,* in which he contended that power tends to concentrate in the hands of the few, and he noted the same interrelationship between government, military, and industry that was just cited from a more recent work by Galbraith. In the same book Mills also presents evidence to prove that there is a "hardening of the arteries" insofar as the ready mobility of Americans from low to extremely high status is concerned. In part of his work he uses the example of only the very wealthiest families in the United States, those with holdings of an absolute minimum of $30 million. Among these families he finds a tendency toward greater and greater stability in position. Of the holders of the greatest fortunes of the nineteenth century, 39 percent were born poor; of the last group in his study, the 1950 generation, only 9 percent were born poor.[12] The Mills analysis contrasts with many studies finding as much mobility as ever in American society, so his analysis must be considered open to controversy. A partial explanation of these differences in findings is that Mills was speaking of only the very wealthiest, and most mobility studies have been done in middle ranges.

The offhand impression of many people is that income and inheritance taxes have had a powerful leveling effect so that change could be noted in the years since Mills wrote *The Power Elite.* In "The Future of Capitalism" Robert Heilbroner looks into this possibility.[13] In his opinion the maldistribution of income is not sufficient to constitute a threat to capitalism, but he thinks it is greater than desirable and is not becoming less. Although a generation has passed since high inheritance and gift taxes were initiated, concentration of stock ownership has "shown no tendency to decline since 1922. The statistics of income distribution show a slow but regular drift toward the upper end of the spectrum.[14]

[12]C. Wright Mills, *The Power Elite,* Oxford University Press, New York, 1958.
[13]Robert L. Heilbroner, "The Future of Capitalism," *Commentary,* vol. 41, April 1966, pp. 23–35.
[14]*Ibid.*

A much more dramatic statement of the unequal distribution of wealth and financial power is contained in Lundberg's statement that "1.6 percent of the population owns more than 80 percent of all stock, 100 percent of all state and local bonds, and 88.5 percent of all corporate bonds."[15] Although much is said in corporation advertising about the thousands of people who jointly own the corporations, their holdings are generally small. Less than 20 percent of all corporate stock is held by small investors, although they number approximately 15.4 million people.[16] In an age of concern over racial and ethnic inequality, it is important also to ask to what extent minorities are represented among the major owner's of America's corporations. The figures are not encouraging. As of 1968 the directorships of 88 percent of the fifty biggest corporations in America were held by WASPs (White Anglo-Saxon Protestants) and nearly all the remainder by white ethnics.[17]

Looking not just at the superrich but at the upper fifth of incomes in America, we see other evidences of very great economic inequality. In 1970 the top fifth of family income exceeded average income by 223 percent; at the same time the bottom fifth of family income was only 28 percent of the average for the country as a whole.[18] Stated another way, the top fifth averaged just over eight times as much income as the bottom fifth. It is true that over the last few decades nearly all incomes have risen; nevertheless, the *absolute* gap between rich and poor has increased. Between 1946 and 1970 the incomes of the bottom fifth of American families increased by $1,000; the incomes of the top fifth (already eight times as large) rose by $4,000.[19]

Unequal Power   Wealth is a source of political power—power to finance candidates and campaigns; power to hire lobbyists and lawyers; power to threaten noncooperating congressmen with support for their opponents; and power to get lucrative government contracts, to grant or withdraw funds from foundations and universities, and even to receive special consideration in antitrust cases. "Since the early 1950s, the law against existing monopolies has been permitted to lapse into a state of desuetude," says John M. Blair,[20] a well-informed student of the problem.

[15]Ferdinand Lundberg, *The Rich and the Super-Rich: A Study in the Power of Money Today,* Lyle Stuart, Inc., New York, 1968, pp. 21–22.

[16]*Ibid.,* p. 22.

[17]Fletcher Knebel, "The WASPS: 1968," *Look,* July 23, 1968, pp. 69–72.

[18]Christopher Jencks et al., *Inequality: A Reassessment of the Effect of Family and Schooling in America,* Basic Books, Inc., Publishers, New York, 1972, p. 209.

[19]*Ibid.,* p. 211.

[20]John M. Blair, *Economic Concentration: Structure, Behavior and Public Policy,* Harcourt Jovanovich, Inc., New York, 1972, p. v.

He continues to say that partly as a result of government leniency the 200 largest corporations, which in 1947 held 47.1 percent of manufacturing assets, had increased their holdings to 60.4 percent by 1968. The size of the largest corporations has grown until they often represent more wealth than entire sovereign nations. The fifty largest American corporations employ almost three times as many people as do the fifty states, "and their combined sales are over five times greater than the taxes the states collect."[21] General Motors alone employs 600,000 people.

The very size of the corporations gives them a type of immunity from possible failure. Could the federal government permit the financial and employment chaos that would result from the collapse of such giants? Apparently not. During the Great Depression one of the first remedial measures of the government was the Reconstruction Finance Corporation, set up to lend cheap money to industries to bail them out of their financial distress. Although the Reconstruction Finance Corporation was finally abandoned decades later, the same government thinking occurred recently. When Lockheed seemed on the verge of collapse, the President appealed to Congress for $250 million to rescue the corporation from bankruptcy. Eventually, in spite of much grumbling and criticism, Congress agreed.[22] The government-sponsored railroad combination known as Amtrak can be interpreted as a similar type of government rescue work.

Not only do giant corporations receive special favors and, apparently, immunity from total collapse, but they can even exert their influence in international affairs. A startling case of the attempt to use such power came to light in 1972 in connection with the International Telephone and Telegraph Company (ITT). ITT is alleged to have collaborated secretly with the CIA and high government officials to interfere in the internal affairs of Chile to prevent the late President Allende from taking office.[23]

It is very commonly supposed that the growth and increasing power of corporate wealth has its beneficial sides. Large corporations, with their impersonal structure of organization, have often responded more easily to requirements of fair hiring practices than have small businesses. Sometimes they become quite benevolent concerns for their employees, especially those in the upper levels. It is also supposed that they must be more efficient than smaller business. This latter idea is often called into

[21] Andrew Hacker, "A Country Called Corporate America", New York Times Magazine, July 3, 1966.
[22] "Lockheed Stirs up the Ghost of RFC," Business Week, July 26, 1971, p. 23. Also, "Lockheed Digs Itself Out of a Hole," Business Week, Jan. 29, 1972, pp. 72–74.
[23] To a degree this episode merged with the Watergate scandals that began to occupy the attention of the press in 1973. An early article explaining the matter clearly appeared in Time, vol. 99, April 3, 1972, pp. 42–44, under the title "Meanwhile Down in Chile: Alleged ITT-CIA Plot to Block Allende's Presidency."

question, however. Can corporations grow so big as to be cumbersome, rigid, and set in their ways? Certainly Ralph Nader has accused the auto industry of this very trait, with its concentration on size and power in automobiles long after a considerable segment of the public was looking for fuel economy. John Blair questions the assertion that giant business is more efficient than smaller business concerns. He cites innumerable examples of the relative indifference of big business to the rapid introduction of new inventions and processes.[24] Often smaller competitors do better. One of the reasons is probably the relative invulnerability of some of the largest corporations to failure, which makes it easier for them to rest on their laurels. By oligopolistic control of markets, they often find themselves in a position where they can raise prices even in the face of a falling market and hence keep profits virtually constant. According to Blair, General Motors was able to maintain a gross return of 20.2 percent from 1953 through 1968; Standard Oil of New Jersey, 12.6 percent; and Du Pont, 22.2 percent. These were almost precisely the figures aimed at by the technostructures of the corporations, and they were maintained regardless of dips in the economy.[25] Occasionally an efficient new competitor will upset the possibility for the artificial control of prices by an industry, or foreign imports will force prices into a competitive position. Arguments exist among economists as to how much power oligopolistic industries have to set prices arbitrarily, but increasingly the consensus is that such powers are considerable.

Because we changed long ago from a land of small farmers and businessmen into one in which almost everyone works for a corporation, government agency, or other formal organization, we must look next to the impact of the modern economy on labor.

THE POSITION OF LABOR AND THE IMPACT OF AUTOMATION

Automation, originally defined as the "automatic handling of parts between progressive production processes,"[26] has come to mean any type of automatic process that replaces or improves human control of production. Sometimes the word "cybernation" is used, meaning full use of computers along with other types of automation. In some respects it is a continuation of the increasing industrial efficiency that started with the first days of the Industrial Revolution and the later growth of assembly line production. One effect of the long process of change in production

---

[24]Blair, *op. cit.,* pp. 228–254.
[25]*Ibid.,* pp. 419–437.
[26]Paul A. Samuelson, *Economics: An Introductory Analysis,* McGraw-Hill Book Company, New York, 1964, p. 333.

techniques has been to make work monotonous, and a corollary effect has been to do away with pride in craftsmanship and identification with the product. The resistance of labor to new techniques and the drive for efficiency is an old story, at least as old as Hargreaves and his spinning jenny that was attacked and destroyed by an angry mob. Will automation also reduce worker satisfaction and increase worker anger, or will it alleviate some of the problems of the industrial system?

Bell shows how management attitude toward labor has gradually changed from speed-up to worker satisfaction. The cult of the efficiency expert reached its heyday around the turn of the century with Frederick W. Taylor and his stopwatch and with Frank Gilbreth (Father in the well-known story *Cheaper by the Dozen*). Gilbreth reduced all mechanical operations to their smallest component parts, called "therbligs" (his name spelled backward), in an attempt to speed up each movement.[27] The compulsive nature of the assembly line was heightened as never before, and the resentment toward management and its efficiency experts was correspondingly heightened. The modern policies of coffee breaks and improved conditions of all kinds, along with more of a labor union's definition of what constitutes a fair day, have changed the situation considerably; still it is difficult to make people happy with most kinds of menial jobs, even by such devices as calling garbage men sanitary engineers. In a 1955 study only small percentages of workers in the following categories said they would choose the same kind of work again: service workers, 33 percent; semiskilled operatives, 32 percent; unskilled, 16 percent. Professional, managerial, and sales personnel indicated greater satisfaction with their jobs,[28] although 10 percent of professionals, 36 percent of managers, and 18 percent of sales personnel expressed almost as much discontentment as the lower-paid workers.

A more recent study of worker satisfaction was conducted by the Survey Research Center at the University of Michigan in 1969.[29] The study found only slight correlation between worker satisfaction and high-status jobs but a little higher correlation between worker satisfaction and pay. In specific questions asked the workers, the most important single response was that they wanted challenging jobs; secondly, they wanted enough freedom to do the job right; thirdly, they wanted agreeable fellow workers. Certainly the better pay, greater challenge, and greater freedom are all associated with jobs requiring fairly high levels of

[27]Daniel Bell, *The End of Ideology*, Collier Books, The Macmillan Company, New York, 1962, pp. 227–272.

[28]Nancy C. Morse and Robert S. Weiss, "The Function and Meaning of Work and the Job," *American Sociological Review*, vol. 20, April 1955, pp. 197–198.

[29]Jencks *et al., op. cit.*, pp. 247–250.

skill. Because automation tends to eliminate some of the dullest assembly line jobs, one enthusiastic automation advocate, Bernard Asbell, writes

> We are engaged . . . in one of history's most grand and pure acts of humanity. We are making it unfeasable for masses of men to live like animals. To those millions still entrapped in the animal pens of our old ways, we are showing the way—even compelling them down the way—to dignity, physical freedom and the joys of intellectual discovery.[30]

Although not many researchers in the field are quite as ecstatic in their praise of automation as Asbell, many others point out its ultimate advantages; fewer monotonous jobs paced by the machine and more jobs in which people are in control of the machines. There will be no more need for Markham's "Man with the Hoe"—"distorted and soul-quenched . . . stolid and stunned, a brother to the ox."

Automation and Job Replacement   One can hardly mention automation without entering into a discussion of job replacement. There are some areas in which the loss of jobs in recent years has been a cause for alarm. There has been a loss of 435,000 railroad jobs, 265,000 jobs in textile mills, 310,000 jobs in coal mining, and 3,600,000 jobs in agriculture.[31] Many of these job losses have resulted from new automated techniques, although some have been caused by the decline in demand in certain industries, coal, for example.

The following advertisement says a lot about the versatility of new equipment and reasons for workers' concern over job losses:

> TransfeRobot 200 will pick up, turn over, insert, transfer, shuttle, rotate, or position parts accurately, and will control secondary operations such as drilling, stamping, heat sealing, welding, embossing, forging.[32]

Such machines are always frightening to the worker and perhaps even to the disinterested layman.

Automation increases the need for technical and professional workers; it produces more goods and services; it elevates the level of management; and it is one of many factors making a stable economy imperative. However, automation leaves little room for the uneducated or those with outworn skills. Jobs are being replaced at the very time that

---

[30]Bernard Asbell, *The New Improved American*, Dell Publishing Co., Inc., New York, 1965, p. 23.
[31]*Ibid.*, pp. 173–174.
[32]Asbell, *op. cit.*, p. 30.

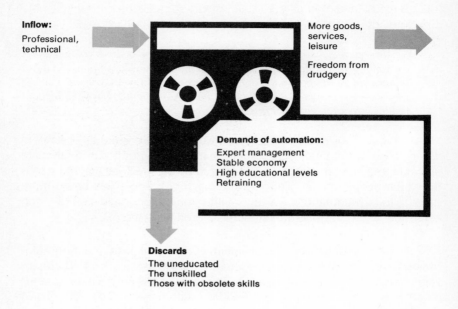

Inflow:
Professional, technical

More goods, services, leisure

Freedom from drudgery

Demands of automation:
Expert management
Stable economy
High educational levels
Retraining

Discards
The uneducated
The unskilled
Those with obsolete skills

many disadvantaged minority groups are most insistent on job equality. The present job situation has helped spur the drive of minority groups for more access to higher education so they will not be left behind in the shrinking field of menial occupations. The following graph from the Labor Department gives a picture of the changing labor situation with its general demand for jobs requiring training beyond the high school level; professional, technical, and service occupations are the fastest-growing ones.

The graph is sufficiently generalized to need a little explanation. The professional and technical category includes business administration, all kinds of engineering, and nearly all kinds of health services, as well as physical, social, and life scientists, teachers, and many more. Many of the next entries are nearly self-explanatory. Operatives, near the bottom of the list, includes many manufacturing jobs. In this area note that the projected increase is barely enough to keep up with population, in spite of an expected growth in production. This slow growth in employment reflects more automation of manufacturing processes. The same is true to a much greater degree for nonfarm laborers and even more for farm laborers.

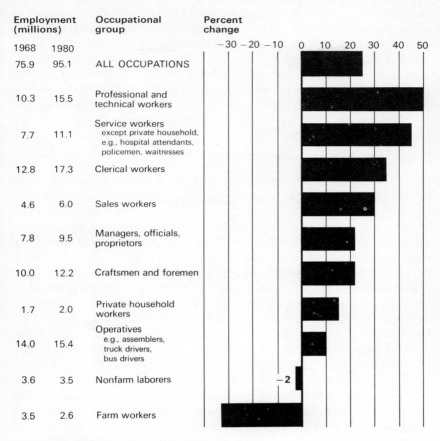

Employment (millions)		Occupational group	Percent change
1968	1980		
75.9	95.1	ALL OCCUPATIONS	
10.3	15.5	Professional and technical workers	
7.7	11.1	Service workers except private household, e.g., hospital attendants, policemen, waitresses	
12.8	17.3	Clerical workers	
4.6	6.0	Sales workers	
7.8	9.5	Managers, officials, proprietors	
10.0	12.2	Craftsmen and foremen	
1.7	2.0	Private household workers	
14.0	15.4	Operatives e.g., assemblers, truck drivers, bus drivers	
3.6	3.5	Nonfarm laborers	−2
3.5	2.6	Farm workers	

Source: U. S. Dept. of Labor, *United States Manpower in the 1970s: Opportunity and Challenge,* Government Printing Office, 1970, p. 13.

The *Occupational Outlook Handbook* of the Labor Department,[33] in its lists of average annual openings between 1970 and 1980, notes in several categories that "Employment decline will more than offset openings from retirements and deaths." Such a statement is a notice of

[33]U.S. Department of Labor, Bureau of Labor Statistics, "Occupational Outlook Handbook in Brief," in *Occupational Outlook Quarterly,* vol. 16, no. 1, Spring 1972.

dying occupations, many of which are in the railroad industry. It is inevitable that some trades will die and others will be born, although it is small satisfaction for a man laid off from work to know that someone with more modern skills is getting a job elsewhere. Part of the solution for technological unemployment is to be found in retraining programs, but such programs are of little use unless the economy is prosperous enough to absorb large numbers of workers, including those laid off from obsolete jobs as well as young people entering the labor force. What economic measures can be taken to ensure a prosperous economy?

STABILIZING THE ECONOMIC SYSTEM

Economic planning, whether by business, government, or an individual householder, is very difficult unless prices remain fairly constant. Inflation cuts into each person's wages and even deeper into the meager incomes of recipients of welfare and old-age pensions. On the other hand, general stability of prices has often accompanied a sluggish economy, with little new investment and therefore unemployment. The resulting problems become more than generalized statistics because unemployment always strikes hardest at certain social groups. In 1969, for example, unemployment among youths aged sixteen to nineteen was 5.5 times as high as for adults of twenty-five to fifty.[34] Demographic factors will reduce slightly the number of sixteen- to nineteen-year-olds in the population in the coming years, but the young age group will continue to be overrepresented among the unemployed. Although black people had made gains in education through the 1960s and more of them had good jobs than before, black unemployment continued to be about twice as high as white. Recession boosts the rate of unemployment for young people and black people and is the worst enemy of both groups, just as inflation is the worst economic enemy of the elderly. For years politicians and economists have tried to grapple with these twin problems, often with little success. The traditional policies have been those of monetary and fiscal manipulation.

Monetary and Fiscal Policy   The age of Woodrow Wilson brought a new concept into the management of the national economy—*monetary policy,* which is the attempt to control inflation and deflation through control of the money supply. The Federal Reserve System can lower or raise rediscount rates, which in turn increases or lowers interest rates to the borrower. The principle is that if money is cheap (interest rates are low), more people will borrow, and if money is costly (interest rates are

[34]U.S. Department of Labor, *U.S. Manpower in the 1970s: Opportunity and Challenge,* Government Printing Office, Washington, D.C., 1970, p. 7.

high), fewer people will borrow. The record indicates that monetary policy has had only a very limited effect. It certainly was not sufficient to control the Great Depression or inflations that have taken place since. More governmental policies were to be tried.

The new policies were started during the Roosevelt administration, without a clear theory or mathematical analysis of just what the result to the economy would be. The vague term "pump priming" was used to describe the intended effect; but soon a new economic analysis of the government role in a depression was provided by John Maynard Keynes of England, and the science of economics has never been the same. Keynes started by discovering an economic dilemma that had been overlooked before his time: individual savings can have the effect of slowing down an economy if there is no outlet for their investment.[35] This slowing down has a snowballing effect that can eventually end in a new equilibrium of permanent depression. Vast new discoveries or other sources of new investment could reverse the cycle, as could the wasteful expenditures of war. The first alternative does not always appear, and the second is too horrible to be a purposeful solution, but there remains a third alternative. Let the government spend large amounts of money, in deficit spending if necessary, to make up for the shrinkage of private investment. The management of the money supply started in Wilson's time is called *monetary policy*; the pumping of money into the economy by direct government action is part of what is called *fiscal policy*.[36]

Distribution of Gross National Product   Neither policy is enthusiastically endorsed by all economists, but they have become so important in governmental policies as to be essential to economic institutions. Even the public is forming the habit of thinking in terms of modern fiscal policy and other words associated with modern *macroeconomics,* that is, large-scale analysis of economic issues. "Gross national product" has become a part of the common vocabulary, although "net national product" is a little more meaningful for the following equation. *Gross national product* is the sum total of all goods and services produced in a single year. *Net national product* equals gross national product minus depreciation and will be referred to as NNP.

$$NNP = C + I + G$$
where C = consumer expenditure
 I = private investment
 G = government expenditures

---

[35]Samuelson, *op. cit.,* p. 242.
[36]*Ibid.,* chap. XII.

To keep the equation balanced it would be necessary to increase G if there is a decline in C and/or I. If C, I, and G all increase rapidly, as in wartime, there are strong inflationary pressures that can be headed off by higher taxes, price and wage controls, or possibly by forced savings of part of income (to reduce C in the formula). Manipulation of the economy is not always successful, but it is hoped that this brief glance at theory will at least help to clarify the methods that are attempted. It can be seen that whereas the individual reduces spending when times are hard, the government, by keynesian logic, should increase spending. (See models illustrating balanced and inflationary economics page 339.

The Failures of Economic Policy   The question undoubtedly arises in the mind of the reader, "If this kind of economic analysis is theoretically sound, why doesn't it work?" Part of the answer can be supplied in thinking about the contrast between economics and sociology. The economist analyzes money problems as though we were all "economic men," working efficiently to make money and governed by people equally wise in economic matters. The total social system, however, generates all kinds of pressures for policies that might not be economically sound. Military spending must go on, even though it is not economically sound. Sometimes the government makes war, which dislocates the economy by creating strong inflationary pressures. Some presidents and congresses are very favorable to spending money to help special interests or regions of the country; others favor heavy spending to combat poverty. At times, also, economic conservatism gains the upper hand in governmental thinking and attempts are made to cut all costs. Much of the public, and many politicians as well, think government should handle money the way individuals do: If times are bad, cut back on spending. It is not unusual to see the government doing precisely the opposite of what economic theory would suggest.

Even the failure to follow keynesian theory, however, does not answer the entire question of why the system fails to remain stable. The early 1970s saw both inflation and a fairly high rate of unemployment, along with plaguing problems of foreign exchange. Because the United States spends many billions of dollars abroad on tourism and in the stationing of troops, money tends to drain out of the country. The only cure for drainage of money is to sell more goods abroad or to cut imports; but cutting imports reduces competition and makes it easier for American manufacturers to raise prices. Similarly, the more goods we sell abroad, the more prices will rise at home, unless the goods are in great abundance or the market is somehow controlled. Generally speaking, if foreign countries will pay high prices for beef or wheat, why would the producer be willing to sell them for less on the home market?

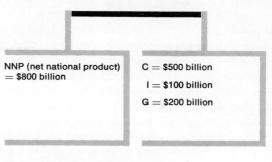

NNP (net national product) = $800 billion

C = $500 billion

I = $100 billion

G = $200 billion

Economy in balance NNP = C + I + G

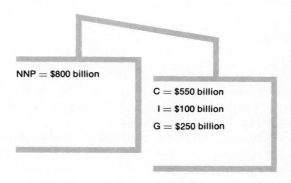

NNP = $800 billion

C = $550 billion

I = $100 billion

G = $250 billion

Economy out of balance NNP < C + I + G

Inflationary pressures at work. Policies to prevent inflation could involve high interest rates to discourage I (investment), or higher taxes to reduce C (consumer spending), or government economies to reduce G (government expenditures).

Yet another complication of the price problem is that many resources are in short supply. If we are cut off from foreign sources of petroleum and must develop our own at higher costs, and look farther and dig deeper for iron, copper, and other minerals, then prices of those commodities will inevitably rise.

Perhaps we are reaching a new phase in economics in which keynesian theory, even if intelligently applied, is not enough. Increasingly over the years the unskilled fail to benefit in new jobs even if the economy is prosperous. For example, 1972 was a very prosperous year; yet unemployment among nonfarm laborers stood at 10.3 percent[37], and that figure was by no means exceptional for a prosperous year. Even if stimulated by high government spending, industry no longer absorbs all the workers. We may eventually have to employ large numbers of people to work on mass-transportation projects, improvement of the environment, reforestation, and development of parks and playgrounds. Such programs, if paid for by taxation, could also drain off surplus funds and slow down inflation.[38] Even if, as many economists believe, there is no way to completely prevent recessions, such policies could at least provide better-than-welfare incomes for the unskilled. Whatever the solutions to our economic problems, few will doubt that new ideas are needed and that present policies are only partial solutions to the problems of economic instability.

SUMMARY

Economic systems are the institutionalized means for production and distribution of goods. Particularly where distribution is concerned, the problem of "just rewards" is viewed by members of society in moral terms; various attempts are made to rationalize uneven reward systems or to change them.

The system that we call modern capitalism emerged slowly out of systems based upon the privileges of feudalism but changed with the advance of the Industrial Revolution. Adam Smith, the best-known early champion of a free-enterprise system, expected capitalism to be a nearly perfect system, distributing goods fairly on a basis of supply and demand. His ideas were widely accepted by rising business interests, but bad conditions in factories and mines caused protests and revolutionary threats. However, capitalism developed such high productivity that it was possible for wages to increase without cutting out profits, and labor reforms gradually came about. Bismarck was the first powerful statesman to grant pensions and other modern benefits to labor, hoping therewith to buy their loyalty for Germany.

As Émile Durkheim pointed out, the intricate division of labor in modern society calls for new norms based upon interdependence and rewards rather than punishments. Greater rewards for labor were a part of the new moral order made possible by high productivity. Even Karl Marx was aware of the great productivity of the capitalistic system and its power to supersede other economic systems, but he expected it to deepen

[37]Melville J. Ulmer, "The Collapse of Keynesianism," New Republic, May 5, 1973, p. 19.
[38]Ulmer, ibid., pp. 17–21.

the poverty of the poor. The system did not lead to the ever-deepening poverty Marx foresaw, but it lacked much of what might have been implied in Durkheim's new moral order.

Despite slowly rising standards of living, new problems arose— waste of natural resources and contamination, business cycles and depressions, monopolistic trends in many industries. In spite of a generally improved standard of material well-being, poverty persisted. Another problem was the increasing involvement of the economic system in military production; a decline in military spending could injure the economy.

Major trends in the economy include greater control by management in large and constantly growing corporations. Although thousands of people own stock in the major corporations, the majority of the ownership is in very few hands. Several sociologists, following the lead of the late C. Wright Mills, have documented a concentration of power in a new "power elite" of business, government, and the military; but their critics would argue that the term "power elite" suggests closer coordination between economic leaders than actually exists.

A worry to labor has been the increase in automation in modern industry. There is no question that many people are replaced in their jobs. New jobs are created, and often the new jobs are cleaner, less monotonous, and more highly skilled than the older jobs. However, for the completely unskilled the employment situation becomes more difficult.

Even more difficult for labor is the threat of economic recessions, with accompanying increases in unemployment. For decades governments have attempted to manipulate economies to prevent recessions and to prevent serious inflation. Economic theory calls for manipulating the money supply and increasing or decreasing the amount of government spending to try to keep the economy on an even keel. The realities of politics, military spending, rising costs of oil and other resources, and problems of international exchange make it difficult to apply keynesian theory. The result is a long-term inflationary trend that continues even in periods of unemployment. Sometimes it is suggested that the government return to the policies of the 1930s by employing people in public works projects, thus ensuring earned incomes and also improving both rural and urban environments.

Chapter 15

Political Institutions

Inherent in all democratic systems is the constant threat that the group conflicts which are democracy's lifeblood may solidify to the point where they threaten to disintegrate the society.[1]

Seymour Martin Lipset
Political Man

Political or *governmental institutions* are societal arrangements for making and enforcing laws, protecting the public health and welfare, distributing public funds and tax burdens, conducting foreign affairs, and deciding the issues of war and peace. Political institutions are the ultimate source of legitimate power in a social system, whether the system is based upon rule by the many or rule by the few. The state seeks to achieve a monopoly of power and a primary claim on the devotion of its people. In return it offers its people a sense of common identity and social cohesion.

[1]Seymour Martin Lipset, *Political Man*, Anchor Books, Doubleday & Company, Inc., Garden City, N.Y., 1963, p. 70.

The word "state" is used here to designate the nation and its government, rather than subordinate governments such as Florida, California, White Russia, or the Ukraine. The word state is used in this way in most parts of the world, referring to a government with full independence or *sovereignty*.

An understanding of political institutions calls for an analysis of the characteristics of the nation-state, the types of leadership that emerge, the interplay of political conflict and national consensus, the patterns of social-class participation, and the possible threats to political systems. Is the force of nationalism too powerful to be subordinated to regional or worldwide interests? Against a background of conflicting interests, can democratic states achieve sufficient agreement to maintain cohesion, give all classes and ethnic groups a sense of belonging and participation, and avoid being torn apart by extremist movements of right and left? Are comparable problems faced by urban-industrial nations whether their governmental systems are democratic or not?

THE NATION-STATE

In an economic sense the modern nation-state is an obsolete institution, because markets and resources cross boundary lines, as do problems of the world economy and money market. Economic turbulence in one country has its repercussions throughout the world. All nations have a vested interest in trade and commerce, although occasionally national ambitions or animosities become so great as to blind people and their leaders to this fact. Despite the economic arguments for a world united, the world is very much disunited, and nation-states remain virtually sovereign; that is, within the limits of their military might, they are able to control all their affairs without the intervention of a higher authority.

Historical forces have welded nations into their present patterns, sometimes suddenly, as for example the independence of the United States or the unification of Italy and Germany. More frequently, nation-states have grown through slow accretion, adding territories, enduring common trials and ordeals, and finding common sentiments and heroes until the bonds of unity are secure. This potential unity does not always materialize and result in nationhood; whether it will do so in such new states as Nigeria and Uganda remains to be seen. If the nation-state is successful, it helps to fill man's need for identity, common cause, and the grouping of ethnocentric attitudes around a center of devotion.

National Fanaticism There are recent cases of devotion to the nation-state rising to fanatical heights. Mussolini spoke of the state as not just an association of people but as a spiritual entity. "Fascism conceives of the State as an absolute," he said, "guiding the play and development, both material and spiritual, of a collective body. The Fascist State is itself conscious and has a will and personality. . . . "[2] Communism, on the other hand, is supposed to be an internationalist movement, one in which the state will eventually "wither away." Nevertheless, the appeal of devotion to Mother Russia seemed to do more for rousing a fighting spirit in World War II than the appeal to ideology. At present the communist states, especially Russia and Red China, cannot maintain monolithic unity as differences in national interest arise. Hitler's Nazi movement was intensely nationalistic, just as was Mussolini's fascism, but it added another ingredient that is a nightmare to the modern world—racism. If race should become the intensely emotional unifying force for human groups, the world could be torn apart in new ways even more devastating than those we have known in the recent past. Whatever the dangers of nationalism may be, it has at least generally united people within their particular territories. Racism has a potential for tearing them apart.

Whether the time will come when people can be united, taking pride in the accomplishments of common humanity, remains to be seen. Fiction writers have foreseen this possibility only in the event of having to unite against a common enemy from outer space. George Orwell saw no possibility for unity but imagined a future world divided into superna-tions, all keeping up a flagrant nationalism to control their people under the rule of Big Brother. A constant state of near-war was necessary, but all the rulers realized that actual all-out war had become an impossibility. Of course, we have no guarantee that states will display even the minimal wisdom Orwell suggests. Certainly we see no sign that the state is about to "wither away."

There are, however, certain centrifugal forces at work within many nation-states, tending to pull them apart. Some of these forces are social-class and regional divisions. Some states, such as the Soviet Union and the United States, contain many racial and ethnic differences. Nearly all modern urban societies face mobile populations with constantly growing economic demands. The complexities of urban-industrial sys-tems call for greater organization to appease all conflicting demands and coordinate efforts. One result of new organizational demands is a changing type of leadership.

POLITICAL LEADERSHIP, POWER, AND BUREAUCRACY

Government is the one institution with the legitimate power to make and enforce decisions and to see that its will is obeyed. At the same time, only

[2]Benito Mussolini, "The State as Life," *International Conciliation,* Carnegie Endowment for International Peace, October 1926.

the most naïve citizen can fail to see that powerful vested interests attempt to pressure the government in one direction or another. When the interests of pressure groups become too great, it can be said that government is run more by influence than by constituted authority.

Power, Authority, and Influence   *Power* is the ability to make and enforce decisions. The most obvious and legitimate type of power is called *authority,* the kind of power legally given to holders of public office, both elective and appointive. Authority is usually limited to certain areas, such as the broad areas of executive, legislative and judicial authority or such very limited areas as those of animal wardens, traffic guards, or inspectors of weights and measures.

There is another kind of power besides that of constituted authority. Much power is wielded by those who are in a good position to convince authorities of their point of view or to pressure them for special favors. This latter type of power is called *influence.* Influence has no special legal status and is hard to detect and measure, but it is always present and must not be overlooked. One who studies only the framework of government without studying lobbyists, campaign contributions, and election techniques is assuming that power is entirely a matter of authority. Those who believe some kind of "establishment" wields all the real power from behind the scenes obviously considers influence more important than authority. Actually both are extremely important. Because influence can be in the form of bribery, graft, favoritism in contracts, and other forms of corruption, it is easy to think of influence as necessarily illegitimate; but many attempts to exert influence are perfeclty honest and legal. Even the concerned citizen who writes to his congressman is attempting to use influence. Reformist movements of the type discussed under collective behavior attempt to exert influence, and the right to be heard certainly cannot be denied to oil, automobile and steel corporations, shipping lines, airlines, labor unions, farmers' groups, and innumerable others with causes to plead. The problem is whether the influence is honest and whether all sides get to be heard. Obviously, those who can make large campaign contributions have an advantage.

An advantage goes also to those who understand and can most easily approach the bureaus through which much of government operates. As governments become more gigantic, they must depend increasingly upon the types of formal organization mentioned in the previous chapter. Government bureaus have the same characteristics as the organizational structures of corporations. They are necessary means for accomplishing the goals of government as well as industry. Max Weber praised bureaucracy highly from the strictly technical point of view, although the word bureaucracy often has bad connotations. Why are bureaucracies necessary, and what connection, if any, do they have with some of the problems of influence?

Weber's Analysis of Bureaucracy   Weber was the classical sociological writer on the subject of bureaucracy, describing its characteristics thoroughly and noting the bureaucratic trend of government and industry. In many respects he was strong in his praise of bureaucracy for its "purely technical superiority over any other form of organization,"[3] although he was pessimistic about the effect of bureaucracy on individualism and liberty. *Bureaucracies,* in his description, are large, hierarchically arranged organizations with precise assignments of duties and powers, well-defined qualifications for positions, and precise rules and directions tending to make them foolproof; they are impersonal in the sense that their services and positions are open to all people irrespective of race, family, or status. Bureaucracy is frequently charged with inefficiency, but Weber attempted to show that it is the most efficient organizational form ever devised. Perhaps the apparent contradiction comes about because earlier forms of administration were much more lacking in efficiency than are modern bureaucracies. A view of the contrasting possibilities for leadership and administration will help to clarify this point.

There are, says Weber, three ways of legitimizing authority: (1) It can be made legitimate on traditional grounds, resting on a belief in the sanctity of custom and inheritance; (2) it can be based on charismatic principles, resting on devotion to the heroic leader; or (3) it can be based on rational grounds, resting on belief in the authority of those who have risen to power through tested competence.[4]

The traditional leaders are best illustrated by systems of monarchy and nobility in which rights to rule are recognized by inheritance. Important administrators and courtiers, and even army and navy officer corps, are recruited from the upper classes, more on the basis of kinship or family tradition than on qualification or efficiency. If the system must adjust to the modern business world, then pressure is exerted for developing an efficient civil-service system based on competitive tests—an administrative bureaucracy.[5]

Charismatic leadership, as we saw in the study of religion, is based upon intense personal loyalty to a magnetic leader. In government this is

[3]Max Weber, *Essays in Sociology,* H. H. Gerth and C. Wright Mills (eds.), Oxford University Press, New York, 1946, p. 240.

[4]Weber, *The Theory of Social and Economic Organization,* A. M. Henderson and Talcott Parsons (trans.), Talcott Parsons (ed.), The Free Press, Glencoe, Ill, 1947.

[5]Lipset, "Bureaucracy and Social Reform," *Research Studies,* Washington State University, vol. 17, 1947, pp. 11–17.

often the revolutionary leader who brings about great changes in the social order. Eventually the charismatic leader dies or is replaced. A successor might try to hold control of the movement entirely in his own hands, but eventually the changes have to be institutionalized and administered through a bureaucracy. Sometimes bureaucratization is a long, slow process, as it was in the United States, where the famous spoils system for recruiting public servants was very evident until the era of civil-service reform after the Civil War. It also should be noted that charismatic qualities are not the monopoly of revolutionists. Many constitutionally elected presidents have had charismatic qualities, exciting strong loyalties and bringing about major changes—Jackson, Lincoln, the two Roosevelts, and Kennedy, for example. The person who sees his role simply as carrying out legislation and avoiding drastic change might be characterized as the *bureaucratic type*. All those presidents whose names no one can remember might be called bureaucratic types, although Weber considered the definitive type of bureaucrat to be an appointive official.

The third means of legitimizing authority, on rational-legal grounds, is characteristic of the trend of the industrial world. Powers and duties are carefully assigned to leaders and assistants in the hierarchical manner typical of bureaucracy. Bureaucracy provides the expertness that traditional arrangements often lack and the continuity that charismatic leadership often fails to provide. It is the most rational means of organization and administration.

Criticisms of Bureaucracy The foregoing discussion, consistent with Weber's views, shows the positive side of bureaucracy and, to some extent, the ideal of a bureaucracy rather than the reality. In actual practice some of the rules of impersonality and impartiality are violated. Even in bureaucracies it often helps to know the right people. Equally important, in terms of the discussion of influence with which we started this section, it helps to have one's friends appointed to important positions in governmental bureaus. Ever since their establishment, certain regulatory commissions have been in a position of great power. If railroads, airlines, the food and drug industries, power companies, and communications networks are regulated by government commissions, it is to their interest to win friends on the commissions or even to exert their influence to get their friends appointed to such commissions. In an age when government is too vast and remote to be watched by the average citizen, it is easy for the public interest to be sacrificed. On the other hand, sometimes the public becomes so roused that various associations are formed to exert their pressure on the side of the consumer. It has always been said that the price of liberty is eternal vigilance. When bureaucracies grow remote and inaccessible, even greater vigilance is needed.

Complaints about who runs a bureaucracy, though, do not amount to a refutation of Weber's idea that bureaucracy is an efficient means of accomplishing the aims of government and industry. A criticism that aims at the very nature of bureaucracy has to do with its latent functions— unforeseen and unintended results inevitable in the system. One latent function is a confusion of ends and means. Bureaucrats can become so absorbed in the rules that they forget the actual purposes for which the rules were made.[6] In schools, for example, the desired end is education; attendance and grades are only means to this end. Yet for some administrators attendance records and grades are the overriding concerns of the institution. Another problem is that bureaucracy consists of so many levels of officialdom that it is hard to reach the person holding ultimate authority. "Going through channels" becomes a tedious process, and often it is necessary to find "unofficial channels" to cut through too much bureaucratic red tape. Thus the person who happens to know the secretary to the top official can save much bother, but this undermines the impersonality that is supposed to be part of the bureaucratic ethic.

Sometimes a bureaucracy seems to proliferate officials, resulting in "more chiefs than Indians." This is the type of situation lampooned by C. Northcote Parkinson in *Parkinson's Law*.[7] Parkinson makes it appear to be a "scientific law" that much of the work of bureaucracies consists of men making work for each other and that the number of bureaucrats increases whether the bureau has anything to do or not. He exaggerates, of course, but voices the feelings of many people about bureaucracy. A writer on the same subject, Laurence J. Peter, has come up with the term "level of incompetence." His idea, which he calls the Peter Principle, is that in a bureaucracy people are promoted if they do their jobs well. They finally get promoted into jobs that they are unable to perform well, and the promotions stop at that point. They have "reached their level of incompetence," and there they remain, inefficient and exasperating.[8]

Lipset shows how the routinization of government bureaucracies makes them conservative and unable to adjust to new ideas.[9] Alfred Weber raises a more disturbing thought about bureaucratization—it is inconsistent with liberty. He decries the growth of great business and

[6]Robert K. Merton, *Social Theory and Social Structure,* The Free Press of Glencoe, Inc., New York, 1957, pp. 19–84.

[7]C. Northcote Parkinson, *Parkinson's Law and Other Studies in Adminstration,* Houghton Mifflin Co., Boston, 1957.

[8]Laurence J. Peter and Raymond Hull, *The Peter Principle,* William Morrow & Company, Inc., New York, 1969.

[9]Lipset, "Bureaucracy and Social Reform," *op. cit.,* pp. 11–17.

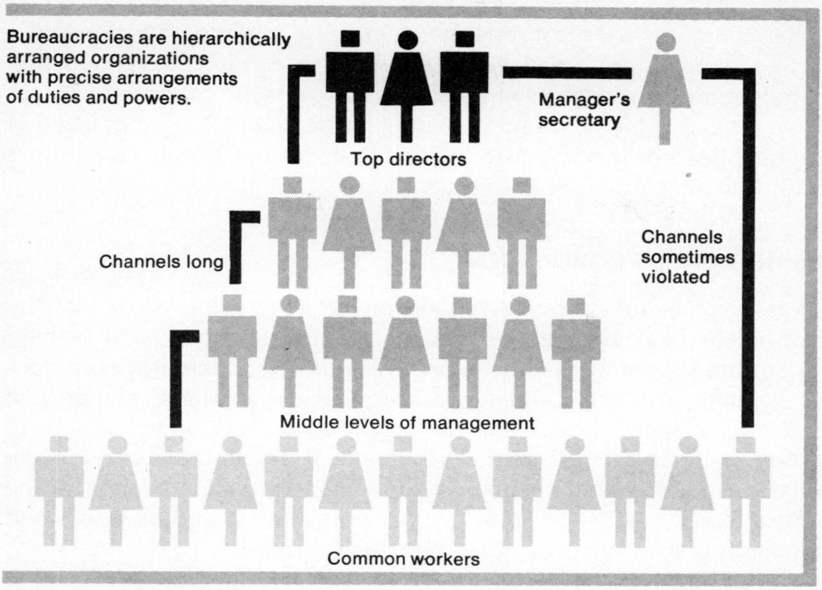

Bureaucracies are hierarchically
arranged organizations
with precise arrangements
of duties and powers.

Manager's
secretary

Top directors

Channels long

Channels
sometimes
violated

Middle levels of management

Common workers

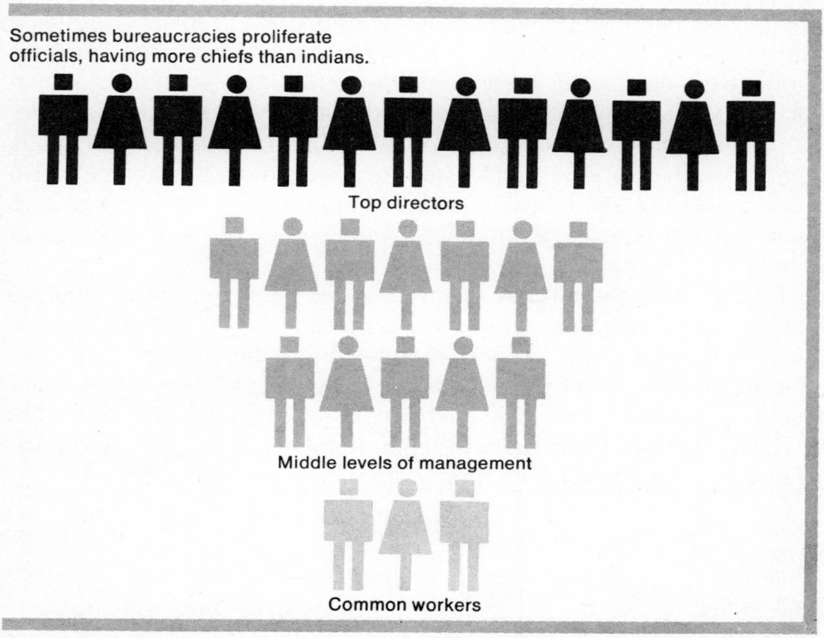

Sometimes bureaucracies proliferate
officials, having more chiefs than indians.

Top directors

Middle levels of management

Common workers

military bureaucracies that promote an increase in standardization and a decline in individual initiative.[10] Bureaucrats tend to become entrenched for long periods of time. One need only consider the history of J. Edgar Hoover, head of the FBI from 1924 until his death in 1972, or of General Hershey, head of the Selective Service System from World War II until 1970, to realize the truth of this assertion.

THE GROWTH OF GOVERNMENT

It was pointed out in the discussion of the economic system that the government has become the regulator of the economy and is held responsible for seeing that the economy flourishes, unemployment does not become excessive, and funds are available for large numbers of programs, including urban renewal, retraining workers, and assistance to depressed areas as well as the astronomical amounts needed for the military establishment. A glance at the federal and state budgets of the United States will show the size of government and give a good indication of the enterprises to which it is committed.

The budget for the 1975 fiscal year called for expenditures of $304.4 billion. (up $100 billion from 1971). Of these expenditures, $95 billion were for national defense (up $22 billion from 1971, in spite of our being at peace when the latter budget was prepared). Other large items (in billions) were health, 28; income security, 104; interest on the national debt, 29; veterans, 14.1; education and manpower, 11.5; agriculture, 7.4; housing and community development, 6.2; and international affairs (largely foreign aid), 4.7.[11] State- and local-government costs have also mounted, totaling $95 billion in 1968. One-third of this amount goes to education, and equal amounts (approximately 13 percent each) go to highways and welfare.[12]

Rising governmental costs is a widespread phenomenon in countries where concern for social programs has become an important political issue. Tax revenues have risen to 28.8 percent of the GNP in the United States. In Germany and France the figure is higher, 34.9 percent and 38.6 percent, respectively, and in Sweden the tax revenues are 41.1 percent of the GNP.[13] Governments perform larger numbers of services, and costs increase even in countries without vast military commitments.

[10]Alfred Weber, "Bureaucracy and Freedom," *Modern Review*, vol. 3, March–April 1948, pp. 176–186.

[11]*The Budget of the United States Government, Fiscal Year 1975, Summary*, U. S. Government Printing Office, Washington, D. C., 1974, p. 40.

[12]*Ibid.*, p. 404.

[13]Alfred G. Buehler, "The Cost of Democracy," *The Annals of the American Acadamy of Political and Social Science*, vol. 379, September 1968, pp. 1–12.

Where it comes from ...

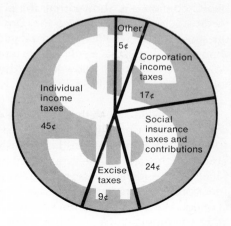

Where it goes ...

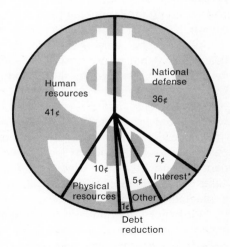

(Source: *The Budget in Brief,* Executive Office
of the President, Bureau of the Budget, p. 1)

*Excludes interest paid to trust funds

There are always complaints about the cost of government, high taxes, and the welfare state. At the same time there is the general feeling that much welfare-type legislation is here to stay. Public-opinion polls in the 1930s found the public to be generally in favor of the New Deal reforms, and similar polls in the 1960s showed support just as strong for similar types of legislation, including antipoverty programs. A 1967

351

public-opinion poll showed half the people in favor of the extension of medicare to all members of the family, not just the aged.[14] Even a questionnaire on whether the federal government wields too much power showed similar results. Only 26 percent of the public said "Yes, federal powers are excessive." However, 52 percent thought we were spending too much money on the military.[15]

The Presidency   Although the powers of the Presidency are enumerated in the Constitution, the office has grown beyond its explicit constitutional limits. Besides his extensive constitutional powers as Chief Executive, his appointment powers, and his powers as Commander-in-Chief, the President wields great power as leader of his political party. His ceremonial powers as Chief of State help make him the center of national attention as no other governmental official can be. Modern television and other communications media have furthered the constant exposure of the President to the public limelight. His messages to Congress have increasingly become the launching platform for extensive legislative programs. Clinton J. Rossiter lists ten roles of the presidential office, including all the traditional ones, and adding "Chief Legislator," "Protector of the Peace,"' "Manager of Prosperity," and "Leader of the World's Free People"—all roles going far beyond the explicit statement of the Constitution.[16]

Such events as the Vietnam war have caused many Americans to have second thoughts about whether the President should assume the role of Leader of the World's Free People. Commager notes that in the past the President's military powers were used only in case of national peril, but now they are used more routinely, on a global scale, and in cases where opinion is divided about whether the national interest is immediately involved.[17]

Of major importance in the growth of the Presidency has been the growth of involvement in foreign affairs. "We may take it as an axiom of political science that the more deeply a nation becomes involved in the affairs of other nations, the more powerful becomes its executive branch."[18] No other branch of government has the access to secret information and the ability to move with sufficient speed in foreign-policy crises. Other types of crises, such as depression or natural disasters, have

[14]Lloyd A. Free and Hadley Cantril, *The Political Beliefs of Americans,* Rutgers University Press, New Brunswick, N.J., 1967, pp. 10–11.

[15]Gallup Poll, *Los Angeles Times,* Aug. 14, 1969, p. 1.

[16]Clinton J. Rossiter, *The American Presidency,* Mentor Books, New American Library, Inc., New York, 1956, chap. 1.

[17]Henry Steele Commager, "Can We Limit Presidential Power?" *New Republic,* vol. 158, Apr., 1968, pp. 15–18.

[18]Rossiter, *op. cit.,* p. 64.

increasingly called for presidential action. The Presidency also seems to symbolize American democracy more than any other branch of government. No other election combines all the talents of showmanship and political manipulation in such blatant ways nor creates such a circus. But no other contest excites public interest to the same degree. Whatever the backstage manipulations, the public has the feeling that its voice is heard most strongly every four years in the Presidential elections, as is apparent in voting patterns, even though it was originally supposed that the House of Representatives would be the governmental body closest to the people. Originally, only the House of Representatives was elected by direct vote of the people.

There is obvious danger in such concentration of power and prestige in a single office. Traditionally, the conservatives have worried over presidential aggrandizement. The breaking of the Watergate and related scandals in the Nixon administration caused liberals to have similar feelings of concern. Unlike the bribery and special favors scandals of the Grant and Harding administrations, the Watergate scandals involved illegal attempts to manipulate elections and thus perpetuate power. However, the problem of concentration of power and prestige goes much deeper than the last administration. In an article titled "The President as King," George Reedy[19] compares the modern presidency with that of fifty years or more ago and finds that many recent presidents have been overly concerned with how strong an impression they will make on the course of history. He decries the growth of presidential libraries, the use of the imperial "we" to describe a president's decisions, and the fleets of airplanes, limousines, and yachts at the disposal of the president. He questions the utility to future historians of the enormous library collections left by recent presidents, but says instead, "They smack far more of the Egyptian Pharaohs, who sought immortality through the erection of stone pyramids."[20]

In his analysis, Reedy agrees with what has already been said about how such crises as depressions and wars automatically add to the president's duties and power. He adds another note of importance: in recent years the Presidency has become an increasingly isolated office. Presidents are too busy to meet the public as much as they did in the days of Jackson. Instead, they trust to public relations, the creation of images, management of the news out of the White House, and press conferences that also seem to have an imperial elegance about them. They are surrounded by staff writers who direct public relations and manipulate their images, until the public no longer sees presidents as real

[19]George Reedy, "The President as King," *Intellectual Digest,* September 1973, pp. 29–35.
[20]*Ibid.,* p. 31.

flesh-and-blood persons but as symbols of power. Ironically, the process can become self-defeating. Presidents can eventually lose touch with the people and lose their popularity so utterly that Congress feels safe in ignoring them. In such a crisis the President can become just as dangerously weak as he is at other times dangerously strong. The greatest hope, as Reedy sees it, is that as the public becomes more aware of public-relations techniques, they no longer work. Suddenly, as in the old fable, somebody realizes that "The emperor has no clothes."

Other Areas of Governmental Growth   Other areas of government have grown too because an executive cannot grow constitutionally without the explicit or implicit approval of Congress and the courts. Government has grown not only because of foreign involvement, war, and crisis but because of the demands of the economy and of various interest groups. Agriculture and labor call for special aid and regulation, as do railroads, airlines, ships, trucks, and all other means of transportation. States demand more aid in welfare programs, road building, water projects, and educational programs. Large, congested cities have brought forth a Department of Housing and Urban Development in the federal government. Because minority groups demand laws for equal treatment, and federal government is the only agency likely to make or enforce such laws in many of the states, the area of race relations has become a concern of federal government. When funds are distributed to aid in welfare, education, disaster relief, or urban planning, the government administrative bureaucracy must grow to provide supervision of such expenditures. For these and other reasons the federal government has become an agency spending over $300 billion/year and employing an administrative bureaucracy of nearly 3 million people. The Labor Department estimates a 10 percent gain in federal government employment and a 52 percent gain in state government employment between 1970 and 1980.[21]

PARTIES, CONSENSUS, AND CLASS VOTING HABITS

Conflicting interests inevitably arise in government. Secure monarchs of the past were able to ignore the problems of the people to a greater degree than now, but even they could not be deaf to all voices. Their ministers and courtiers were attuned to the more powerful conflicting interests within the kingdom. Modern dictatorships often give little official recognition to conflicting pressures, but behind the scenes there are

---

[21]U.S. Dept. of Labor, *U.S. Manpower in the 1970s: Opportunity and Challenge,* Government Printing Office, Washington, D.C., 1970, p. 17.

struggles for influence, and there are often factional struggles for succession when a dictator dies.

Democratic systems require effective political parties—parties that give the voter a choice but are not so far apart ideologically as to result in strong polarization into ideological extremes. There must be enough clash of interest to challenge leadership, but the differences still must be within a general area of agreement or *consensus* on democratic principles and the functions of the state. When a party turnover takes place there must not be a vengeful undoing of all the previous legislation, as happened in the short-lived Spanish Republic and has sometimes happened in France.

Political Parties   Political parties, as everyone learns in government classes, serve the function of presenting candidates and issues to the people, publicizing elections and programs, getting voter turnout, and, in principle at least, trying to guarantee that their banner carriers will perform well in office. A more subtle function that is sometimes overlooked was stated cleverly by Bernard Shaw.[22] In an imaginary conversation between William III and his crafty advisor, the Earl of Sunderland, Shaw pictures the King as being at his wit's end as to how to settle his problems with Parliament and his English subjects. Sunderland advises him to choose all his ministers from the majority party; then, when things go wrong, it will not be in any way the fault of the King, but simply of that inept political party. From that day on, Shaw continues, failures have resulted in change of parties but have not reflected on the monarchy or the country. In the United States we do not have the device of monarchy, but the failure of the party in office does not, in the public mind, reflect too strongly against the country. We simply "throw the rascals out" and try again.

Although Shaw's suggestion might sound somewhat facetious, a party system undoubtedly helps to maintain national morale as well as to serve the generally recognized function of making shifts in policy possible. Russia, in contrast, had to go through a ritual "destalinization" after the death of Joseph Stalin to convince her people that the new leadership would not be as ruthless as the old. No change of parties was possible, however, and the only political party in Russia could not avoid coming out tarnished. American and British parties also are sometimes tarnished in reputation, but the public can turn to the opposite party for a number of years while shifts in party leadership come about and the old party reemerges, none the worse for wear, after catching up with the times.

[22]Bernard Shaw, *Everybody's Political What's What,* Constable & Co., Ltd., London, 1944, pp. 25–28.

Consensus and Class Difference Not all voters shift their party alignment, regardless of declining popularity of the party in office. To a great degree the political identifications of people are based upon factors other than the particular party leader or his platform. There are regional and ethnic differences in party preference as well as a notable difference on a social-class scale. Since 1932, poorer people have tended to identify with the Democratic party more than with the Republican, thinking of it as the more "liberal" of the two.

The word "liberal" has a variety of meanings. It once referred to the laissez-faire philosophy of as little government as possible. In popular usage the word "liberal" now refers to almost the opposite philosophy, and it is this type of definition that will be used here, following the analysis of Free and Cantril,[23] who speak of two types of liberal philosophy: *operational* and *ideological*. *Operational liberal* refers to the person who approves minimum wages, social security, medical care, and antipoverty programs—in general, a large government commitment to the handling of social problems. Free and Cantril find an actual majority of the American voters favorable to most such programs, so there seems to exist a liberal consensus on the operational level. There are inconsistencies in this respect, however, with a resentment of the high taxes and governmental bureaucracies resulting from such programs. *Ideological liberals* are those who state views favorable to increasing the size of government, more regulation of property rights, more of the welfare state, and little worry about a drift toward socialism. The majority rejects this type of liberalism. Whereas 65 percent are operational liberals, only 16 percent are ideological liberals in this sense of the word.[24]

In spite of a possible overall consensus, class differences are marked. Of those who call themselves members of the propertied class, 40 percent are operational liberals; of those claiming middle-class identification, 57 percent are operational liberals; and of the working class, 74 percent are operational liberals.[25]

On a political-party basis, the same differences in viewpoint are to be inferred. Eleven percent of Republicans identify themselves as of the propertied class, and only 2 percent of Democrats do so; 35 percent of Republicans are of the working class, whereas 65 percent of Democrats are of that class.[26] A 1969 Harris Poll presents somewhat different information from that found by Free and Cantril, especially in its emphasis on public outrage against taxes and inflation. Even in the Harris

[23]Free and Cantril, *op. cit.*, pp. 23–40.
[24]*Ibid.*, pp. 31–32.
[25]*Ibid.*, p. 18.
[26]*Ibid.*, p. 142.

Poll, though, the major problem seems to be "the public loss of faith in the government's judgment and priorities" rather than a rejection of domestic programs. Those interviewed were 69 percent in favor of cutting expenditures in foreign aid (oddly enough, at an all-time low), 64 percent in favor of cutting Vietnamese expenditures, and 51 percent in favor of cuts in the space program, in spite of spectacular successes. On the other hand, only 37 percent said to cut federal welfare spending first, and 60 percent said the last thing to cut should be aid to education. Sixty-seven percent resented "the way my tax money is being spent," and there was a strong feeling that taxes were being rigged for the rich.[27]

All the above data reflect expressions of attitude. To what extent these attitudes are translated into action depends partly upon the voting habits of the people. It will be seen that actual voter turnout may be more favorable to the conservatives than the above statistics would imply.

Who Votes   Our political parties are not successful in getting a unanimous turnout for elections. In 1896, 80 percent of those eligible to vote went to the polls in a presidential election; in 1920 the figure dropped to a low of 49 percent of those eligible to vote. The 1920 case was unusual in that women had just been enfranchised by the Nineteenth Amendment, but many of them were not yet prepared to participate in the vote. In recent years voting has fluctuated greatly, always being higher than in 1920, but lower than in 1896. The vote is always higher in presidential-election years than in "off-year" elections, indicating that people see the presidency as more important than the legislative branch of government.[28] For example, in 1960, 64 percent of the electorate voted for President, and 59.6 percent voted for representatives, but two years later, without a presidential election to stimulate interest, only 46.7 percent of the people voted for representatives. Voter turnout is irregular, but it has been over 60 percent in all recent presidential elections.[29]

In the number of people voting, there are some well-marked categorical differences. Men vote in larger percentages than women, and whites more than blacks, although the male-female and black-white differences are declining rapidly. Middle-aged people vote more than the old or the young, which can have a strong effect in elections. For example, in the 1972 presidential election, McGovern had hoped for a very large vote from the newly enfranchised eighteen- to twenty-year-old voters, but the turnout of the young voters was very light and not as

[27]Joe McGinnis, "The Dollar Squeeze," *Life Magazine,* vol. 67, no. 7, Aug. 15, 1969, pp. 18–23.
[28]Lipset, *Political Man;* p. 85.
[29]Richard M. Scammon, "Electoral Participation," *Annals of the American Academy of Political and Social Science,* vol. 371, May 1967, pp. 59–77.

More likely to vote	Less likely to vote
Men	Women
Middle-aged	Young and very old
Northerners	Southerners
The educated	The uneducated
Whites	Blacks
The rich	The poor

What keeps people from the polls?
Health problems
Jobs out of town
Transportation problems
Less perception of importance
Less access to information
Less group pressure to vote
Racial disabilities
More cross pressures

heavily Democratic as had been expected. These demographic differences in voting helped to make Nixon's victory even larger than it otherwise would have been. Other voting differences are regional and economic. More Northerners than Southerners vote, and the voting rate goes up with both education and income. The well-to-do are better represented at the polls than the poor,[30] which helps to give them more political influence than would be expected from their numbers.

Several circumstances surrounding nonvoting show a certain amount of hardship on the poor. Health problems, lack of transportation, or having to be at work are frequent reasons for nonvoting among the poor. Military personnel have difficulty voting and help to account for a relatively low percentage of voters among the young. Racial discriminations in the disguised form of literacy tests or in the overt form of intimidation have been very prominent in keeping down the size of the Afro-American vote. Discrimination against the black voter has declined greatly in recent years, with favorable results in voting records. In at least a few recent city elections, black people have voted in larger percentages

[30]*Ibid.,* pp. 59–77.

358

than whites. Other reasons for nonvoting are often summed up as apathy, but this may be merely an emotionally charged term by which the voter condemns the nonvoter. The poorer people often feel that the system is rigged and that they have only a choice between two parties which are both indifferent to their interests. Frequently the viewpoint is correct, but in many cases it is not. Even when one of the candidates has a favorable record of support for economic opportunity programs, labor laws, social security and welfare, it still takes a great amount of effort to get out the vote in poorer districts. S. M. Lipset has a number of explanations of nonvoting among the poor, based on data from many countries.

According to Lipset, people are more apt to vote if they perceive the importance of government policies to them. The importance is seen most clearly by the educated and well-to-do (who would like to keep down taxes and maintain policies favorable to business) and in the special case of government employees, who have the highest voting record of any occupational group. Access to information is another variable that aids the educated upper and middle classes and helps the workers only when intensive political work is done by parties or unions. Group pressures to vote also have their impact, and these pressures are greatest in the middle class where voting is considered a norm of good citizenship. Finally, cross pressures are very important. Lipset[31] cites cases where left-wing unions almost monopolize the time and interests of workers, as in parts of France, and produce a high turnout of working-class voters, sometimes even higher than that of other classes. On the other hand, a voter may have only a vague working-class identification, along with the conflicting feeling that he is moving toward middle class. His church or neighborhood may be traditionally conservative, exerting counterpressures on him, or such pressures may come from the newspapers or magazines he reads. In cases of strong cross pressures he may decide not to vote at all, feeling uncertain and confused about his own interests. Lipset shows that these confusions are greater for working-class than for upper-class citizens and are among the reasons for lower voter turnout and a resultant underrepresentation of the poor in elections. Whether differences in social-class attitudes and participation in the election process are a threat to democracy is one of the questions now to be examined.

THREATS TO THE POLITICAL SYSTEM

In addition to general worries about taxes and inflation, unequal voter turnout, and the growth of bureaucracy and executive power, there are other worries about democracy. Can true democracy survive in a mass

[31]Lipset, *Political Man,* pp. 183–229.

society? What effect do economic crises and frequent wars have upon democratic societies? Are there antidemocratic groups and attitudes that menace our way of life?

Alienation in the Mass Society   The idea of alienation in mass society is prominent in modern literature as well as in psychology and sociology. The concept of alienation is found among writers of various political persuasions, from socialists and social democrats to ultraconservatives. Basically, the mass society of today alienates people from each other and from meaningful groups in various ways, making the people prone to look for new meanings. Eric Fromm[32] and Hannah Arendt[33] attribute much of the psychosocial background for the rise of hitlerism to the alienation of men from their old traditions, communities, and sources of identity as Germany changed into a modern mass society. In their search for a new identity the Germans chose rampant nationalism and *der führer*, losing themselves and their problems in a great new cause.

Bell gives an analysis of several writers who take the mass-society approach (Ortega y Gasset, Karl Mannheim, Karl Jaspers, and others), and tries to sum up their concepts.[34] He finds certain inconsistencies: people are linked more closely by the mass media and interdependence, yet the theory holds that they are more alienated from one another. Americans are described as lonely and isolated, and yet we are also characterized as a ''nation of joiners.'' Specialization makes modern people develop along different lines, and yet they are characterized as a faceless, homogeneous mass. The concept of mass society, Bell goes on to say, may have its merits, but it misses much of the variety of American life with its regional, ethnic, and occupational groups, and its clash of interests and ideas. It also overlooks the remarkable persistence of primary groups in the mass society. It becomes questionable whether the mass-society concept is sufficient to explain such a phenomenon as hitlerism or extremist groups in American society.

Extremist Groups in a Pluralistic Society   Joseph R. Gusfield views American society in a manner similar to Bell's.[35] He does not try to demolish the picture of mass society, but he does contend that the traditional analytical tool of political science—the view of a democratic government as a system for reconciling pluralistic pressures and interests—is still valid. Extremist politics can be expected but not because

[32]Eric Fromm, *Escape from Freedom,* Farrar & Rinehart, Inc., New York, 1941.
[33]Hannah Arendt, *The Origin of Totalitarianism,* Meridian Books, Inc., New York, 1958.
[34]Daniel Bell, *The End of Ideology,* The Free Press, Glencoe, Ill.,1950, pp. 21–38.
[35]Joseph R. Gusfield, ''Mass Society and Extremist Politics,'' *American Sociological Review,* vol. 27, February 1962, pp. 19–30.

of mass society. After all, there have been extremist groups in much more traditional societies. If we define *extremism* as an unwillingness to abide by democratic rules of the game, then we might define the Whiskey Rebellion of Washington's administration as our first national experience with extremist politics. Certainly the decision of the South not to accept the Presidency of Lincoln was a case of extremist politics in this sense of the word, but not at a time when the United States was thought of as a mass society. Extremist politics emerge from social situations in pluralistic societies, Gusfield argues, because of disenfranchised classes (until recently black America, for example), competing interests that see no hope (labor unions at times), doomed classes (the small farmer), or periodic crises where compromise breaks down (the Civil War). Our present concern most likely is to be with doomed classes and with groups previously excluded from the political process.

Harold Lasswell, writing during the days of the rise of Hitler, commented on the winning over to nazism of certain groups who saw themselves as doomed classes, largely in lower-middle-class positions—small farmers, small shopkeepers, clerks, and craftsmen. These people saw themselves overshadowed by the upper bourgeoisie and by unionized labor.[36] A case can be made for calling them "alienated in mass society," but an equally good case could be made for viewing them as pressure groups with complaints to be mediated by a pluralistic society. A more recent study concludes that these people did not vote for Hitler in a majority of cases until late in the period of his rise,[37] apparently after hope for aid from the Weimar Republic had been abandoned.

The last important revival of the Ku Klux Klan in the late 1950s can be thought of as an attempt to save a doomed class of white supremacists. An analysis of members (not too large a group was available because of the secrecy of the organization) revealed that most of them belonged to a marginal lower-middle-class group undergoing rapid change and status disorientation because of community change and differences in job requirements.[38]

So far as the disturbance on the part of those people previously excluded from the system—the black Americans—is concerned, the subject has been discussed in Chapter 10. Frustrated and not knowing how to achieve legitimate political influence, some of their numbers turned to violence, as did labor groups before they achieved recognition.

[36]Harold Lasswell, "The Psychology of Hitlerism," *The Political Quarterly*, vol. 4, 1933, pp. 373–384.
[37]Karl O'Lessker, "Who Voted for Hitler," *American Journal of Sociology*, vol. 74, July 1968, pp. 63–69.
[38]James W. Vander Zanden, "The Klan Revival," *American Journal of Sociology*, vol. 65, March 1960, pp. 456–462.

An interesting note on the behavior of groups with a legitimate complaint, but one ignored by holders of political power, was reported by Harvey Molotch.[39] An oil slick, caused by leakage from offshore wells, for a time virtually ruined the beaches of Santa Barbara, a city with many wealthy residents. Unable to obtain their aim of closing the wells and bitter over their inability to influence the government, they turned to direct action: "sit-downs blocking oil trucks, yacht sail-ins circling offshore wells, 'nonnegotiable demands,' " and even murmurs about blowing up oil rigs. It seems that even a wealthy group excluded from the system can turn to nonconventional forms of collective behavior. The lower classes, however, are more likely to feel excluded more frequently. Are they a potential source of danger?

Working-class Authoritarianism   Some conservatives worry about the possibility of movements on the extreme left. If threatened middle classes under some circumstances join movements of the right, will working-class members join movements of the left? Working-class people have just been characterized as "more liberal" than middle or propertied classes, but it must be recalled that "liberal" has a variety of meanings. Working-class people, according to the data from Free and Cantril, are liberal in economic issues, especially wage and welfare measures. In the political sense "liberal" can be a synonym for tolerance of a wide range of views and of the gradualist processes of democracy. It is in this respect that the working class is characterized as less liberal than the middle and upper classes. A combination of political liberalism and the *authoritarian* desire for strong leadership and the suppression of the opposition would predispose people to radical extremism.

In a discussion of lower-class authoritarianism, Lipset notes that in many countries the Communist party has had greater appeal to the workers than the Socialist party. Both are oriented to the working class, but the Communist party is rigid and authoritarian, and the Socialist party is not.[40] The implication is that the rigid, simplistic doctrines appeal more to the less educated segment of the population, a segment that is also more isolated from groups and associations and has had less experience with the give and take of organization life. Lipset argues that education is positively associated with tolerance, and because the lower class is less educated, it is not surprising to find it less tolerant of dissension. A lack of knowledge of the roles of other people is also closely associated with

[39]Harvey T. Molotch, "Oil in Santa Barbara and Power in America," paper presented at the American Sociological Association Convention, San Francisco, Sept. 2, 1969. (Also reported in *The San Francisco Chronicle*, Sept. 3, 1969, pp. 1, 26, under the title "Rich Become Radicals.")
[40]Lipset, *Political Man*, pp. 89–90.

authoritarianism[41] and is more likely to be a problem of the less educated lower class than of the well-educated.

However, the working class of the United States has not followed the Communist party line as in France and Italy. One reason is the traditional feeling that upward mobility is possible; thus the more hopeful members of the working class take on a feeling of middle-class identity. Probably another reason is that the United States has had a particularly strong cultural orientation to democratic processes. It is also likely that the greater amount of sectarian- and revivalist-type religion in America, which, like political extremism, tends to be simplistic and anti-intellectual, may "drain off the discontent and frustration which would otherwise flow into channels of political extremism."[42]

It is also possible that the very factors that make for working-class authoritarianism are gradually declining and that such authoritarianism might be less evident in the future. The isolation of rural counties is less marked than in the past, and fewer people live in such counties. The years of schooling, even for children of the poor, are increasing. Dissemination of information (admittedly along with much nonsense) through television and other mass media certainly reduces isolation and increases social awareness.

Upper-class Authoritarianism If the working class is narrowly authoritarian in its attitudes, we might expect it to look upon society in conspiratorial terms and to agree that a small inside group of big businessmen really run the country. Actually a study by Form and Rytina found the poor taking a very different point of view, generally agreeing that the country is pluralistically run by various business, labor, religious, and political groups.[43] In comparing the rich with the poor, the researchers found certain respects in which the rich seemed more narrow-minded. They were unable to see that some strata of the population need special governmental help; 72 percent felt that the government had already done too much for the poor. The rich also were likely to choose "business and the rich" as the most powerful elements in society and to feel that this was the way it should be. They showed strong class consciousness and out-group antipathy, conclude Form and Rytina. "A good case can be made for upper-class authoritarianism."[44]

[41]Don Stewart and Thomas Hoult, "A Social Psychological Theory of the Authoritarian Personality," *American Journal of Sociology,* vol. 65, November 1959, pp. 274–279.

[42]Lipset, *Political Man,* p. 200.

[43]William H. Form and Joan Rytina, "Ideological Beliefs in the Distribution of Power in the United States," *American Sociological Review,* vol. 34, February 1969, pp. 19–30.

[44]*Ibid.,* p. 30.

Perhaps the reference to upper-class authoritarianism seems to be a nagging case of charge and countercharge, but the point is that people are most likely to be closed-minded in matters that affect their welfare, whether they are rich or poor. Lower-class authoritarianism has appeared historically in attempts to keep out foreigners who compete on the labor market and in "white backlash" against blacks in recent elections. It undoubtedly was one of the factors showing up in the Wallace vote of 1968, but that vote was not too impressive except in a few states of the South. If the wage earner voted for Wallace in the hope of keeping his neighborhood white, he was admittedly showing narrow-mindedness, but is it a type of narrow-mindedness unknown to the middle or upper classes?

Any type of change that may lead to unemployment is naturally feared by the workingman, and unemployment is associated with strong class consciousness and militancy.[45] Radical sentiments, much greater militancy of labor unions, and a tendency to join visionary movements were characteristic of the unemployed during the Depression period. However, government action eventually relieved unemployment, ameliorated poverty for those out of work, and began to reduce the intensity of radical feelings. The two-party system, beginning to respond to the socioeconomic problems of the people, undoubtedly helped to prevent the rise of a radical party at that time. The Socialist and Communist parties failed to capture the working-class loyalty. There was some fear of the social movement of Father Coughlin and of the demagoguery of Senator Huey Long, but their influence eventually waned. With a government more readily geared to coping with the socioeconomic problems of the poor than in those days, there is reason for hope that radicalism would fare no better in a future depression than in the past.

There is ample evidence for narrow-minded and authoritarian attitudes in various parts of society. It is, however, the lower class that is submitted to the greatest number of frustrating pressures making for anger and extremism. If we are to avoid the possibility of frustration and anger showing up in a form threatening to democracy, we must try to avoid the types of crises that might bring forth such emotions. The crafty Machiavelli observed centuries ago that a republic must beware of war because if the war is lost, the leaders might be overthrown by a dictator, and if the war is won, the leader will be so heroized as to be made into a dictator. In spite of our propensity for electing military heroes to the Presidency, we have never had the disaster that Machiavelli foresaw, but

---

[45]John C. Legget, "Economic Insecurity and Working Class Consciousness," *American Sociological Review*, vol. 29, April 1964, pp. 226–234.

the passions of war have brought other problems for democracy. Free speech and freedom of the press have been drastically abridged. In World War I, we attacked and vilified German Americans and socialists. In World War II, we incarcerated thousands of Japanese-Americans without trial. All segments of a population become more authoritarian in times of war, more fearful of the outsider and of the nonconformist. Although wars are bitter experiences for all nations, politically they are especially dangerous for democratic systems.[46]

SUMMARY

Political institutions are the ultimate source of legitimate power in societies. Regardless of the system of government, the state seeks to achieve a monopoly on power and a primary claim on the devotion of its people. In return it offers a sense of common identity and social cohesion—sentiments that can sometimes rise to the level of national fanaticism.

Although nationalism continues to be a powerful force in most of the world, many nation-states are faced with certain divisive forces from within. Many countries face ethnic, racial, and regional divisions. In modern societies urban, mobile populations develop increasing economic demands, and there are always conflicts of interest between social classes.

The complexities of urban-industrial systems call for greater organizational effort that is met by increasing bureaucratization in both government and industry. Government grows in both size and expense because it must regulate the economy and provide for the welfare of its people. The growing regulatory functions of government, and in many cases mobilization for war, lead to greater concentration of executive power, as exemplified by the American Presidency.

Conflicting interests inevitably arise in government. Firmly established monarchical states of the past were relatively immune to pressures from the common people, but even they had to take notice of the varied interests of the powerful. In dictatorships there are usually factions competing for influence at governmental centers. In operating democracies, political parties attempt to win the allegiance of various interest groups by promising to serve their cause.

Democratic systems seem to function best in cases where there is a fair degree of consensus. A general acceptance of some types of welfare measures illustrates a degree of consensus in the United Sates, but there

---

[46]Robert M. McIver, *The Ramparts We Guard,* The Macmillan Company, New York, 1950, pp. 84–92.

remain strong social-class differences in opinion as to how far welfare-state measures should go. Although working-class people have a stake in elections, they are less likely to vote than are middle- and upper-class people, for a variety of reasons.

In periods of rapid change, political systems can be placed under serious threat. In the opinion of some observers, alienation in mass society is a major source of political danger, leading to the politics of extremism and impatience with democratic processes. Seymour Lipset presents evidence that authoritarian attitudes are most prevalent among lower-class people, both in Europe and the United States. Other researchers find strongly authoritarian attitudes among the well-to-do, characterized by a very blurred perception of the problems of other classes. Authoritarian attitudes are not just matters of social-class position, however. Times of threat and crisis tend to limit tolerance and increase the fear of dissension in all economic levels of the population.

PART FIVE ART: Vishnu (on the left), intending to preserve the social order, grips it so hard that he actually uproots it, as Siva (on the right) sweeps the masses across the barrier of the unknown (dark) to overpower the established order which represents only a few.

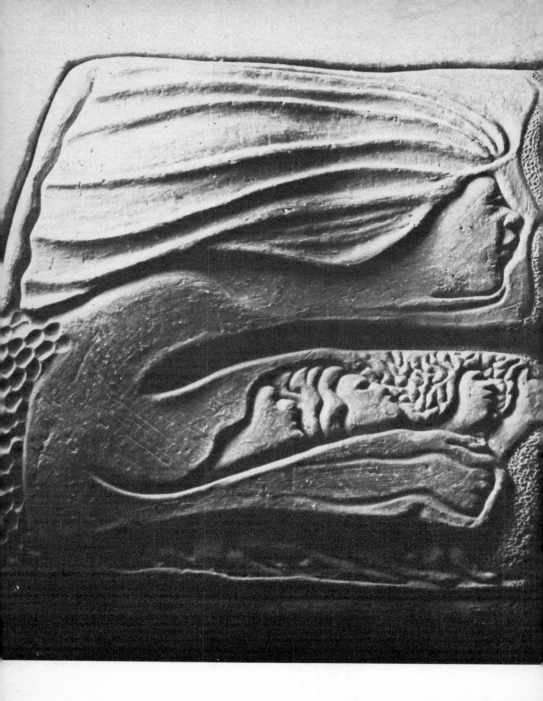

Part Five

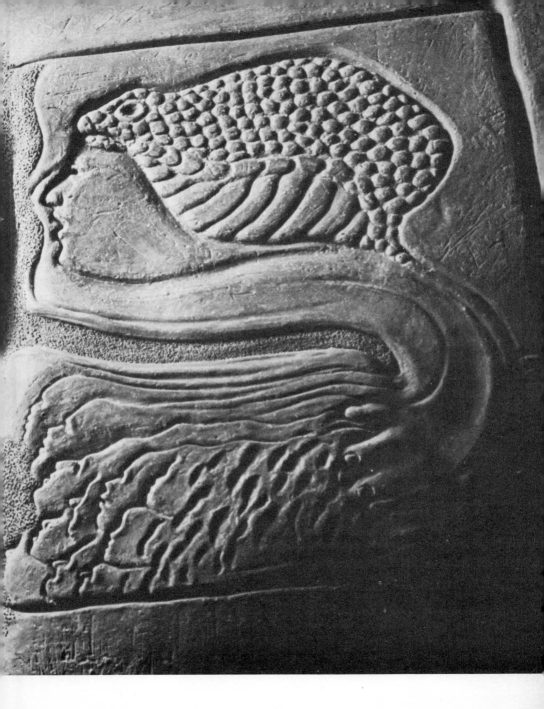

Sociology and Social Change

During the period of history ushered in by the Industrial Revolution, people have been extremely aware of social change, thinking of it as an inevitability and probably a positive good. Yet there have been societies in which little change has occurred over periods of centuries. Our question in the final chapter, then, will be "What motivates change?" Is there any perceptible direction of social change? Why does the pace of change accelerate? Why is the God of Preservation increasingly foiled in all his efforts?

We are fellow passengers on a flight whose destination we do not know but whose velocity seems to increase with time and distance, like the speed of the galaxies the astronomers describe. We are fleeing from the simple life of band and local community that was so long our spiritual home while seeking new levels of integration and new rules of life. Many convergent pressures drive us on, including the growth, congestion, differentiation, and institutional changes of which we have spoken, but, more importantly, a scientific technology that has become both a servant and a master force driving us toward ever greater technological complexity. Things once familiar to the aged have now disappeared, and no one can guess the way of life of the next generation.

Many have tried to analyze the direction in which we are traveling—some by comparisons with past history, some by trying to project along a perceived line of progress, and others by a point-by-point analysis of the factors causing change. In the following pages we shall examine a few of the historically based theories of social change, which are still pursued by some sociologists, but not as commonly as in the past. Are there repetitious cycles in civilizations? Do certain historical developments provide a key to the future; or does Siva keep his intentions forever hidden from our view?

Next we shall review some of the areas of change already covered in previous chapters, looking for their interrelationships and asking if one type of change necessarily precedes another. For example, is social change compelled by population growth, by new patterns of socialization and education, by political and economic systems, or are all these changes ultimately traceable to changes in technology? Our next questions concern factors in change and resistance to change—invention and diffusion on the one hand and vested interest on the other.

Finally, we must ask if there are conditions under which cumulative forces of change become explosive and revolutionary. Or are revolutions a result of stubborn resistance to change? Or do they represent an imbalance of forces, alternately raising hopes and dashing them? Whatever the case, the changes that began with the Industrial Revolution continue to spread throughout the world, making ours a fast-moving, exciting, and extremely perilous age.

Chapter 16

The Pressures of Change

No single thing abides, but all things flow
Fragment to fragment clings;
The things thus grow
Until we know and name them. By degrees
They melt, and are no more the thing we know.

Lucretius

Throughout the major portion of human history the process of change has been extremely slow, often deliberately retarded by such cultural devices as the subordination of the young to the old, reverence for departed ancestors and their ways, and avoidance of the ways of the stranger. At times the catastrophes of war and famine have doubtlessly forced migrations and adjustment to new ways, but the new adjustments have been disturbing, breaking up the small measure of tranquility that man has been able to attain through fixed status, beliefs, values, and folkways.

372

Then came the development of agriculture and settlement into permanent villages and towns. These developments were the hallmark of the so-called neolithic revolution—one of the two great ages of invention, the other being the modern phase of history.[1] Animals were domesticated, the wheel was invented, writing began, and the use of metals was discovered. The debris of the past reveals a story of the rise and fall of civilizations, of invasion and counterinvasion, of pillage and looting, captivity and slaughter. There is another side to the story, however. Behind all the conflict and destruction, invention of new culture traits was progressing, and new ideas were diffusing from centers in the Near East, India, and China. Social and technical inventions were increasing, opening many possibilities that the Old Stone Age had never known.

CONFLICTING THEORIES OF SOCIAL CHANGE

Many of the writers of theories of social change have looked upon one or the other of these two aspects of human history: the rise and fall of civilizations and the gradual accumulation of new inventions, ideas, and possibilities. We can hardly take an interest in history wihtout speculating about the destiny of our own little segment of humanity, wondering whether we can defy the common fate of nations or whether we too will be "as one with Nineveh and Tyre."

Cyclical and Struggle Theories Those writers most impressed with the growth and destruction of civilizations have tended to look on social change in terms of futile cycles or even as a decline from some kind of a mythical golden age to the miseries of today. One of the well-known works on cycles of development is Oswald Spengler's *Decline of the West*.[2] Spengler thought of civilizations as similar to living organisms, with their youth, maturity, and inevitable old age and death. Each had its original inspiration and ideal, which was destined eventually to fade in the pursuit of more materialistic interests, presaging the demise of the civilization.

Many optimistic Western historians, on the other hand, have tended to give an upward-and-onward view of history and to consider history merely the history of the Western world. The cyclical theorists have avoided this easy optimism and Western ethnocentrism but have not been able to explain the mechanisms of rise and fall to the satisfaction of modern sociologists.

[1] Claude Lévi-Strauss, *The Savage Mind*, The University of Chicago Press, Chicago, 1966, p. 15.
[2] Oswald Spengler, *Decline of the West*, Alfred A. Knopf, Inc., New York, 1928.

Futile cycles (Spengler)

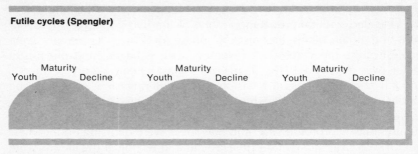

Youth Maturity Decline Youth Maturity Decline Youth Maturity Decline

A common Western view

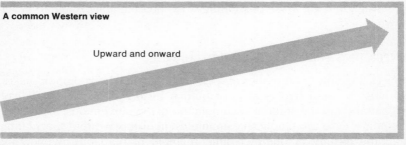

Upward and onward

A struggle theory (Hegel)

Conflicting forces / New synthesis / Diverging interests / New conflict / New synthesis / Diverging interests

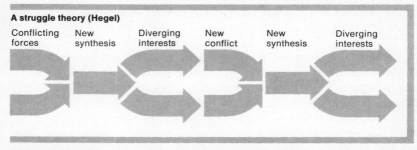

Parallel developments at different rates (Lewis Henry Morgan)

Western civilization / Eastern civilization / Aztecs, Mayas / Polynesians / Australian aborigines

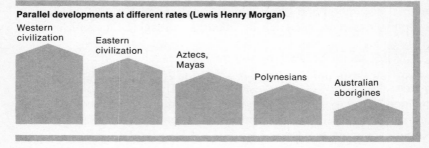

Another alternative view of history is that of various "struggle theorists." Hegel, for example, saw all social change as the result of struggle between opposing forces, eventually producing a "new synthesis" that would itself find new opposing forces to renew the struggle. Marx, in his theory of class struggle, was strongly influenced by the view of Hegel.

Arnold Toynbee: Challenge and Response   Probably the best-known contemporary philosopher of history is Arnold Toynbee, whose monumental work *A Study of History*[3] seeks the general causes of rise and decline of civilizations. The idea of challenge and response as causative forces runs strongly through his work, and he makes interesting comparisons between the Greco-Roman world of antiquity and contemporary Western civilization. His work amounts to a vast summary of historical cultural systems but has been criticized for proving points by a careful selection of examples. It also ends in a kind of historical mysticism, expecting a new age of religion to save man from his impending doom but not explaining how this new age of faith is to come about.

Sociologists and anthropologists, as well as philosophers and historians, have attempted to make sense and order out of the human record. In the nineteenth century they often looked at social change from the perspective of *cultural evolution*—the idea that cultures evolve in a way comparable to the evolution of species in the biological world. Evolution was central to the thinking of the sociologist Spencer and the anthropologist Lewis Henry Morgan. Morgan's theory, stated briefly, was that all cultures evolve along similar lines and with an inevitability resulting from the "psychic unity of man." His point of view was consistent with modern ideas of the potentialities of all peoples to build advanced cultures, but it failed to explain different rates of growth and the enormous range of cultural differences.

Functionalism   *Functionalism* became a prominent concept for analyzing cultural change in the early twentieth century. Functionalism tries to understand cultures in terms of how their various parts contribute to the maintenance of the total system. For example, absolutist governments served an important function in early civilizations, harnessing the energies of the people to control rivers and develop irrigation systems. It would be easy to use functionalism to explain various practices repellent to the modern world. For example, female infanticide (killing girl babies) functions to keep down the population, slavery functions to increase the

[3]Arnold Toynbee, *A Study of History*, abridgment of vols. I-X by D. C. Somervell, Oxford University Press, New York, 1947–1957.

power of the slave-holding class, and warfare functions to eliminate inefficient social systems. Naturally, functionalists would not go this far in a "whatever is is right" philosophy, but functional analyses do run into this problem.

Functionalism, however, makes some important advances in the understanding of social change. It helps to explain why customs persist unless new customs can serve the same functions. For example, polygyny will persist if it functions as a prestige system for important men, regardless of missionary teachings. It could possibly change, though, if a new and equally desirable status symbol could be found. Functionalism also raises the question of why change occurs at all.[4] Change can occur in two ways: as a result of strains within the system or as a result of outside forces. There are always strains within a social system resulting from individual variations. The younger generation is never a perfect duplicate of the old. Rulers attempt to solve problems in different ways. Sometimes population increase puts a strain on resources. Sometimes something new is invented. The outside forces can be the infusion of new ideas from surrounding people, competition with other groups for control of land and resources, or the crisis of war. The question remains, though, whether there is a patterning of these changes into a type of increasing complexity and specialization that can be called cultural evolution.

CONTEMPORARY THEORISTS: TALCOTT PARSONS, LESLIE WHITE, AND PITIRIM SOROKIN

Several modern theorists are reexamining cultural evolution. The new theories are improved upon by many years of research and by new theoretical perspectives. Different models of analysis are used, sometimes viewing a society in terms of *structural functionalism,* as a *moving equilibrium* (Parsons), or, as suggested by Wilbert Moore, a *tension-management mechanism.*[5] The terms "moving equilibrium" and "tension-management mechanism" suggest that cultural and social systems can undergo considerable change and that readjustments of various institutions are needed and made, but behind all the changes is a certain persistence—a very different perspective from that of "decline and fall" or "old age and death."

White's Energy Theory Two modern theorists of society who are interested in revised forms of cultural evolution are the anthropologist

[4]Kenneth E. Bock, "Evolution, Function, and Change," *American Sociological Review,* vol. 28, April 1963, p. 232.
[5]Wilbert E. Moore, *Social Change,* Prentice-Hall, Inc., Englewood Cliffs, N.J., 1963, p. 10.

Leslie White and the sociologist Talcott Parsons. Both would agree that the earlier cultural evolutionists had made a marked contribution to our understanding of human cultures, but these modern theorists depart from the simple unilineal evolutionary theory of Lewis Henry Morgan. Both recognize that the course of cultural evolution is complex and that not all societies evolve in exactly the same direction; but insofar as there has been a trend from the simple to the complex in human societies, the word "evolution" is appropriate. Parsons speaks of the advanced societies as those that "display greater generalized adaptive capacity."[6] Of the two theorists, White lays the greater stress on invention and technology. Because cultural diffusion of inventions occurs, the place of origin of a new idea is irrelevant to him. His view of cultural evolution is of the entire human species, not of any particular society. A major point of his analysis is the *energy theory of evolution,* the idea being that as people have tapped greater sources of energy they have developed greater potential for cultural advancement. Until the time that animal power was harnessed for doing the work of humans, nearly all available energy and time had to be expended in earning a living, and all people were directly engaged in food production, whether in hunting or gardening. With greater energy available, much more differentiation of labor became possible as many former gardeners were released to do some of the other work needed for cultural development—organization of effort, the building of forts and temples, advances in the arts, military protection, and so forth. Thus it was the period of human history when we first attached the ox to the plow that can be called the first great breakthrough, and the second great breakthrough came with the Industrial Revolution. Naturally, White sees other sources of variation in cultural possibilities, including the level of organization, the tools invented, and the environment. He uses the formula

$$E \times T \times V = P$$
$$\text{where } E = \text{energy}$$
$$T = \text{tools}$$
$$V = \text{environment}$$
$$P = \text{potential[7]}$$

Culture does more than provide a means for economic support; it gives people a set of values, customs, beliefs, and a system of organization. White does not omit any of these ideas. He elaborates especially on

[6]Talcott Parsons, *Societies: Evolutionary and Comparative Perspectives,* Prentice-Hall, Inc., Englewood Cliffs, N.J., 1966, p. 110.

[7]Leslie A. White, *The Evolution of Culture,* McGraw-Hill Book Company, New York, 1959, p. 49.

the state-church phase of cultural evolution, in which societies are often organized under the control of a godlike king.[8] Such a structure, accompanied by a belief system, functions to make the social system expand far beyond that of a tribal group and gives cohesion to the system. Strong kings, upper classes, and laws attributed to the gods all help to serve the function of controlling a heterogeneous population, but much of the old freedom of earlier times disappears.

White insists that societies could not have grown without an expansion of the amount of energy available for human use, increasing production and making possible a division of labor and social-class differentiation. As the modern phase of civlization is entered, the energy available increases manyfold, not only making tremendously more production possible but making it possible wihtout slavery or divine rulers, although man is still organized and regimented far more than in his early primitive state. Technological factors, then, especially available energy, are seen as the underlying elements in social change.

Parsons: Adaptive Capacity   Parsons is more inclined to stress social structure and ideology first, for the advancement of adaptive capacity depends upon ever-widening bases for social structure, that is, advance from the mere band or tribal organization to that of city-state, nation, or empire. Writing is a first step in this direction, taking societies out of the primitive state. Belief systems that legitimatize authority and law in the larger societies are also basic to such organizational advance.[9] Thus the divine pharaohs of ancient Egypt represented a great advance over primitive tribal organizations because they were able to hold together large populations under one system (as White recognizes in the state-church phase). Because the divinity of the pharaohs was closely tied in with continuity, changelessness, and the Nile, the system could not easily expand to societies outside of Egypt. It also lacked the degree of separation of the supernatural sphere from the natural that Parsons contends is necessary for innovation and cultural change.[10]

Rome later supplied a legal and citizenship system that extended over a vast empire, but it failed in some ways in the legitimization of its authority, and it always had some people who were not assimilated into the system: slaves and the downtrodden. With regard to religion, Rome was in some ways archaic. Too sophisticated to truly adhere to the god-king idea, it nevertheless fell short of developing a religious system with universal appeal. Hence Rome witnessed a bewildering profusion of

---

[8]*Ibid.,* pp. 303–328.
[9]Parsons, *op. cit.,* p. 11.
[10]*Ibid.,* pp. 51–61.

White's energy theory: E × T × V = Potential

(Adapted from Leslie A. White, *The Evolution of Culture:*
The Development of Civilization to the Fall of Rome,
McGraw-Hill Book Company, New York, 1959, pp. 33-57.)

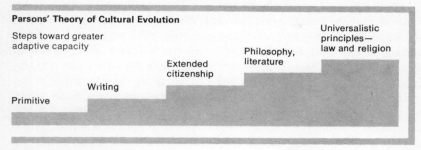

Parsons' Theory of Cultural Evolution

Steps toward greater
adaptive capacity

Universalistic
principles—
law and religion

Philosophy,
literature

Extended
citizenship

Writing

Primitive

(Adapted from Talcott Parsons, *Societies:*
Evolutionary and Comparative Perspectives,
Prentice-Hall, Inc., Englewood Cliffs, N.J., 1966, p. 110.)

Eastern cults of various kinds. Christianity was finally accepted through-out the empire, but only after Rome was already in the twilight of its development.[11]

A universalistic type of religion had been brought into the Eastern world by Buddha, but because the eventual technological breakthrough into modernity occurred in the West, Parsons gives this less importance than the religious development of ancient Palestine. The Hebrew nation was never impressive in size, and its period of glory was very short, but the Hebrews developed a religious and legal concept with a universality that made it adaptable to later Christian and Moslem people: the concept included a legal system that flowed out of the will of a universal God, as their prophets saw it, and was therefore superior to any particular society or ruler.[12] Future generations could fight over just what the will of God was, but the principle had great possibilities for generalization into many cultures, both as a religious and a legal principle.

Another people whose period of political glory was short, the Greeks, also made one of the universalistic contributions that would be necessary before larger systems of organization could develop. Ancient Greece developed a cultural system of philosophy and literature that

[11]*Ibid.*, pp. 86–94.
[12]*Ibid.*, pp. 96–102.

extended far beyond the boundaries of her city-states, influenced the Roman Empire, and later influenced all Europe with the revival of Greek learning in the period of the Renaissance. Greece also made an important contribution to the concept of citizenship. Although citizenship was limited to old families, all adult male citizens were considered virtual equals.

In the theories of both White and Parsons there is the obvious implication that cultural evolution differs from physical evolution in that cultural diffusion is possible. Some societies have made considerable advance along one specialized line or another but have left no apparent heirs. Others have come forth with the inventions—in the cases cited by Parsons, nonmaterial inventions—that have made higher levels of organization possible and that have increased cultural capacity to adapt. When these organizational capacities are combined with scientific technology the modern phase of man's development is reached. White suggests that the next phase may be one in which computers make not only greater organization but better thinking processes possible.[13]

Sorokin: A Theory of Flux Sorokin views society as a "supersystem" that includes a social structure, culture, and groups of individuals. This supersystem is in a continual state of social change, but, unlike many of the theorists preceding him, Sorokin sees the possibility of societies changing in many different directions according to the values of the individuals within the system. Previous theories generally portrayed social change as moving in one direction, for example, Durkheim's idea that "primitive societies" would increasingly move toward "civilized societies" because of a division of labor. Sorokin explains that societies may move back and forth from one type of "civilization" to another and that human beings were beginning to gain the knowledge needed to control the direction of change.

To understand the "flux" of social change, students of sociology must first become acquainted with the various possible types of society that can exist. Sorokin supplies descriptions of three basic "civilizations," *sensate, ideational,* and *idealistic,* which exist only as "ideal types" and never in their pure forms. Sensate culture exists when the mentality of its populace accepts as real only those things that can be perceived by the sense organs. Therefore sensate civilizations are not interested in acquiring or seeking "absolute knowledge" and tend to use empiricism (observability) as the source of truth. Such cultures would likely be atheistic or agnostic because of a lack of a belief system that transcends the individual.

[13]R. P. Cuzzort, *Humanity and Modern Sociological Thought,* Holt, Rinehart, and Winston, Inc., New York, 1969, pp. 232–233.

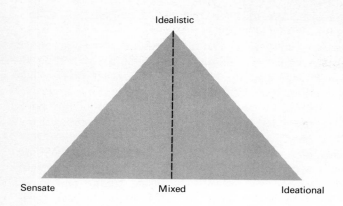

Idealistic

Sensate   Mixed   Ideational

All the opposite characteristics typify the ideational culture. The adherents to the culture of an ideational civilization view reality in a spiritual sense. These civilizations are deeply religious in orientation and depend upon faith and revelation as sources of truth and are not preoccupied with the empirical aspects of existence. The sensate person might want to gain knowledge about observable phenomena so that he can manipulate it to his own gratification, but the ideational person simply conforms to the existing patterns and conditions in this world and sets his sights on the visionary prophecies of the "next world." Reality, in ideational culture, is everlasting and absolute.

Idealistic culture is a perfect blending of sensate and ideational types; however, this third civilization is raised above the other two because of the addition of "reason" as a source of truth. Of course, for idealistic culture to exist, the elements of sensate and ideational culture must coexist in a harmonious fashion. This creates an epistemological triangle within which societies can fluctuate. To classify a society, one need only to examine the works of its philosophers or its art forms, analyze them, and then categorize them according to the descriptions given above. However, the sociologist may find that a given civilization might not "fit" Sorokin's scheme:

> Simple arithmetical calculations result in findings that take the following form: In the Nth century, "A" percent of Western philosophy was sensate and "B" percent was idealistic. Such findings support Sorokin's theory of social change, but they also demonstrate a limited possibility of quantifying data on cultural style.[14]

[14]Nicholas S. Timasheff, *Sociological Theory: Its Nature and Growth*, Random House, Inc., New York, 1957, p. 238.

A fourth type of culture must be imagined to complete Sorokin's system of thought, a "mixed" culture. Mixed culture would be a combination of sensate and ideational cultures without reason as a source of truth. Mixed culture would depend partly upon empiricism and partly on asceticism (faith) and would represent the midpoint of the line separating sensate and ideational cultures at the base of the triangle.

Sorokin believed that societies were continually "bouncing" back and forth between sensate and ideational civilizations, sometimes rising to great heights and nearly achieving idealistic culture and other times passing through mixed culture in a sort of schizophrenic fashion. Writing some time before his death in 1969, Sorokin observed that Western culture had nearly reached the extreme of sensate culture and might begin to turn toward ideational mannerisms. This, of course, is speculation, and, in fact, many contemporary sociologists believe that all of Sorokin's theory regarding "culture types" or "civilization types" is highly speculative and geared more toward philosophy than toward sociology. But, as Becker and Boskoff remind us,

> Two features give Sorokin's work importance: one, it approaches a sociology of knowledge that attempts to show that mental factors determine existential factors, rather than vice versa; second, quantitative techniques were applied to long-range historical data for the purpose of achieving statements of general relationships.[15]

THE INTERRELATIONSHIPS OF SOCIAL CHANGE

As functional analysis emphasizes, one complexity of the study of social change is the fact that the elements of a culture are interrelated in such a way that a change in one element of the society leads to corresponding changes in others. This is most easily seen in the impact of mechanical inventions, to which we shall return; but for the sake of a summary of the field we have covered in this text, it will be interesting to review some of the interrelationships already mentioned or implied in the preceding pages.

Alternative Reference Points in Change   Chapter 2 discussed human groups and the drift from gemeinschaft to gesellschaft society. The whole trend of the modern world could be analyzed fairly well in terms of these changes in group relationships, and as a matter of fact many of the people most worried about modern mass society actually do analyze our problems in this way. Changes could also be analyzed in terms of the socialization problems discussed in Chapter 4. There is an often-noted

---

[15]Howard Becker and Alvin Boskoff, *Modern Sociological Theory: In Continuity and Change*, Holt, Rinehart and Winston, Inc., New York, 1957, p. 409.

tendency for the older generations to feel that the younger generation is not being socialized properly and that this is the reason for disturbing changes. Another analysis of social change starts with the differentiation of human societies by division of labor and status and class. Some of our most obvious recent changes have been in the area of greater specialization. The change in relationships between majority and minority racial and ethnic groups is another focal point in the study of social change. We also could use the growth of population as a starting point in the study of social change, for increasing population means there is no possibility of a return to simple agricultural existence. Instead, there is a compulsion toward further increasing industrial production in order to take care of the people. Population pressures, along with urbanization, also create a society that calls for more controls over the lives of people—they must abide by zoning laws and building codes, pay increasing property taxes, submit to allocation and rationing at times, and increase their police forces.

Interrelationships of Changing Institutions The family gradually changes to fit the conditions of society, as was noted in the contrast between consanguineal family and restricted conjugal family. However, even the family is sometimes taken as a starting point for change. The family system that frees the individual for the competitive struggle, and hence emphasizes individualism, is more congenial to modern capitalism than a more restrictive family, and there are probably even cases where family change has preceded economic change. Religious attitudes also change, perhaps in response to changing conditions, but recall that Weber saw the religious orientation of Calvinism as at least one cause of the rapid development of capitalism. In other words, religious change motivated economic change. Education also becomes a powerful force for change, and yet it is complementary with the rest of society. It is the society whose values and economy require education that develops a modern educational system. Some underdeveloped countries train a small, educated elite that can hardly be used, and it becomes a restive element, often radical and revolutionary. Recall Benjamin and Kautsky's study showing that in the countries not yet entering industrialization the few communist members are likely to be part of the educated elite.

As Chapters 14 and 15 demonstrated, economic and political institutions are closely interwoven, especially with the mixed economic system of today. Economic changes are basic and underlying as seen from one perspective, but at the same time it is possible for poor governmental systems to greatly retard economic growth. Values and beliefs are also basic to economic change, retarding such changes if the society believes too strongly in the sacredness of the old ways. Political changes in the direction of a stronger state are of overwhelming importance today, as are changes in the equalization of political power. Whichever way we turn we see this entangling relationship between one institution and another. It is also demonstrable that certain important inventions have their impact on practically all customs and institutions, and an understanding of the interrelationships of the various aspects of society will aid to analyze the impact of one such invention.

In analyzing the impact of a particular invention, we are using the ideas of the late William Fielding Ogburn[16] but exemplifying those ideas in our own ways. In starting with a particular invention, it is first necessary to deny complete *technological determinism*—the idea that technology is always the first cause in social change. There must be favorable attitudes in a society before it will accept an invention, and even our own technically oriented society has allowed some important inventions to go without takers—the first modern submarines, for one example.

It was Ogburn's point of view that an important new invention would act on a society very much as ripples spreading across a pond until every part of the society was somehow affected. If we start with the automobile, we can demonstrate the point, although other starting points would do just as well—the railroad at one time, or the airplane more recently.

Derivative Effects of the Automobile The invention of the automobile and its increasing production called for new products from the area of international trade. It was one of the industries that concentrated labor in large plants and helped to give rise to the labor movement. New supportive industries had to grow, especially petroleum and rubber, and old industries died out; buggies, horses, and hitching posts were seen no more. The government also had to become involved, making new laws for the regulation of traffic and building the roads that the new means of transportation required. Higher levels of government had to take over more of the duties imposed by the new transportation system. Local governments could not bear the cost, nor could they coordinate a national transportation system.

There are many other ramifications of the invention of the automobile. Urban growth was no longer confined to suburbs strung out along railroad lines or water courses; now the city could explode in all directions. Motels began to replace the city hotels and drive-in restaurants, drive-in movies, and even drive-in banks and drive-in churches appeared. Dating patterns and the time of coming-of-age were affected. The age at which the state law permits a driver's license is a crucial age for the young man, allowing him to join the dating whirl. Probably too much has been made of automobiles and the morals of the young, for

[16]William Fielding Ogburn, *Social Change*, The Viking Press, Inc., New York, 1950.

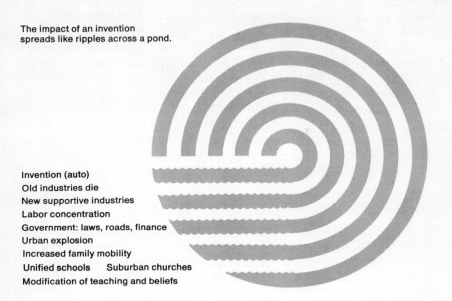

The impact of an invention
spreads like ripples across a pond.

Invention (auto)
Old industries die
New supportive industries
Labor concentration
Government: laws, roads, finance
Urban explosion
Increased family mobility
Unified schools   Suburban churches
Modification of teaching and beliefs

there is no doubt that the good old horse and buggy were quite agreeable to young couples too, but maybe the horse had an annoying habit of going home when the hour got too late!

Family mobility increased, although moving around the country was already a part of the American pattern of living. The little red schoolhouse disappeared as bus transportation made possible consolidated schools. The "little brown church in the wildwood" was replaced by the urban or suburban church. In both institutions the growth in size had further implications. Better trained teachers and ministers began to do away with some of the distinction between rural and urban, although some rather backward rural areas still remain. Religion became less fundamentalist; educational standards became more uniform. One could also add to the list of effects of the automobile a number of unpleasant latent functions, especially smog and pollution, a worldwide struggle for oil resources, gasoline shortages, and a frantic search for alternative fuels.

Not all inventions have been as thorough in their effects as the automobile, but many have been. The invention of gunpowder eventually brought the whole age of medieval castles to an end. An earlier chapter discussed the tremendous impact of automation on employment and education. No one knows what the ultimate effects of the discovery of atomic energy may be, but it will probably dwarf the importance of all previous inventions.

As noted, social change can be described in terms of long-range theories of history and cultural evolution. It can be described in interrelational terms and as the result of the acceptance of particular inventions. These perspectives, however, fall short of explaining all the factors involved in social change. Undoubtedly there are many that escape the attention of analysts, such as Hans Zinsser's germs, or mutation, radiation, DDT, and a host of others. However, a more practical understanding of social change can be gained by discussing a few of the commonly noted factors in social change and resistance to change.

A FACTOR ANALYSIS OF CHANGE AND RESISTANCE

Invention is one of the most important factors in social change, but it needs little elaboration because it has already been discussed. The kinds of inventions described (automobile, gunpowder, and atomic reactors) are *material inventions* and are the types usually thought of first. There are also important *nonmaterial inventions:* writing, money, credit, banking, social security, monarchy, "divine right," democracy, slavery, insurance, corporations, consumers' cooperatives, and credit cards, to name but a few. The nonmaterial inventions creating better systems of organization and universalistic principles of law, it will be recalled, are a part of Parsons' analysis of cultural evolution.

Diffusion is even more important than invention. Diffusion is the process of borrowing cultural elements from another culture. All societies have borrowed more than they have invented because many inventions are ancient and have spread throughout most of the world: the bow and arrow, wheel, plow, beasts of burden, weaving, use of metals, most types of clothing and food, languages and writing, paper and ink, glass, silverware, chinaware—the vast majority of the objects of everyday use, even including the stories we tell and the religions we follow.

Crises as Change Agents   *War* increases the demand for the inventions of weapons of death, very obviously, and it also increases the demand for materials from all parts of the world. Armies spread new ideas—and bad habits—from one part of the world to another. The French armies of Napoleon's time have been credited with spreading the ideas of the French Revolution wherever they went. Earlier, the Crusaders had learned much from the Saracens, and this learning helped to usher in the Renaissance in Europe.

The *crises* of flood, drought, and other natural disasters have led to new societal adjustments. In earlier times they led to migration to new territories; now they result in greater efforts to control nature. *Depressions* are types of business crises that have resulted in many social inventions in Western societies, especially in the United States—social security and insurance of bank deposits being some of the most prominent inventions.

Deliberate Promotion of Change   In the historic past it is likely that many inventions have been the result of accident rather than deliberate seeking of new ways of doing things. Accidental inventions occur even today, but most of our present-day inventions are a result of *deliberate efforts at change*. Giant corporations hire thousands of researchers to find new products, and governments do the same.

Laws are used to institute change. We are used to the idea of smog-control devices on cars and may have to get used to a substitute for the internal-combustion engine. Laws insist upon education of the young. Laws promote racial equality in more and more aspects of life. Laws insist that people save toward their old age through the social-security system. Laws often tell young men they must join the service, although most youths rarely express any desire to do so.

Resistance to Change   There are also many kinds of *resistance* to social change. One resistance is simply the force of *habit* and another has to do with *uncertainty* about the new invention. Some people took many years to get used to television sets, having been fairly well-satisfied with radios. Sometimes peculiar stories arise about the possible ill effects of a new invention. "Good old-fashioned methods" are preferred. In earlier times many people saw inventions as somewhat sacrilegious—"If God had intended us to fly, He would have given us wings."

Costs are important as a resistance to change. Spectacular achievements in space are purchased at such a high price that some taxpayers would like to slow down the pace. Ingrained habits and costs often combine as resistance factors. Nothing could facilitate some types of learning more than to simplify the spelling of the English language and also to change to a metric system instead of the cumbersome measuring system used by the United States. Yet there is very slow progress toward a metric system, and virtually none in spelling. Much new printing would have to be done, and there would have to be the unlearning of old ways and the learning of new ones. Resistance to the improvement of notational systems can be a serious detriment to a civilization. China has been "stuck" with a writing system that is extremely cumbersome compared with our Western alphabetical system.

Vested interest is very important in resistance to social change. Petroleum interests would not be happy to see a change to electrical cars. Workers are not happy about inventions that make their jobs unnecessary. The railroad interests were successful for decades in resisting the St. Lawrence Seaway because of the competition it would bring. All these are examples of vested interest, a financial stake in the old order.

Sacred values and beliefs often cause resistance to change. The Amish still think of automobiles as worldly wickedness and refuse to use them. Printing, invented in China, spread to the Arabic lands but was rejected on the grounds that it would be sacrilegious to print the holy Koran rather than write it by hand.[17] Insecticides were resisted in Iran because "If we kill the pests Allah sends against us, who knows what He'll send next!"[18]

Sometimes *attitudes* of society will be resistant to a new element even though the attitudes are not what could be called sacred beliefs. For example, most American people will not adopt such delicacies as snails, fried grasshoppers, pickled octopus, or goats' eyeballs. We have borrowed various cultural traits from Mexico—a few words, styles of architecture, art, dress, decoration, and food—but bullfights, no! Our sensitivities would not permit us to watch the killing of a bull. We like to watch prize fighters beat each other into insensibility and to watch people get broken and maimed in auto races, but we would not kill a bull, except in the slaughterhouse.

Resistance to change sometimes seems to be solid and immovable, and then it collapses rather suddenly, as was the case with resistance to medicare for the aged. Wilbert Moore uses the word "thresholds" to describe this situation of a poorly perceived threshold of change.[19] His example is of the sudden breakdown of resistance to birth control in some countries that have been adamantly opposed to it. The process of change here seems to be the gradual absorption of new ideas, a slow rationalization of old attitudes, and a final willingness to take action in a new direction.

Cultural Lags   *Cultural lags* are periods of maladjustment created by the failure of some social traits to change fast enough to keep up with change in other parts of the social system. Technology often leads, and customs and ideas have to catch up. The idea of cultural lags was first used by Ogburn, and one of his examples was the failure to develop conservation methods in American forestry.[20] His forestry example em-

[17] Paul Frederick Cressey, "Chinese Traits in European Civilization: A Study in Diffusion," *American Sociological Review*, vol. 10, no. 5, October 1945, pp. 595–604.
    [18] Margaret Mead, *Cultural Patterns and Technical Change*, New American Library, Inc., New York, 1962, p. 233.
    [19] Wilbert E. Moore, "Predicting Discontinuities in Social Change," *American Sociological Review*, vol. 29, June 1964, pp. 331–338.
    [20] Ogburn, *op. cit.*, pp. 200–213.

phasizes the persistence of an old belief that was no longer true: "There will always be plenty of trees." The cultural-lag concept has many applications. The United States was slower than most countries to adopt social-security laws because of a persistent belief in the duty of the individual to take care of all of his own economic needs. This belief had become a cultural lag in an age of unemployment caused by technology or by a downturn in the business cycle. Until recently, public interest has lagged behind the rapid pace of river, lake, and air contamination, the attitude having been that "There will always be clean water and air."

Sometimes major aspects of a culture can be cultural lags, as with governmental systems that cannot keep pace with technical, scientific, and economic change. Certain governmental systems have collapsed in the twentieth century, partly for this reason—the Ottoman Empire, the Austrian Empire, the Manchu Empire, and the czarist regime in Russia. In the case of old systems overthrown by revolution, various undermining forces were at work, and it is necessary to go beyond the concept of cultural lag to explain them.

SOCIAL CHANGE AND REVOLUTION

The word "revolution" has several meanings. *Revolution* can mean a fairly complete change brought about by different methods of production or by the acceptance of new ideas such as the Industrial Revolution. Another example is "revolution of rising expectations," a phrase frequently used to describe attitudes in the underdeveloped areas of the world as they begin to hope for the same material comforts that have been attained by Europe and the United States. A second type of revolution is a simple overthrow of government, with one group of rulers replacing another. A synonym for such a revolution is *coup d'etat* (literally, "stroke of state"). From the point of view of the majority of common people, little has changed as a result of such an overturn of leadership. The social order remains basically the same.

Revolution as Basic Social Change The word "revolution" also describes basic change in a social system, usually, but not always, brought about by such uprisings against the existing government as the American Revolution of 1776, the French Revolution of 1789, and the Russian Revolution of 1917. All these revolutions resulted in more than a simple change in the ruling faction. The French and American Revolutions replaced monarchy with republican forms of government, although the first French Republic did not last long. The Russian Revolution not only replaced the political system but made a drastic change to a communist system of economic production. In the United States some of the causes of revolution were the tax issue, the controls of the mercantile system, and the general feeling of being crippled and frustrated by English rule. In each of the other cases the list of grievances was lengthy, but they were grievances that had long been in existence without having brought their nations to the breaking point in the past. What were the conditions that precipitated revolution at the particular point in history when it occurred?

Theories of Revolution: Crane Brinton   Crane Brinton, James E. Davies, and Talcott Parsons have all presented interesting analyses of revolutions. Brinton,[21] drawing on information from the American, French, and Russian Revolutions, and the English Revolution of the seventeenth century, finds that in none of the cases were conditions growing steadily worse. Our American ancestors were making economic progress at the time of the Revolutionary War. It is true that France was undergoing crop shortages at the time of her revolution, but she had experienced a century of rather rapid progress in total output before then. Russia was embroiled in World War I and had suffered defeat at the hands of the Japanese in 1905, but the peasants had received their freedom in 1861, and their overall conditions seem to have been improving. Russia also was making progress in steel and oil production. The earlier English Revolution seems to have been led by a rising class of Puritans who were making considerable advances in business. In all cases, however, there was crisis at the governmental level. A need for new taxes, combined with governmental ineptitude, at a time when there was a rising class of able and determined people demanding more rights, played a part in each of the revolutions. With each revolution there was middle-class leadership and an abandonment of the old order by the leading intellectuals, but only in Russia was there outright appeal to class interest.

Theories of Revolution: James C. Davies   Davies,[22] using a slightly different group of revolutions for illustrative purposes, adds an important factor. Although there is usually a general increase in the well-being and hopes of the revolutionary elements involved, something occurs that seems to shatter their hopes. There is a downturn in prosperity or employment or a serious threat of such a downturn. In neither the Brinton nor the Davies analysis is there the implication that misery alone will lead to revolution. Many societies have existed in a state of misery too long to make this seem to be the single ingredient of revolution.

[21]Crane Brinton, *The Anatomy of Revolution,* W. W. Norton & Company, Inc., New York, 1938.
[22]James C. Davies, "Toward a Theory of Revolution," *American Sociological Review,* vol. 27, February 1962, pp. 5–19.

What seems obvious in much of today's world, especially in the underdeveloped areas, is a situation in which knowledge of better possibilities is at hand, especially among the educated groups. At the same time, social change in the form of new technologies, new products, foreign trade, and a movement from farms to cities strongly dislocates old ways of life. Old norms and rules of behavior are no longer applicable. A situation of anomie exists. It is easy to see the explosive potential of the modern world, but it would be rash to predict revolutions in particular cases.

Theories of Revolution: Talcott Parsons   In Parsons' analysis of the revolutionary movement[23] it is pointed out that a revolutionary movement demands a complex set of circumstances. The rise of a revolutionary movement demands large "widely distributed alienative elements" who are able to pull together, united by a vision of the future. This vision might be of a religious nature, in which case it will result in a religious rather than a revolutionary movement. Under the right circumstances, however, these elements can be united behind a charismatic leader with an exciting ideology of change. Even at this point there must be a weakness in the power structure or a revolution is impossible. This governmental weakness, it will be recalled, was an important point in the analyses of both Brinton and Davies.

Parsons carries his analysis of revolution a step further, showing that there is an *adaptive transformation* so that the new order retains some elements of the old. It is not surprising that communist Russia should have retained a secret police force such as had existed in the days of the Czars, nor that in foreign policy she should again cast hungry glances at Eastern Europe and the Dardanelles, nor that a military elite would again be very prominent in the system. This is not to deny that revolutions make great and sweeping changes, but it does remind us that there is a certain persistence to a social system and a culture.

Summarizing briefly these various viewpoints, a rapidly changing world helps to create the tensions, dislocations, and feelings of alienation that can be mobilized by a successful revolutionary leader. It also should be added that there are ready-made philosophies of revolution exported from Russia, Red China, and elsewhere. At the same time, even moderately effective governments are not easily overthrown. No revolution has occurred in France or Italy in spite of strong Communist parties, even though their governments have suffered a number of leadership crises. Sweeping revolutions in various Latin American countries have long been

[23]Talcott Parsons, *The Social System*, The Free Press, Glencoe, Ill., 1952, pp. 520–535.

predicted, but only a few have come about. Even the incredibly corrupt regime in Haiti still is, at this moment, being maintained by the son of its founder. The study of social revolutions has clearly not brought us to a state of easy predictability. More analyses of the forces of resistance seem to be needed.

Change: Despair and Hope Whether people live in the most progressive modern society or in one of the world's underdeveloped areas, they feel the pressures of change. New products, new technologies, new ways of organizing social institutions, new values and new aspirations are everywhere in evidence. Old ways are gradually abandoned. Cut adrift as they are from the moorings of tradition, modern people can easily feel a confused sense of hopelessness, for the very currents of change that they have set in motion seem now to have a power of their own, sweeping them along almost against their will. The literature of our times is full of nostalgia for a simpler past. Leslie White says, for example, in comparing our plight today with that of the primitive world:

> However crude and ineffectual primitive cultures were in their control of the forces of nature, they had worked out a system of human relationships that has never been equaled since the Agricultural Revolution. The warm, substantial bonds of kinship united man with man. There were no lords or vassals, serfs or slaves, in tribal society. . . . No one kept another in bondage and lived upon the fruits of his labor. There were no mortgages, rents, debtors, or usurers in primitive society, and no one was ever sent to prison for stealing food to feed his children. Food was not adulterated with harmful substances in order to make money out of human misery. There were no time clocks, no bosses or overseers, in primitive society, and a two-week vacation was not one's quota of freedom for a year.[24]

There is, fortunately, another side to the story. People living today in the world described by White would find it a world of unendurable boredom. Day would follow day with little happening and nothing but petty gossip to talk about, together with old superstitions and myths, and an argument about who bewitched whom. Whatever the forces of change have brought there is no way back. We live in an age when the moon and planets beckon us, and our first steps on extraterrestrial bodies have been taken. The task before us is to so organize our societies on earth that we shall be free to turn our attention to the exploration of the unknown, ever increasing the freedom of the mind of man, without the fear that our

[24]White, op. cit., p. 277.

planet will explode behind us in the primordial hatreds and fears that we have been unable to conquer.

SUMMARY

Change was once extremely slow in human societies, but the pace of change increases as technology grows and one development leads to another. Theorists have long attempted to explain social change in various ways, often looking for the cause that underlies all other causes. Spengler saw the cause of change as a kind of vitalistic principle, similar to growth, maturity, and decay of the individual life. Hegel and Marx both emphasized struggle as the motivating force in history, with Marx seeing the struggle as basically economic. Other theorists have tried to relate social change and the rise of civilizations to challenge and response, or climatic change.

Functionalism and cultural-evolutionary perspectives have received more attention from sociologists and anthropologists than most other explanations of change. Functionalism is more concerned with explaining how systems work and how new elements are incorporated into social systems than in grand theories of underlying causes of change.

Modern cultural evolutionists display a variety of viewpoints, but they generally look for certain uniformities in social change and for some of the factors that account for these uniformities. Leslie White sees the increasing amount of energy available to man as the basic factor that unfolds new possibilities. Talcott Parsons emphasizes the importance of greater general adaptability in evolving social systems and the ideologies that support them.

Nearly all explanations of social change have a degree of plausibility, but none is complete enough to satisfy all critics. What makes theory difficult is that social change can be analyzed by viewing any of several factors as prime causes: the drift toward gesellschaft society, new socialization patterns, the intricate division of labor, war and struggle, industrialization, population growth, and many more. All such developments are closely interrelated and are, perhaps, most easily understandable in modern technical societies if viewed from the perspective of the derivative effects of inventions. The automobile makes a good starting point for demonstrating how one invention can affect all the institutions of a society.

Although the analysis of an invention clarifies much about social change, it is not to be concluded that invention is the one and only cause of social change. To clarify this, an analysis of various factors contributing to change has been used—invention, diffusion, crises, and deliberate promotion of change through law. These factors must be weighed against resistances—habit, fears, costs, vested interests, and attitudes and beliefs. Resistance often leads to the disparities in rate of change called cultural lags.

The vast majority of social change takes place without violent revolution, but sometimes a wide gulf between aspirations of the people and their present condition can lead to such upheavals. Uniformities in great revolutions are found by such analysts as Crane Brinton, James E. Davies, and Parsons. Parsons also sees an adaptive transformation that prevents the revolution from being as complete as its supporters would have hoped. Nevertheless, old orders are never completely restored.

The pace of change has become rapid enough to be disturbing to many people, and sometimes a nostalgia for the past is expressed. Sociology, however, must concern itself with an understanding of social systems that cannot be made to stand still or to move backward. Sociologists seek to explain the reasons for social change and its probable direction, but they do not claim to have a special ability to evaluate.

INDEX